A
SOCIALISME OU BARBARIE ANTHOLOGY

A
SOCIALISME OU BARBARIE ANTHOLOGY

Autonomy, Critique, and Revolution
in the Age of Bureaucratic Capitalism

Helen Arnold, Daniel Blanchard, Enrique Escobar, Daniel Ferrand, Georges Petit, and Jacques Signorelli have participated in the selection of the articles as well as the drafting of the introductory texts. The main writer of the introductory text for each part has signed his or her work, but all of these texts have been discussed at length among these participants. Sébastien de Diesbach and Claude Lefort participated in a few meetings and offered useful advice about certain parts.

ERIS

86-90 Paul Street
London EC2A 4NE

Translated from the French and edited anonymously as a public service. Originally published
in France by Acratie in 2007. This first edition
published in Great Britain by Eris in 2018 adheres
to formatting rules, including paragraph indenta-
tion and similar stylistic conventions, that depart
from other existing versions of the text.

Jean Amair, Hugo Bell, Cornelius Castoriadis,
S. Chatel, Claude Lefort, Jean-François Lyotard,
Daniel Mothé, Panonicus, Paul Romano, Albert
Véga, Jack Weinberg

Printed and bound in Great Britain

ISBN 978-1-912475-13-1

Contents

French Editors' Preface

"Préface"
Socialisme ou Barbarie—Anthologie, 7–14

For anyone who participated in the group Socialisme ou Barbarie at any moment in its long—nearly 20-year—history (from 1949 to 1967), seeing it described today, in various places, as "legendary," "famous," or "mythical" stirs up strangely ironic feelings. The irony stems from the fact that, throughout its existence, this group—and the review of the same name, of which it published forty issues—remained invisible, or nearly so, and yet now, once dead, it has become mythical. A bitter irony: invisible or mythical, what is denied it is reality—*its* reality; for, mythical, it remains unrecognized; or worse: it becomes unrecognizable. Thus, to this irony is joined a strange impression: through this legendary aura, anyone who really knew this now-defunct group and journal no longer recognizes the deceased.

What has happened is that the S. ou B. group, though almost unknown during its lifetime, has been reconstructed after its death as the virtual point of origin wherefrom the trajectories of Claude Lefort, Cornelius Castoriadis, and Jean-François Lyotard—who appeared in the Parisian intellectual firmament in the course of the 1970s—are said to have diverged. Yet, rather than *appeared*, it would be fitting to say that they then became *visible*, the firmament's configuration having wholly changed at that point in time. The group and its stars remained invisible so long as the *left-wing*, Marxist or anarchist, critique of the USSR, of Communist parties, and of their various subsidiary operations was subject, in the press, in publishing, and in the University, to the same censorship and to the same sorts of intimidation as in the factories. Only in the course of the 1950s and

1960s did the truth about the regimes of the Eastern-bloc countries little by little start to come out. Soon, though, that truth became so widespread that it rendered untenable any defense of those regimes and vain the intimidation and blackmail of being called *reactionary*. The intelligentsia rediscovered "democracy" and "human rights" and, in the 1970s, saw itself seized with a new mission: the denunciation of Communist totalitarianism. And so, this intelligentsia acknowledged its predecessors, including, among others, Lefort, Lyotard, and Castoriadis, who were, moreover—for those who retained some scruples—highly unlikely to be suspected of being reactionaries. Thus did the S. ou B. group find itself, years after its dissolution, suffused with a glory and a legend that were as blinding to its reality as the darkness to which it had been confined when it was alive.

This legend is deceptive on two key points. First of all, the group was not exclusively preoccupied with the critique of so-called Communist regimes; it was just as concerned with that of so-called liberal Western societies, and it never stopped working out a unitary critique of the two regime-types. In the second place, it was not a coterie of intellectuals but, instead, a group of revolutionaries for whom theoretical work was meaningful only with a view to action on the social and political level. And it was precisely because they considered themselves revolutionaries that they could not be satisfied with denouncing what was going on elsewhere but had to fight right here.

True, the reality of the group, especially its ambitions, is such that the reader of today who becomes aware of it through the texts brought together here will experience this same sense of strangeness and, undoubtedly too, irony. That is because this reality belongs to a now seemingly quite bygone period in the intellectual, political, and anthropological history of the workers' movement. It carries on a tradition that dates back at least to Marx, who, in a logic considered absolutely necessary, connected theoretical analysis, militant activity, and the genuinely historical action of the masses. And it is this tradition that, in the minds of the twenty or so persons who founded the group in 1949, legitimates the exorbitant and—in the view of disenchanted people today—the odious or ridiculous ambition to work for the construction of an organization whose goal would be nothing less than worldwide proletarian revolution.

In fact, the group's origin dates back to 1946, when the "Chaulieu-Montal" (Castoriadis and Lefort) Tendency was set up within the Trotskyist Fourth International. We will lay out the circumstances of the group's birth in the Introduction to Part 1 of the present collection.

Let us state here only that, at the end of World War II, it no longer appeared tenable to support the Trotskyist thesis that made of the USSR a "degenerated workers' State"—that is to say, the necessarily ephemeral product of a momentary balance between the forces of the proletarian revolution and those of counterrevolution. Castoriadis, Lefort, and their comrades noted that the Soviet regime had survived the test of a terrible war and that, far from being on the verge of disappearing or metamorphosing, it was gaining strength and was on its way to expanding into Eastern Europe and, soon thereafter, the Far East. One thus had to look reality straight in the face and denounce Stalinist Russia as a society in which a new class, the bureaucracy, had collectively seized the means of production, imposing on the proletariat and the peasantry an exploitation and oppression that were worse than under bourgeois capitalism. One thus had to see, too, in parties and unions in the West that were the vassals of the Soviet Communist Party (CP), not instruments of working-class and popular emancipation but, instead, kernels of a future bureaucratic class and instruments in the service of its interests.

Stating this, backing it up with a well-documented, rigorous analysis still claiming to be strictly Marxist, and bringing out the implications this new assessment of reality entailed for upcoming social and political struggles—such was the task the group set for itself at the time of its foundation. In fulfilling that task, a lot of room was made for theory—that is why this group chose the review as the instrument for spreading its ideas—but the ultimate aim was practical, since these ideas were to help working-class militants to orient their struggle against their true adversaries, which were just as much the apparatuses of so-called working-class organizations as the capitalists and their States. This at-once theoretical and practical approach, which was *political* in the sense the workers' movement gave to this word, carried the group until its self-dissolution in 1967. It was also expressed through an imperative, one the workers' movement has not always imposed upon itself, far from it: constantly to examine critically and, if need be, to challenge ideas one has formulated oneself.

The break with Trotskyism was an inaugural emancipatory gesture. It afforded the initial impetus to a journey that could be described as *an exploration of modernity* and that was lived by those who followed it as an intellectual adventure, certainly, but also as a passionate one. When one gave oneself the shivers by noticing that "the emperor has no clothes" and shouting it out, when one shook off received ideas in order to get closer to reality and try to grasp it and comprehend it—and certainly, this was something to begin over again [*recommencer*] constantly—one could no longer do without such pungent pleasures.

Here we have another trait that surely makes it difficult today to grasp the reality of the S. ou B. group. Though anchored in the tradition of political groups, its adventurous spirit distinguished it from many extreme or ultraleft groupuscules, which furiously tried to turn a profit on their tiny (and usually inherited) capital made up of firm, nay fixed, ideas in order to carve out a place for themselves in a miniature and, in fact, fictive political field.

This adventurous spirit was carried forth by a sort of underlying vehicle of the age, which could be described by the rather inane word *optimism*. At the time, we would have indignantly denied such optimism, as would most of our contemporaries. How could one call *optimistic* an era upon which the threat of atomic war was still weighing and during which every spontaneous collective initiative seemed doomed to be distorted, diverted to the benefit and for the use of one or the other of the two blocs? For, this was an era of bloody acts of repression, ferocious colonial wars, and harsh social struggles.

And yet, seen from here and now—that is to say, early in the twenty-first century in the West, where the prevailing sense is that of a rush toward catastrophe with no possible way out—the optimism of that bygone time is striking—and astonishing.

This was, first of all—as has been said often enough!—a period of economic growth, and especially of a kind of growth that, unlike what is happening today, was expressed in a general rise in "living standards" in the developed countries, that is to say, for the working classes, through access to consumer goods that were not just gadgets, and with relative financial security. True, while this was, for most people, the source of a certain amount of optimism, the group, for its part, analyzed such "progress" as a rationalization of capitalism, the least of the conditions capitalism had to fulfill in order to endure, and not a threat to its survival.

Much more revealing of a possible challenge to the capitalist order, as much the bureaucratic one as the bourgeois one, it seemed to us, were the new forms of revolt that arose during those same years—they, too, being signs and sources of optimism. Of highest importance were the workers' insurrections that broke out in the People's Democracies during the 1950s. They dazzlingly confirmed the existence of class struggle under bureaucratic regimes, as had been foreseen in S. ou B.'s analyses. And—a still more precious contribution—the ephemeral Hungarian Revolution sketched out the project of an entirely self-managed society, thus giving a new, profoundly emancipatory meaning to the word *socialism*.

Simultaneously, in the immense Third World, the uprisings of peoples oppressed and exploited by the Western powers via colonialism or by other means restored dignity to a huge portion of humanity, invented new modes of struggle both violent and nonviolent, and seemed to open up a bit, for the simple folk of those countries, the possibility of some mastery over their lives. Of course, S. ou B. never yielded to the charms of Third Worldism, but the group endeavored to understand and to bring to light, in their very ambiguities, the liberatory potentials these multiform movements harbored within themselves.

In the developed countries, too, though in less spectacular fashion, manifestations of a contestation of the bureaucratic-capitalist order began to surface, and S. ou B. endeavored to detect them and to clarify their meaning. In the factories, daily resistance, on the job, to the way work was organized, to production norms, and to the hierarchy sometimes, particularly in England, took a sharp turn. More often than before, social movements called into question labor conditions and set forth egalitarian demands. Youth began to protest against its subjection within the family, work, and education, as well as against the boredom and absurdity of the existences they were destined to live. Finally, the young people of that time, especially student youth, more and more often made itself the spearhead of political opposition movements in England (with the Campaign for Nuclear Disarmament), in the United States, in Japan, and so on.

In fact, more than from the Third World, and perhaps even more than from the countries of the Soviet Bloc, it was from the most modern parts of the West that the group expected to see the forerunners of potential social upheaval, and in its effort to bring to light the traits that revealed the underlying nature of our world and presaged its future, one example inspired us: that of Marx and Engels, who dissected mid-nineteenth-century English society and discovered at work therein what was being manufactured for all modern societies. Our England was the United States. With burning curiosity, we followed what was going on there—not only, with the help of our comrades from the Detroit-based group *Correspondence*, the various movements of contestation (wildcat strikes, the Black Movement, the Youth Movement, etc.) but also the innovations of capitalism and the ideas it was working out so that it might understand itself, in particular via "industrial sociology." America was, back then, much more critical of itself than it is today. In cinema, music, and literature many themes were being sketched out that would soon become those of a radical critique of "everyday life." We most certainly were not blinkered, like Communist militants or so-called *progressiviste* intellectuals, who rejected as reactionary, nay even fascistic, everything that came from the United States. Yet our primeval Marxism left aspects of reality out of our field of vision, and in a way America taught us about life, this America that forthrightly displayed its investigations into the concrete organization of time and space, into the relations between men and women, young people and adults, into the forms and contents of education, and so on.

Herein resides the basic originality of the S. ou B. group: it lies in its bid to base a revolutionary perspective on the very movement of modernity. This bid was consciously taken up from the start, but only gradually did the group become aware of what it actually required. And this, too, unfolded like an adventure—an adventure that, however, did not advance *aimlessly* [à l'aventure], but in accordance with a tough-minded logic.

The break with Trotskyism over the "question of the nature of the USSR," as was said at the time, brought with it from the start, that is to say, as early as the first issue of the review, two theoretical consequences. First of all, to characterize the Soviet bureaucracy as a class under the same heading as the bourgeoisie required that one abandon the criterion of the private appropriation of the means of production as a way of defining a capitalist society's dominant class. Property is only the juridical form, as Chaulieu brought out in "The Relations of Production in Russia" (no. 2). The key thing is the effectively actual and exclusive exercise of the management of the means of production, including labor power. The pertinent distinction, therefore, is no longer between property owners and proletarians but between directors or "order givers" and executants or "order takers" [*dirigeants et exécutants*].

In the second place, if one denies that Communist parties and unions are the authentic representatives of the proletariat or its *avant-garde*, the question arises as to where the proletariat is, what it does, what it wants. S. ou B.'s response, which marks its deep break with Leninism, is that the proletariat exists nowhere else but in itself and that it is up to itself to manifest what it does and what it wants. In other words, these responses must be sought at the root, on the shop floor, where consciousness of exploitation and alienation is formed in the worker, but also consciousness of his capacities for creative interventions and self-organization in production as well as in his struggles. Here we have a line of research S. ou B. inaugurated in the very first issue, with the publication [in translation] of Paul Romano's *The American Worker*, and that was to be pursued for a long time, particularly with the publication of texts by Daniel Mothé on his own experience as a worker at the Renault automobile factory. Lefort theorized its political import in "Proletarian Experience" (no. 11, December 1952). *Correspondence* in the United States, *Unità Proletaria* in Italy, and a bit later, *Solidarity* in England worked along this same path.

These initial theoretical innovations led in turn to other, more radical ones that would, around 1960, bring Castoriadis and a part of the group to break explicitly with Marxism. In the early years, however, and until 1958, the theoretical framework of Marxism appeared to the whole group as not only useful but sufficient for understanding the new realities—as the few militants coming from the Bordigist current, like Alberto Véga, who joined in 1950, insisted. It can nevertheless be stated that, even during this period, the slippage away from Marxism, or at least from a certain kind of Marxism, was becoming more pronounced. The decoupling of the notion of class from that of the ownership of the means of production, which had allowed the USSR to be described as a capitalist society, necessarily pushed into the background the role of the objective mechanisms flowing from the intrinsic necessities of capital and the imposition of the *commodity form* on all exchanges. The main motive force of present-day history was thenceforth the struggle between the two blocs and, more profoundly, class struggle.

On the other hand, the opposition between directors and executants, which was read as a class struggle, was in no way confined, as the opposition between capitalists and proletarians basically was, to the sphere of production. It may be located at all levels and in all manifestations of social reality. Here, this opposition meets up again, in some respects though not explicitly, with the basic substance of anarchist thought, which is centered around the struggle against *domination*. It was to become, for the group, the crucial analytical tool [*analyseur*] for everything that happens in capitalist society, which was bureaucratic in the East and liberal in the West—so much so that, little by little, S. ou B. would implement a critique not only of the relations that are formed at the point of production and that obviously retain their central importance but also of relationships between generations, between the sexes, in education, during leisure time, and so on.

A justification for the group's gradual distancing of itself from the economistic and "productivist" side of Marxism may be found in the observation that modern capitalism no longer seemed doomed to collapse beneath its insurmountable objective—economic—contradictions (falling rate of profit, pauperization of the laboring masses, etc.). More and more clearly, Marxism could be summed up, for a large portion of the group, in the idea that men make their own history and that the history of societies, and in any case of modern society, is the history of class struggle.

Throughout the 1950s, little by little this idea was radicalized. Class struggle ended up no longer simply playing the role of motive force for changes in modern society. It was its very crisis; it was its analyzer, and it was the womb in which the project of a revolutionary—that is to say, an autonomous—society was formed. From this perspective, the only justifiable criterion the revolutionary might formulate with regard to the society in which he lives was the one whose elements are furnished to him by the struggle people conduct against it, from the elementary and sometimes unconscious resistance they put up against their being manipulated in their laboring lives and in many other life circumstances all the way up to massive confrontations against the established order. Likewise, the ideas the revolutionary might develop apropos of the society in which he aspires to live will not be found by him either in utopian concoctions or in an alleged science of history but in the creations of the workers' movement, in its egalitarian demands, and in its self-organizational and direct-democratic practices.

All these ideas went, to say the least, beyond the bounds of Marxism. When Castoriadis brought them together into a coherent bundle in "Modern Capitalism and Revolution" (1960–1961) and then in "Marxism and Revolutionary Theory" (1964–1965), these bounds burst. The discussion to which those theses gave rise was quite lively within the group between, on the one hand, mainly Castoriadis and Mothé, and, on the other, Lyotard, Véga, Pierre Souyri, and Philippe Guillaume (not to be confused with [the negationist] Pierre Guillaume). It culminated in 1963 in a split. The S. ou B. group continued on, around Castoriadis and the review. The group Pouvoir Ouvrier (Workers' Power) retained the monthly bulletin of the same title that had been put out for several years already. S. ou B. dissolved itself in 1967; Pouvoir Ouvrier would survive until 1969.

In 1958, the group had experienced another split, as expressed in the departure of Lefort, Henri Simon, and several other members. The disagreement, which had troubled the group since its creation, touched on its praxis, its politics. It flowed from the group's analysis of the nature and role of so-called working-class organizations and bore, precisely, on the question of organization: Was it necessary to get organized and, if so, how? Opposed to the advocates of a—democratically, it was understood, and not hierarchically—structured organization (some were still saying *party*), one with defined contours and a program—that of the autonomy of the proletariat—were those who were denouncing the risk of bureaucratization of every organization that was distinct from the proletariat's own self-organization in its struggles, that is to say, the risk that the organization might seek to play a directive leadership [*d'une direction*] role over the proletariat. In the first camp, notably, were Castoriadis and Véga; in the other, mainly Lefort and Simon. This disagreement is worth noting not only because, despite its, so to speak, fictive character (given the numbers in, and the marginality of, the group), it contributed, at least until 1958, to the structuring of the life of the group and was manifested on several occasions within the pages of the review, but also because it covered over a divergence that itself was never truly expressed therein, though it weighed upon the relationships between Lefort and Castoriadis in particular. That disagreement bears on the very nature of the postrevolutionary regime, such as it might be imagined and wished for. It goes without saying that the whole group violently rejected the idea of dictatorship by a party, even an "authentically" proletarian one, and unreservedly subscribed to the project of a full, active, direct democracy, the democracy of Councils. Yet when, in the final days of the Hungarian insurrection, the Greater Budapest Council defined the principles that were to ground a new kind of socialism, Lefort was the only one, within the group, to hail, among those principles, that of national representation, a Parliament, therefore, one that, alongside the Councils, would be the specific site of the political. He was also the sole one to use, in his analyses of bureaucratic society, the notion of *totalitarianism*. Yet it is in referring to Lefort's subsequent writings on the political, democracy, and totalitarianism that one could, retrospectively, shed some light on what his thinking was when he was still participating in the S. ou B. group.

* * *

In presenting here a selection of texts that appeared in the S. ou B. review, we have wanted to offer to the reader of today the possibility of becoming acquainted with a collective effort at engaged political reflection that, though it bears on a past that is in many regards bygone, still appears to us to be capable of shedding light on many aspects of the present. For the most part, these texts are no longer accessible. The review's forty issues are now unobtainable. The Christian Bourgois edition, in the Éditions 10/18 collection, of articles Castoriadis had published there is out of print.[1] Some articles by Lefort and those by Lyotard on Algeria are still available, since they were reprinted in books, as is Mothé's *Journal d'un ouvrier*.[2] Yet, presented in such ways, those writings do not yield an idea of the collective elaboration to which they contributed and from which, in part, they proceeded.

In order to give due recognition to the collective character of this group effort—whose importance Castoriadis, in particular, was later to underscore when he noted how it had affected his own thinking—it would have been necessary to reproduce numerous articles and notes dealing with current events, including analyses of political events, social struggles,[3] "social trends," and critiques of books and films. It also would have been necessary to accompany the published texts with working documents, minutes of meetings, and so forth. But that was not possible within the framework of a one-volume publication. We thus had to limit our selection to the articles that are most revealing of the theoretical development of the group and, therefore, often to the authors that are recognized today. And yet, we were not able, in many cases, to furnish the full text of the articles retained, some of which are of book length.

On several levels, we therefore had to make choices, indeed highly restrictive ones. What guided us in these choices was basically the *inside* knowledge we have of the group's thinking and of its development, since the six persons who carried through this work had all been members of the group. True, not all of us followed Castoriadis at the time of the 1963 split. We have endeavored to be impartial, aided in this effort by the benefit of time. This same benefit of time exposed us to the temptation to make retrospective judgments about this or that idea or position taken by the group: we have refrained from doing so.

We have divided the present collection into seven thematic sections that cover the main preoccupations of the group. These sections follow in an order that corresponds pretty much to the chronological order in which the themes broached came to the fore in S. ou B.'s work. In addition to the selection of texts, our intervention has been limited to rather brief introductory notes that set these texts back within their context and to summaries of portions of articles that had to be cut.

D. B.

Notes

1. Translator/Editor (henceforth: T/E): Since the publication of this Preface in 2007, Éditions du Sandre (Paris) has begun republishing, in a multivolume set entitled *Écrits politiques* 1945–1997, Castoriadis's S. ou B.-era writings that had been reprinted by 10/18 from 1973–1979, along with additional political writings by Castoriadis. All forty issues of *S. ou B.* are now available online at soubscan.org and the ambitious project of soubtrans.org will be to provide extensive translations, in a number of languages, of S. ou B. texts, including full versions of all the translations in the present English-language volume.

2. On the other hand, Philippe Gottraux's thesis was published by Payot (Lausanne) in 1997 under the title *Socialisme ou Barbarie. Un engagement politique et intellectuel dans la France de l'après-guerre*. In its first part, it offers solid documentation about the group's history, but its interpretation of that history is highly debatable. [T/E: See now also Stephen Hastings-King's groundbreaking 2014 study: *Looking for the Proletariat: Socialisme ou Barbarie and the Problem of Worker Writing* (Leiden and Boston: Brill).]

3. In 1985, Acratie published a volume in which are to be found a number of articles, reprinted from the review, that dealt with workers' struggles from 1953 to 1957. [T/E: *Socialisme ou Barbarie. Organe de Critique et d'Orientation Révolutionnaire. Anthologie. Grèves ouvrières en France 1953–57* (Mauléon: Acratie).]

Translator/Editor's Introduction

What if the ways in which ordinary people lived their everyday lives and struggled against exploitation, oppression, and alienation were themselves bases for and prefigurations of social change? Theory would not need to be inculcated by outside specialists. And, like the actions of the State itself, attempts by political and labor organizations as well as by managers at all levels to substitute for people's activity would constitute not just misrecognition of their tendencies toward autonomy but veritable power grabs—themselves subject to perpetual challenges from below.

Performing this radical reorientation, Socialisme ou Barbarie (Socialism or Barbarism, S. ou B.), an obscure, consistently shunned postwar French revolutionary organization since become "legendary,"[1] concluded that the popular response to "rationalized" forms of outside control in a world divided into two competing "bureaucratic-capitalist" camps would be *workers' management*—as was stunningly confirmed, against traditional Left expectations, by workers' revolts in the Fifties in the East (East Germany, Poland, and Hungary) and by increasingly widespread challenges to established society in the Sixties in the West (including the May '68 student-worker rebellion).[2] Such critical thought not only examined the overall crisis of systems of domination but explored their contestation at the workplace, in changing relations between the sexes and generations, as well as within national liberation movements, bringing out "the positive content of socialism" while remaining clear-eyed about potential rebureaucratization of emancipatory struggles.

Initially formed in 1946 as the Chaulieu-Montal (Cornelius Castoriadis-Claude Lefort) Tendency within the Parti Communiste Internationaliste (PCI, the French section of the Trotskyist Fourth International), the group Socialisme ou Barbarie, which took its name from a Rosa Luxemburg formula,[3] became, two years later, an independent revolutionary organization that endured, amid various internal controversies and splits, until its self-dissolution in 1967. From 1949 until 1965, its journal of the same name published forty issues of what are now recognized as some of the most creative and incisive analyses and visionary programmatic revolutionary texts of the second half of the twentieth century.

Seven decades after its inception, five decades after its "suspension *sine die*," and one decade after the publication in France of a selection of the group's writings, a *Socialisme ou Barbarie Anthology* has finally appeared that translates the complete French *Anthologie* while incorporating, for the English-speaking public, *S. ou B.* articles on American and British workers' struggles. This collection restores the *collective* nature of the group's adventure, where manual and intellectual workers, in contact with like-minded revolutionary organizations worldwide, reflected and acted together in anticipation of a nonhierarchical, self-governing society. The present volume also commences the Soubtrans Project www.soubtrans.org, an online multilingual collective effort to translate an ever-increasing number of the extant *S. ou B.* texts.

* * *

"Struggle" lies at the *center* of the S. ou B. experience as well as of the present *Anthology*. In the middle of the central fourth part of its seven-part thematically-organized selections, Chaulieu declares, "Those who look only at the surface of things see a commodity only as a commodity." A traditional Marxist would anticipate here a long excursus on the "law of value" sure to evoke how, via "commodity fetishism," "every product [is converted] into a social hieroglyphic"—that is, a mysterious code requiring a specialized caste of decoders. Instead, Chaulieu objects, "They don't see in it a crystallized moment of the class struggle." Recalling the *theme of struggle at the point of production*—present from the review's very first issue and as adapted from Johnson-Forest (C.L.R. James-Raya Dunayevskaya) Tendency worker narratives—he asserts, "They see faults or defects, instead of seeing in them the resultant of the worker's constant struggle with himself"—that is, his[4] struggle both to participate in the collective labor he is obliged to perform and to parry irrational orders emanating from external management of that labor. "Faults or defects embody the worker's struggles against exploitation. They also embody squabbles between different sections of the bureaucracy managing the plant." Struggle here is *historical* in a strong sense and *open-ended* in ways that the "laws" of "scientific socialism" never were.

Struggle involving serious political commitment also marks the *prehistory* of this group later often retrospectively mistaken for a debating society that would have prepared the "intellectual" careers of some subsequently famous members. "Albert Véga"[5] battled both Francoists and Stalinists in Civil War Spain. In France, Pierre Souyri fought in the Resistance as a teenager; "Daniel Mothé" and Benno Sternberg were active clandestinely under the Occupation. Lefort was organizing Parisian high-school students clandestinely during the War while in Greece Castoriadis, who had joined the Communist Youth at age fifteen, created a clandestine oppositional group and review by age nineteen. Georges Petit, a self-described "sympathizer and fighter for a crypto-Communist organization," struggled, after his Gestapo arrest and deportation to German concentration camps, to combine imperative outward submission with an ongoing critical take on his internment, including the Communists' role within the prisoners' hierarchy. Jean-François Lyotard was one of several "suitcase carriers" in the group who were supportive of the Algerian FLN. Students who joined later viewed S. ou B. as dispensing the education they could not receive at University.

The Chaulieu-Montal Tendency was set in motion one evening in 1946 when Lefort, who had been "holding weekly meetings that drew, on average, one hundred people" at Lycée Henri IV and later created a "network of work groups," attended a PCI meeting. Hearing Castoriadis speak there, he was won over by the latter's nonorthodox argument about the Russian bureaucracy even before the presentation ended. Lefort's companion urged him to introduce himself and soon the three were living together. This growing tendency fought for two years to alter Trotskyist analyses and policies from within,[6] garnering praise for Castoriadis from Trotsky's widow Natalia Sedova, collaborating with the Gallienne and Munis tendencies, and beginning a longstanding, fruitful collaboration with the Johnson-Forest Tendency (later *Correspondence*) when members Raya Dunayevskaya (Trotsky's former secretary) and "Ria Stone" (Grace Lee [Boggs]) visited Paris in 1947 and 1948.

A form of struggle we might call *creative internal conflict* already appeared as the Chaulieu-Montal Tendency prepared to leave the Fourth International. Castoriadis advocated a delayed but decisive public break designed to maximize recruiting efforts and build a new revolutionary organization committed to struggle for workers' autonomy; Lefort demurred, to the point of briefly suspending his participation, as he wished, instead, to constitute quietly but immediately a separate group of reflection that recognized the autonomy of workers' struggles. The journal's subtitle, "Organ of Critique and Revolutionary Orientation," perhaps expresses in part an overlapping compromise as well as an ongoing tension between these contrasting visions. That first short-lived split was followed over the years by others—key ones of which are presented below through competing texts published in the review by the opposing protagonists—starting with a struggle in April 1949, when Lefort again temporarily departed, over how to position the group in relation to the sudden, promising but limited appearance of antibureaucratic, working-class "Struggle Committees."[7] Indeed, the inaugural "Presentation" (March 1949) had stated that "the classic saying ['Without revolutionary theory, no revolutionary action'] has meaning only if it is understood to be saying, 'Without *development* of revolutionary theory, no development of revolutionary action.'"[8] So, the struggle over how to further revolutionary theory was central to the group's disputatious and fecund history from the first text in that first issue until Castoriadis's final *S. ou B.* text, "Marxism and Revolutionary Theory,"[9] where he concluded that one must choose either to remain Marxist or to remain revolutionary.

Even the group's self-dissolution a year before May '68 (a decision preceded by two years of arguments)[10] did not end the strife. Some joined an effort to reconstitute the group during the events,[11] while others, like Lyotard to his subsequent regret, bitterly rejected all cooperation.[12] More relevant to *S. ou B.*'s republication history,[13] Lefort soon decided to reprint his *S. ou B.* texts separately, along with other writings, in *Éléments d'une critique de la bureaucratie* (1971). This unilateral decision by a prolific cofounder (who definitively left the group in 1958) made it difficult to envision an exhaustive reprinting.[14] Thus began, the next year, the compiling and then the reissuance of Castoriadis's principal contributions to the review in eight volumes (1973–1979).[15] Later, Lyotard published his main *S. ou B.* texts in *La Guerre des Algériens* (1989).[16] The anarchist publisher Acratie made a first, quite limited effort in 1985 to bring together a collection of texts from the review: *Socialisme ou Barbarie: Chronique des grèves en France en 1953 et 1957.*[17] It was only in 2007 that Acratie brought out, initially via private subscription, the more comprehensive *Anthologie*, where one could read for the first time in one place an illustrative sampling of the review's contents as well as the various sides of the group's main disputes.

* * *

This strife has extended even into the preparation of the present translation.[18] Upon completion in 1992 of the last volume of Castoriadis's *Political and Social Writings* (*PSW*), I announced a project Castoriadis enthusiastically supported: "to publish [a volume of *S. ou B.*] translations in the not-too-distant future."[19] That hope was long delayed, first by publication difficulties with my other Castoriadis translations in the years prior and then subsequent to his 1997 death.[20] Finally, in 2001, after identifying a potential publisher, I began to approach former members but encountered, sometimes, a longstanding animus, especially toward Castoriadis, dating back at least to their early exits or after the group's breakup—some of which rubbed off on me, his translator, by association.[21] Leaving the selection of texts for a potential anthology in French and then in English translation to a group of certain former members, I discovered that my interlocutors, who had unresolved feelings toward Castoriadis and thus, it would seem, toward me, had misrepresented my intentions to this group, and I was eventually barred from translating the *Anthologie* I had helped instigate, which finally appeared a half decade later. Even the generous offer of the University of Michigan Library (which houses the world-renowned Labadie Collection of Social Protest Material) to scan for free all forty *S. ou B.* issues in collaboration with the Cornelius Castoriadis/Agora International Website www.agorainternational.org aroused suspicions, and an anonymous collective instead had to initiate the Soubscan Project www.soubscan.org. Only in 2013, when the Victor Serge Foundation obtained Acratie's green light after certain former members relented, did the current translation project start to become a concrete possibility.

Of course, translation itself is disturbing.[22] The process whereby "foreign ideas [are introduced] into what we think of as a determinate yet evolving literary community or 'body politic,' so as to open that body to the possibility of a considered assimilation of something that is not (yet) itself"[23]—thereby also transforming the text beyond recognition for readers in the original language—involves struggle, as it inherently creates suspicions and opens issues on both sides of the linguistic divide. My friendly and supportive predecessor, "Maurice Brinton" (London Solidarity's late cofounder Christopher Agamemnon Pallis), endeavored to adapt Castoriadis's *S. ou B.*-era writings to a working-class audience within Britain's specific context. Brinton had given the 1957 version of "On the Content of Socialism"[24] a more workerist bent than was warranted by the French original while here and there altering the text and inserting defensive footnotes regarding certain points, e.g. Castoriadis's recognition that some form of money ("signs") would continue to exist in a self-managed society based on the principles of "absolute wage equality" and "consumer sovereignty." At the time, even this altered translation drew the ire of some sectarians.[25] As recently as 2011, the Socialist Party of Great Britain declared its position (unchanged since 1904) "vindicated" against both Castoriadis and Solidarity, while misrepresenting "On the Content of Socialism" as simply a "blueprint" (though every French and English version explicitly denied this)[26] and avoiding any substantive dialogue.[27]

When editing this and other Brinton translations for *PSW*, I tried to bring them closer to the originals while respecting his excellent work. I have now gone even further toward restoring the original, and without including, for the *Anthology*, those notes and comments Castoriadis added later. Readers are urged to consult them (found in *PSW*), but in keeping with the French Editors' avowedly antianachronistic aim, the present translations may be read as better reflecting the original context.[28]

Brinton chose evocative terms—"order-givers"/"order-takers"—to translate *dirigeants/exécutants*, which designate the principal classes engaged in struggle, starting in the workplace, during the age of bureaucratic capitalism, when the conflict between the property-owning bourgeoisie and propertyless proletarians gave way to the division between those who manage production, the economy, and society and those who must carry out "fundamentally contradictory" managerial commands. Brinton's militant translations were not concerned with presenting Castoriadis's writings as a whole and in historical context. In *PSW*, I adopted "directors"/"executants," so that the reader would understand the connections with "execution" and *direction*—which translates variously as "(giving) direction," "management," and "leadership," depending on the context, and sometimes with multiple overlapping meanings. This more literal choice becomes even more significant when Castoriadis's *S. ou B.* texts are reset alongside others'. The extended struggle between Castoriadis and Lefort over *la direction révolutionnaire*—"revolutionary leadership"—becomes clearer: In what sense can one speak of leadership (*direction*), even a generally noncoercive one of "ideological struggle and exemplary action," if, from the very first issue, overcoming bureaucratic capitalism entailed the suppression of the directors/executants division? Their lively and shifting exchanges over the "organization question" reveal an imperfect but true dialogue of far-reaching implications, in both content and form, for today's radicals.[29]

* * *

Highlighting the group's "creative internal conflict" should not leave one with the impression that a Castoriadis/Lefort rivalry adequately symbolizes its concerns and accomplishments. Many other voices may be heard here. Hearing those voices helps round out people's understanding and appreciation of S. ou B. as a revolutionary group concerned with: "Proletarian Experience" (not limited here to Lefort's eponymous editorial but also including writings by American and French working-class authors Paul Romano—a Johnson-Forest Tendency member and factory worker—and "Mothé"—a worker at Renault); the workers' struggle against the "Communist" bureaucracy ("Hugo Bell"—a pseudonym for Sternberg—and "Véga" on East Germany, plus a broad array of texts on the 1956 "Hungarian Insurrection," which S. ou B. can be said to have foreseen); as well as anticolonial struggles and the tendency toward bureaucratization in such struggles ("François Laborde"—pseudonym for Lyotard—on the Algerian War), along with resistance thereto ("Pierre Brune"—pseudonym for Souyri—on "The Class Struggle in Bureaucratic China").

Despite not having previously translated these authors, their texts posed few problems.[30] I shall mention just one. Mothé uses the reflexive verb *se débrouiller*—which can generally mean "to manage" (not in the sense of "management" but of "getting by")—to describe how workers in a work collective engage in "improvisational coping" (my improvised suggestion for coping with the translation of this word) and how managers in the hierarchy also practice—individually—such improvisational coping. In order to cope with this verb's richness, I have also occasionally translated it as "to make do."[31] This bit of colloquial near-redundancy should foster philosophical interrogations as much as highlight how—in the grips of a managerial bureaucracy that mandates worker participation at the same that it strives to undermine all such attempts at participation by excluding or circumventing autonomous decision-making[32] (effective exercise of autonomy rendering the manager's role *redundant*, in both the British and general meanings of that term) and in the face of technical changes designed to remove the human element from production—workers express, through their collective activity, the maxim "Necessity is the mother of invention." *Necessity* refers here to the unfree nature of work when managed from the outside, and *invention* refers both to executants' organizational creativity and to their constant adaptation to as well as adaptation of technical production processes (themselves technical innovations).[33]

Nor should the fact that public recognition of S. ou B. was mostly[34] belated leave one with the impression that the group was detached, spinning utopias in isolation. Besides previously mentioned cooperation with the Gallienne, (Grandizo) Munis, and Johnson-Forest tendencies, let us note that "Véga" and "Mothé" were among the Bordigists who entered the group in 1950 (much to Lefort's consternation). Communication and collaboration with James and Dunayevskaya of *Correspondence* continued into the 1950s, and well beyond then with Grace Lee and her Detroit autoworker husband Jimmy Boggs, who influenced the group's views on the woman and minorities questions. A significant discussion between Chaulieu and Council Communist Anton Pannekoek on workers' councils and revolutionary organization appeared in the review in 1954. Free radicals such as anti-Algerian War activist Pierre Vidal-Naquet—who secured publication for Mothé's first book—and artist/poet Jean-Jacques Lebel—who penned for the review an obituary of Munis comrade Benjamin Péret—actively sympathized. Along with André Breton and members of *Arguments*, Castoriadis and Lefort helped found a "Committee of Revolutionary Intellectuals" at the time of the Hungarian Revolution. Even after Lefort's definitive departure, he joined Castoriadis in a "Cercle Saint-Just" along with historians Vidal-Naquet[35] and Jean-Pierre Vernant as a way of developing broader outside ties and new themes when the group was wracked in the early 1960s by conflicts between "the Tendency" and an "Anti-Tendency" (Véga, Lyotard, Souyri). As Pouvoir Ouvrier (the name of its popularized monthly until the 1963 split), S. ou B. published a joint text with Unità Proletaria (Italy), Socialism Reaffirmed (later Solidarity; Great Britain), and Pouvoir Ouvrier Belge (Belgium) following a May 1961 "conference of revolutionary socialists."[36] Solidarity was key to S. ou B.'s emphasis on the shop stewards' movement in Britain, and Solidarity pamphlets containing *S. ou B.* translations were smuggled aboard trawlers into Poland where they were read by some Solidarność founders. Castoriadis's 1995 "Raoul" (Claude Bernard) obituary recalls the group's ongoing efforts to draw disaffected Trotskyists and others into a wider coalition.[37] There were contacts with the "All-Japan League of Student Self-Government" (Zengakuren) and, via Solidarity, with Berkeley Free Speech Movement (FSM) leader Mario Savio. And let us not allow subsequent invectives to make us forget that *L'Internationale Situationniste* cofounder Guy Debord, who saw his political education transformed through contact with the review in the second half of the 1950s, penned in 1960, with "Canjuers" (Daniel Blanchard), the "Preliminaries Toward Defining a Unitary Revolutionary Program"[38] between *IS* and *S. ou B.* before himself briefly joining the latter group.

This wider engagement with like-minded revolutionaries worldwide may be read in the pages of *S. ou B.* and this *Anthology* via articles whose inspiration and actual words originated abroad. In addition to Romano's and Stone's *The American Worker*, serialized in the first eight issues, and Jack Weinberg's FSM article in the last issue, the text now titled in English "Wildcat Strikes in the American Automobile Industry" translates a *Correspondence* account of autonomous labor action and "The English Dockers' Strikes" draws heavily upon an article published in *Contemporary Issues*, a magazine published in London and New York by Josef Weber's post-Trotskyist American/British/ German "Movement for a Democracy of Content."

* * *

Of course, any one-volume *Anthology* and this short Introduction cannot satisfactorily summarize two decades of contributions from a highly heterogeneous and contentious collective. Nor could any such limited publication persuasively present what the American historian of the group, Stephen Hastings-King, calls the overall "collage" effect *S. ou B.* successfully created—through editorials, articles, and analyses, worker narratives and strike reports, polemics and programmatic texts, book and film reviews, letters to the editor and reprinted clippings from establishment and alternative presses, etc.—in order to depict a "mounting wave" of revolutionary activity in the age of bureaucratic capitalism.[39] The French Editors considered several ways of presenting the review through various choices of texts before adopting the thematically-organized selections to be read here. This, too, was a struggle—one well executed, for it forms a positive basis for the larger Soubscan and Soubtrans projects mentioned above, where that effect becomes much more evident.

In conclusion, I mention that this translation project was not simply an individual undertaking. My heartfelt thanks to Bill Brown, Andrea Gabler, Stephen Hastings-King, Clara Gibson Maxwell, and Harald Wolf, whose exemplary encouragement and support helped ensure a successful outcome to this modest quarter-century struggle.

—David Ames Curtis, March–April 2016

[N.B.: Curtis's original translations from the French and his editing of extant English-language texts and translations ultimately have been edited anonymously as a public service for the present nonprofit print and online publication.]

Notes

1. Or still *ignored*: an entire volume devoted to *The Politics of Jean-François Lyotard* (London and New York: Routledge, 1998) lacks all mention of Lyotard's Socialisme ou Barbarie involvement.

2. May '68 student leader Daniel Cohn-Bendit, along with older brother Gabriel (who had attended S. ou B. meetings), publicly acknowledged their and others' debt to S. ou B. in *Obsolete Communism: The Left-Wing Alternative*, trans. Arnold Pomerans (London: André Deutsch Ltd., 1968), 18.

3. This formula had antecedents in Engels and the young Marx and was also voiced by Trotsky; see: David Ames Curtis, "Socialism or Barbarism: The Alternative Presented in the Work of Cornelius Castoriadis," *Autonomie et autotransformation de la société. La philosophie militante de Cornelius Castoriadis*, ed. Giovanni Busino (Geneva: Droz, 1989), 293–322 http://www.academia.edu/13495706/Socialism_or_Barbarism_The_Alternative_Presented_in_the_Work_of_Cornelius_Castoriadis

4. So as to avoid anachronism, we retain throughout the translation the sexist "he" and "him" extant at that time.

5. For "Véga" (Alberto Masó) and "Daniel Mothé" (Jacques Gautrat), we follow their own practice of continuing to use their publishing pseudonyms. See the second Annex for a list of pseudonyms.

6. Lefort was elected to the PCI's Central Committee.

7. Despite their conflicts over organizational and philosophical matters, "in the face of major events (French politics, East Berlin, de-Stalinization, Poland, Hungary and Algeria)," Lefort stated in a 1975 interview (*Telos*, 30 [Winter 1976–77]: 177), "Castoriadis and I

found ourselves so close that the texts published by either of us were also in large part the product of the other."

8. *CR*, 36. (See the third Annex for a list of Abbreviations of Castoriadis Volumes.)

9. Now in *IIS*.

10. A small group calling itself alternatively "Communisme ou Barbarie" and "Groupe Bororo" was the "quite slender, but significant, thread of historical continuity" between S. ou B. and the March 22 Movement that helped instigate the May '68 protests. See *PSW3*, 122, n. 1.

11. A longer version of a mimeographed text distributed during the protests—"Reflect, Act, Organize" (the first part of "The Anticipated Revolution," now in *PSW3*)—appeared in June 1968 as *La Brèche*—the first published book to reflect on the events—under Castoriadis's pseudonym Jean-Marc Coudray and accompanied by texts from Lefort and Edgar Morin.

12. See *PSW3*, 85–87, for my note analyzing Lyotard's retrospective take on his behavior.

13. Based on an early 1990s interview with former S. ou B. member Alain Guillerm who subsequently passed away.

14. With far better connections and fewer direct conflicts, *Arguments* (1956–1962), the review cofounded by S. ou B. collaborator Morin, was, by contrast, able in 1976 to reprint its issues in their entirety, reorganized topically, with French government aid.

15. This selection, extensively translated in the three-volume *PSW* series, included unsigned editorials, anonymous texts, and articles that Chaulieu/Paul Cardan/etc. coauthored with other members, as well as Chaulieu-Montal Tendency texts and new post-*S. ou B.* Castoriadis essays and introductions, several of which were written expressly for this collection.

16. Sternberg and Mothé were able to rework some of their *S. ou B.* articles into books published while the review was still in existence.

17. Acratie's publisher, Jean-Pierre Duteuil, helped found the March 22 Movement with Daniel Cohn-Bendit.

18. In recounting forthrightly the difficulties I faced in executing the present translation project (honesty being the translator's duty when making self-reflective contributions to the International Republic of Letters), I feel no animosity toward erstwhile participants in the group. Those who struggled therein have my full esteem and merit other people's critical admiration for their lonely but steadfast engagement in such an exemplary, original undertaking riven by creative conflicts that took their emotional toll. If any former members wish to add their

views in an ongoing dialogue, I will be glad to print such contributions at www.soubtrans.org, where the present Introduction will also appear.

19. *PSW3*, 87–88, n. 3.

20. The year of his death finally saw the publication of *World in Fragments, The Castoriadis Reader,* and a *Thesis Eleven* Festschrift I edited. *On Plato's "Statesman"* appeared in 2002.

21. Thus, a "transference" *away* from the psychoanalyst Castoriadis had become and *toward* me. Unrelated to the *S. ou B.* translation project, former member Henri Simon, confusing me with a professor at an "American academic review," went so far as to point to Castoriadis's association with me to claim that Castoriadis had become a dreaded "intellectual." See n. 46 in *Correspondance Chaulieu (Castoriadis)-Pannekoek 1953-1954*, ed. Henri Simon (Paris: Échanges et Mouvement, 2001). Simon promised to correct this gross case of mistaken identity but instead posted the text online: http://www.mondialisme.org/ spip.php?article934. [*June 2017 addition*: Interpreting the "animus" mentioned in the body of this Introduction in purely personal and "sentimental" terms (whereas the context was primarily political and organizational, since it related to certain former members' "early exits" from S. ou B. or their time "after the group's breakup"), Simon took exception to this "animus" statement as well as the present footnote. His proof that he remained on good "personal" terms with Castoriadis? Castoriadis continued to send *him* books with "amicable" dedications! In fact, Simon's mention of the "American academic review" in question (*Telos*) was part of a laughably absurd theory he had devised around a typo ("1915," placed in sequence *after* 1917), which Castoriadis, with my alleged help, would have supposedly introduced in order to avoid mentioning "1919" and thus to block the "historical current" of "council communism." In fact, this 1976 text—typed directly in English by Castoriadis many years before I had ever met him—was simply badly edited and sloppily typeset by *Telos*, as was its custom; the correct date ("1919") appears in both the 1979 French translation and my subsequent English-language editing (*PSW3*). Despite having been exposed in this way as both ridiculous and the fomenter of an instance of mistaken identity involving my name, Simon refuses, even today, to remove from the internet this false identification. Yet I do not take the matter personally: Simon equally refused to acknowledge, let alone reply to, a devastating, in-depth critique of his entire pamphlet (Jean-Luc Leylavergne's February 2003 "Remarques sur la brochure: *Correspondance Pierre Chaulieu–Anton Pannekoek 1953-1954; présentée et commentée par Henri*

Simon (Échanges et Mouvement 2001)," https://collectiflieuxcommuns.
fr/160-remarques-sur-la-brochure?lang=fr). What we can retain
from this minor contretemps, mentioned for illustrative purposes, is
that *struggle* continues to underlie the internal and external relations
of this now-defunct group, sometimes in the most profound and
productive ways, sometimes in the pettiest of fashions. Of additional
note: Simon informed me that he, too, was excluded (like me, but
also other of his fellow former S. ou B. members) from providing
input to the self-selected French editorial committee that prepared
the *Anthologie*.]

22. See my 2004 Castoriadis conference paper: http://1libertaire.free.fr/
    Castoriadis45.html.

23. See my Translator's Foreword to Lefort's *Writing: The Political Test*
    (Chapel Hill: Duke University Press, 2000), x.

24. *Workers Councils and the Economics of A Self-Managed Society* (London:
    Solidarity, 1972).

25. Adam Buick, "Solidarity, the Market and Marx," [*Libertarian
    Communist*], 2 (April 1973): 1–4 http://socialismoryourmoneyback.
    blogspot.com/2009/12/solidarity-market-and-marx.html.

26. Solidarity's added diagrams, with illustrated hedgehogs, perhaps fos-
    tered the false impression that "On the Content . . . " was meant as a
    "blueprint" (rather than the summary and extrapolation of workers'
    struggles it explicitly declares itself to be), but, unlike Isaiah Berlin's
    dour underground Archilochus-inspired hedgehogs that allegedly
    "know one thing" alone, Solidarity's hedgehogs—said to be "prickly"
    and resistant to "being interfered with"—gambol about, read "Poetry
    by Benjamin Péret," collectively discuss specific factory blueprints,
    and are even seen among the stars in Solidarity's illustrations.

27. ajohnstone, "Vindicated: Solidarity's 'market socialism'" http://
    socialismoryourmoneyback.blogspot.com/2011/02/vindicated-
    solidaritys-market-socialism.html (February 18, 2011).

28. The libertarian publisher Acratie studiously made no copyright
    claims to the material it published in its *S. ou B. Anthologie*, and
    thus the present translations of *S. ou B.* articles (differing from texts
    published later in French and English), as well as translations of
    the *Anthologie*'s introductions and apparatus, proceed on that same
    basis: a radical educational public service.

29. The knowing reader will nevertheless be amused, retrospectively,
    to see Castoriadis, later the critic of representation and elections,
    declaring in 1957: "councils will be composed of representatives who
    are elected by the workers"—even when followed by the provisos

"responsible for reporting to them at regular intervals, and revocable by them at any time, and unit[ing] the functions of deliberation, decision, and execution"—and Lefort, the philosopher of "representation" and of "the political" as expression of inevitable "social division," asserting that the "working class . . . cannot *divide itself* . . . cannot alienate itself into any form of stable and structured representation without such representation becoming autonomized." Moreover, "Democracy is not perverted by the existence of bad organizational rules" may sound like it came from Castoriadis's 1996 critique of Habermas/Rawls/Berlin ("Democracy as Procedure and Democracy as Regime," now in: http://www.notbored.org/RTI.pdf), but it is Lefort who employs this argument against Castoriadis during their 1952 confrontation over "revolutionary leadership."

30. My thanks to Stephen Hastings-King (and *Viewpoint Magazine*) for allowing me to use his online translation of "Proletarian Experience" as the basis for the version published here.

31. Neither should "to make do" be confused with "to make/do," my translation for Castoriadis's key *IIS* term *faire*, wherein both "making" and "doing"—the imaginary dimension of creative human action, or *teukhein* (as contrasted with "representing/saying," or *legein*)—are involved. After completing the first draft of this Introduction, it was pointed out to me that "making do" is also offered as a translation for *se débrouiller* by Deborah Reed-Danahay in "Talking about Resistance: Ethnography and Theory in Rural France," *Anthropological Quarterly*, 66:4 (October 1993): 221–29.

32. In his 1971 obituary of S. ou B. member Benno Sternberg, surreptitiously published in *Les Temps Modernes* (Sartre, who had refused to acknowledge S. ou B.'s existence in print, was already blind by that time, and the obituary was signed simply "C.C.," as former member Christian Descamps has pointed out), Castoriadis attributed to Sternberg and to his early 1950s studies of the East German proletariat under Stalinism the formulation of the participation/exclusion dichotomy that lies at the base of bureaucratic capitalism's "fundamental contradiction." (See now "Benno Sternberg-Sarel," translated in: http://www.notbored.org/PSRTI.pdf, 256.)

33. "The action of the proletariat, in fact, does not only take the form of a resistance (forcing employers constantly to improve their methods of exploitation), but also that of a continuous assimilation of progress and, even more, an active collaboration in it. It is because workers are able to adapt to the ceaselessly evolving pace and form of production that this evolution has been able to continue. More basically, because

workers themselves offer responses to the myriad detailed problems posed within production, they render possible the appearance of the explicit systematic response called *technical innovation*. Aboveboard rationalization is the self-interested takeover, interpretation, and integration from a class perspective of the multiple, fragmentary, dispersed, and anonymous innovations of men engaged in the concrete production process" (Lefort, "Proletarian Experience," in Part 2).

34. At its height after the Hungarian Revolution, S. ou B. had approximately one-hundred members and the review printed 1,000 copies per issue. Nevertheless, as Castoriadis jestingly said, "If all [the people who *later* claimed to be supporters] really had been with us at the time, we would have taken power in France somewhere around 1957."

35. Pierre Lévêque and Vidal-Naquet's *Cleisthenes the Athenian: An Essay on the Representation of Space and of Time in Greek Political Thought from the End of the Sixth Century to the Death of Plato* (1964), trans. David Ames Curtis (Atlantic Highlands, New Jersey: Humanities Press, 1996), was one fruit of this dialogue.

36. "Socialism or Barbarism," now available at: http://www.notbored.org/PSRT1.pdf

37. "Raoul," translated in ibid. This list of international contacts and collaborators is far from exhaustive.

38. Translated by Ken Knabb in the *Situationist International Anthology* (Berkeley, CA: Bureau of Public Secrets, 1981), 305–10, now available at: http://www.bopsecrets.org/SI/prelim.htm. Blanchard's remembrances of his collaboration with Debord appears in translation as "Debord, in the Resounding Cataract of Time" here: http://www.notbored.org/blanchard.html

39. *Looking for the Proletariat: Socialisme ou Barbarie and the Problem of Worker Writing* (Leiden and Boston: Brill, 2014).

PART ONE

BUREAUCRATIC SOCIETY

"La Société bureaucratique"
Socialisme ou Barbarie—Anthologie, 15–18

There are two reasons, of different natures, why the present *Anthology* opens with a section devoted to bureaucratic society. On the one hand, the critical analysis of bureaucratic society—that is, the society of the so-called socialist countries—and then of the phenomenon of bureaucracy as the essential trait of all modern societies was at the center of the theoretical work of the Socialisme ou Barbarie group from beginning to end. On the other hand, this theme lies at the very foundation of this group's first principles: in a way, the phrase *bureaucratic society* can be said to offer, in condensed form, the response the group's founders, those young revolutionary militants, gave to what was then called *the Russia question*—the question the degeneration of the October Revolution and the bureaucratization of the workers' movement posed for so-called Left Marxist currents (Workers' Opposition, Councilists, Bordigists, Trotskyists, etc.).

The Socialisme ou Barbarie group was set up in 1946 as a "tendency" within the Parti Communiste Internationaliste (PCI)—that is, the [French section of the] Trotskyist Fourth International. It was known as the "Chaulieu-Montal Tendency," from the pseudonyms for Cornelius Castoriadis and Claude Lefort, its main organizers. This tendency officially broke from the PCI in 1949 in order to become the "Socialisme ou Barbarie group," which was meant to be the kernel of a new revolutionary organization.

Why, in 1946, was there this initial distancing from the Trotskyist movement? At the end of World War II, the face of the "Soviet bureaucracy" (the phrase then in use within the Trotskyist current to describe the set of social groups that had exercised power in Russia since the end of the

Russian Civil War) had taken on a quite different appearance from the one that could be attributed to it in 1923. Back then, Trotsky had characterized it as the product of a momentary balance between the forces of world revolution and those of counterrevolution—in other words, as a necessarily ephemeral historical product, since it was destined to be swept away by the victory of one or the other of those two protagonists. Now, here one was seeing this social formation exiting from the war victorious over the Third Reich, just like the ruling classes of the capitalist countries, while the dictatorship it was exercising in Russia itself had become more uncontested than ever, and, finally, it was swarming into Eastern Europe—and would soon do the same in the Far East. The Trotskyist thesis had proved untenable, and so the Soviet bureaucracy had to be unmasked as an exploitative and oppressive stratum, the same as the bourgeoisie, and the USSR as a capitalist society of a new type. Consequently, the task of the revolution in Russia, as elsewhere, would not simply be, as the Trotskyists claimed, to drive from power a group of parasites but to overthrow established social relations. Such appeared (very schematically) to be, in the view of the young militants of the "Chaulieu-Montal Tendency," the new realities of 1946.

Nineteen-Forty-Seven and 1948 were going, again from their standpoint, to clarify the world situation and its prospects for the future. The hopes and illusions raised by the Resistance and the Liberation, particularly in France and in Italy, had very quickly vanished. In all the countries exiting from the war, the living conditions and labor conditions of the working classes were quite harsh indeed (with the exception, to some extent, of North America). People were slaving away at work, starving and, in winter, freezing to death. In France, for example, "bread riots" broke out in 1947 and, in October, the daily bread ration was lowered to 200 grams, or less than the level set at the height of the War.

Little by little, the division of the world decided at Yalta was becoming a reality. In Eastern and Central Europe, the Communist parties tightened the USSR's grip on these States. As for France and Italy, they became firmly anchored within the Atlantic camp. Suddenly, the powerful CPs of those two countries (in France, the Parti Communiste Français [PCF] was garnering nearly a third of the vote in elections) abandoned their pro-Reconstruction policy of national unity and entered into opposition. This new strategy had been dictated by the Kremlin. Yet it was also a tactical necessity: in France, the Spring '47 strike at the Renault automobile factory and those that followed during the Summer and Fall, particularly in the coalfields, obliged the PCF to side with its proletarian base against the Government. Already, the hegemony of the Confédération Générale du Travail (CGT, General Confederation of Labor) over the working class appeared threatened: anti-Communist elements brought about a split within this French labor union confederation and created, in April 1948, the Confédération Générale du Travail-Force Ouvrière (CGT-FO, General Confederation of Labor-Workers' Force).

Nineteen-Forty-Eight was when the world truly entered into the Cold War. In February, there was the "Prague Coup"—that is, the seizure of power by the CP, but also and straight afterward the escalating and intensified exploitation of working-class manpower. In June began the Berlin Blockade, initiated by the Soviets. The United States soon found itself in the grip of McCarthyist fever and the American military budget exceeded the total amount of credits allotted for the Marshall Plan over a five-year period. To many, beginning with Charles de Gaulle, World War III seemed unavoidable.

In the first issues of the review, many ideas that seemed vital at the time and that astonish us today express how much one was in the grip of circumstances during this dark period: society and even capitalist civilization were said to have entered into a phase of decline; the ruling classes were said to be capable of survival only by imposing on the proletariat overexploitation, which would inevitably entail, in the end, lowered labor productivity and therefore a regression in productive forces; it was said, moreover, that these ruling classes would no longer tolerate democratic freedoms, however illusory those freedoms might have been; and, finally, they were said to be readying to hurl humanity into a new war, one infinitely more destructive than the one from which humanity had barely just exited.

Unless, that is, the proletariat transformed "their" war into "its" war—that is to say, revolution. Here was an idea the group endeavored to elaborate during this period on the theoretical level, and which it condensed into the formula "socialism or barbarism." In the event of a new war, it did not suffice to advocate revolutionary defeatism in both camps. One had to help the proletariat become aware of the means this war would place into its hands for its own liberation. This is the thesis expounded upon in particular by Philippe Guillaume (Cyrille Rousseau) in "La Guerre et notre époque" (War and our era), published in issue 3: The proletariat is the principal actor in modern production as well as the collective repository of technology, and it retains this role in times of modern industrial and mechanized warfare.

"We regard this war," wrote Guillaume,

as a decisive moment for the world system of exploitation, and that is so not only because, there, it will shake the material and political foundations of the opposing exploitative regimes but also because the masses will experience capitalism and the bureaucracy for themselves on a scale and at a level that are without comparison to everything that has gone before. Of course, having that experience under those conditions includes some profoundly negative aspects, but such experience will also be had precisely at the moment when the masses will have at its disposal weapons and techniques that are indispensable for drawing decisive conclusions about the effective seizure of power by the proletariat. War may be the path of barbarism; that is undeniable. But a revolutionary policy with respect to modern warfare can also give the proletariat the weapons it needs to achieve ultimate power for itself.

Trotsky had already written in 1939:

[I]f the international proletariat, as a result of the experience of our entire epoch and the current new war, proves incapable of becoming the master of society, this would signify the foundering of all hope for a socialist revolution, for it is impossible to expect any other more favorable conditions for it.[1]

In the present part of this *Anthology*, we reprint large excerpts from three texts: the article entitled "Socialism or Barbarism," drafted by Castoriadis but published as the Editorial for the first issue of the review and therefore reflecting the positions of the group as a whole; "The Relations of Production in Russia," signed "Pierre Chaulieu" (Castoriadis) and published in the second issue of the review; and, finally, "Stalinism in East Germany" (nos. 7 and 8), signed Hugo Bell (Benno Sternberg).

D.B.

Notes

1. T/E: Leon Trotsky, "The USSR in War" (September 1939), first published in *The New International*, 5:11 (November 1939): 325–32. Reprinted in *In Defense of Marxism* (New York: Pioneer Publishers, 1942), 9.

Socialism or Barbarism

"Socialisme ou Barbarie"
Socialisme ou Barbarie, 1 (March 1949), 7–12, 32–46
Socialisme ou Barbarie—Anthologie, 19–35[1]

The Editorial for the first issue, which took as its title the terms of the dilemma posed in 1915 by Rosa Luxemburg, draws a picture of the world situation in early 1949 from the revolutionary, Marxist, anti-Stalinist standpoint. Yet at the same time, it marks the ideological point starting from which the group's thinking was going to evolve, as the rest of this Anthology will show.

This text was meant to remain firmly anchored in Marxist thought. Society is analyzed there in terms of classes; classes are defined by the collective relations that are formed at the point of production; the dynamic of capital and, in particular, the movement that tends toward its concentration constitute the main engine of modern history, and so on. This text also remains to a large extent Leninist: it takes up again the Leninist theory of imperialism—correcting it, however, in the light of the results of World War II, since that war did not culminate in a new unstable coalition of powers but in the polarization of world capital around two antagonistic blocs. Likewise, this text does not challenge the idea of a dictatorship of the proletariat, in the aftermath of the revolution, on the condition that this not be the dictatorship of the party.

This editorial no less manifests its striking originality. Such originality stems not so much from the characterization of the Soviet bureaucracy as a new class. That idea was in the air since well before the War and discussed openly within the Trotskyist movement. What gives this editorial its unique accent and the force that was going to propel the group onto an original theoretical path is that it recognizes in the proletariat the role of principal protagonist of its history, including its defeats—for example, for having let the 1917 Revolution give birth to a new exploitative regime—this being the recognition of the proletariat's capacity to manage production and organize socialist society.

After an introduction that synthesizes a characterization of the situation "a century after the Communist Manifesto," and which we reprint below, the first part, "Bourgeoisie and Proletariat," opens with a reminder of the way world capitalism had evolved up to and including World War II, putting the accent on the process of capital concentration and on the growing role of the State. The situation in the aftermath of the War may be summarized in two traits: concentration of world capital into two poles, and a difference in the nature of these two poles: in one, Russia, capital and the State have organically merged; in the other, centered around the United States, "big business [le grand capital] has not yet become completely identical with the State." Yet capital is destined to amalgamate on a world scale and the two systems to merge, a process that can come about only through war.

The second part, "Bureaucracy and Proletariat," reexamines the evolution of the workers' movement up to 1914. The creation of powerful organizations allowed one to obtain reforms and to better the condition of at least a portion of the proletariat (the "workers' aristocracy"). Yet that, too, culminated in the constitution of a bureaucracy and of a stratum linked to the bourgeoisie, whence the Sacred Union in 1914. The proletariat reacted to the catastrophe of war only afterward: in the Autumn of 1917 in Russia, then in Germany, Hungary, and so on. The author next inquires into the reasons for the defeat of the European revolution between 1918 and 1923. We reprint below, after the introductory pages, his analysis of the degeneration of the Russian Revolution, which closes the second part, then the entire third part, "Proletariat and Revolution."

A century after the *Communist Manifesto* was written and thirty years after the Russian Revolution, the revolutionary movement, which has witnessed great victories and suffered profound defeats, seems somehow to have disappeared. Like a river approaching the sea, it has broken up into rivulets, run into swamps and marshes, and finally dried up on the sands.

Never has there been more talk of "Marxism," of "socialism," of the working class, and of a new historical era. And never has genuine Marxism been so distorted, socialism so abused, and the working class so often sold out and betrayed by those claiming to represent it.

The bourgeoisie, in various superficially different but basically identical forms, has "recognized" Marxism and has attempted to emasculate it by appropriating it, by "accepting" part of it, by reducing it to the rank of one of a number of possible doctrines. The transformation of "great revolutionaries into harmless icons," of which

Lenin spoke forty years ago, is taking place at increasing tempo. Lenin himself has not escaped the common fate.

"Socialism," we are told, has been achieved in countries numbering four hundred million inhabitants, yet that type of "socialism" appears inseparable from concentration camps, from the most intense social exploitation, from the most atrocious dictatorship, and from the most widespread brutish stupidity. Throughout the rest of the world the working class has been faced for almost twenty years now with a heavy and constant deterioration of its basic living standards. Its liberties and elementary rights, achieved only through years of struggle against the capitalist State, have been abolished or gravely threatened.

On top of all this, millions of people are now realizing that we have no sooner emerged from the Second World War than we face a third one, which, it is generally held, will be the most catastrophic and terrible ever seen.

In most countries the working class is organized in gigantic trade unions and political parties, numbering tens of millions of members. But these unions and parties are every day more openly and more cynically playing the role of direct agents of the bosses and of the capitalist State, or of the bureaucratic capitalism that reigns in Russia.

Only a few minute organizations seem to have survived the general shipwreck, organizations such as the "Fourth International," the Anarchist Federations, and a few self-described "ultraleftist" groups (Bordigists, Spartacists, Council Communists). These organizations are very weak, not only because of their numbers (numerical strength by itself is never a criterion), but above all because of their political and ideological bankruptcy. Relics of the past rather than harbingers of the future, they have proved themselves utterly incapable of understanding the fundamental social transformations of the twentieth century and even less capable of developing a positive orientation toward them.

Today the "Fourth International" uses a spurious faithfulness to the letter of Marxism as a substitute for an answer to the important questions of the day. Some vanguard workers are to be found, it is true, in the ranks of the Trotskyist movement. But there they are constantly twisted and demoralized, exhausted by an activism devoid of all serious political content, and, finally, discarded. With the small amount of strength it can muster, the "Fourth International" plays its comical little role in this great tragedy of the working class's mystification when it puts forward its class-collaborationist slogans, like "Defense of the Soviet Union," for a Stalino-reformist government, or, in more general terms, when it masks the reality of today behind the empty formulas of yesterday.

In some countries, the Anarchist Federations still enjoy the support of a number of workers with a healthy class instinct—but those workers are very backward politically, and the anarchists keep them that way. The anarchists' constant refusal to venture beyond the sterile slogan "No Politics," or to take theory seriously, contributes to the confusion in the circles they reach. This makes anarchism one more blind alley for workers to get lost in.

Meanwhile, various "ultraleftist" groups cultivate their pet sectarian deviations, some of them (like the Bordigists) even going so far as to blame the proletariat for their own stagnation and impotence, others (like the Council Communists) living happily in the past and seeking therein their recipes for the "socialist" kitchens of the future.

Despite their delusional pretensions, all of them, the "Fourth International," anarchists, and "ultraleftists," are but historical memories, minute scabs on the wounds of the working class, destined to be shed as the new skin readies itself in the depths of its tissues.

A century ago, the revolutionary workers' movement was constituted for the first time when it received its first charter, the *Communist Manifesto*, from the brilliant pen of Marx and Engels. Nothing shows better the strength and depth of this movement, nothing can give us more confidence as to its future than the fundamental and all-embracing character of the ideas on which it was founded.

The imprescriptible merit of the *Communist Manifesto* and of Marxism as a whole was that it alone provided a granite foundation upon which a solid, unassailable edifice could be built. The *Manifesto* had the everlasting merit of helping us understand with blinding clarity that the whole history of humanity—until then presented as a succession of chance events, as the result of the action of "great men," or even as the product of the evolution of ideas—was the history of *class struggle*. It showed that this struggle between exploiters and exploited has gone on in each epoch, within the framework set by given levels of technical development and given economic relations created by society itself.

The *Manifesto* showed that the present period is that of the struggle of the proletariat against the bourgeoisie, of the productive, exploited, and oppressed class against the idle, exploitative, and oppressing class; that the bourgeoisie develops the productive forces and the wealth of society ever further, unifies the economy, the conditions of life, and the civilization of all peoples while at the same time it increases both the misery and the oppression of its slaves.

The *Manifesto* proclaimed that the bourgeoisie is developing not only the forces of production and social wealth but also an ever more numerous, more cohesive, and more concentrated class of proletarians. The bourgeoisie educates this class and even drives it toward revolution. The bourgeois era allowed one, for the first time in history, to raise the question of the total abolition of exploitation and of the building of a new type of society, and to raise it not on the basis of the subjective wishes of social reformers but on the basis of the real possibilities created by society itself. Finally, the *Manifesto* showed that the proletariat alone can be the essential motive force for the social revolution. Driven forward by the conditions of its life and disciplined over a long period of time under the capitalist system of production and exploitation, the proletariat would overthrow the ruling system and reconstruct society on a communist basis.

From the very outset, Marxism outlined a framework and orientation for all revolutionary thought and action in modern society. It even succeeded in foreseeing and predicting many of the delays and difficulties the proletariat would encounter on the road to its emancipation. But the evolution of capitalism and the development of the workers' movement itself have given rise to new difficulties, unforeseen and unforeseeable factors, and previously unsuspected tasks. Weighed down by these new difficulties, the organized revolutionary movement folded. At the present time, it has disappeared.

The first job confronting those who wish to rebuild the revolutionary proletarian movement is to become aware of the tasks confronting the movement today and to respond to these problems.

Roughly speaking, we can say that the profound difference between the situation today and that of 1848 is the appearance of the bureaucracy as a new social stratum tending to replace the traditional bourgeoisie in the period of declining capitalism.

Within the framework of a world system based on exploitation, new economic forms and new types of exploitation have appeared. While maintaining the most fundamental features of capitalism, these new forms differ significantly from traditional capitalism in that they have superseded and broken radically with such traditional capitalist forms as the private ownership of the means of production. These new economic forms even superficially resemble some of the objectives the workers' movement had set itself, objectives such as the statification or nationalization of the means of production and exchange, economic planning and the coordination of production on an international scale.

At the same time, and intimately connected with these new forms of exploitation, appeared the bureaucracy. This is a social formation that previously existed in embryonic form, but which now, for the first time in history, has crystallized and established itself as the ruling class in a whole series of countries.

The bureaucracy was the social expression of these new economic forms. As traditional forms of property and the bourgeoisie of the classical period are pushed aside by state property and by the bureaucracy, the main conflict within society gradually ceases to be the old one between the owners of wealth and those without property and is replaced by the conflict between directors and executants in the production process. In fact, the bureaucracy justifies its own existence (and can be explained in objective terms) only insofar as it plays a role deemed essential to the "management" of the productive activities of society and, thereby, of all other forms of activity.

The importance of this replacement of the traditional bourgeoisie by a new bureaucracy in a whole series of countries resides in the fact that, in the majority of instances, the roots of this bureaucracy seem to lie within the working class itself. The core around which the new ruling strata of technicians, administrators, and military personnel crystallized was none other than the leadership strata from the trade unions and "working-class parties" who have achieved various degrees of power after the first and second imperialist wars. This bureaucracy, moreover, seems capable of achieving some of the original objectives of the workers' movement, such as "nationalization" and "planning." And these achievements seem to provide the bureaucracy with the best basis for its continued domination.

The clearest result of a whole century of economic development and of the development of the workers' movement itself appears to be as follows. On the one hand, the traditional organizations (such as trade unions and political parties) that the working class continually created for its emancipation regularly transformed themselves into the means for mystifying the working class. Oozing out of every pore came the elements of a new social stratum. Climbing onto the backs of the workers, this social stratum sought to achieve its own emancipation, either by integrating itself into the capitalist system or by preparing and finally achieving its own accession to power.

On the other hand, a whole series of measures and programmatic demands, once considered progressive and even radically revolutionary (such as agrarian reform, nationalization of industry, planning for production, monopolization over foreign trade, international economic coordination), have been fulfilled, usually by the actions of the workers' bureaucracy, sometimes by capitalism itself in the course of its development. This has taken place without there resulting for the toiling masses anything other than a more intense, better coordinated, and, in a word, rationalized exploitation.

The objective outcome of this evolution has been a more efficient and more systematic organization for exploiting and enslaving the proletariat.

These developments have given rise to an unprecedented ideological confusion concerning the problems of how the proletariat should organize for struggle and of how working-class power should be structured and even of what the program for the socialist revolution should be.

Today it is this confusion concerning the most fundamental problems of the class struggle that constitutes the main obstacle to rebuilding the revolutionary movement. To dispel it, we must analyze the main features of capitalist development and of the evolution of the working class during the last hundred years.

[...]

A fundamental question therefore has to be answered on the morrow of every successful revolution. Who will be the master of society once it is purged of the capitalists and their tools? The power structure of the new regime, its political form, the relationship between the working class and its own leadership, the management of production, the type of system prevailing in the factories, all these are but particular aspects of this general problem.

Now, in Russia this problem was resolved quite rapidly when a new exploitative stratum, the bureaucracy, came to power. Between March and October 1917, the struggling masses had created organs that expressed their aspirations and that were to express their power. These organs, the soviets, immediately came into conflict with the provisional government, which was the instrument of the capitalist class. The Bolshevik Party was the only organized group advocating the overthrow of the government and the conclusion of an immediate peace. Within six months it had acquired a majority in the soviets and was leading them toward a successful insurrection. But the result of this insurrection was the enduring establishment of the Party in the seat of political power and, through the Party and as it degenerated, of the bureaucracy.

Once the insurrection was over, the Bolshevik Party showed that it conceived of the workers' government as its own government. The slogan "All Power to the Soviets" soon came to mean, in reality, "All Power to the Bolshevik Party." The soviets were quickly reduced to the role of mere organs of local administration. They retained for a while, it is true, a certain autonomy. But this was only because of the needs of the Civil War. The "dispersed" form the Civil War took on in Russia often made it difficult, if not downright impossible, for the central government to exercise authority.

This relative autonomy of the soviets was to prove quite temporary. Once normal circumstances were reestablished, the soviets were forced to become once again local executive organs, compelled to carry out without dissent the directives of the central power and of the party in command. They progressively atrophied through lack of use. The increasing antagonism between the masses and the new government found no organized channels through which it might express itself. Even when this antagonism took on a violent form, sometimes reaching the point of armed conflict (as in the Petrograd strikes of 1920–1921, during the Kronstadt insurrection, during the Makhno movement), the masses of the workers opposed the Party as an unorganized mass and not through the soviets.

Why this antagonism between the Party and the class? Why this progressive atrophy of the soviets? The two questions are intimately interconnected. The answer to both is the same.

Long before it took power, the Bolshevik Party contained within itself the seeds of the developments that could lead it into complete opposition to the mass of the workers. It based itself on Lenin's conception (outlined in *What Is to Be Done*) that the Party alone possessed a revolutionary consciousness (which it inculcates into the working class). The Party had been built on the idea that the masses themselves could attain merely a trade-union consciousness. It had been built of necessity under the conditions of Czarist Russia as a rigid clandestine apparatus of cadre elements, carefully selecting the vanguard elements of the working class and of the intelligentsia. The Party had educated its members in the conceptions of strict discipline and in the notion that whatever others might say, the

Party was always right. Once in power, the Party identified itself completely with the Revolution. Its opponents, whatever ideology they might advocate or whatever tendency they might belong to, could then only be "agents of the counterrevolution" as far as the Party was concerned.

From these conceptions it followed quite easily that other parties should be excluded from the soviets and made illegal. That these measures most often were unavoidable cannot be disputed. But the fact remains that "political life" in the soviets was soon reduced to a monologue—or to a series of monologues—by Bolshevik representatives. Other workers, if they wished to oppose the policy of the Party, could neither organize to do so nor oppose the policy of the party effectively without organization.

Thus the Party very rapidly came to exercise all power, even at the lowest levels. Throughout the country it was only through the Party that one could gain access to higher positions. The immediate results were twofold. On the one hand, many Party members, knowing themselves to be uncontrolled and uncontrollable, started "achieving socialism" for themselves: They started solving their own problems by creating privileges for themselves. On the other hand, all those throughout the country who had privileges to defend within the framework of the new social organization now entered the Party en masse, in order to defend these privileges. Thus it came about that the Party rapidly transformed itself from an instrument of the laboring classes into an instrument of a new privileged stratum, a stratum the Party itself was exuding from its every pore.

Confronted with these developments the working class was quite slow to react. Its reactions were feeble and fragmented. We are now approaching the key to the whole problem. The new duality between soviets and Party was quickly resolved in favor of the Party. The working class itself often actively assisted this evolution. Its best militants and most devoted and class-conscious offspring felt the need to give the Bolshevik Party everything they had and to support it through thick and thin (even when the Party was clearly opposing the will of the masses). All this proved possible because the working class, taken as a whole, and in particular its vanguard, still conceived of the problem of its historical leadership in terms that, however necessary they may have been at this stage, were nonetheless false.

Forgetting that "there is no supreme savior, neither God nor Caesar nor tribune," the working class saw in its own tribunes, in its own Party, the solution to the leadership problem. It believed that once it had abolished the power of the capitalists, it had only to confide this leadership role to the Party to which it had given its best people for that Party to act automatically in the class's exclusive interests.

To start with, the Party did in fact act in the interests of the working class and for rather longer than might have reasonably been anticipated. Not only was the Party the only one constantly on the side of the workers and peasants between February and October 1917, not only was it the only one to express their interests at the critical juncture; it was also the indispensable organ for the final crushing defeat of the capitalists, the one to which the workers and peasants are indebted for the successful outcome of the civil war. But already, in playing this role, the Party little by little was becoming detached from the masses. It finally became an end in itself, the instrument of and the framework for all the privileged members of the new regime.

When considering the birth of this new privileged stratum, one must distinguish the purely political aspects, which are only its expression, from the far more important economic roots.

In a modern society the major part, and in particular the qualitatively decisive part, of production is the part carried out in factories. For a class to manage a modern society, it must actually manage the factories themselves. The factories determine the overall orientation and volume of production, the level of wages, and the pace of work—in short, all the problems whose solution will determine in advance the direction in which society's structures will evolve.

These problems will be solved in the interests of the working class only if laboring people solve them themselves. But for this, it is necessary for the proletariat as a class to be before all else master of the economy, both at the level of the general management of industry and at the level of the management of each particular enterprise. These are but two aspects of the same thing.

This management of production by the workers themselves assumes an additional importance in modern society. The entire evolution of the modern economy tends to replace the traditional distinction between owners and the propertyless with a new division and opposition between directors and executants in the productive process. If the proletariat does not immediately abolish, together with the private ownership of the means of production, the management of production as a specific function permanently carried out by a particular social stratum, it will only have cleared the ground for the emergence of a new exploitative stratum, which will arise out of the "managers" of production and out of the bureaucracies dominating economic and political life.

Now, this is exactly what happened in Russia. Having overthrown the bourgeois government, having expropriated the capitalists (often against the wishes of the Bolsheviks), having occupied the factories, the workers thought it quite natural to hand over management to the government, to the Bolshevik Party, and to the trade-union leaders. By doing so, the proletariat was abdicating its own essential role in the new society it was striving to create. This role was inevitably to be taken over by others.

Around the Bolshevik Party in power, and under its protective wing, the new boss class gradually took shape. It slowly developed in the factories, at first disguised as directors, specialists, and technicians. This took place all the more naturally as the program of the Bolshevik Party left the door open to such an evolution, and at times even actively encouraged it.

The Bolshevik Party proposed certain economic measures that later formed one of the essential points in the program of the Third International. These measures consisted first of all in the expropriation of the big capitalist trusts and in the forced merger of certain smaller enterprises; second, in the essential field of the relations between the workers and the apparatus of production, the measures centered around the slogan "Workers' Control." This slogan was based on the alleged incapacity of the workers to pass directly to the management of production at factory level and above all at the level of the central management of the entire economy. "Control" was to fulfill an educative function. It was, during the transitional period, to teach the workers how to manage, and they were to be taught by ex-bosses, technicians, and production "specialists."

But "control" of production, even "workers' control" of production, does not resolve the problem of who really directs production. On the contrary, it implies quite clearly that, throughout this entire period, the problem of effective management was actually being resolved in quite a different way.

To say that the workers "control" production implies that they do not *manage* it. The Bolsheviks called for workers' control. They had little confidence in the workers' ability to manage production. There was a fundamental opposition of interests, at first latent, between the workers, who "control," and others, who actually manage production. This antagonism created in the production process what amounted to a duality of economic power. Like all situations of dual power, it had to be resolved quickly: Either the workers would press forward, within a short period, toward total management of production, reabsorbing in the process the "specialists," technicians, and administrators who had risen from their ranks, or the latter would finally reject a type of "control" that had become an encumbrance to them, a control that was increasingly a pure formality, and would install themselves as absolute masters over the management of production. If the State cannot tolerate a condition of dual power, the economy can tolerate it even less. The stronger of the two partners will quickly eliminate the other.

During the period preceding the expropriation of the capitalists, "workers' control" had a positive meaning. As a slogan, it implies the working class's invasion into the command stations of the economy. *After* the expropriation of the capitalists, such control can give way only to the complete management of the economy by laboring people. Otherwise "workers' control" will merely prove to be a protective screen used to conceal the first steps of the nascent bureaucracy.

We now know that in Russia "workers' control" led precisely to this last development. The conflict between the mass of workers and the growing bureaucracy was resolved in the interests of this bureaucracy. Technicians and "specialists" from the old regime were kept on to perform "technical" tasks. But they rapidly merged with the new strata of administrators that had risen through the ranks of the Party and of the trade unions. They soon began to demand unchecked [*sans contrôle*] power for themselves. The "educational function" of workers' control played right into their hands. It did not help the working class at all. Instead, it laid the economic foundations for the new bureaucracy.

There is little mystery about the subsequent growth of the bureaucracy. Having dealt first with the proletariat, the bureaucracy then turned against the privileged elements in town and country (the NEPmen and the kulaks) whose privileges were based on traditional bourgeois types of exploitation. The extermination of these remnants of the old privileged strata proved quite easy for the bureaucracy. In its struggle against these elements, the bureaucracy had at its disposal even more advantages than a trust enjoys in its struggle against small, isolated entrepreneurs.

The bureaucracy embodies the natural tendency of the modern economy toward the concentration of the forces of production. It rapidly overcame the resistance of the petty capitalist and the rich peasant strata, which are hopelessly doomed to disappear even under capitalism. After a bourgeois revolution, the development of the economy itself precludes a return to feudalism. Similarly, a return to the traditional, disjointed, and anarchic forms of capitalism was no longer an option in Russia. The return to a regime of exploitation as a result of the degeneration of the revolution could express itself only in new forms, in the accession to power of a new stratum expressive of the new economic structures, themselves imposed by the natural tendency toward ever more complete concentration.

The bureaucracy rapidly proceeded to the complete statification of production and to "planning." It initiated the systematic exploitation of both the economy and the proletariat. In the process, it proved capable of developing Russian production to a considerable extent. This development was imposed upon it by the need to increase its own unproductive consumption and especially by the need to expand its military potential.

The clear significance for the proletariat of this type of "planning" appears when we look at the real wages of the Russian worker. As a result of the October Revolution, wages had increased 10 percent between 1913 and 1928. Later on they fell to half their prerevolutionary levels, and at present they are even lower. The aforementioned development of production indeed is being held back more and more by the contradictions of the bureaucratic regime and above all by the drop in labor productivity. This is the direct result of bureaucratic overexploitation.

As the bureaucracy consolidated its power in Russia, the parties of the Third International underwent a comparable evolution. They became completely detached from the working class and soon lost entirely their revolutionary character. Bearing down upon them were the dual pressures of decaying capitalist society and of the centralized apparatus of the Third International, which itself reflected the bureaucratization of Russian society. The International increasingly came under the control of the Russian bureaucracy.

The "Communist" parties gradually became completely transformed. They were becoming converted into instruments of the foreign policy of the Russian bureaucracy at the same time that they were beginning to serve, in their respective countries, the interests of those broad strata of the trade-union and political bureaucracies that were emerging from within the ranks of labor. It was the capitalist regime's crisis and decay that were forcing these strata to break with capitalism and with its traditional reformist representatives. Together with an increasing number of technicians in the bourgeois countries, these strata began to see the bureaucratic-capitalist regime that had come to power in Russia as the perfect expression of their own interests and aspirations. The high point of this development was reached at the end of World War II. Taking advantage of the conditions left by the war, of the collapse of entire sections of the bourgeois regime in Europe, and of the military support of the Russian bureaucracy, Communist parties took over political power in a number of European countries and set up regimes based on the Russian model.

World Stalinism today binds the ruling strata of Russia and the satellite countries with the cadres of the "Communist" parties of other countries. Stalinism represents the point of intersection of three distinct trends: the structural evolution of world capitalism, the disintegration of traditional society, and the political development of the workers' movement.

From the economic point of view, Stalinist bureaucratism expresses the fact that it is becoming more and more difficult to continue to produce within the outdated framework of bourgeois property relations and that the exploitation of the proletariat can be organized to infinitely greater advantage within a "nationalized" or "planned" economy.

From the social point of view, Stalinism expresses the interests of new strata, born of the concentration of capital and labor and of the disintegration of traditional social formations.

In the production process, Stalinism tends to group around itself the technicians and the bureaucrats in the economic and the administrative fields, and those responsible for "managing" the labor force, namely, the "working class's" trade-union and political cadres. Outside production, Stalinism exerts an irresistible attraction on declassed and lumpenized petty bourgeois elements and on "radicalized" intellectuals. These elements can become a social class again only after the old regime is overthrown (since that regime offered them no collective prospects) and after a new regime based on privilege is instituted.

Finally, from the point of view of the labor movement in the countries where they have not yet taken power, the Stalinist parties express that particular stage of development of class consciousness where the proletariat, having perfectly well understood the need to overthrow the capitalist system of exploitation, still is prepared to entrust this task to a Party it considers its "own." The Party is entrusted with the unchecked responsibility for leading the struggle against capitalism and administering the new society.

But the labor movement will not stop forever at this particular stage of its ideological development.

The fact that the Stalinist bureaucracy is an exploitative stratum is perceived, instinctively at first, and later on more and more consciously, by a growing number of advanced workers. Despite the quite understandable absence of precise information about what is going on in the Russian orbit, it is becoming clear to many workers that the striking silence of the masses in the East reflects the deep hatred the laboring people there have for their jailers. Stalinist demagogy will not be able to conceal forever the monstrous terror being exerted against the masses.

It is difficult to imagine that workers there have many illusions left about a regime that exploits them—or that they will have any illusions about any other system that does not specifically express their power. In the capitalist countries, likewise, workers who have for many years followed the Stalinist parties are beginning to see that the policies of these organizations simultaneously serve the interests of the Russian bureaucracy and the interests of the local Stalinist bureaucracy, but never their own interests as workers. In France and Italy in particular, this still-confused awareness of what has gone wrong manifests itself in a progressive disaffection of the workers from "Communist" parties.

But something else is also clear. Despite the chronic and deepening crisis of capitalism, despite the threat of a war of unprecedented destruction, the workers are not prepared to reorganize themselves along conventional lines or to follow new parties, whichever ones they may be and whatever their program may be. We have here not only an understandable sense of distrust resulting from the negative conclusions drawn from all previous experiences. We also are witnessing a demonstration of unquestionable maturity that marks a decisive turning point in the working class's political and ideological development. Far more profoundly than in the past—and in light of the lessons it has learned from its past experience—the working class is beginning to raise the crucial problems of how it should organize and what its program should be. These are the problems of how to organize and how to exercise power on a proletarian basis.

PROLETARIAT AND REVOLUTION

Both in its bourgeois and in its bureaucratic forms, capitalism has created the objective premises for the proletarian revolution on a world scale. It has accumulated wealth. It has developed the forces of production. It has rationalized and organized production up to the very limits permitted by its own regime of exploitation. It has created and developed the proletariat, whom it has taught how to handle both the means of production and weapons, while at the same time imbuing it with a hatred of misery and slavery.

But modern capitalism has exhausted its historical role. It can go no further. It has created an international, rationalized, and planned economic structure, thus making it possible for the economy to be directed consciously and for social life to blossom freely. But capitalism is incapable of achieving for itself this conscious management of the economy, for it is a system based on exploitation, oppression, and the alienation of the vast majority of humankind.

The supplanting of the traditional bourgeoisie by the totalitarian "workers' bureaucracy" in no way resolves the contradictions of the modern world. The basis for the existence and might of the old bourgeoisie and of the new bureaucracy is to be found in the total degradation and brutalization of man. Bourgeois and bureaucrats can develop the forces of production and increase or just maintain their profits and their might only by increasing their exploitation of the masses to an ever greater extent. For the working class, the accumulation of wealth and the rationalization of the economy simply mean the accumulation of misery and the rationalization of their exploitation.

Both capitalists and bureaucrats try to convert the producer into a mere cog of their machinery. But in so doing they kill in him what they need most, productivity and creative ability. The rationalization and accentuation of exploitation bring in their wake a terrible decline in labor productivity, as may be seen especially in Russia. The waste that used to occur as a result of competition between enterprises now is produced on an infinitely vaster scale as a result of struggle on the international level. And further wastefulness occurs with each new periodic massive destruction of the productive forces, which now is taking on unprecedented proportions.

Should a Third World War lead to the unification of the world system of exploitation, the civilization and social life of humanity would be threatened with total collapse. The unlimited totalitarian domination of a single group of exploiters (whether Yankee monopolists or Russian bureaucrats) would give them free rein to plunder the earth. The fall in the productivity of labor under such a regime of ever-increasing exploitation and the complete transformation of its dominant stratum into a parasitic caste no longer having any need to develop the forces of production would lead to a massive regression in social conditions and to a prolonged setback in the development of human consciousness.

But the proletariat can still rise up and challenge capitalist and bureaucratic barbarism. Over a period of a century of capitalist development, the workers have seen their specific weight in society constantly increase. Problems are now posed in the clearest and most objective terms before the working class. This clarification demands not only a complete rejection of all regimes of exploitation, whether bourgeois or bureaucratic, but also an awareness of the proper tasks of the proletarian revolution, of what methods of struggle are needed, and of the objectives of working-class power. This clarification will become complete and definitive as we approach this terrifying war.

The *apparent* result of a century of proletarian struggle can be summarized as follows: The working class has struggled, but it has succeeded only in placing in power a bureaucracy that exploits it as much as or more than the bourgeoisie did. The *profound* result of these struggles, however, is to be found in the process of clarification that will be their consequence.

It now is objectively apparent to laboring people in a material and palpable way that the goal of the socialist revolution cannot simply be the abolition of private property. This objective is gradually achieved by the monopolies and (especially) the bureaucracy themselves with no other result than an improvement in its methods of exploitation. The goal of the socialist revolution must be the abolition of all fixed and stable distinctions between directors and executants, in relation to both production and social life in general.

In the political sphere, the objective of the proletarian revolution can only be the destruction of the capitalist or bureaucratic State and its replacement by the power of the armed masses. Already this is no longer a State in the usual sense of the word (i.e., the State as organized coercion), and as such it will immediately begin to wither away. Likewise, the objective of the revolution in the economic sphere cannot be simply to remove the management of production from the hands of the capitalists in order to place it in those of the bureaucrats. It must organize management on a collective basis as a matter of vital concern to the entire working class. By moving in this direction, the distinction between managerial personnel and executants in the production process should start to wither away beginning on the very morrow of the revolution.

Only the proletariat, acting as a whole, can achieve the aims of the proletarian revolution. No one else can do the job for it. The working class cannot and should not entrust anyone with this task, and especially not its own "cadres." It cannot drop its own initiative and abdicate its responsibility for instaurating and managing the new society by passing the task on to anybody else. If the proletariat does not itself, as a whole, assume at every moment the initiative and the leadership of every aspect of social activities, both during and more especially after the revolution, it will only have succeeded in changing masters. The system of exploitation will reappear, perhaps under different forms, but fundamentally with the same content.

We must now give concrete form to this general idea by providing more precise details about and by modifying the program for revolutionary power, that is, the political and economic system implied by the dictatorship of the proletariat. Similar changes are necessary in relation to the working-class problems of how to organize and struggle under the capitalist system.

The program of the proletarian revolution cannot remain what it was before the experience of the Russian Revolution. It must take this experience into account. It must also take into account the changes that have occurred in Eastern Europe and in the other countries that entered the Russian zone of influence after World War II. It can no longer be held that the expropriation of private capitalists is equivalent to socialism—or that it is sufficient to statify or "nationalize" the economy to render exploitation impossible.

We have now clearly established that even after the expropriation of the capitalists, the development of a new exploitative stratum is quite possible—that it is, moreover, inevitable if the expropriation of the capitalists is not accompanied by the direct takeover and management of economy by the working class itself. We also have seen that statification and nationalizations, whether undertaken by the Stalinist bureaucracy (as in Russia and in the Russian zone of influence), by the Labour Party bureaucracy (as in Britain), or by the capitalists themselves (as in France), far from eliminating or lessening the exploitation of the working class, serve only to unify, coordinate, rationalize, and intensify this exploitation. We also have established that economic "planning" is but a means to an end, that in and of itself it has nothing fundamentally progressive to offer the working class, and that, if it is carried out while the proletariat is economically and politically dispossessed of power, it can amount only to the planning of exploitation itself. Finally, we have seen that neither land reform nor the "collectivization" of agriculture is incompatible with a modern, rationalized, and highly scientific exploitation of the peasantry.

We must conclude then that the expropriation of private capitalists (as expressed in statification or nationalization) is but the negative half of the proletarian revolution. Such measures can have a progressive content only if they are linked with the positive half of the program: the management of the economy by laboring people. This means that the management of the economy, whether at the center or on the factory level, cannot be entrusted to a stratum of specialists, technicians, "capable people," or bureaucrats of whatever ilk.

Management must be carried out by laboring people themselves. The dictatorship of the proletariat cannot be merely a political dictatorship. Above all, it must be an economic dictatorship of the proletariat. Otherwise, it will serve only as a front for the dictatorship of the bureaucracy.

Many Marxists, and Trotsky in particular, already have shown that unlike the bourgeois revolution, the proletarian revolution cannot confine itself to eliminating obstacles left over from the previous mode of production. For the success of the bourgeois revolution, it was necessary—and sufficient—that the obstacles left over from the feudal regime be abolished (obstacles such as feudal corporations and monopolies, the feudal ownership of land, etc.). From that point on, capitalism built itself up and developed all by itself through the automatic process of industrial expansion. The abolition of bourgeois property, on the other hand, is the necessary—but not the sufficient—condition for the building and development of a socialist economy. After the abolition of bourgeois property, socialism can be built only in a conscious manner, that is to say, through the *conscious* actions of the masses, constantly resisting the natural tendency of the economy bequeathed by capitalism to revert to a regime of exploitation.

But there is a second and even more important distinction between the proletarian revolution and all previous ones. For the first time in history, the class taking power cannot exert this power through "delegation," it cannot entrust its power for any lengthy and enduring period of time to its representatives, to its "State," or to its "Party." The socialist economy is built up through constant, conscious action. The question is, *who* is this consciousness? Historical experience as well as an analysis of the conditions for the existence of the working class and of the postrevolutionary regime point to the conclusion that this "consciousness" can only be that of the class as a whole. "Only the masses," said Lenin, "can really plan, for they alone are everywhere at once."

To avoid failure, the proletarian revolution cannot be confined to nationalizing the economy and entrusting its management to "competent people" or even to a "revolutionary Party," even if these measures contain some more or less vague idea of "workers' control." The revolution must entrust the management of the factories and the overall coordination of production to the workers themselves, to responsible workers who are checked on continually and who can always be recalled.

In politics, likewise, the dictatorship of the proletariat cannot mean the dictatorship of a single party, no matter how proletarian and revolutionary it is. The dictatorship of the proletariat means democracy for the proletariat. Every right must be granted to the workers and above all the right to form political organizations having their own specific viewpoints. It is inevitable that the militants of the majority fraction in the mass organizations will be called upon more frequently than others to positions of responsibility. The essential thing, however, is that the entire laboring population should be able to monitor them constantly, to recall them, to withdraw its support from the fraction that until then was in the majority, should it so wish, and give it to another. Under these circumstances, the distinction and opposition between political organizations proper (parties) and mass organizations (soviets and factory committees) will quickly lose their significance. The perpetuation of this opposition could only be the harbinger of a degeneration of the revolution.

Right now we can only begin to trace the main lines of orientation that the working class's previous experience sets down for all future revolutions. The concrete forms of organization the working class will adopt can be defined only by the mass itself. The question, for instance, of what kind of economic centralization should be combined with a certain necessary amount of decentralization can only be decided by the mass itself as it comes to grips with these problems in the course of its struggle.

The problems of how the proletariat should organize and struggle within the framework of capitalism should be considered in much the same light. The conclusion that it is useless or harmful to organize the vanguard politically before the revolution has begun does not follow, either from the fact that the class as a whole has to go through the objective experiences that will raise its consciousness and lead it to revolution or from the fact that workers' organizations have served till now as fertile breeding grounds for the bureaucracy.

It is historically indispensable to organize the advanced section of the class politically. This is based on the need to maintain and to propagate among the workers a clear understanding of the development of society and of the fundamental objectives of proletarian struggle. This must be done both through and in spite of temporary fluctuations of the working class's level of consciousness and amid local, national, and craft differences.

The organized vanguard will consider its first task to be the defense of working-class conditions and interests. It will constantly strive, however, to heighten the workers' struggles, and ultimately it will come to represent the interests of the movement as a whole during each stage of struggle. Moreover, the objective constitution of the bureaucracy as an exploitative stratum makes it obvious that the vanguard can organize itself only on the basis of an antibureaucratic ideology, on the basis of a program directed mainly against bureaucracy and its roots, and by constantly struggling against all forms of mystification and exploitation.

But from this point of view, the essential thing for a political vanguard organization to do, once it has become aware of the need to abolish the distinction in society between directors and executants, is to seek from the outset to abolish this distinction within its own ranks. This is not just a simple question of better bylaws, but involves above all raising the consciousness and developing the talents of its militants through their ongoing and permanent theoretical and practical education along these lines.

Such an organization can grow only by preparing to link up with the process by which autonomous mass organs are created. In this very limited sense, it might be correct to say that the organization represents the ideological and political leadership [*direction*] of the working class under the conditions extant in the present exploitative regime. It is essential to add, however, that this leadership is constantly preparing its own dissolution through its fusion with the working class's autonomous organs. This will happen as soon as the class as a whole enters the revolutionary struggle and ushers onto the historical stage the real leadership of humanity, which is none other than the proletarian masses themselves as a whole.

Only one force can arise today to challenge the continuing decay and increasing barbarism of all regimes based upon exploitation: that of the producing class, the socialist proletariat. Constantly increasing in numbers through the industrialization of the world economy, ever more concentrated in the process of production, trained through ever greater misery and oppression to revolt against the ruling classes, having had the chance to experience the results of its own "leaderships," the proletariat, despite an increasing number of difficulties and obstacles, has ripened for revolution. The obstacles confronting it are not insurmountable. The whole history of the past century is there to prove that the proletariat represents, for the first time in human history, not only a class in revolt against exploitation but a class positively capable of overthrowing the exploiters and of organizing a free and humane society. Its victory, and the fate of humanity, are in its hands.

Notes

1. T/E: Reprinted in *SB1*, *SB(n.é.)*, and *EP5*. Originally translated as "Socialism Reaffirmed" by Bob Pennington and printed as a Solidarity Pamphlet (1961) and then, in revised form, in *PSW1*.

The Relations of Production in Russia

Pierre Chaulieu

"Les Relations de production en Russie"
Socialisme ou Barbarie, 2 (May 1949), 1–3, 31–51, 61–66
Socialisme ou Barbarie—Anthologie, 36–52[1]

"The Relations of Production in Russia" endeavors, on the one hand, to refute on the theoretical level the arguments of those who continued to maintain that the bureaucracy is not a class and that Russian society retains a socialist foundation and, on the other hand, to gather material proof of the contrary position. Here is how Chaulieu poses the problem:

The question of the class nature of economic and hence social relations in Russia has a political importance that cannot be exaggerated. The great mystification that prevails around the allegedly "socialist" character of the Russian economy is one of the principal obstacles to the proletariat's ideological emancipation, an emancipation that is the fundamental condition for the struggle toward its social emancipation. Militants who are beginning to become aware of the counterrevolutionary character of the policies of the Communist parties in bourgeois countries are slowed down in their political development by their illusions about Russia. The policy of these Communist parties appears to them to be oriented toward the defense of Russia—which unquestionably is true—therefore as being already decided upon and, in a word, agreed to in terms of Russia's defense requirements. Even for the most highly conscious among them, the case of Stalinism always boils down to that of Russia, and in judging the latter, even if they accept a host of individual criticisms, the minds of the great majority of these militants remain clouded by the idea that the Russian economy is something essentially different from an economy of exploitation, that even if it does not represent socialism, in comparison with capitalism at least, it is progressive.

We also should point out that everything in present-day society seems to conspire to maintain them in this grand illusion. It is instructive to see the representatives of Stalinism and those of "Western" capitalism—who disagree on all other questions, who are capable even of disagreeing on whether two plus two equals four—concurring with astonishing unanimity that Russia has realized "socialism." Obviously, in their respective techniques of mystification, this axiom plays different roles. For the Stalinists, identifying Russia with socialism serves to prove the preeminence of the Russian regime, whereas for the capitalists it demonstrates the execrable character of socialism. For the Stalinists, a "socialist" label serves to camouflage and to justify the bureaucracy's abominable exploitation of the Russian proletariat, an exploitation that bourgeois ideologues, mellowed by a sudden attack of philanthropy, highlight in order to discredit the idea of socialism and revolution. Now, without this identification, their respective tasks would be much more difficult. Nevertheless, in this work of mystification, the Stalinists as well as the bourgeoisie have been aided by the Marxist or allegedly Marxist currents and ideologues who have defended and helped popularize the mythology of the "socialist bases of the Russian economy."[2] This has been done for twenty years with the aid of apparently scientific arguments that boil down essentially to two ideas:

1. Whatever is not "socialist" in the Russia economy is—in whole or in part—the process of income distribution. By way of compensation, production (as the foundation of the economy and society) is socialist. That this distribution process is not socialist is after all normal, since in the "lower phase of communism," bourgeois right still prevails.

2. The socialist—or in any case, as Trotsky would say, "transitional"—character of production (and consequently the socialist character of the economy and the proletarian character of the State as a whole) is expressed in the state ownership of the means of production, in planning, and in the monopoly over foreign trade. [...]

The article then demonstrates at length, while relying on numerous quotations from Capital *and the Preface to* A Contribution to the Critique of Political Economy, *that production, distribution, exchange, and consumption are inseparable aspects of a single process: "If, therefore, the relations of distribution in Russia are not socialist, the relations of production cannot be either. This is so precisely because distribution is not autonomous but rather subordinated to production." As for the juridical form of property ownership, whether it is state-run or private changes nothing in the relations of production: the latter "are concrete social relations, relations of man with man and of class with class, as they are realized in the constant, daily production and reproduction of material life." It is these relations, on the contrary, that give a content to the form of property ownership: "What confers a socialist character or not upon 'nationalized' property is the structure of the relations of production." Now, those relations are, in Russia, characterized by the bureaucracy's absolute domination over the whole production process. Chaulieu summarizes this in the following paragraph:*

> *We have seen that statification is in no way incompatible either with class domination over the proletariat or with exploitation, here in its most perfected form. We can understand too—it will be shown in detail later on—that Russian "planning" has no less the same function: It expresses in a coordinated fashion the interests of the bureaucracy. This appears on the level of accumulation as well as on that of consumption, these two being, moreover, absolutely interdependent. With respect to its general orientation, the concrete development of the Russian economy under the domination of the bureaucracy differs in no way from that of a capitalist country. In place of the blind mechanism of value, it is the mechanism of the bureaucratic plan that assigns some specified portion of the forces of production to the production of the means of production and some other specified portion to the production of consumer goods. What guides the action of the bureaucracy in this domain obviously is not the "general interest" of the economy—a notion with no concrete or precise meaning—but rather its own interests. This is shown by the fact that heavy industry is oriented essentially toward the fulfillment of military needs—and, under present conditions and especially for a relatively backward country, this signifies that the entire productive sector needs to be developed; that the consumer-goods industries are oriented by the bureaucrats' consumer needs; and that, in carrying out these objectives, laborers have to produce the maximum and cost the minimum. We see therefore that in Russia, statification and planning serve only to advance the class interests of the bureaucracy and to aid in the exploitation of the proletariat, and that the essential objectives as well as the fundamental means (the exploitation of laborers) are identical to those of capitalist economies.*

The article's third part, "Proletariat and Bureaucracy," broaches a factual analysis of Russian society. We offer below large excerpts thereof.

PROLETARIAT AND BUREAUCRACY

1. General Characteristics

Let us now examine the fundamental relation of production in the Russian economy. This relation exhibits itself, juridically and formally, as a relation between the worker and the "State." As we know from sociology, however, the juridical "State" is an abstraction. In its social reality, the "State" is first of all the set of persons that makes up the State apparatus in all its branches (political, administrative, military, technical, economic, and other). Before all else, therefore, the "State" is a bureaucracy, and the relations of the worker with the "State" are in reality relations with this bureaucracy. We have limited ourselves here to recording a fact: the stable and irremovable character of this bureaucracy as a whole. It has this character, not from an internal point of view (i.e., not from the standpoint of real or possible "purges" or of other such dangers facing the individual bureaucrat), but from the standpoint of its opposition to the whole of society, that is, from the fact that there is straightaway a division of Russian society into two groups: those who are bureaucrats and those who are not and never will become bureaucrats. This fact, which goes hand and hand with the totalitarian structure of the State, deprives the mass of laborers of any possibility of exerting even the most minimal amount of influence over the direction of the economy and of society in general. As a result, the bureaucracy as a whole has the means of production completely at its disposal. We will have to return later to the sociological signification of this power and to the class character of the bureaucracy.

By the mere fact that a part of the population, the bureaucracy, has the means of production at its disposal, a class structure is immediately conferred upon the relations of production. In this connection, the absence of capitalistic "private property" plays no part. Having the means of production at its collective disposal, having the right to use, enjoy, and abuse these means (being able to build factories, tear them down, contract them out to foreign capitalists, having their product at its disposal, and determining how production will proceed therein), the bureaucracy plays vis-à-vis Russia's social capital the same role that the major stockholders of a joint-stock company play vis-à-vis its capital.

Two social groups therefore find themselves face-to-face: the proletariat and the bureaucracy. These two groups enter into determinate economic relations as regards production. These relations are class relations insofar as the two groups' relationship to the means of production is totally different. The bureaucracy has the means of production at its disposal; the proletariat has nothing at its disposal. The bureaucracy has at its disposal not only machinery and raw materials but also the society's consumption fund. The worker consequently is obliged to "sell" his labor power to the "State"—that is, to the bureaucracy—but this sale assumes a special character, to which we will return soon. In any case, through this "sale" the indispensable coming together of the workers' living labor with dead labor (the market for which has been cornered by the bureaucracy) is achieved.

Let us examine more closely this "sale" of labor power. It is immediately evident that the possession of the means of production and the means of coercion, of the factories and the State, confers upon the bureaucracy a predominant position in this "exchange" process. Just like the capitalist class, the bureaucracy dictates its conditions in the "labor contract." But the capitalists hold sway economically within very precise limits defined by the economic laws regulating the market, on the one hand, and the class struggle, on the other. Is it the same for the bureaucracy?

It clearly is not. No objective obstacle limits the bureaucracy's possibilities for exploiting the Russian proletariat. In capitalist society, Marx says, the worker is free in a juridical sense, and he adds, not without irony, in every sense of the term. This freedom is first of all the freedom of the man who is not shackled by a fortune, and as such it is equivalent, from a social point of view, to slavery, for the worker is obliged to labor to avoid starvation, to labor wherever work is given to him and under conditions imposed upon him. However, his juridical "freedom," while serving all along as an enticement into the system, is not devoid of significance, either socially or economically. It is this "freedom" that makes labor power a commodity that can, in principle, be sold or withheld (by striking), here or elsewhere (by availing oneself of the possibility of changing firms, towns, countries, etc.). This "freedom" and its consequence, the intervention of the laws of supply and demand, allow labor power to be sold under conditions not dictated exclusively by the individual capitalist or his class as a whole, but rather under conditions that are also determined to an important degree, on the one hand, by the laws and the state of the market, and, on the other hand, by the relation of forces between the classes. We have seen that, during capitalism's period of decadence and organic crisis, this state of things changes and that, in particular, the victory of fascism allows capital to dictate imperatively to the workers their labor conditions. We will return to this question later, but it suffices for us to remark here that a large-scale, lasting victory for fascism would certainly lead not only to the transformation of the proletariat into a class of modern-day industrial slaves but also to profound structural transformations of the economy as a whole.

In any case, it can be stated that the Russian economy finds itself infinitely closer to this model than to the one of the competitive capitalist economy when it comes to the conditions for "selling" labor power. These conditions are dictated exclusively by the bureaucracy; in other words, they are determined solely by the internal need to increase the surplus value of the productive apparatus. The expression "sale" of labor power has no real content here: without mentioning what is actually called "forced labor" in Russia, we can say that the "normal," "free" Russian laborer does not have his own labor power at his disposal in the sense that the worker in the classical capitalist economy has his labor power at his. In the overwhelming majority of cases, the worker can leave neither the enterprise where he works, nor his town, nor his country. As for strikes, it is well known that the least grave consequence is deportation to a forced-labor camp. Domestic passports, labor passes, and the MVD [Soviet Ministry of Information, or secret police] make all job transfers and changes of work impossible without the consent of the bureaucracy. The worker becomes an integral part, a piece of the equipment of the factory in which he works. He is attached to the enterprise more rigidly than is a serf to the land; he is attached to it as a screw nut is to a piece of machinery. Henceforth, the working class's standard of living can be determined—along with the value of its labor power—solely as a function of the dominant class's accumulation and unproductive consumption.

Consequently, in the "sale" of labor power, the bureaucracy unilaterally and without any possible discussion imposes its conditions. The worker cannot even formally refuse to work; he has to work under the conditions imposed upon him. Apart from this, he is sometimes "free" to starve and always "free" to choose a more interesting method of suicide.

There is therefore a class relationship in the production process, and there is exploitation as well. Moreover, this specific type of exploitation knows no objective limits. Perhaps this is what Trotsky meant when he said that "bureaucratic parasitism is not exploitation in the scientific sense of the term." For our part, we thought we knew that exploitation in the scientific sense of the term lies in the fact that a social group, by reason of its relation to the production apparatus, is in a position both to manage productive social activity and to monopolize a portion of the social product, even though it does not directly participate in productive labor, or else it takes a share of this product beyond the degree of its actual participation. Such was slave-based and feudal exploitation, such is capitalist exploitation. Such also is bureaucratic exploitation. Not only is it a type of exploitation in the scientific sense of the term, it is still quite simply a scientific kind of exploitation, the most scientific and the best-organized kind of exploitation in history.

To note the existence of "surplus value" in general certainly does not suffice to prove the existence of exploitation, nor does it help us understand how an economic system functions. It was pointed out a long time ago that, to the extent that there will be accumulation in socialist society, there also will be "surplus value," or in any case a gap of some sort between the product of labor and the income of the laborer. What is characteristic of a system of exploitation is the use of this surplus value and the laws that regulate it. The basic problem to be studied in the Russian economy or in any class-based economy is to be found in how this surplus value is distributed into funds for accumulation and funds for the dominant class's unproductive consumption as well as in the character and orientation of this accumulation and its internal laws. But before we grapple with this problem, we ought to examine the limits of exploitation, the real rate of surplus value, and the evolution of this exploitation in Russia as well as begin to examine the laws regulating the rate of surplus value and its evolution, understanding that the definitive analysis of these laws can be done only in terms of the laws of accumulation.

2. The Limits of Exploitation

In formal terms it can be said that the determination of the rate of "surplus value" in Russia rests upon the arbitrary will, or rather the discretionary power, of the bureaucracy. In the classical capitalist regime, the sale of labor power is formally a contract, whether it is arrived at by individual or by collective bargaining. Behind this formal appearance we discover that neither the capitalist nor the worker is free to discuss and to set on their own the conditions for this labor contract. In fact, through this juridical formula the worker and the capitalist only give expression to economic necessities and express the law of value in a concrete way. In the bureaucratic economy, this "free" contractual form disappears: wages are set unilaterally by the "State"—that is, by the bureaucracy. We will see that, in this case like nowhere else, the will of the bureaucracy obviously is not "free." Nevertheless, the very fact that the setting of wages and labor conditions depends upon a unilateral act of the bureaucracy, on the one hand, enables this act to express the bureaucracy's interests in an infinitely more advantageous way, and, on the other hand, ensures that the objective laws regulating the determination of the rate of "surplus value" will be fundamentally altered by it.

The extent to which the bureaucracy has discretionary power over the overall determination of wages and labor conditions immediately raises an important question. If we assume it tends to pursue maximum exploitation, to what extent does the bureaucracy encounter obstacles in its efforts to extort surplus value; to what extent are there limits to its activity as an exploiter?

As we have shown, the limits resulting from any application of the "law of value" in a competitive capitalist economy cannot exist in a bureaucratic economy. Within this economic framework (where there is no labor market and no opportunity for the proletariat to resist), the "value of labor power"—in short, the Russian working class's standard of living—becomes an infinitely elastic notion subject almost to the whims of the bureaucracy. This has been demonstrated in a striking manner since the inception of the "five-year plans"—that is, ever since the economy became completely bureaucratized. Despite the enormous increase in national income following the onset of industrialization, a huge drop in the masses' standard of living has come to light. This drop in working-class income obviously goes hand in hand with an increase both in accumulation and in bureaucratic income.[3]

One might suppose that there would be some inevitable "natural" limitation imposed upon bureaucratic exploitation, as dictated by a laborer's "minimum physiological" standard of living, that is, the elementary needs of the human organism. Actually, notwithstanding its unlimited willingness to go on exploiting, the bureaucracy is constrained to allow the Russian worker two square yards of living space, a few pounds of black bread a month, and some rags of clothing as needed for the Russian climate. But this restriction does not signify much. First, this physiological limit itself is surpassed often enough, as is shown by such manifestations as prostitution among working-class women, systematic theft from the factories and a bit everywhere else, and so on. On the other hand, having at its disposal about twenty million laborers in concentration camps on whom it spends practically nothing, the bureaucracy controls a considerable mass of manpower free of charge. Finally, what is most important, nothing is more elastic than the "physiological limit" of the human organism—as has been demonstrated by the recent war, even to those who might have doubted it. Experience has shown (in the concentration camps as well as in the countries that suffered most under the Occupation) how thick a man's skin is. In another connection, the high productivity of human labor does not always require recourse to a physiologically taxing reduction in the standard of living.

Another apparent limitation on the bureaucracy's efforts at exploitation seems to result from the "relative scarcity" of certain types of skilled labor. If such a limitation were real, it certainly would be obliged to take the problem of skilled-labor shortages into account. Consequently, so the argument goes, it would have to regulate wages in these branches of work according to the relative shortage of these types of skilled labor. But this problem, which affects only certain types of work, will be examined later, for it directly concerns the creation of semiprivileged or privileged strata and as such it touches much more upon the question of bureaucratic income than on that of the working class's income.

3. The Struggle over Surplus Value

We have said that the class struggle cannot interfere directly with the setting of wages in Russia, given that the proletariat as a class has been bound from head to foot, that it is impossible to strike, and so on. Nevertheless, this in no way means either that the class struggle does not exist in bureaucratic society or, in particular, that it does not have any effect upon production. But its effects here are completely different from the effects it can have in classical capitalist society.

We will limit ourselves here to two of its manifestations, which are tied, more or less indirectly, to the distribution of the social product. The first of these is theft—theft of objects directly pertaining to productive activity, theft of finished or semifinished goods, theft of raw materials or machine parts—insofar as it assumes massive proportions and insofar as a relatively large proportion of the working class has made up for their terribly inadequate wages with proceeds from the sale of such stolen objects. Unfortunately, a lack of information prevents us at this time from detailing the extent of this phenomenon and consequently its social character. However, to the degree that this phenomenon has grown to any significant extent, it obviously expresses a class reaction—subjectively justified but objectively a dead end—that tends to alter the distribution of the social product to a certain extent. It appears that this was especially the case between 1930 and 1937.[4]

The second manifestation we might mention here is an "active indifference" toward the results of production, an indifference manifested on both quantitative and qualitative levels. Production slowdowns, even when they do not take a collective, conscious, and organized form (a "work slowdown" strike), but rather retain an individual, semiconscious, sporadic, and chronic character, already are, in capitalist production, a manifestation of working-class reaction against capitalist overexploitation, a manifestation that becomes increasingly important as capitalism can react to the crisis resulting from the falling rate of profit only by increasing relative surplus value, that is, by intensifying more and more the pace of production. For reasons (to be examined later) that are in part analogous and in part different, the bureaucracy is obliged to push this tendency of capitalism to the maximum in the area of production. It is therefore understandable how the overexploited proletariat's spontaneous reaction would be to slow the pace of production to the extent that police-state coercion and economic constraints (piece-rate wages) allow them to do so. The same goes for product quality. The bewildering amount of bad workmanship in Russian production, and particularly its chronic character, cannot be explained merely by the "backwardness" of the country (which might have played a role in this connection at the start, but which already before the War could no longer seriously be taken into consideration) or by bureaucratic disorder, notwithstanding the increasing scope and character of this latter phenomenon. Conscious or unconscious bad workmanship—the incidental fraud, if it may be called that, committed when it comes to the results of production—only gives material expression to the attitude of the worker who faces a form of economic production and a type of economic system he considers completely foreign and, even more than this, fundamentally hostile to his most basic interests.

It is impossible, though, to end this section without saying a few words about the more general significance of these manifestations from the historical and revolutionary point of view. While these are subjectively sound class reactions that cannot be criticized, their objectively retrograde point of view nevertheless ought to be understood in the same light as, for example, we view desperate workers in the early capitalist era smashing machines. In the long run, if the class struggle of the Soviet proletariat is not afforded a different way out, these reactions can only bring with them this class's political and social degradation and decomposition. Under the conditions of the Russian totalitarian regime, however, this different outcome obviously cannot be built upon battles that are partial with respect either to their subject or to their object (like strikes for wage demands, which have been rendered impossible under such conditions), but only upon revolutionary struggle. We will return later at great length to this objective coincidence of minimal and maximal goals, which also has become a fundamental characteristic of the proletarian struggle in capitalist countries.

These reactions lead us to raise another problem, one that is fundamental for the bureaucratic economy: the problem of the contradiction found in the very term "complete exploitation." The tendency to reduce the proletariat to a simple gear in the productive apparatus, as dictated by the falling rate of profit, can only bring along with it a terrible crisis in the productivity of human labor. The only possible result is a reduction in the volume, and a lowering of the quality, of production itself, that is, the accentuation, to the point of paroxysm, of the crisis factors of an exploitative economy. We will merely indicate this problem here, and will examine it at great length later.

4. The Distribution of Consumable National Income

It is clearly impossible to undertake a rigorous analysis of the rate of exploitation and the rate of surplus value in the Russian economy today. Statistics concerning the composition of the income and living standards of various social groups, or statistics from which these figures could be deduced indirectly, ceased being published for the most part immediately after the five-year plans began to be written, and the bureaucracy systematically hides all the relevant data both from the Russian proletariat and from world opinion. From this fact alone we may infer on a moral basis that this exploitation is at least as grievous as it is in capitalist countries. But we can arrive at a more exact calculation of these figures based upon general data known to us that the bureaucracy cannot hide.

Indeed, we can arrive at some sure results based upon the following data: the bureaucracy's percentage of the population and the ratio of the average bureaucrat's income to that of the average laborer's income. Obviously, such a calculation can only be approximate, but as such it is indisputable. There is also another way in which the challenges and protests of Stalinists and crypto-Stalinists are inadmissible: Let them ask the Russian bureaucracy first for the publication of verified statistics on this matter. The matter can be discussed with them afterward.

Concerning first of all the bureaucracy's percentage of the population, we refer to Trotsky's calculation in *The Revolution Betrayed*.[5]

Trotsky gives figures ranging between 12 and 15 percent and up to 20 percent of the whole population for the bureaucracy (state functionaries and upper-level administrators, managerial strata in firms, technicians and specialists, managerial personnel for the kolkhozy, Party personnel, Stakhanovites, non-Party activists, etc.). Trotsky's figures have so far never been contested. As Trotsky pointed out, they were calculated giving the bureaucracy the benefit of the doubt (i.e., by reducing its size) in order to avoid arguments about secondary points. We will retain the average result of these calculations, granting that the bureaucracy constitutes approximately 15 percent of the total population.

What is the average income of the laboring population? According to official Russian statistics, "the 'average' annual wage per person, if you join together the director of the trust and the charwoman, was," as Trotsky observes,

> about 2,300 rubles in 1935, and was to be in 1936 about 2,500 rubles. . . . This figure, very modest in itself, goes still lower if you take into consideration that the rise of wages in 1936 is only a partial compensation for the abolition of special prices on objects of consumption, and the abolition of a series of free services. But the principal thing is that 2,500 rubles a year, or 208 a month, is, as we said, the *average* payment—that is, an arithmetic fiction whose function is to mask the real and cruel inequality in the payment of labor.[6]

Let us pass over the repugnant hypocrisy of publishing "average wage" statistics (imagine if, in a capitalist country, the *only* statistics published concerned average individual income and then one tried to make judgments about the social situation in this country based upon this average income!) and let us retain this figure of 200 rubles a month. In reality, the minimum wage is only 110 to 115 rubles a month.[7]

What now of bureaucratic income? According to Charles Bettelheim, "Many technicians, engineers, and factory directors get 2,000 to 3,000 rubles per month, this being twenty to thirty times more than the poorest paid workers."[8] Speaking later on of even "higher salaries" that are, however, "less common," he cites income figures ranging from 7,000 to 16,000 rubles a month (160 times the base wage!), which assistant movie directors and popular writers can easily earn. Without going to the heights of the political bureaucracy (president and vice-presidents of the Council of the Union and the Council of Nationalities receive 25,000 rubles a month, 250 times the base wage:

this would be equivalent in France to 45 million francs a year for either the president of the Republic or the president of the Chamber, if the minimum salary is 15,000 [old] francs a month; in the United States, if the minimum wage is 150 dollars a month, it would be equivalent to 450,000 dollars a year for the president. The latter, who receives only $75,000 a year, ought to envy his Russian colleague, who has an income comparatively six times higher than his. As for Mr. Vincent Auriol, who receives only six million francs a year [as President of the Republic], that is, 13 percent of what he would receive if the French economy were "collectivized," "planned," and "rationalized," in a word, truly progressive, he appears to be a poor relation indeed), we will confine ourselves just to deputies' pay, "which is 1,000 rubles a month, plus 150 rubles a day when meetings are held."[9] If it is assumed that there are ten days of meetings in a month, these figures yield a sum of 2,500 rubles a month, that is, twenty-five times the lowest wage and twelve times the "theoretically average wage." According to Trotsky, average Stakhanovites earn at least 1,000 rubles a month (this is precisely why they are called "the Thousands"), and some of them earn even more than 2,000 rubles a month, that is, ten to twenty times the minimum wage.[10] Taken as a whole, these estimates are more than confirmed by the data in Kravchenko;[11] his information establishes that the highest figures given here are extremely modest and should be doubled or tripled to arrive at the truth concerning money wages. Let us emphasize, on the other hand, that we are not taking into account perquisites and indirect or "in kind" benefits granted to bureaucrats, which as such (in the form of houses, cars, services, special health care, well-stocked and even better-priced buying cooperatives) are at least as important a part of the bureaucracy's income as its cash income.

Therefore, a ratio between average working-class and bureaucratic incomes of 1 to 10 may be used as the basis of our calculations. Doing this, we really will be acting on the bureaucracy's behalf, since we will take the "average wage," as provided by Russian statistics, of 200 rubles, which includes a significant proportion of the bureaucracy's income in this index of *working-class* wage levels for 1936, and since we also will take 2,000 rubles a month (the least high figure cited by Bettelheim) as the *average* income for the bureaucracy. Indeed, we would be justified in taking 150 rubles a month as the average worker's wage (i.e., the arithmetic mean of the minimum salary of 100 rubles and the "average wage," which includes the bureaucracy's salaries as well) and at least 4,500 rubles a month as the average salary for the bureaucracy, which we arrive at if the "standard" salary of engineers, factory managers, and technicians—which Bettelheim indicates to be 2,000 to 3,000 rubles a month—is added to an equal amount of services from which the bureaucracy benefits as a result of their position, but which are not contained in their salaried income. This would yield a ratio of 1 to 30 between the average worker's wage and the average bureaucrat's salary. The ratio is almost certainly even greater. Nevertheless, we will base the calculations we make in the remainder of this essay upon these two bases, retaining only those figures that are the least damning for the bureaucracy, that is, those based upon a ratio of 1 to 10.

If we suppose, therefore, that 15 percent of the population has an income on average ten times higher than the rest of the population, the ratio between the total incomes of these two strata of the population will be 15 x 10 : 85 x 1, or 150 : 85. The consumable social product is therefore distributed in this case in the following manner: 63 percent for the bureaucracy, 37 percent for the laboring population. This means that if the value of consumer products annually is some 100 billion rubles, 63 billion is consumed by the bureaucracy (which makes up 15 percent of the population), leaving 37 billion rubles worth of products for the other 85 percent.

If we now want to take as a more realistic basis for our calculations the ratio of 1 to 30 between the average worker's income and the average bureaucrat's income, we arrive at some startling figures. The ratio between the total incomes of the population's two strata will be in this case 15 x 30 : 85 x 1, or 450 : 85. The consumable social product therefore will be distributed in a ratio of 84 percent for the bureaucracy and 16 percent for the laboring population. Based upon an annual production valued at 100 billion rubles, 84 billion will be consumed by the bureaucracy and 16 billion by the laboring population. Fifteen percent of the population will consume 85 percent of the consumable product, and 85 percent of the population will have the other 15 percent of this product at their disposal. We can understand therefore why Trotsky himself ended up writing, "In scope of inequality in the payment of labor, the Soviet Union has not only caught up to, but far surpassed, the capitalist countries!"[12] Still we should point out that it is not a matter of the "payment of labor"—but we will return to this.

The author next comes to the question of the payment of simple labor and skilled labor, the enormous inequality of incomes in Russian society often having been justified by the "shortage of skilled labor." After a theoretical examination of the problem as it is posed in a capitalist society and in what a socialist society should be, he considers the case of Russian bureaucratic society.

Let us now see how the problem occurs within the framework of Russian bureaucratic society. Let us say straight off that in drawing up this antithetical parallel, our intention is not in the least to oppose Russian reality to the mirage of a "pure" society, however socialist it may be, or to provide recipes for a future socialist kitchen, but rather to lay down a barrage against the barefaced lies of those who, positively or through a subtle combination of affirmations and omissions, of empty talk and periods of silence, try cynically and shamefully to justify bureaucratic exploitation through "Marxist" economic arguments.

First of all, what are the facts? According to the figures Mr. Bettelheim himself cites (figures that are well known from other sources and can be confirmed by a host of data from the most varied authorities), "the range of salaries" in Russia runs from 110 rubles a month at the base for the simple manual worker to 25,000 rubles for the summits of the state bureaucracy. This was so in 1936. The latter amount, indeed, absolutely is not an exception or unrelated to other incomes, since, according to Mr. Bettelheim, "many technicians, engineers, and factory directors get 2,000 to 3,000 rubles per month, this being twenty to thirty times more than the poorest paid workers";[13] he also says here that other groups occupy intermediary echelons, with incomes of 7,000, 10,000, or 15,000 rubles a month.

We therefore find ourselves standing before a pyramid of incomes running from 1 to 250, if only monetary wages are taken into account. If "social" wages—which, "far from compensating for them (these inequalities), increase them, for these ('social wages') mostly benefit those who receive the highest salaries"[14]—are taken into account, the distance between the base and the summit of this income pyramid would easily double. Let us nevertheless make a present to the bureaucracy of its "social wage" and retain the *official* figure of 1 to 250, which is amply sufficient for what we are trying to prove.

What are the "objective" arguments aimed at "justifying" or "explaining" this enormous disparity?

First, the value of labor power ought to differ according to the degree of specialization. We will not belabor this point: We have just shown that a differentiation based upon the difference in value of labor power can only range within limits going at most from a single amount to double that amount. That is to say, from the point of view of the law of value as it was conceived by Marx, the higher strata of Russian society benefit from incomes of 10, 15, and up to 125 times higher than those the value of their labor power would necessitate.

Second, the incomes of "skilled workers" (from now on, we will have to put this entirely theoretical expression in quotation marks) had to be raised above their value in order to attract into these professions the workers lacking there.

But why the devil is there a dearth of these kinds of workers? On account of the arduous, unsafe, or disagreeable character of the types of jobs in question? Not at all. We have never heard anyone say that in Russia there was a lack of hands for this kind of work. If that indeed is what was lacking, the "labor camps and re-education camps" (read: concentration camps) would be (and actually are) there to remedy the situation. In fact, the best-paid jobs obviously are the least arduous, the most comfortable, and (the possibility of purges excepted) the least dangerous that can be found. No, these jobs on the whole are jobs for "trained staff [*cadres*]," and the problem is promptly reduced by the bureaucracy and its advocates to the "shortage of trained staff." But we have shown already that faced with the possibility of a similar shortage, raising the pay of categories experiencing "scarcity" is no help at all, for it alters in no way the particulars of the problem. How else, indeed, can one explain the fact that after twenty-five years of bureaucratic power this "shortage of trained staff" persists and is becoming more marked, unless it is looked at in terms of the constant widening of income ranges and the permanent accentuation of privileges? Here is an amply sufficient illustration of what we have said about the absurdity of this procedure that supposedly is intended to mitigate the dearth of trained staff. In particular, how else can one explain the fact that, since 1940, the bureaucracy has brought back heavy tuition expenses for secondary education? Even though it has adopted this policy of exorbitant income differentiation in order to "resolve the problem of a dearth of trained staff"—one knows not why this policy has been adopted (or rather one knows only too well why)—it clearly has not precluded itself (or rather it has not at all absolved itself) in the least from trying to increase, through centralized means, the production of the kinds of skilled labor power in question here. Beyond this, the bureaucracy (which by itself alone consumes at least 60 percent of Russia's national consumable income under the pretext of "mitigating the dearth of trained staff") prevents those who are the sole concrete hope for overcoming this dearth (i.e., all those who are not children of bureaucrats) from acquiring those skills about whose scarcity the bureaucracy is always bitterly complaining! Just one-tenth of the income swallowed up by the bureaucratic parasites would suffice in five years to bring forth a historically unprecedented superabundance of trained staff, *if* it were earmarked for the education of the people.

Far from remedying the dearth of trained staff, as we have said, this differentiation of incomes in reality only increases it. We encounter here the same sophism found in the problem of accumulation: The historical justification of the bureaucracy supposedly is to be found in Russia's low level of accumulation, whereas in fact the bureaucracy's unproductive consumption and its very existence are the principal brakes put on the process of accumulation. Likewise, the bureaucracy's existence and its privileges supposedly are justified by the "dearth of trained staff," when in fact this bureaucracy consciously acts to maintain this dearth! Thus the bourgeois go around all the time talking about how the capitalist regime is necessary because the workers are incapable of managing society, without adding at any point that there is no reason for this alleged "incapacity" other than the conditions to which this system itself condemns the workers.[15]

During the first postrevolutionary years, when higher pay was offered to "specialists" and technicians, it was a matter first of all of retaining a large number of trained staff who otherwise would have tried to flee, basically for political reasons. Later on, it was a matter of a purely temporary measure intended to allow workers to learn from them[16] and to win time in order for the training of new staff to yield results. But that was thirty years ago. What we have seen since is the "self-creation" of privileges by and for the bureaucracy, the accentuation of the former, the crystallization of the latter, and the "castification" of its strata, that is, the preservation of the socially dominant position of these strata through a de facto monopoly over education. This monopoly over education goes hand in hand with the complete concentration of political and economic power in the hands of the bureaucracy and is connected with a conscious policy oriented toward selecting a stratum of privileged people in every field. Such a stratum is economically, politically, and socially dependent upon the bureaucracy proper (a phenomenon of which the most astonishing example is the creation ex nihilo of a monstrous kolkhoz bureaucracy, once agriculture was "collectivized"). This policy was topped off with a trend toward intense stratification in every field, presented under the ideological mask of the "struggle against egalitarian cretinism."

In summary, we find ourselves faced with a differentiation of incomes absolutely without any relation either to the value of labor power furnished or to a policy "designed to orient workers toward the various branches of industry and toward various skills in conformity with the exigencies of the plan."[17] How then can we characterize those who have recourse to economic arguments in order to justify this state of affairs? Let us say simply that, with respect to bureaucratic exploitation, they are playing the same role of shabby apologists as Bastiat was able to play opposite capitalist exploitation.

It will perhaps be said that this is their right. Most incontestably so, we would respond. But in doing so, it is not their right to present themselves as "Marxists." For, after all, it cannot be forgotten that arguments that justify the incomes of exploitative strata by the "scarcity" of a factor of production these strata have at their disposal (interest by the "scarcity" of capital, ground rent by the "scarcity" of land, and so on—bureaucratic incomes by the "scarcity" of skilled labor) have always been the basis of bourgeois economists' arguments aimed at justifying exploitation.

For a revolutionary Marxist, however, these kinds of reasons do not justify anything. They do not even explain anything, for their own premises themselves demand an explanation. In allowing, for example, the "scarcity" (or the supply and demand) of cultivatable land to "explain" ground rent and its fluctuations, one wonders: (1) upon what general foundations does this system regulated by supply and demand rest; what are its social and historical presuppositions; and (2), above all, why must this rent, which plays this allegedly objective role, be transformed, be "subjectivized" into the income of a social class, of the landowners? Marx and Lenin have already observed that the "nationalization of the land"—that is, the suppression not of ground rent but of its transformation into the income of a social group—is the ideal capitalist claim; indeed, it is obvious that the bourgeoisie, even if it admits in principle that ground rent acts as a means "of balancing supply and demand in the use of nature" and of eliminating from the market "non-solvent needs," does not understand why this charge ought to benefit landowners exclusively, seeing that, for the bourgeoisie, no monopoly is justified save for the one it itself has over capital. Obviously, this ideal bourgeois claim is never lodged, for general political reasons first of all, and in particular on account of the rapid merger of the capitalist classes and landowners. All the same, this theoretical example proves that even if this "scarcity" is admitted in principle as a regulating principle of the economy—in reality, it is merely a reactionary mystification—the distribution of the revenue resulting from this "scarcity" to certain social categories in no way can be deduced therefrom. This was understood even by the "neosocialist" school, which tried to uphold both the regulative character of the "scarcity" of goods and services and, at the same time, the allotment to society of the resulting revenues.

In the case before us, none of these "explanations" concerning the "scarcity of skilled labor in Russia" either justifies or explains the bureaucracy's appropriation of the revenues allegedly resulting from it, *except if one refers to the class character of the Russian economy*, that is, to the monopoly the bureaucracy has over the conditions of production in general, and over the production of skilled labor in particular. When the class structure of Russian society has been understood, everything is explained and everything even is "justified" in one stroke. But this justification—similar to the one that can be given historically to the capitalist regime and, in a word, even to fascism—does not go very far. It ends where the exploited class's possibility of overthrowing the exploitative regime begins—whether this regime calls itself the "French Republic" or the "Union of Soviet Socialist Republics"—a possibility whose only test is revolutionary action itself.

<h3 style="text-align:center">Notes</h3>

1. T/E: Reprinted in *SB 1*, *SB(n.é.)*, and *EP5* and translated in *PSW1*, with a Postface.
2. In connection with this, Trotsky has contributed the most—with no one else being his equal on account of the immense authority he enjoyed in anti-Stalinist revolutionary circles—toward maintaining this confusion within the vanguard of the working class. His erroneous analysis of Russian society continues to exert an influence that has become positively pernicious to the extent that it continues to be maintained with infinitely less seriousness and semblance of scientific underpinnings by his epigones. Let us note again the influence that certain freelance Stalinists such as Mr. Charles Bettelheim—usually considered "Marxist," for the great amusement of future generations—exert due to the fact that they dress up their apologia for the bureaucracy in a "socialist" jargon.
3. A study of the evolution of exploitation through the five-year plans will be made in another article. [T/E: Such a text was never published in *S. ou B.*]
4. On theft during this period, see the works of Ante Ciliga, Victor Serge, etc.
5. Leon Trotsky, *The Revolution Betrayed* (New York: Pathfinder Press, 1972), 135–43.

6. Ibid., 124.
7. Bettelheim, *La Planification soviétique*, 62. [T/E: This is presumably the 2nd rev. ed. (Paris: M. Rivière et Cie., 1945).]
8. Ibid., 52.
9. Ibid., 62.
10. *The Revolution Betrayed*, 125.
11. T/E: Victor Kravchenko was a Russian bureaucrat who left the USSR and became known for his book, *I Chose Freedom* (New York: Scribner's, 1946).
12. *The Revolution Betrayed*, 125.
13. *La Planification soviétique*, 62.
14. Ibid., 63.
15. We would need all the richly violent language of a Lenin responding to Kautsky in order to characterize with a minimum of justice the ventures of people such as Mr. Bettelheim, who purposely gets lost in all the technical details of Russian "planning" and who cites a wealth of charts and figures in order to make himself forget and to make others forget what is, from the revolutionary Marxist point of view, the crux of the matter: What is the class significance of such planning; what is the class significance of the monstrous disparity of incomes in Russia? But we have decided once and for all to ignore the very person of Mr. Bettelheim—we think this is the best thing that could happen to him—in order to lay hold of the thing itself.
16. V. I. Lenin, *Selected Works* (New York: International Publishers, 1943), vol. 7, 372–76.
17. T/E: Chaulieu had quoted earlier, in a part of the present text not reproduced here, this passage from Bettelheim's *Les Problèmes théoriques et pratiques de la planification* (Paris: Presses Universitaires de France, 1946); see: 3n.

Stalinism in East Germany

Hugo Bell

"Le Stalinisme en Allemagne orientale"
Socialisme ou Barbarie, 7 (August–September 1950): 28–33, 42–45
Socialisme ou Barbarie, 8 (January–February 1951): 34–35
Socialisme ou Barbarie—Anthologie, 53–61

This text, signed by Hugo Bell (Benno Sternberg), illustrates, through a concrete historical analysis, the theses expounded in the theoretical texts presented above. It was later to be included in a book, La Classe ouvrière d'Allemagne Orientale. Essai de chronique (1945–1958) *(Paris: Éditions Ouvrières, 1958), with the author listed as Benno Sarel. This work is the fruit of several years of experience in both postwar occupied Germanies, supplemented by meticulous documentary work.*

The author begins by painting a picture of East Germany, ravaged by war and subjected by the Russian Army to terror, first, and then to devastating exploitation under the pretext of reparations owed by the German people as a whole to the Soviet Union. In this "hunger zone," where the death rate was reaching its heights and where the birth rate was plummeting, the Russians dismantled and brought back home with them machinery, rails, and entire factories and then, after having noted the waste that accompanied this pillaging, endeavored to relaunch local production, tapping it through "Soviet Joint-Stock Companies" (Sowjetische Aktiengesellschaften, or SAGs). At the same time [1946], they pieced together a new Communist party, the Socialist Unity Party of Germany (SED), around a core of pure Stalinists who had returned from their exile in Russia, while systematically excluding the revolutionaries who had remained in Germany. Little by little, through promotions within the working class and by making the most of the extreme dearth of basic necessities in order to create a stratum of relatively privileged persons, a veritable bureaucratic ruling class was constituted that relied, obviously, on the Soviet occupier and endeavored to assume leadership of society.

That did not go without difficulties. We give below two examples of this. The first relates to this Stalinist Party-State's relations with the bourgeoisie. With the line laid down by the Kremlin ruling out any genuine "socialist revolution" in East Germany, the bureaucracy in no way sought to expropriate all the capitalists; it believed, on the contrary, that it could rely on a certain number among them, the "progressive elements" of the bourgeoisie, to put production back on track while keeping them closely in check. Here is what happened in reality.

Everything was organized so that a certain number of capitalists might live and work, though within very strict bounds and under very strict surveillance. The general goal was to profit from the experience of the capitalists in order to run the country's economic machinery with a view toward delivering reparations to the USSR and consolidating the SED regime. Yet the Stalinist party proved politically myopic when it thought that one could, with the help of the state apparatus and propaganda about the "progressive fraction of the bourgeoisie," divert an entire social class from its goal.

The Bourgeoisie's Resistance

As early as 1946, cartels and free capitalist associations were re-formed. The small glass manufacturers of Thuringia grouped together and then united with the glass polishers who had emigrated from Bohemia and grouped together on their own. They came to an agreement to push up prices for their production. Yet this association, as well as other similar ones, were sporadic in character, for they were quickly discovered. Other capitalist groupings had more luck and grew in scope; thus, textile manufacturers and dealers in Saxony had also created a community of clandestine labor back in 1946. Unlike their Thuringian colleagues, they were clever enough to occupy the main posts in the textile section of the industrial syndicate of Dresden as well as the latter's subsidiary in Chemnitz. Moreover, and especially, they were able to work their way into the respective department of the Saxon Minister of the Economy. Quite often, these industrialists and big merchants were SED members and took advantage of the theory, then in vogue, of the progressive current in the bourgeoisie. Thanks to their administrative and political relationships, and their cleverness, the weavers and sweater manufacturers of the Chemnitz region made a fortune. They commandeered quantities of raw materials and fuel above what they required. They resold these on the black market. They sold a portion of their production secretly to West German or Berlin capitalists, or else did offsets in the Russian Zone. The case of the weavers of Saxony was far from isolated, and other lesser-scale scandals broke out in other branches, too.

Only a few months after the creation of the syndicates, the capitalists not only succeeded in transforming into their own instruments those bodies the SED meant to use to control them but they also, with the help of those bodies, sabotaged planning efforts and broke up the economic administrative apparatus. It thus proved impossible to make the bourgeoisie work against itself, and the theory of the progressive capitalist current collapsed.

For, in another way the entire economic situation was favoring capitalism's clever and secret resistance. After the destructions of war, the dismantlings [of factories, etc.] and the reparations had brought about general shortages. The market was inundated with paper money, and prices were kept artificially at the low level of 1944. Anything was bought and sold. One had to be rather clever to find even poor-quality raw materials and, amid the ruins, some rudiments of means for manufacturing. Many small- and middle-sized businesses were thus founded between 1945 and 1947 by former capitalists, who made the most of their commercial experience and their business connections. For the same reason—shortages and general distress—functionaries could be corrupted rather easily. A ministry editor made 300 to 400 marks a month, and the tiniest manufacturer, before the monetary reform, juggled many tens of thousands of marks. Again for the same reason, the capitalists succeeded in influencing or corrupting the works councils [*Betriebsräte*] in their factories. Those councils agreed that a portion of production would be subtracted from the plan and "compensated for," that is, swapped, through private channels, for other commodities or fresh supplies for the workers. Often, the works council agreed to cover up the operation if it obtained benefits for itself.

Thus, far from "remaining in their place and working," as the Soviet command would have wanted, the capitalists moved about, wrestled around, and scored points, for they succeeded in winning over or corrupting the very apparatus that was meant to keep them in check. Of course, in doing this, they felt encouraged by the rebirth of capitalism in West Germany and in general by the superiority of the forces of capitalism over those of the USSR on the world level.

Profitability of Private and Nationalized Companies

That was only a part of the weight the capitalist sector exerted upon the Russian Zone's economy. For, often, and especially at the beginning, private companies succeeded, from the standpoint of profitability, in beating the nationalized companies. The March 7, 1948 issue of *Der*

Morgen, which is the Liberal-Democratic Party's organ in the Soviet Zone, demonstrated that, for 1947, the nationalized companies of Saxony, which showed a profit of around five million marks, had in reality lost 18.5 million, for the financial administration made them a gift of 23.5 million in the form of taxes on capital it did not receive but reportedly claimed from private companies. The nonprofitability of the LEBs [*Landeseigene Betriebe, Land*-owned companies] was all the more striking as they enjoyed, in relation to private companies, still other advantages beyond a different taxation. They received subsidies to maintain 1944 prices and were given favorable treatment in the distribution of raw materials.

Yet the private sector displayed greater commercial cleverness, and the profits brought in by offset deals were incomparably higher than legal profits.

**The Spirit of Capitalism Spreads to the
Nationalized Sector and Public Institutions**
Simply in order to live and be able to feed their workers, the nationalized companies, too, had to resort to offsets. Behind the back of party organs and of the regional industrial grouping to which it belonged, the factory sold a portion of its production for its own benefit. Often, such operations, which were strictly forbidden, were carried out in order to fulfill some tragically pressing need. From time to time, real distress calls from the personnel of nationalized companies made their way even into the SED press, like the one sent by the Maximilianshütte's worker-correspondent to the Stalinist newspaper of Thuringia:

> Those who are in the administration ought to imagine what it means to fill a blast furnace by flashlight. The men on the blast furnace's night shift are in danger of dying on account of the inadequate lighting caused by the lack of electric light bulbs.

The lot of the manager of a nationalized company was often no more enviable. He was forced to feed and clothe his workers, for otherwise they were unable to produce. He had to procure raw materials and equipment, for the failure to achieve the Plan could mean for him dismissal if not arrest. Moreover, the same fate could befall him if his "offsets" were too apparent. Of course, growing corruption of the administration's cadres accompanied "offset deals."

The Party made desperate efforts to combat such habits. It strongly condemned "company selfishness" and advocated "emulation for democratic reconstruction." It launched appeal after appeal and threat after threat, instituting a multiplicity of monitoring bodies. Yet its struggle looked like tilting at windmills, for the evil resided in the distress and in the general atmosphere created by the Occupation and by Soviet levies on current production. On the other hand, the system of "offsets," the benefits and the easy living these offsets occasioned, gradually spread to the upper-level administration and party cadres. For, in fact, "selfishness" was far from limited to companies and extended to the cooperatives, to "democratic organizations," to towns, and further along to the governments of the *Länder*. It was not rare to see cooperatives fighting with the Peasants Mutual Aid Association or with a municipality over a factory that had just been appropriated and that would have enlarged each's respective domain. Other times, one witnessed real cold wars between *Länder* governments. Thus was Saxony-Anhalt for a time exploited by its neighbors who had coal, textile raw materials, and chemical products delivered to them while furnishing nothing in exchange. Was that because Saxony-Anhalt was the sole *Land* to have a Liberal-Democratic president? Yet, among governments led by the SED, the dealings were the same: in Spring 1947, Thuringia had sent to Saxony thread to be woven; the latter, however, instead of returning it to Thuringia in the form of fabric, delivered the manufactured product under the heading of reparations and thus saved its own assets from Russian levies. In exchange, Thuringia later arranged so that its deliveries to Saxony scheduled as part of the three-month plan would be deferred until the quarter had elapsed and the deliveries became null and void.

During the years 1946 and 1947, the central administrative offices had no authority over the *Länder* governments in their planning and coordination efforts, and true particularism and regional selfishness, whose cause was poverty and the lack of future prospects, developed in the Russian Zone.

Thus, less than a year after the nationalizations of 1946, the bourgeoisie, after having suffered a serious defeat, was on its way to taking its revenge. Far from limiting itself to the sphere assigned to it, it circumvented the constraints to which it was subject, and, above all, its spirit and methods won over the opposing camp. Individualism and the quest for profits overrode the collectivist feelings one was trying to imprint. Once again, it proved to be the case that individualism is naturally born of poverty and that poverty ill lends itself to planning.

The Stalinist party, which thought that it could master social reality through edicts and police tactics, saw the failure—at the very least, the partial failure—of its policy and, particularly, of its attempt to "utilize" the bourgeoisie. True, an SED card had become the key to every social position, but the Stalinist party's policy contained a fundamental contradiction that condemned it to Sisyphean tasks. It created collectivist-type bodies under its domination, like the LEBs, and supported them with all its energies, but at the same time it re-mitted 100 percent of the Russian levies and thus helped to generate the accompanying poverty: "company selfishness," "local selfishness," and, in general, bourgeois-type individualism. Between Spring 1947 and Spring 1948, the Party went to great lengths to surmount this contradiction, but that would again be through administrative mea-sures and police tactics. […]

Hugo Bell's study particularly well highlights the process by which the instau-ration of the Communist Party dictatorship radically transformed its relations with the working class and revealed its nature as an exploitative class. It was not rare, in the aftermath of the Reich's collapse, for the workers to mobilize themselves spontaneously in order to restart their factories. The Party prompt-ly put things to rights. Under the authority of a reliable hierarchy, it sought to reinstaurate industrial discipline everywhere. Yet it was difficult to motivate workers to work by letting them die of hunger and by levying the better part of their production in order to send it to Russia. Also, the Party sought to rely on the Works Councils (Betriebsräte) the Allied Control Council had set up [as a possibility] in April 1946.

Once again, the Stalinist party tended to imprison social reality within a fiction that was made up from start to finish. The workers grudgingly produced goods that were going away to the USSR. Were they hostile to a party that remitted these levies? One would endeavor to convince them through propaganda that everything was alright. At the same time, all opposing opinions were stifled. Through a sleight of hand, one got the workers to elect Stalinist representatives in the Works Councils. Those Councils would then conduct the Party's policy while claiming to represent the workers. In accordance with their principles of confidence in the apparatus and the cadres and with their habit of holding the masses in contempt, the Stalinist leaders were ready to think that, by "holding" the representatives of the workers, they would be able to influence and "hold" the latter, as well.

Reality would soon show how inflexible it was to the Party's maneuvers.

The Works Councils Split Along the Line
of the Stalinist Party/Working Masses Divide

Elections for the Works Councils unfolded predictably. Made skeptical about everything, the workers approved, generally without discussion, the candidate lists that had been offered them by the trade-union factory committee after having been drawn up by the Stalinist cell bosses with the approval of local party leaders.

Once elected, the *Betriebsräte* had to apply the production program on which they had run. Quite quickly, it was noticed that most of the factory cells had been obliged to take on some undependable elements in order to complete the lists. Too disconnected from the mass, they did not really have enough cadres to control the council. Many people who had run were in reality apolitical, though formally members of the SED, or else old Communists who felt closer to the workers than to the bureaucratic directors.

Only in a few cases did the *Betriebsrat* try to apply the "work first" policy the Party was applying particularly in the VEBs [*Volkseigene Betriebe*, Publicly or People's Owned Companies] and the SAGs, but then the *Betriebsrat* was transformed almost automatically into an auxiliary of the cell and even of the police. The workers paid no attention to the *Betriebsrat's* harangues about production. So the *Betriebsrat* was obliged to introduce piece rates, reinforce labor discipline, and sometime frisk workers at the factory's gates to discover "saboteurs and thieves." Of course, in that case, the *Betriebsrat* no longer had anything in common with the workers; it had failed in its mission to link workers with the nascent bureaucratic stratum and had placed itself deliberately into the latter camp.

Most often, the *Betriebsrat* was composed of workers who remained close to the concerns of their working comrades. That was rather clearly apparent in the month of November 1946, when the *Betriebsräte* issued their first quarterly report. Most complained of the bad food for the workers and declared that, under such conditions, production could not be increased. There were instances where the *Betriebsrat* warded off resolutions formulating such a demand that had been adopted by the Trade-Union Committee or the SED cell. The result was that, thenceforth, much less publicity was given to quarterly balance sheets and that, later on, those balance sheets were practically no longer drawn up.

In late 1946, the trade unions undertook an investigation into one hundred nationalized companies' *Betriebsräte*. Only 16 had calculated the cost price of production and had raised the issue of balancing the company's budget. The Councils' concern lay elsewhere: procuring food for the personnel to eat. But that was possible only illegally or through personal relationships, and the Council then inevitably entered into conflict with the Party and sometimes the factory's Stalinist cell and management. It would sometimes happen that the *Betriebsrat* would grant the workers two days' leave per week just so that they could go to the countryside to load up on food, and management would just cancel the measure. Most often, the *Betriebsrat* sold on the black market or "offset" a portion of its production against provisions. It would sometimes happen that the cell would then threaten to arrest the *Betriebsrat*. Often a genuine enmity arose between these two bodies. This fact was acknowledged by the Berlin SED's internal bulletin, *Wille und Weg*, of February 1947. One year after their official creation, the nationalized companies' *Betriebsräte* had certainly escaped party control. Not only had they not succeeded in sealing the break that existed between workers and bureaucrats, but the Works Councils had themselves divided along the lines of this very break.

Betriebsrat, Stalinist Cell, and Company Management

Speaking schematically, one can state that, within a nationalized company, the *Betriebsrat* represented the workers; the Stalinist cell represented the interests of the Kremlin, established order, and the general interests of the nascent caste, while management was most often beset by "company selfishness." The Trade-Union Committee generally found itself under the influence of the cell.

The workers' hostility to the bureaucrats rarely expressed itself through highly developed forms of struggle: there were in all only three or four strikes for better nourishment, which were quickly repressed. The *Betriebsrat* represented not only the workers but also their dead-end situation, their lack of future prospects, and their lack of hope in the destiny of their class. At no moment was there a serious attempt to unite the working class against the bureaucracy. The working class remained dispersed and simply endeavored to stay alive.

Within each factory, however, the workers sometimes succeeded in influencing not only the *Betriebsrat* but, as we have seen, the cell and management, as well. All three got along in order to cover unofficial business. Great was the Party's dismay in such cases. This feeling was expressed, for example, in the September 1947 issue of the trade union's theoretical review, *Arbeit*, which wrote: "The *Betriebsräte* and the company's trade-union or political groups tend to find themselves under pressure and be pulled along by unpoliticized and discontented portions of the personnel." Yet, most often, the Party did not publicize such feelings and sometimes its dismay was expressed through arrests.

There also were tense situations between management and cell. Management's members belonged to the cell yet did not generally come to meetings. Grappling with tremendous problems, they ran up against the requirements of the Party, represented here by the secretary of the SED group. Not being able to oppose it overtly, they feigned ignorance of the cell. Yet in their attitude, a tinge of contempt was not lacking as an accompaniment for their hostility. The current managers—former revolutionary workers—had made a new step toward the acquisition of caste consciousness. Caught up in their managerial preoccupations, they felt themselves superior not only to the mass of laborers but also to their old party comrades who had remained workers continuing to live as before, day-to-day, engrossed by the problems of their existence.

Often there was a personal connection between company management and the cell's leadership. This corresponded to the lack of mid-level party cadres, the consequence of which almost always was to subordinate the cell to management. The Party then reacted, handing back real management to reliable elements, even at the risk of letting production collapse, but the situation always remained quite unsteady.

The Stalinist party had therefore far from mastered the domestic situation of the "People's Owned Companies." There were, on the one hand, workers, who were dispersed, hostile, and resorting to individual solutions; on the other, the bureaucratic directorial group, united by a concern for production for which it was solely in charge, but torn between the need not to distance itself from the workers and the need to follow the party line. The old individualistic spirit of capitalism was also represented by the bureaucratic group's need to have recourse to offsets. Corruption and the desire for enrichment were not lacking, either, and extended even to the members of the Works Council.

[...]

The Stalinist Party's Reaction

The Stalinist attempt to revive, with the *Betriebsräte's* aid, both the illusions of the workers' vanguard and the zeal for work from the Summer of 1945 had failed. Despite its political amorphousness, the working class had established how the majority of Councils would behave. Faced with its weight and its desire to live, the network of Stalinist cadres proved too feeble.

The SED was increasingly considered an organization of Quislings, and labor productivity, which was in early 1947 (according to official sources) 40 percent of what it was in 1936, was not on an upward curve.

The *Betriebsräte* constituted, at the very least in form, a democratic means for resolving the problem of labor productivity; thenceforth, the Party would resort to ever more purely bureaucratic and forceful means. It gradually was going to restrict the rights of the *Betriebsräte* until it dissolved them; it was going to introduce into the factory the exploitative methods known in the USSR under the name *Stakhanovism*; finally, it was going to create out of thin air police-state supervisory bodies, which it would name *popular* and which it was then going to present as stemming from laboring people's own initiatives. Each measure was going to be presented as a democratic victory, but its propaganda no longer found any echo among the workers, and increasingly this propaganda was to become a simple political excuse for Communists-turned-bureaucrats. Combined with the attraction of material advantages, the teaching of Stalinism in schools was to become the way to recruit new political leadership cadres and economic managers. [...]

PART TWO

THE WORLD OF WORK

"Le monde du travail"
Socialisme ou Barbarie—Anthologie, 63–65

The great majority of the working class as well as the revolutionary minority have long accepted the idea that the condition of being exploited was the mere consequence of the capitalist organization of production. The workers thought of themselves as belonging to a dependent class, one fully determined by the decisions of the opposing bourgeois class. Work, where such dependency was blatant, was experienced by them as a kind of curse. Now, according to the standard morality, such work was treated as the very foundation of society, and that, too, was something the workers believed. Pride in a task well done and disgust at the life lived in the factory, jealous protection of the tools of the workplace and occasional destruction of modern machinery, contempt as well as nostalgia for the old crafts were all tearing at workers' consciousness. The major working-class organizations had done nothing to reduce this ambivalency or to foster in laboring people a fairer appreciation of their place within society. Treating them sometimes as minors in need of guidance and education, sometimes as a mass of unskilled labor to be used according to the political needs of the moment, these organizations had, instead, heightened the state of dependency in which the division of labor had maintained them. Rebellious as a result yet feeling profoundly discouraged about any prospects for changing their fate, workers accepted with resignation that the current way in which their productive activities were being organized was something beyond their competency, thinking that responsibility for such organization legitimately fell to the employers' managers.

Now, as soon as it was formed, the S. ou B. group combated this division of labor and affirmed laboring people's capacity to make modern production techniques their own, to invent their own means of resistance, and to go beyond the narrow framework of their particular work unit. The image of the proletariat communicated in the review was thus one of a class whose creativity in struggles and its talent at responding collectively to problems that arose throughout the production process rendered it capable of managing, first of all, production and then the overall operation of society. The working class was thus becoming, in the full sense of the term, an autonomous class upon which a revolutionary project could be founded anew.

We give here three excerpts from articles indicative of the group's renewal of thought and action.

The first one is drawn from Paul Romano's *The American Worker*, a booklet published in 1947 by the Johnson-Forest Tendency, an American group with which S. ou B. had, from its beginnings, maintained a close relationship. This text, published over the first five issues, constituted for many years a model for the interpretation of struggles conducted in France.

The second one is drawn from Claude Lefort's "Proletarian Experience," which appeared as the unsigned editorial in issue 11. This text is made up of two parts: first, a close discussion of the nature of the proletariat, of the meaning of its opposition to the capitalist organization of production, and of the universal import of its struggle; second, an attempt to define the concrete activities (surveys, gathering of testimony) that would suit the statements enunciated in the first part. In the opening discussion, the author shows that the proletarian's class consciousness is not a result of his mere situation of being exploited, as this situation tends merely to assign him a place, a subordinate one, within society; the proletarian's class consciousness is formed through the activity and reflection he has to deploy, the objectives he has to set for himself, and the obstacles he has to surmount—in a word, through the experience he has of his exploitation.

The third excerpt is drawn from "The Factory and Workers' Management," by Daniel Mothé (*S. ou B.*, no. 22). Mothé, who at the time was a milling-machine operator in a tool-making shop at the Renault factory and the organizer, alongside Raymond Hirzl, of the factory newspaper *Tribune Ouvrière*, shows that the workers in his shop, when confronted with an organization that had been created with the goal of directing their slightest gestures, are for this very reason led, so that production might keep going, to circumvent the directives imposed on them, to coordinate their activities among themselves, and to subvert constantly Management's basic principles: division of labor and compartmentalization of tasks. They organize mutual aid, both within their shop and with shops cooperating in the same manufacturing processes; they short-circuit the lines of command, negotiate with the methods agents and the hierarchy over times and deadlines, and impose upon everyone the rules of social etiquette [*savoir-vivre*] at work. Ultimately, production in the shop appears as the result of innumerable acts of improvisatory coping [*débrouillardise*] and social etiquette, cunning and conflict, which are constantly being replayed at all levels. The relationship between management and the workers does not appear to be conditioned on the shop floor only by the massive relation of force usually invoked, but just as much by the result of the multiple confrontations production activities themselves occasion. Mothé concludes with some thoughts about the unsuitability of the system of hierarchy, the ineffectiveness of controls and checks imposed from without, and the need to abandon the compartmentalization of tasks. He then ends lucidly with some thoughts about the difficulties that will arise when workers attempt to extend their conception of production activities from the shop-floor level first to the factory and then to the overall operation of society.

G.P.

[T/E: To these three texts have been added in chronological order, for English-speaking readers, three key *S. ou B.* studies of workers' struggles in Great Britain and the United States.]

The American Worker

Paul Romano

"L'Ouvrier américain"
Socialisme ou Barbarie, 5–6, (March–April 1950): 124–34
Socialisme ou Barbarie—Anthologie, 66–75[1]

[…]

THE CONTRADICTION IN THE FACTORY

Lowered Productivity of Labor

I had discussions with several workers on the lowered productivity of labor.

Worker "R" agrees. Especially concerning the assembly lines. Says workers do not want to exist as slaves. Says production could be upped 20% or 30% if workers were given a free hand. Complains of the insuperable number of obstacles which a worker encounters during the day. Says if all red tape and annoying supervisory help were eliminated, and if workers' ingenuity were allowed full play, production could be considerably upped. He says it is very difficult to know what the individual worker thinks as he isolates himself mentally in many respects from his fellow worker. He does not often say what he thinks. He says workers hold back on their production and never give their fullest.

Just Putting in Time

I spoke with two other workers on the same subject. One worker says production could be doubled. The other is in doubt. Seems to think it means more work for the workers. I approached the subject on the basis of a 4-hour day, 5-day week and asked if that goal was possible. I tried to impress them with a plant-wide conception of cooperation.

I explained what was in reality workers' control. One said that during the war in his section of the plant, the fellows used to knock out work fast deliberately and then spend a few hours in horse-play. They enjoyed themselves and at the same time got the work out. He claims the mental attitude was entirely different then. Now the monotony is extremely evident. It is just a question of putting in time. He resents the pressure of the foreman when the production norm is completed and he is kidding around. The foreman, it seems, cannot stand workers being idle even though the norm has been filled. (The other worker in reference to this noted that the miners had not been paid for a full day's work in their walk-out, although the production quota for the day had been filled.) He spoke of the many skillful tricks applied by workers during the war.

The steel gang distributes steel wherever it is needed throughout the plant. This job often consists of several workers pushing about large skids of steel. It is plain to see that the foreman over that group feels that these workers are holding back. He constantly, in moments of impatience, lends his own strength to pushing the skids. The workers distinctly resent this. They do not mind when I, another worker, help them. When I add my weight, the skid of steel rolls smoothly. This may mean that only another worker is needed. But from the look on the faces of the steel gang, it might also seem that they had adjusted their strength to keeping the skid moving at a slow pace.

A laborer one day confided in me the following: "You know, kid, being a laborer is really an art. The idea is not to be around when you are needed. There is a way to time all this, and the clever laborer need not exhaust himself."

I will add that this may have been much more true during the war. It appears that since some have been laid off, the laborers must work harder. But when the opportunity presents itself, the laborer will still seize it to lighten his load.

As the tempo of work increases and the oppression of the worker becomes greater, at a certain point in the process a change comes over the worker. At the moment the machine is inflicting its greatest damage on him, and when he is reaching the bottom depths of his despair, a sudden sense of defiance and then freedom envelops him. This happens at rare moments but leads inevitably to lowering the productivity of labor as it exists under the present factory setup.

On the other hand, I have seen workers almost wear themselves into the ground trying to put out an extra number of pieces purely from the desire to see how much they could do. In these instances, there was no extra money involved. In contradiction to this, workers will deliberately burn out tools in the machine at quitting time, by turning off the lubricant. Sometimes this is done to chastize the incoming worker for something ill-natured he has done.

The Division of Labor

The worker labors under contradictions. He may often wish to help another worker in some task, but because of the classifications and the fear of risking the resentment of his fellow workers, he refrains from doing so.

At the same time there is the ever present threat of the company using the worker's action against him in attempts to further the amount of work a man must do.

The wage scales and classifications in the shop are extremely numerous. It is a continual battle to reach a higher classification and more money, with one worker competing against another. Much anger is generated between workers and against the company over upgrading or promotions to new jobs. Every time a new job is open, a bitter wrangle takes place. It is not predominantly a question of the nickel raise involved, as it may seem on the surface, but a desire for recognition and a chance for exploitation of one's own capabilities.

In factories where different classifications of work are set up, workers confine themselves to their own classifications. For example, a machine operator runs the machine, the laborer sweeps and cleans, lifts, etc. This is usually the case. I have noticed, however, the distinct tendency on the part of workers to break these classifications by doing work not in their jurisdiction, so to speak. An operator does some laboring work, etc. This infraction of the rules is done on the workers' own initiative. That is, they take on the added tasks as long as they do it of their own accord. If the company orders them to do these things, immediately the men rebel and refuse. It is almost impossible to stop them when they decide of themselves.

Seniority regulations of the union very often prevent workers with real qualifications from getting ahead. For instance there are workers with a few years of experience who have outdistanced old-time workers in ability and imagination. This is traced fundamentally to the type of technical and academic training they have received in the modern school system. I have heard even workers with seniority talk about how the seniority system is a brake on production.[2] At the same time they would fight against the company's trying to override seniority.

They are in a contradiction because they realize that workers need seniority as a defense and yet feel that such defensive measures do not allow the best productive talents of the workers to emerge. The workers say that if they had the opportunity in the ranks to decide who should be upgraded, they would be able to make better choices.

The last several months have shown signs of a swift development in the workers. They are stirred and moved by a deep unrest. They want a better life in the factory. Their desire to solve the frustrating contradictions of production can be seen everywhere. For example the worker who, sick to his stomach from the stench of his machine, shuts it down and shouts "To hell with my classification. I can't stand it. I am going to clean out this goddamn machine."

The Creativity of the Workers

When a worker has the opportunity to sneak away, he investigates the other sections of the plant. Rarely does this happen. The longing to vision the whole of which he is a part is never satisfied. He does not get to know the routine and full mechanics of the next departments. When he can, the worker will stop at a machine which intrigues him, pick up a piece of work and comment on it. He will question the operator about it. An exceptional yearning can be seen in the watchful eyes of those whose job it is to perform some sort of laboring or unskilled manual task. It is not uncommon to hear one worker say to another, "Boy, that job's a good one to have."

However, when a worker is upgraded, the new job soon becomes routine and once again he feels the same dissatisfaction. Many workers express the hope to get into the tool room, but even in the tool room the work has been broken down into routine operations. One of the highest-skilled men in my department is a set-up man. He does a variety of jobs in the course of the day, changing set-ups, devising fixtures, etc. Yet he is bored with his work. He says: "If you think this is such a good job you can have it. I'm fed up with it."

During the war, there arose a type of worker creativity known as a "Government Job."[3] I don't think there is a worker who at some time or another has not made a "Government Job." It was always natural to observe a worker making something for himself during working hours. Hundreds of thousands have made rings, lockets, tools, and knick-knacks. If the foreman or boss would come over and ask "what are you doing?", the reply was "a Government Job." Many beautiful things were made and the workers used to show them to each other. This has carried over and it appears that it will remain. The term applies to anything the worker makes for himself on company time. But it also appears that the workers today don't have as much patience for this type of work and something more is needed.

The worker doesn't want to know how to do many things just for the sake of doing them. One worker will refer to another as a good all-round man. He would also like to be one but even that is not enough.

At lunch time, workers will often discuss how a job could be done more efficiently from beginning to end. They will talk about what stock to use, how to machine it, how to do certain operations on various machines with various set-ups. But they never get a chance to decide how and why things should be done. However, if they can't use all they know, they try to use some of it.

In order to make production, many workers devise ingenious adaptations. Some change gears when the foreman is not about. Some make special tools and fixtures for their machines to make it easier for themselves. They keep these improvements secret so the company doesn't benefit. At times they help each other and at other times they do not.

The other day the worker on the next machine devised something of skilled nature to better his machine performance. He insisted on showing it to me and explaining to me what he had done. He was pleased with his accomplishment but was frustrated that there were no others he could show it to.

Operators on steel-cutting machines have desires to speed up R.P.M.'s on them and then increase the feed to the maximum cut to see how far they can go. This is characteristic on lathes, boring mills, etc. I've done the same myself many times. Although destruction may result, the workers seek in this way, completely to master the machine.

Since the workers are unable, in the shop, to express fully their creative instincts, outside the factory and in the home, they seek to give free rein to these instincts.

Many workers seek relief from tension of the shop on their off hours by working on their cars. Cleaning and polishing them. Tinkering with the motor and other parts. Workers continually paint and fix up their own homes.

But here too they feel that something is missing. They may interrupt such a project for weeks because they have lost interest and, unless they force themselves to finish, it remains undone. Many workers say to their friends in the shop: "When I finish a day's work here I have to go home and do the same thing there."

When a worker sees a new piece of machinery he eyes it with professional skill. "What a piece of machinery that is," he says. His appreciation is not based on a monetary calculation of the machine, but on its performance under his own command.

The Community of Labor

The miserable life in the factory is universal, so when some workers whine and continually complain to their fellow workers, it antagonizes them. Gripers are not liked and wherever possible avoided. The workers say to a griper: "Don't complain to me. Go tell it to the boss."

The average capable worker respects another good worker. It is his way of building up respect among his fellow workers in recognition of his capabilities. The community of labor brings this forth as part of an unstated code.

Workers have ways of testing each other. Sometimes a whole day will be spent plaguing a worker; for example, putting bluing on his machine,[4] stopping his machine continually, upsetting his tool box, hiding his tools, etc. . . . This is to determine if the worker will squeal to the boss and also to determine if he has a sense of humor and is a good guy.

Often a worker takes satisfaction out of coming to work on a very hazardous day. The initiative is his and he chooses to come as this is one day he is not expected to come to work. Those workers who do come that day find a certain enjoyment out of having arrived, especially if there are workers absent. There is then a certain camaraderie or light-heartedness apparent.

Workers in each department visit the toilet for a smoke and rest at certain periods during the day. No one has set the time, but in my department, we have set a custom of our own. The day is divided into sections. First smoke is at 10:00 A.M., second is at 2:00 P.M. At these specific times, some of the other workers will be there and there is company to talk with.

When a worker moves from one factory to another, a temporary feeling of being lost seizes him, and unsureness of whether he will be able to make good on the next job. One day in the new plant among the workers again and his confidence in himself and his ability immediately returns.

When tragedy befalls a worker, death in the family, illness, or some such personal sorrow, the workers express deep sympathy. Often it is difficult to console such a worker in words, so in order to show his sympathy, the average worker will attempt some way in the day's work to aid the bereaved worker. When tragedy strikes a worker, he finds some relief back in the factory away from the sorrow at home.

As Though They Were Somebody
At lunch, one day, workers were discussing and lamenting the fact that there is so little real friendship amongst people. One was speaking in terms of what really amounted to comradeship. He remarked that it was tragic that relations between men were not harmonious.

All employees are numbered. Badge numbers are systematically re-placing names of individual workers. Pay envelopes, work charts, etc., are all figured on the basis of number. Even workers begin to refer to each other as numbers. "No. 402 worked on my machine last night."

There are many workers in the shop who search for some expression of their importance as individuals. The company, knowing this, institutes a certain type of uniform. It is in the form of a smock or light work coat with the company insignia on it, usually worn by set-up men, inspectors, etc. I took care to notice the effects of this rose on a few workers. For the first few days, they seemed to adopt a self-important air as though now they were somebody. After a few days, the coat was dirty, and added to this, from the very beginning the other workers ignored the new distinction which those who wore the coats seemed to think they had. The novelty soon wore off as no change was brought to their status and work continued in the same monotonous manner as before.

Workers now and then wear their names on their shirts. Many workers become identified by the distinct type and color of the clothing they wear.

I described above the conveyor system and the hostility of the workers to it. There are some other aspects to this situation. Previously, the checkers came to the workers' machines and in a relationship exchanged receipts for the work which the operator created. Now the worker places his work on a conveyor from whence it travels to a central pay point. At various intervals during the week he receives his receipts. The old relationship no longer exists of contact between worker and checker. (This is very satisfactory to the checker.) The old system gave the worker a feeling of individual contact with the recipients of his work. The worker is angry at the new system and demands that the old relation be established. He insists that he be paid for his work at his machine. His reason is that otherwise he is cheated of some of his day's work. But this is no more the case than usual. The company goes to extremes to see no one is cheated. The new system as stated proves in many respects more satisfactory than before. But the worker, not understanding himself or his reason, is angry because he is becoming further divorced from, and automatized in, his work. He attempts to protect his individuality and resents the regimentation of his labor into a sterile path. So he protests not the fact that he is required to lift the work onto the conveyor, but the further divorce of himself, from the end result and the receivers of his efforts.

Teamwork

Production as it exists today in the shop seeks to divide the white from black, Jew from Gentile, worker from worker. But the shattering of the division can take place right at the point of production. As I have stated previously, workers have a basic respect of other good workers. The community of labor establishes a pride in this type of activity which is deeply rooted in the worker. No matter how much modern production distorts the worker, this instinct remains always there. This becomes a universal trait and cuts through barriers of race, creed, and religion. But there is no way for the worker to express this trait today in any productive manner. The result is that it appears in other ways.

At times, a wonderful camaraderie develops in the shop amongst the workers. Usually this is discernible in some sort of horseplay. Many times workers will sing songs together to lighten the day's work. Or many will talk everlastingly of the baseball teams, their standings and who is playing. Specific detail is given to individual players and many know very exact information on some of the players and their health. Workers will use any subject as a means of maintaining a bond of interest between them, e.g. baseball, betting, women.

A good worker always likes to keep his place of work clean. The conflict of classifications often prevents him from doing so.[5]

One day the floor along the row of machines has become soaked with oil. Sawdust has been thrown down to absorb it. The result is a thick, heavy mess on the floor. Although this condition almost always exists, this one day the operators find a broom and clean about their machines. Then systematically the broom is passed on down the line. The company always exhorts the men to do this, but very rare are the times when they do, although they want very much to keep their places of work clean.

One day the temperature soared to the top of the thermometer. The plant is stifling. The top row of windows in the plant is closed. The chain has broken and has not been fixed. Workers up and down the shop complain continuously to the foremen. They are helpless for some reason and are not able to get the windows opened. No one puts in a grievance. I look for the committee-man, but he has not come in. I approach one worker and say, "Let's open the goddam windows ourselves. If we wait for the company to do it nothing will be done." He says, "Come on." I mentioned it to a few workers and they agree. Two of us went up to the bathroom window which was suspended from the ceiling and looked over the situation. It was impossible to fix it from there. We went back down and had to return to our machines. What had become crystal clear to me was the fact that a half-dozen workers would instantaneously have responded to a call to get a ladder ourselves and go up and fix the window.

The workers are ready to act together to better their life in the factory.

CONCLUSION

The basic machine in production is the lathe. It was on the basis of the first crude lathe that the advanced machinery of modern production has developed. Almost all machinery is a modification of the lathe, e.g. the huge boring mills, or of the drill press, e.g. the thread-cutting machine, or of the lathe and the drill press. Most every worker who understands machinery knows this. The point which I wish to make is this: The mastery of any of these machines automatically prepares the worker to gain mastery easily over the others. I have seen this hundreds of times in the last 7 years. I as well as other workers have at some time or other, been put on machines which we had never run. Most often it took about a half hour to be able to run them satisfactorily. This is a frequent occurrence in most factories. When work runs out on one machine, the worker is often put on another. I see it every day in the factory. In my present plant, during the first two months, I ran a drill press, air-chuck lathe, automatic-screw, foot press, etc. Two of these machines I had never run before.

I recall that during the war this was much more so. Another fact shown by the war was the ease with which newcomers to machinery could learn in a comparatively short space of time. This was proved to me by the fact that in the first three years of the war, I alone trained some twenty-odd workers, white and Negro, ranging in age from 17 to 50, in running engine and turret lathes.

It is clear, then, that the present-day organization of production itself develops certain strata of workers in a multiplicity of abilities. But this multiplicity of abilities the worker can never develop to its fullest in the factory as it is today.

The worker uses his five senses in the day-to-day labor in the factory. Every one of them is distorted and mutilated. The terrible frustration which is the product of years of exposure to an inhuman production apparatus drives relentlessly toward the overthrow of that apparatus and its replacement by a productive system which will enable the worker to give fullest expression to his senses.

In modern production, the worker is isolated on an island in the midst of men and machines. So divorced has the worker become from himself that he is divorced from his fellow worker. He cannot stand the chattering of men in the cafeteria, and can find ease better, alone at his machine. The anxiety of the worker is due to the fact that he is forever caught between the contradiction of wanting to let his instinct, to do a good job and be close to his fellow workers, have its way, and then having to reverse himself.

The deep undercurrent of protest which exists in the factory is slowly but surely beginning to concretize itself. The deepest hostility exists everywhere. It can be seen in the slumped shoulders of a worker trudging down the length of the factory; in the way in which a worker walks up to a drinking fountain and wearily bends over to meet the rising stream of water; and in the set lips and drawn features of the worker towards midnight on the second shift. What more profound expression of all this can be given than the words of worker X who, in speaking to his foreman, says, "thought Lincoln freed the slaves." Later in the company of several shopmates, he mentioned something to the effect that it was time that someone came and freed us from the machines. [. . .]

Notes

1. T/E: *The American Worker*—which includes Romano's "Life in the Factory" and Ria Stone's (Grace Lee Boggs's) "The Reconstruction of Society" and which was first published as a pamphlet in 1947—was reprinted by Bewick (Detroit) in 1972, with Romano's part now available at: http://www.prole.info/texts/americanworker1.html. The present excerpt reprints Romano's seventh and last chapter, plus part of the Conclusion. Original spelling, punctuation, etc. have been retained, with very slight corrections.

2. One can indeed speak of a *seniority system* in America, because it is the only way for the unions to be able to struggle against the enormous and arbitrary fluctuations in demand for manpower that exist in that country. But, conversely, the role of the unions in capitalist production, on the one hand, and the bureaucratic hold of the unions over the workers, on the other hand, end up being tremendously

increased by this practice. [French Editors: These notes were introduced by the militant who translated the text in the review. Some instances of clumsiness or abstruseness may be noted, though we have not deemed it useful to correct them.]

3. In France this is what is called *la perruque*, which has existed from time immemorial. It is nevertheless to be noted that here the objects produced are generally utilitarian objects (racks for bikes, baby carriages, etc.), obviously for personal use. During the Occupation, however, one could witness objects genuinely being produced for sale or barter.

4. T/E: "Bluing is a passivation process in which steel is partially protected against rust, and is named after the blue-black appearance of the resulting protective finish." https://en.wikipedia.org/wiki/Bluing_(steel)

5. What the author is trying to say is that one is either unable or unwilling to do what is outside one's job.

Proletarian Experience
Editorial

[Claude Lefort]

"L'expérience prolétarienne"
first published as the Editorial for
Socialisme ou Barbarie, 11 (November–December 1952): 6–16[1]
Socialisme ou Barbarie—Anthologie, 77–87[2]

If it is true that no class can ever be reduced solely to its economic function and that a description of concrete social relations within the bourgeoisie is a necessary component of a comprehension of that class, it is truer still that the proletariat requires a specific approach that would offer access to its *subjective development*. Despite some reservations concerning what is entailed by this term, it summarizes better than any other the dominant trait of the proletariat. The proletariat is subjective in the sense that its conduct is not the mere result of the conditions of its existence. More profoundly, its conditions of existence require of it a constant struggle for transformation, thus a constant distancing from its immediate fate. The progress of this struggle and the elaboration of the ideological content that enables such distancing together compose an experience through which the class constitutes itself.

To paraphrase Marx again, one must above all avoid fixing the relation of the proletariat to the individual as an abstraction. One must search for how its social structure emerges continually from the vital process of determinate individuals because what is true, according to Marx, of society is all the truer of the proletariat, which represents *the* eminently social force within the present historical stage as the group that produces collective life.

It nevertheless must be recognized that the indications we find in Marx of an orientation toward the concrete analysis of the social relations constitutive of the working class have not been developed within the Marxist movement. What for us are the fundamental questions have not been directly broached: How do men, placed under the conditions of industrial labor, come to appropriate that labor? How do they strike up specific relations among themselves? How do they perceive and practically construct relations with the rest of society? And, in a singular manner, how do they compose a shared experience that makes of them a historical force? These questions have ordinarily been left aside in favor of a more abstract conception, the object of which is, for example, Capitalist Society (considered in its generality), and the forces that make it up, while situated at a distance, are placed on the same level. So it was for Lenin, for whom the proletariat was an entity whose historical meaning had been established once and for all, and which was (with the exception that one was for it) treated like its adversary by virtue of its outward characteristics. Excessive interest was accorded to the study of the "relation of forces," which was conflated with class struggle itself, as if the essential problem were to measure the pressure one of its two masses exerted on the opposing mass. For us, this does not at all mean that we reject the objective analysis of the structure and institutions of the social totality, nor are we claiming, for example, that the only true knowledge that can be given has to be elaborated by the proletarians themselves as a function of their rootedness in the class. This "workerist" theory of knowledge—which, let it be said in passing, would reduce the work of Marx to nothing—must be rejected for at least two reasons: first, because all knowledge claims objectivity (even as it may be conscious of being socially and psychologically conditioned); second, because the aspiration to a practically and ideologically universal role—that of in fact identifying itself with society as a whole—belongs to the very nature of the proletariat. But the fact remains that objective analysis, even when conducted with the greatest rigor, as was done by Marx in *Capital*, remains incomplete because it is constrained to be interested only in the results of social life or in the fixed forms into which that life is integrated (for example, technical development or capital concentration) and to ignore the human experience that corresponds to this material or, at the very least, external process (for example, the relations of men to their labor in the steam age or the age of electricity, in the age of competitive capitalism, and in that of state monopoly capitalism). In a sense, there is no way to separate material forms and human experience because the latter is determined by the conditions in which it is made, and these conditions, which are the result of social evolution, are the product of some human labor. Yet from a practical viewpoint, objective analysis is eventually subordinated to concrete analysis, for it is not conditions that are revolutionary, but human beings, and the ultimate question is how human beings appropriate and transform their situation.

The urgency of and interest in concrete analysis are forced upon us from another viewpoint as well. Sticking close to Marx, we have just underscored the producer-role in the social lives of workers. More must be said, however, for that same statement could apply in a general way to any class in history that has borne the burden of labor. Yet the proletariat's tie to its producer-role is unlike that of any other class in the past. That is because modern industrial society can be compared only partially to the other societal forms that preceded it. The idea, fashionable today among many sociologists, that, for example, the most archaic types of primitive societies are closer to feudal Europe of the Middle Ages than the latter society is to the capitalist society from which it was born has not yet gotten around to showing that idea's importance as concerns the role of classes and their relations. There is a twofold relationship in any society, one of man to man and another between man and the thing he transforms, but with industrial society the second relationship takes on a new import. There is now a sphere of production governed by laws that are to a certain extent autonomous. Of course, that sphere is situated in a total social sphere since the relations between classes are eventually constituted within the production process, but it cannot be reduced to that, for technical development and the rationalization process that has characterized capitalist evolution since its origins have had an import that goes beyond the strict framework of class struggle. To take a banal example, the industrial usage of steam or electricity entails a series of consequences—for a mode of the division of labor, for the distribution of firms—that are relatively independent of the general form of social relations. Of course, rationalization and technical development are not realities in themselves: there is so little to them that they can be interpreted as defenses erected by the bosses whose profits are constantly threatened by proletarian resistance to exploitation. Nonetheless, even if the motivations of Capital suffice to explain those origins, they still cannot account for the content of technical progress. The deeper explanation for the apparent autonomy in the logic of technical development is that such development is not the work of capitalist management alone: it is also the expression of proletarian labor. The action of the proletariat, in fact, does not only take the form of a resistance (forcing employers constantly to improve their methods of exploitation), but also that of a continuous assimilation of progress and, even more, an active collaboration in it. It is because workers are able to adapt to the ceaselessly evolving pace and form of production that this evolution has been able to continue. More basically, because workers themselves offer responses to the myriad detailed problems posed within production, they render possible the appearance of the explicit systematic response called *technical innovation*. Aboveboard rationalization is the self-interested takeover, interpretation, and integration from a class perspective of the multiple, fragmentary, dispersed, and anonymous innovations of men engaged in the concrete production process.

From our viewpoint, this last remark is fundamental because it incites one to place the emphasis on the experience that unfolds at the level of production relations and on the perceptions workers have of these relations of production. This does not entail a radical separation of this specific social relation from those expressed at the level of society overall but, rather, just a recognition of its specificity. In other words, if we say that industrial structure wholly determines social structure and that it has acquired such permanency that every society—whatever its class character—has to model itself on certain of its traits, then we must understand the situation into which it places the men who are integrated therein out of full necessity—that is, the proletarians.

So in what might a concrete analysis of the proletariat consist? We will try to define it by enumerating various approaches and evaluating their respective interest.

The first approach would be to describe the economic situation in which the class finds itself placed and the influence the latter has on its structure. Ultimately, it would require a total social and economic analysis. In a more restricted sense, we would want to talk about the class's labor conditions and living conditions—modifications within its concentration and differentiation, changes in the methods of exploitation (intensity of work, length of the workday, wages and labor markets, and so forth). This is the most objective approach in that it is focused on apparent (and, indeed, essential) class characteristics. Any social group can be studied in this way, and anyone can devote a study to it independently of any revolutionary commitments whatsoever.[3] There is nothing specifically proletarian about such a method—even as it can be said that such an investigation is or will generally be inspired by political motives since it necessarily does a disservice to the exploitative class.

A second approach, the inverse of the first, would typically be labeled *subjective*. It would focus on all expressions of proletarian consciousness, or on what one ordinarily refers to as *ideology*. For example, early Marxism, Anarchism, Reformism, Bolshevism, and Stalinism have represented moments of proletarian consciousness. It is very important to understand the meaning of their succession, to understand why broad strata of the working class have rallied around their flag[s] at different historical stages and how these forms continue to coexist within the present period. In other words, it is important to understand what the proletariat is trying to say by way of these intermediaries. While we make no claim for its originality—numerous examples can be found in Marxist literature (in Lenin's critiques of Anarchism or Reformism, for example)—such ideology analysis could be taken quite far, in the present period, when we benefit from the distance that allows us to gauge transformations in doctrines, despite their formal continuities (that of Stalinist ideas from 1928 to 1952 or that of Reformism over the past century). However, whatever its interest, such a study is as incomplete as it is abstract. We utilize here an external approach, using information that can be gathered through publications (the programs and writings of the major movements of interest) but that does not necessarily impose upon us a proletarian perspective. And we allow what, at this level, is arguably most fundamental about worker experience to escape. We show interest here only in explicit experience, only in what is expressed, what is formatted in programs or articles, without worrying whether the ideas exactly reflect the thoughts or real intentions of the working-class strata in whose name they seemed to speak. While there is always a gap that separates what is experienced from what is elaborated and transformed into a thesis, this gap is particularly wide in the case of the proletariat. This is first of all because this class is alienated—not only dominated but also totally excluded from economic power and thereby rendered incapable of representing any status at all. This does not mean that ideology would be unrelated to its class experience, but in becoming a system of thoughts, it presupposes a break with that experience and an anticipatory attitude that allows nonproletarian factors to exert an influence. Here we encounter once again a basic difference between proletariat and bourgeoisie to which we have already alluded.

For the latter, the theory of Liberalism in a given era meant just an idealization or rationalization of its interests: the programs of its political parties generally expressed the status of certain of its strata. For the proletariat, Bolshevism, although to some extent it represented a rationalization of the working-class condition, was also an interpretation performed by a fraction of the vanguard associated with an intelligentsia that was relatively separate from the class. In other words, there are two reasons for the distortion of worker expression: that it is the work of a minority external to the class's real life or constrained to adopt a relation of exteriority thereto; and that it is utopian—not in a pejorative sense, but in the sense that it is a project designed to establish a situation, not all of whose premises are contained in the present. Of course, the various ideologies of the workers' movement represent that movement in a similar way since the movement recognizes them as its own, but they represent it in a derivative form.

A third approach would be more specifically historical. That approach would consist in seeking a continuity within the great manifestations of the workers' movement since its advent, demonstrating that revolutions and, more generally, diverse forms of worker resistance and organization (associations, unions, political parties, strike committees or struggle committees) are moments of a progressive experience and showing how this experience is linked to the evolving economic and political forms of capitalist society.

Finally, there is a fourth approach, which we deem the most concrete. Rather than examining the situation and development of the proletariat from the outside, this approach would from within seek to restitute its attitudes toward its labor and toward society and to show how its capacities for invention and its ability to organize itself socially manifest themselves within its everyday life.

Prior to any explicit reflection, to any interpretation of their lot or their role, workers have spontaneous comportments toward industrial labor, exploitation, the organization of production, and social life both inside and outside the factory. By any account, it is in such comportments that their personalities are most completely manifested. At this level, the distinctions between subjective and objective lose their meaning: such comportments eminently contain ideologies that to a certain degree constitute their rationalization, just as they presuppose economic conditions whose ongoing integration and elaboration such comportments achieve.

As we have said, such an approach has yet to really be explored. No doubt there are valuable lessons in the analysis of the nineteenth-century English working class presented in *Capital*. However, Marx's basic preoccupation was to describe workers' labor and living conditions, so he stuck to the first approach we mentioned. Since Marx's time, we could cite only "literary" documents attempting to describe the worker personality. True, over the past few years and primarily in the United States, a "worker" sociology has appeared that claims to do concrete analyses of social relations within companies while proclaiming its practical intentions.

This sociology is the work of the bosses. "Enlightened" capitalists discovered that material rationalization had its limits, that men-objects had specific reactions that had to be taken into account so that one might get the most out of them—that is, get them to submit to the most efficient forms of exploitation. This admirable discovery brought back into service a previously Taylorized form of humanism and made a fortune both for pseudopsychoanalysts, called upon to liberate workers from their resentment as a harmful obstacle to productivity, and for pseudosociologists, tasked with inquiring into individuals' attitudes toward their labor and their comrades and with perfecting the best methods of social adaptation. The misfortune of this sociology is that by definition it cannot reach the proletarian personality, for it is condemned, by virtue of its class perspective, to broach it from without, seeing nothing but the personality of the producing worker, a simple executant irreducibly tied to the capitalist system of exploitation. The concepts used in these analyses, like *social adaptation*, have for workers a meaning opposite to that of the investigators (for the latter, there can be adaptation only to existing conditions; for workers, adaptation implies a lack of adaptation to exploitation). The results generated are worthless. This failure shows the presuppositions that would shape a genuinely concrete analysis of the proletariat. It is fundamental that such labor be recognized by workers as a moment of their own experience, an opportunity to formulate, condense, and collate a type of knowledge that is usually implicit, more "felt" than thought, and fragmentary. What separates this effort shaped by revolutionary aspirations from the industrial sociology we spoke about is what separates the situation of time-study men in a capitalist society from that of the collective determination of production norms in the case of workers' management. To the worker, an investigator sent to examine his cooperative tendencies or his mode of social adaptation must look like a time-study man trying to measure his "psychological durations." In contrast, the kind of effort we are proposing is grounded on the idea that the proletariat is engaged in a progressive experience that tends to explode the framework of exploitation itself. This effort would be meaningful only for those who participate in that experience themselves. Chief among those people are the workers.

In this respect, the radical originality of the proletariat manifests itself once again. This class can be known only through itself and only on the condition that whoever inquires about it acknowledges the value of proletarian experience, is rooted in its situation, and makes his own this class's social and historical horizons—on the condition, therefore, that he break with the immediately given, that is, with the conditions of the system of exploitation. Things go quite otherwise for any other social group. American researchers have studied with considerable success, for example, the Midwestern petty bourgeoisie as if they were studying the Papuans on Alor Island. Whatever the difficulties encountered (we are still discussing the relationship of the observer to his object of study), and however much the investigator needs to go beyond the simple analysis of institutions in order to restitute something of the meanings they have for concrete human beings, it is nonetheless possible in these cases to acquire a certain amount of knowledge about the group under study without sharing its norms and accepting its values. This is because the petty bourgeoisie, like the Papuans, has an objective social existence that, good or bad, is what it is, tends to persist in the same form, and offers its members a set of conducts and beliefs that are solidly linked to conditions in the present. As we have emphasized throughout, the proletariat is not only what it seems to be: the collectivity of the executants of capitalist production. Its genuine social existence is hidden: it is of course of a piece with present conditions but also in stark contradiction to the current system (of exploitation). We witness the advent of a role that differs at every point from the one contemporary society imposes on it.

This concrete approach, which we deem instigated by the very nature of the proletariat, implies that we might be able to gather and interpret testimonies from workers. By *testimonies* we especially mean narratives recounting life, or, better, individual experience that are done by the interested parties and that are capable of providing insights into their social lives. Let us list a few of the questions we think are the most interesting to see broached in such testimonies, questions that have been shaped in significant measure by already existing documents:[4]

One would seek to specify:

a) The worker's relationship to his work—his function within the factory, level of technical knowledge, and understanding of the production process. For example, does he know where the piece comes from that he works on and where it goes? His occupational experience:

Has he worked in other factories, on other machines, in other branches of production, etc.? His interest in production: How much initiative does he bring to his job; is he curious about the techniques employed? Does he have a spontaneous sense of the transformations that should be brought to the structure of production, to the pace of work, and to the context and conditions that shape life in the factory? Does he have a generally critical attitude toward the employers' rationalization methods? How does he welcome attempts at modernization?

b) Relations with other workers and people from other social strata within the company (differences in attitudes toward other workers, foremen, employees, engineers, and management); his conception of the division of labor. What do hierarchies of function and wage represent? Would he prefer to do some of his work at a machine and some in an office? How does he accommodate his role as simple executant? Does he consider the social structure within the factory to be necessary or, in any case, as "going without saying"? Are there tendencies toward cooperation, competition, isolation? A taste for working as an individual or in a team? How are relations among individuals distributed? Personal relations, the formation of small groups—on what basis are they established? How important are these relations for the individual? If they are different from social relations that take shape in offices, how are the latter perceived and evaluated? What importance does he attribute to the social physiognomy of the factory? Does he know the layout of other factories and does he make comparisons? Does he have exact information about wage levels for other functions throughout the company? Does he compare pay stubs with other workers? Etc.

c) Life outside the factory and knowledge about what arises in the wider social world. (Impact of life inside the factory on life outside it: How does his job materially and psychologically influence his personal and family life, for example? Which milieu does he frequent outside the factory? To what extent are these patterns imposed on him by his work, by the neighborhood in which he lives? What are the characteristics of his family life, relations with his children, the education they receive, his extra-occupational activities? How does he occupy his leisure time? Does he have a special taste for particular types of entertainment? To what extent does he use mass media for news and culture: books, newspapers, radio, cinema? What are his attitudes about them? What are his tastes . . . not merely what newspaper does he read, but what does he read first in the newspaper? To what extent is he interested in what is happening in the world and does he discuss that: accounts of political or social events, technological discoveries, bourgeois scandals? Etc.)

d) Links to properly proletarian history and traditions. (Knowledge of the workers' movement in the past and familiarity with that history; actual participation in social struggles and the memories they have left; knowledge of workers' situations in other countries; attitude toward the future, independent of any particular political assessment, etc.)

Whatever the interest of such questions, it is nonetheless important to ask about the import of individual testimonies. We well know that we will be able to gather only a relatively limited number of texts: On what basis can one generalize from them? A piece of testimony is by definition singular: that of a 20- or 50-year-old worker who works in a small plant or large facility, a developed militant, someone with extensive trade-union and political experience, one with set opinions or bereft of any training or experience in particular. Without resorting to artifice, how can one entirely discount these differences of situation and derive from such differently motivated narratives lessons of universal import? On this point, criticism is largely justified, and it seems clear that the results it would be possible to obtain would necessarily be limited. At the same time, it would be equally contrived [*artificiel*] to deny all value to such testimonies. First, no matter how great the individual differences, they play out within a single frame: the situation of the proletariat. Through these singular narratives, we aim at that situation much more than the specificity of this or that life. Two workers placed under very different conditions have in common the fact that both have endured one or another form of labor and exploitation that is essentially the same and absorbs three-quarters of their personal existence. Their wage gap might be appreciable, their housing conditions and family lives may not be comparable, but it remains the case that they are profoundly identical both in their roles as producers or machine operators, and in their alienation. In fact, all workers know that: this is what yields that sense of familiarity and social complicity (even when the individuals do not know each other) that is clear at first glance for a bourgeois entering a working-class neighborhood. It is therefore not absurd to look among these particular examples for traits with a more general signification, given that they all have resemblances that together suffice to distinguish them from those of any other strata of society. To that must be added that this method of collecting testimony would be much more susceptible to criticism were we interested in gathering and analyzing opinions, for those would necessarily be of a great diversity—but as we have said, we are interested in worker *attitudes*. These attitudes are sometimes expressed, of course, in the form of opinions, and are often disfigured by them, but they are in every case deeper and necessarily simpler than the opinions proceeding therefrom. This would present a clear obstacle were we to try to use a limited number of individual testimonies to infer the proletarian opinion about the USSR or such a precise issue as wage spreads. But it is a much simpler matter, it seems to us, to perceive worker attitudes toward the bureaucrat, spontaneously adopted inside the production process. Finally, we should note that no other mode of knowledge would allow us to respond to the problems we have posed. Even if we had available a vast apparatus for a statistically based investigation (the data for which would be gathered by quite numerous worker comrades willing to pose thousands of questions to other workers in various factories, given that we have already ruled out any investigation carried out by researchers from outside the working class), that apparatus would be useless, because responses gathered from anonymous individual respondents that could only be correlated numerically would be without interest. Only responses attributed to a concrete individual can be brought into relation with each other; their convergences and divergences enable the isolation of meaning and evoke experiences or systems of living and thinking that can be interpreted. For all these reasons, individual narratives are invaluable.

This does not mean that we would thereby claim that we could define what the proletariat is in its reality after having rejected all the ways of representing its condition while glimpsing itself through the distorting prism of bourgeois society or of the political parties that purport to speak in its name. A worker's testimony, no matter how evocative, symbolic, or spontaneous it might be, remains conditioned by the situation of the witness himself. We are not alluding here to distortions that may arise from the individual's interpretations, but rather to the distortion testimony necessarily imposes on its author. To tell a story is not to act within it. Telling a story even entails a break with the action in ways that transform its meaning. For example, narrating a strike is not at all the same as participating therein, if only because, as a participant, one does not yet know the outcome of one's actions, and the distance entailed by reflection allows for judgments about that which, in real time, had not yet had its meaning fixed. In fact, there is in this case something much more than a gap of opinion: there is a change of attitude—that is, a transformation in the way of reacting to situations in which one finds oneself placed. In addition, a narrative puts the individual into what is for him an equally unnatural isolated position. A worker typically acts out of solidarity with the other people who participate in the same situation; without even talking about overt social struggles, there is the ongoing everyday struggle within the production process to resist exploitation, a struggle hidden but ongoing and shared among comrades. The attitudes most characteristic of a worker toward his job or toward other social strata are not found by him within himself, as would be the case with the bourgeois or the bureaucrat who sees his conduct dictated by his individual interests. Rather, the worker shares these attitudes with others as collective responses.

The critique of a worker narrative has to allow one to glimpse, within individual attitudes, the aspect that involves group conduct. However, in the final analysis, these registers do not entirely overlap in a narrative, with the result that we can derive only an incomplete knowledge from them. To finish—and this last critique connects back to the first while deepening it—the historical context in which these narratives are published must be bought out. There is no eternal proletarian who testifies, but a certain type of worker who occupies a definite historical position, situated in a period characterized by a significant retreat of worker forces all over the world and by the struggle between two forces within exploitative society to reduce gradually to silence all other social manifestations, which tends to develop into both open conflict and a bureaucratic unification of the world. The attitude of the proletariat (even that essential attitude we are searching for which transcends to some extent these particular historical circumstances) is not the same in a period in which the class works with a view toward achieving emancipation in the short term, on the one hand, and one in which it is momentarily condemned to contemplate blocked horizons and to maintain a historical silence, on the other.

It is enough to say that the approach we have characterized as *concrete* remains abstract in many respects, given that the three aspects of the proletariat (practical, collective, historical) are broached only indirectly and are thereby distorted. In fact, the concrete proletariat is not an object of knowledge: it works, it struggles, and it transforms itself. One cannot in the end catch up with it at the level of theory, but only at the practical level by participating in its history. Yet this last remark is abstract, too, for it does not take into account the role of knowledge in this very history, which is an integral part thereof, along with work and struggle. It is a fact as manifest as others that workers ask themselves about their condition and the possibility of transforming it. One can therefore only increase the number of theoretical perspectives, which are necessarily abstract, even at moments of their convergence, and postulate that all progress toward the clarification of worker experience ripens that experience. So it is not by way of some standard formula that we said that the four approaches we criticized in succession were in fact complementary. This did not mean that their results could usefully be added together but, rather, that their convergence across different paths communicates, in a more or less comprehensive manner, the same reality we have already called, for lack of a better term, *proletarian experience*. For example, we think that the critique of the evolution of the workers' movement, of its forms of organization and struggle, the critique of ideologies, and the description of worker attitudes necessarily overlap. For, the positions that expressed themselves in systematic and rational ways in the history of the workers' movement and the organizations and movements that have followed one another all coexist, in a sense, as interpretations and potential realizations within the proletariat today. Beneath (so to speak) the Reformist, Anarchist, or Stalinist movements, there is among the workers, proceeding directly from the relation to production, a projection concerning their fate that makes these elaborations possible and contains them at the same time. Likewise, the techniques for struggling that seem to be associated with phases of worker history (1848, 1870, or 1917) express types of relationships among workers that continue to exist and even to manifest themselves (in the form of a wildcat strike with no organization, for example). This does not to mean that, by its very nature alone, the proletariat contains all the episodes of its history and all possible ideological expressions of its condition. For, our remark could be flipped around to say that the material and theoretical evolution of the proletariat has led it to be what it is and that that evolution has come to be condensed in its actual conduct by creating for it a whole new field of possibilities and reflection. In analyzing worker attitudes, it is essential not to lose sight of the fact that the knowledge thus obtained is itself limited and that, being more profound or more comprehensive than other modes of knowledge, such knowledge not only does not undermine their validity but still has to be connected up with those modes or risk becoming unintelligible.

[. . .]

Notes

1. T/E: Reprinted in *Éléments d'une critique de la bureaucratie* (Geneva: Droz, 1971); 2nd ed. (Paris: Gallimard, 1979).
2. T/E: The present edited excerpt is based on the translation by Stephen Hastings-King, which appeared online in *Viewpoint Magazine*, 3 (September 30, 2013).
3. Think, for example, of Georges Duveau's book *La Vie ouvrière en France sous le Second Empire* [T/E: Paris: Gallimard 1946].
4. *The American Worker*, translated in *S. ou B.*, 1 (May 1949) [T/E: a later part of Paul Romano's text is included in the present *Anthology*], and Eric Albert, "Témoignage," in *Les Temps Modernes* (July 1952).

Wildcat Strikes in the American Automobile Industry

Anon.

"Les grèves sauvages de l'industrie automobile américaine"
Socialisme ou Barbarie, 18 (January–March 1956): 49–60[1]

Bourgeois and reformist propaganda in Europe makes deliberate reference to the situation of the American proletariat. It claims to show with this example that the "absence of class struggles" and a "friendly collaboration" between workers and bosses—involving a "socially responsible attitude" on the bosses' part, and support for the interests of the business enterprise on the workers' part—lead to the good fortune of all concerned, for, this propaganda claims, production is increased and a higher standard of living is granted to the working class. And when the contracts between the American automobile trade unions and first Ford, and then General Motors, were settled, the most "serious" French journalists did not hesitate to speak of the end of capitalism in the United States and of a new era of social history that was about to dawn.

Obviously, American reality is utterly different from this primitive, comic-strip view. Certainly, American capitalism has been able, for more than a century, to develop without any domestic or foreign obstacles on a virgin continent richly endowed by nature, thus bringing production to levels that no one else has been able to attain. This comfortable position has allowed it to grant relatively high wages at the same time, it must be added, that the availability of free land compelled them to do so, up to the beginning of this century.[2] But relatively high wage levels far from constitute the sole, or even the most important, characteristic of the condition of American workers. Without mentioning the celebrated but unfortunate "depressed third of the nation"—fifty million Americans living in poverty, even according to

European standards—we need only recall that the American worker pays for his wage through a much greater exploitation of his labor power in production, a soul-destroying work pace, and complete enslavement to machines and the assembly line. And yet, contrary to the assertions of bourgeois propaganda—which on occasion is akin to that of the Stalinists[3]—the bosses have not given up anything that was not extracted from them by force or imposed by the threat of struggle any more in the United States than elsewhere; the history of the American proletariat is filled with battles that, while they have not attained till now the political level of those of the European proletariat, at times have surpassed them in their violence and in the effectiveness of their organization.[4] But from a long-range perspective, the most important thing undoubtedly is that the class struggle at the point of production, the proletariat's revolt against the structure of the capitalist factory, its methods of organizing production, and the labor conditions these methods entail are livelier and profounder here than anywhere else. It is no accident that, after Taylorism, the "human relations" movement developed in the United States with the aim of inventing techniques capable of taming the workers' incessant revolt against capitalist production relations in a tactful way—since one cannot be tamed by brute force.[5]

Nevertheless, faced with this set of conditions and a growing proletarian combativeness, it remains true that American capitalism has been led to follow a policy that can be summarized in schematic terms by saying that, when it is forced to make concessions, it shows itself to be disposed, more than European capitalism, to give in on wages, while making up for these wage increases by increasing production and by stepping up productivity.

Since the War this policy has enjoyed the total complicity of the trade-union bureaucracy. Incapable of defending the workers' demands on the level of the concrete relations of production, of the organization of labor, and of labor conditions—since these demands, taken together, amount to a challenge to capitalist power in the factory and whose sole possible outcome would be workers' management of production—this labor bureaucracy uses the workers only as a means to force its own way into the administrative authority that controls production, and it tries to appease them by "satisfying" their wage demands. But its whole policy results more and more in the following contradiction: Trying to maintain its grip on the workers, without which it would again become nothing, it compensates for its inability to satisfy their basic demands by winning more or less real economic advantages, though such advantages are now becoming less and less important as the workers' material and cultural levels are raised.

Thus the American trade-union bureaucracy successively has obtained from the capitalists a kind of sliding scale that ties wages first to the cost of living, then to the rate of productivity increases, then a "pension plan," and finally, in June 1955, the "guaranteed annual wage."

Of course, all these "reforms" are far from really containing everything their names imply. Although this is a relatively secondary point, we will try to show it briefly in the case of the "guaranteed annual wage," the attainment of which has provoked the strikes to which this article is devoted.

American workers are bound to their employers by collective agreements or "contracts" of a set length of time. Beyond wage rates, they specify in extremely detailed fashion what jobs workers can be assigned to, based upon the skills they possess, as well as overall labor conditions. In addition, these contracts, which are negotiated between the trade-union leadership and the employers each time they come up for renewal, usually include no-strike clauses that remain in effect for the duration of the agreement. In cases where it is still possible to strike, it has to be done under the auspices of the "legal" or "official" trade union. If not (i.e., if it is a "wildcat" strike), the strikers are left to fend for themselves: The trade union will not support them financially, the courts will stop them from picketing, and so on.

The renewal period for these contracts is the occasion for arduous negotiations between trade unions and employers. During this period, the threat of a strike hangs over the negotiations, in case they fail and the contract expires.

This past year, as the UAW's contracts with the industry's "Big Three" (Ford, General Motors, and Chrysler) were just about to expire, Walter Reuther, the UAW's president (who at the same time is president of the CIO), made the centerpiece of his negotiation demands his plan for a "guaranteed annual wage" (GAW), that is, an unemployment fund supported by employer contributions that would pay to unemployed workers the equivalent of a full wage for a year. The State already pays unemployment compensation for twenty-six weeks, equivalent to around a third of one's pay; according to Reuther's plan, the employers would have to contribute to the workers' unemployment compensation fund in order for it to reach 80 percent of one's wage for a year. Assuming that half of the workers are unemployed one year in six, this would be equivalent to an increase in the company's wage outlays (or total worker payroll) on the order of 6 percent.

The employers did not agree to this proposal, and what Reuther eventually "obtained" was an employer contribution limited to twenty-six weeks and lower than the one demanded, so that the unemployed worker would receive a total of 65 percent of his pay for four weeks and 60 percent for twenty-two weeks. The "guaranteed annual wage" thus is in fact a "guaranteed wage for less than two-thirds of one's wages during a six-month period," and it is financed in half by employers with the rest coming from public contributions. Using the hypothetical figures introduced earlier (half of the workers unemployed one year in six), it amounts to an increase in the company's wage outlays on the order of 1.5 percent.[6]

Thus having surrendered a full three quarters of the ground on which he had taken his stand without once asking the workers their opinion, Reuther not only publicly declared victory but also tried to convince the workers of the "historic" importance of the new contract.

Without consulting anyone and least of all the interested parties, Reuther and his bureaucracy had decided that what the workers needed was neither a wage increase nor a slowdown in the speed of work nor a half-hour daily work break, no, none of those things. Rather they decided that what the workers needed was what Reuther himself *knew* they needed: his "historic" plan for a guaranteed annual wage. To this decision the workers responded with an explosion of wildcat strikes, which were directed as much against the trade-union bureaucracy as against the bosses and which demonstrated that Reuther is committing fraud by talking "in the name of the workers."

The description of these strikes given in the pages that follow provides firsthand testimony published by two American working-class journals, *Correspondence* and *News and Letters*,[7] both of which come out in Detroit, the center of the American automobile industry.

REUTHER'S STRATEGY AND
THE ATTITUDE OF THE WORKERS

The strategy Reuther employed to obtain the guaranteed annual wage consisted of a plan to negotiate in succession with the "Big Three" of the American automobile industry: Ford, General Motors, and Chrysler. All he asked of the workers was to pay five dollars a month until a strike fund of $25 million was built up and to get ready "in case the union needed them." As for the negotiations, they were conducted in secret between the trade-union leadership and Ford's management. At the same time, Reuther called on the workers to give him a strike-authorization vote. In the past, under similar circumstances, the workers have always authorized a strike in order to reinforce the union's bargaining position. But this time endless arguments broke out in the factories.

At the Rouge (Ford) factory, which employs 48,000 workers, most of the workers thought they had no alternative but to vote for a strike; otherwise, "the company might smash the union." Another group of workers felt they could not vote for a strike, but they also could not vote against the union; so they decided not to vote at all. We must note here the great contrast with the past: In the past when workers would not vote, they would be ashamed to admit it or they would find some excuse to justify themselves.

A few advanced workers (neither Stalinists nor Trotskyists) went even further. They said they would vote against the strike. They were not against the "guaranteed annual wage," but they were not for it either. They rejected Reuther's program and his strategy to win it from top to bottom. They said that they were fed up with the union's unbroken record of giving in on working conditions and with its policies that ended up giving more and more power to the company.

Ever since the pension plan of 1950 and the five-year contract that went along with it, the workers have been learning what Reuther's big economic packages mean to them. Every worker under fifty felt that Reuther's pension plan was tying him down to fifteen, twenty-five, or forty-five more years of the same kind of work in the same plant. These workers wanted guaranteed working conditions, not a guarantee that they would have to work the same old way for the rest of their lives.

They were opposed to the "guaranteed annual wage" as well as to Reuther's strategy of striking one plant while the others kept working. The majority of Ford workers felt that for any strike to be effective, the whole CIO should go out.

As many workers said, "The company and the union decide what we'll get—and we have to vote for that. If the union really represented us, they'd ask us what we want. Then they'd negotiate for that." They are fed up with the union deciding what they should fight for.

Nevertheless, as the vote drew closer, many workers who wanted to vote against the strike authorization changed their minds. One reason was that the union published a pamphlet entitled *We Work at Ford*, which pointed out the evils at Ford before the days of the union. This was typical bureaucratic demagogy. The pamphlet told, in 1955, of conditions at Ford before 1935, conditions that had been changed, of course, only by the great working-class battles of 1935–1937. Some workers, however, were swayed by such demagogy. One fellow said he had changed his mind and would vote for the strike authorization because "we work for such a ratty company."

The majority of the Ford Rouge workers had no confidence in Reuther and Co. But a strike vote left no choice, so they voted yes to make clear their opposition to the Ford Company. The vote for the strike was 45,458 to 1,132, with about 10,000 abstentions.

A few days before the first strike deadline at Ford, the company handed the union a counterproposal on the "guaranteed annual wage." It was an offer whereby workers could buy company stocks at half-price.

The workers took every opportunity to joke about this management proposal. Workers ran around calling each other "Mr. Stockholder." One worker ordered the foreman to go away because "we're holding a stockholders' meeting." Actually, they had detected management's trick; if workers owned company stock, management could speed up the line and tell them "it's for your own benefit."

Reuther had carefully chosen Ford rather than GM as his first target. Henry Ford II and the men around him belong to the same generation of "planners" as Reuther himself. The "guaranteed annual wage" is as natural to Ford's thinking as it is to Reuther's. Rather than haggling over a nickel increase for the workers, both Ford and Reuther preferred to put aside five cents an hour for the workers' "security"; then the worker would not be able to "waste" his money.

In agreeing to the "guaranteed annual wage," Henry Ford II was continuing his father's tradition of controlling the lives of the company's workers. The only difference was that the elder Ford did it through private spies and the Bennett Service Department, while Reuther and Ford II planned to do it through a closely cooperating corps of union, company, and government administrators.

In preparing the "guaranteed annual wage" proposal, Reuther had gotten together a staff of 250 administrators. In order to work out the economics of GAW, he had gone into the universities and hired some of the best brains of sociologists and economists. Step by step, and as he was taking the union away from the workers, Reuther set up an administrative and bureaucratic apparatus to rival that of industry and the State.

WILDCAT AT FORD ROUGE

The labor accord between Ford and the CIO's automobile union, the UAW, was signed June 6. While Reuther and Bugas, Ford vice-president and chief company negotiator, were triumphantly posing for photographs, explaining how many hours of sleep they had lost and how many cups of coffee they had drunk, each bending over backward in mutual congratulations to give the other credit for statesmanship, wildcat strikes erupted in Ford plants all over the country.

The 4,300 tool-and-die workers at Rouge started the strike and 6,000 maintenance workers immediately went on strike in support of these first strikers. The workers said that they were not interested in the "guaranteed annual wage," and demanded a thirty-cent (105-franc) an hour increase. But the widespread nature of the wildcat strikes showed that much more than thirty cents was involved. Ford Motor Co. has plants in twenty-three major cities all over the country. At the peak of the strikes, on June 7 and 8, there were stoppages in thirty-seven plants, and 74,000 of Ford's 140,000 workers were not working. In a number of cases the strike developed around "local grievances" (safety, health, rest periods, wage inequities, etc.). This was the first time this expression was used. GM workers were soon to send it ringing around the entire country.

The president of the local union at the Rouge plant (Local 600) is Carl Stellato, who gained his reputation as a "left-wing" opponent of Reuther, but when it comes to strikes, his policy was no different from Reuther's. At midnight on June 5, Stellato had issued an appeal to local officers to "keep the men on the job."

Stellato's speech on June 6 needs to be recorded for history. To the thousands of jeering and booing workers, Stellato said, "Don't boo me. Go boo Ford. . . . You cannot boo security. That's what you are getting, security. This contract will go down in history."

Television newscasts brought knowledge of this meeting to people throughout the country. The cameras traveled over the thousands and thousands of workers, occasionally picking out a jeering and hooting face until it reached the platform where Stellato was speaking. But his impressive speaking lost all meaning against such a background. He was just one man. However, when a rank-and-file member came to the TV microphone saying the committeemen were being paid by the company to sell them out, he was part of the thousands and all the men around him shouted in agreement. On newscasts later in the evening, these speeches by rank-and-file workers were often cut and the sound of the booing was subdued, but the impact of thousands of workers against one union leader was never completely lost.

Every parking lot and street corner around the Rouge plant became a meeting place, with the union leaders distributing back-to-work leaflets informing strikers that under the constitution they had to work until the contract had been voted up or down. Skilled workers demonstrated, crying out, "G.R.R." (Get Rid of Reuther); "Reuther and Stellato have sold us down the river for GAW." This revolt of the skilled workers is of particular significance because, ever since Reuther lost the confidence of the production workers, he has been building up a base among the skilled tradesmen. The skilled workers issued a release saying that they were not just putting up a narrow fight for themselves but that the struggle "was being transferred into the new field of waging a campaign against the adoption of the new contract." They appealed to "all Ford workers to join in this campaign."

The resumption of production at Ford depended on the attitude of the maintenance workers. Their discussions had been lively. Some said, "We don't want the committeemen setup, but what can we do?" Others said, "If we ask for more money, all that will happen is that the prices of cars will go up." They asked each other, "What is the concrete alternative? If we don't accept this agreement, the whole contract will have to be rewritten."

The skilled workers finally went back to work June 8. On June 20 and 21, the Rouge local vote on the new Ford contract was taken. It was accepted, 17,567 votes to 8,325; 30,000 workers did not vote, however, because they were opposed to the contract but saw no alternative. The contract was actually approved by less than a third of the work unit.

Stellato hailed the vote for the contract as "complete evidence that the members failed to heed the swan song of those elements who have tried to make political capital at the expense of the Ford workers and their families." This ambitious politician was the only one who dared to imply that politicians had started the strike. Unlike any other big actions by American workers in recent history, this was the first time that it was impossible for anybody to talk about "Communist agitators."

A few days after the signing of the Ford contract, Henry Ford II proposed that industry-wide bargaining be the next step. Reuther's reply was that that really would be a way to make small crises into big ones. The nightmare of a general strike now hangs over Reuther and the auto companies.

THE GM STRIKES

Reuther's success with Ford had unquestionably softened up General Motors. Reuther therefore prepared for a new "victory."

General Motors has 119 plants in fifty-four cities employing about 350,000 wage workers. During June 6–13, the week of negotiations with GM, the Ford strikes were taking place. They gave the signal for an outbreak of wildcat strikes in a dozen GM plants in several states (Massachusetts, Pennsylvania, New Jersey, Missouri, Kansas, Michigan, and California). Most of the time they were aimed at satisfying "local grievances."

At the Buick-Oldsmobile-Pontiac (BOP) plant in Southgate, California, strikers said that the union was not discussing with the company what they wanted. One worker said,

> We want four things locally. We want a 15-minute break in the morning and afternoon to get a cup of coffee. Is that asking a lot?

> We want a decent relief system so that a guy can tend to his physical needs when he must. You just would not believe men have to wait hours to get excused from the line for a couple of minutes.

> We want protective clothing at company expense.

> We want a few minutes at company expense to clean our hands and put away our tools.

The local president and the regional director tried to force the workers back, but the workers voted 10 to 1 to remain out. The local president admitted that the ranks were in control. "The membership is running things," he said. "They told me that they were going to stay out until they get some satisfaction over the issues." The International sent a special representative from Detroit to try to persuade the men back to work. The men voted to put an ad in the Detroit papers stating their demands. These California workers were looking for a way to establish contact with the Detroit workers independently of the union structure.

Enraged by the wildcats, Reuther and Livingston (GM UAW director) sent a telegram on June 8 to local union officials accusing the GM strikers of "sabotaging national negotiations." Reuther demanded loyalty from his machine. "Entire principle of unionism, teamwork, and mutual responsibility is at stake," he told them. "There can be no excuse for any leadership deserting these principles at this time, regardless of any existing situation. Local leaders are therefore mandated under the constitution to notify the membership of these instructions and to work tirelessly towards ending these unauthorized stoppages."

As a result of this barrage from the International, the local leaders at the Chevrolet plant in Cleveland issued a back-to-work circular. "We know that you are demonstrating against bad working conditions in this shop," they said. "If GM does not give in to our just demands, we will shut the plant down in a legal authorized orderly manner."

Except at the BOP plant in Southgate, California, the GM wildcat strikes that had occurred prior to the expiration of the pact ended on Friday, June 10. At the Southgate plant, the strikers finally went back to work on June 14, after staging an hour and a half stop-work meeting.

The pact with GM was signed on June 13. Reuther and Livingston immediately issued a victory release, concluding, "The credit, of course, goes to the rank-and-file workers in GM plants whose maturity, whose willingness to stand up for the principles in which they believe, was the biggest single force on the union's side of the bargaining table."

The response of the rank-and-file workers to Reuther was immediate: 125,000 GM workers were out on this same Monday, June 13.

Almost everywhere workers brought up "local issues" concerning working conditions. The biggest GM strikes in Detroit were in the Cadillac plant and the Fleetwood plant, which makes Cadillac bodies. The Fleetwood workers presented the company with thirty-four local grievances, including company supply of gloves, boots, and aprons; coffee breaks; washup time; and so on.

In a statement signed by Anthony Kassib (Fleetwood local president) and the executive board, Reuther was notified that "bodies will not roll off the assembly lines until our local issues are resolved." The forty-eight officers said they would resign unless the International recognized that the strike was legal. An International officer said that if the local officers resigned, the union would probably appoint an administrator to run the local. At the local meeting, strikers proposed picketing Solidarity House, the International's headquarters. The motion was defeated, but while local officers were presenting the plant's demands on the International, 150 Fleetwood strikers gathered outside Solidarity House. They jeered the local leaders and threatened to bring down the strikers unless the International authorized their strike.

The local leaders invited Reuther, Livingston, and other International officers down to the local. The International officers declined. Reuther was not showing his face anywhere except at the green company bargaining tables, the International offices, and on the cover of *Time*.[8]

At the neighboring Cadillac plant, thirty-two local issues were presented: against speed-up, wage inequities, more wash-up time, paid lunch break, etc. The Cadillac strikers sent a delegation to the Fleetwood strikers. All the union ever does is send down orders and representatives from the International headquarters to the locals. The locals, on the other hand, are constantly trying to organize means of communication with one another.

All over the country during the week of June 13–17, GM workers were out. Meanwhile, however, the capitalist press could not adjust itself to the fact staring it right in the face that Reuther no longer represented the auto workers. The press was totally unprepared for this wave of strikes. The *Detroit Free Press*, for example, carried a lengthy feature by its labor expert under a big front-page headline, saying that GAW means "BIG AUTO STRIKES ARE DEAD."

By Monday, June 20, the union already had forced most of the strikers to return. However, a new strike broke out at the GM plant at Willow Run (near Detroit). This plant manufactures the automatic transmissions for all Pontiac, Oldsmobile, and Cadillac cars.

The strike again was over "local issues." On Friday, June 24, at a local meeting strikers jeered and hooted local and International leaders ordering them back to work. They voted to continue their strike and said they would picket Solidarity House as well as the plant because the UAW "is trying to force the contract down our throats." They demanded to know "what is happening to the five-dollar-a-month strike assessments."

After this meeting, the International called another meeting for the following Sunday because it "was confident a true expression of the majority of the membership will mean an immediate return to work." Detroit workers, attentively following these events, expected that the union would be up to its usual trick of packing the meeting with hacks and holding it at a time and place when workers could not attend. But at the Sunday meeting, with more than a thousand workers in attendance, the vote was 9 to 1 to continue the strike. The meeting also voted 514 to 367 against accepting the GM contract. On Monday, June 27, the workers rushed the plant, got their paychecks, and left. GM, realizing that the International leadership was no longer able to control the ranks, went to court and got an injunction against picketing. The CIO International leadership went along with court action against a strike for the first time in its history. Individual strikers were named as defendants. Before the judge, attorneys for the union argued that the International and local officers were blameless in the strike. "We repudiate the people engaged in this picketing. We do not represent them in this picketing. They are on a frolic of their own."

Finally, at a stormy meeting held June 28, a vote for going back to work carried. Livingston threw the book at the tool sharpeners who had instigated the strike, threatening them with suspension from the union and a trial. Strikers shouted that they could win "regardless of the International." The vote to return to work was finally 1,259 to 513, with approximately 1,400 not voting.

As the Willow Run strike was nearing its end, the workers at the Ternstedt plant in Flint, which makes hardware and fittings for GM cars, walked out, led by the skilled tradesmen. At a meeting of the local, the GM contract was rejected and the local officials had to call for another meeting and another vote.

Since these strikes, 2,000 skilled workers from Michigan, Indiana, and Ohio have met in Flint to set up machinery for possible withdrawal from the UAW-CIO and for the formation of a new union.

Let us mention, in closing, a conclusion drawn by one of the American workers' papers we have used to present these events: "A movement is now under way," writes *Correspondence*, "to break from the stranglehold of the CIO bureaucracy by establishing new forms of organization. No one knows exactly what will happen next or the many forms this revolt will take. Rank-and-file auto workers have now learned that they can lead a nationwide strike without the assistance of the bureaucratic machine."

Notes

1. T/E: Reprinted, with additional notes not included here, in *EMO1* and *EP1* and translated in *PSW2*. Most of Castoriadis's article consists of his abridged translation of an article in *Correspondence*, 2 (August 1955), which we have relied upon here.

2. The famous "closing of the frontier" actually did not take place until a short time before the beginning of World War I; till then, the abundance of free land and great opportunities for migration within the country meant that the real wages of the industrial worker could

not be lower than the real income of an independent landowner who had at his disposal as much land as he and his family could cultivate.

3. The "passivity" of American workers often has been invoked by Stalinist and crypto-Stalinist propagandists, especially at the height of the Cold War, in order to create an anti-American psychology toward the entire population of the United States. Likewise, during World War II, their propaganda, which came to be directed against Germans as such, presented the German proletariat as completely integrated into Nazism.

4. The great factory-occupation strikes of 1935–1937, which led to the formation of the CIO, are only one example of these kinds of battles.

5. Romano's document, "L'Ouvrier américain," and Ria Stone's study, "La Reconstruction de la société," published in *S. ou B.* issues 1–8, grippingly illustrate these aspects of the class struggle in the United States and their enormous importance for the future. [T/E: See Romano and Stone's *The American Worker* (1947; reprinted, Detroit: Bewick Editions, 1972) and the excerpt from Romano's text, above.]

6. The hypothetical figures given in the text concerning the duration of unemployment and the percentage of workers affected are equivalent to assuming an average level of regular unemployment equal to 1/12 of the total work force, or 8.33 percent—a percentage much higher than the actual one. In view of this, GAW actually represents for the employers an even smaller cost. The percentage increases given in the text concerning the company's wage outlays are based upon simple arithmetic. Before this contract was signed, the company spent in six years, 5½ years of wages, or 286 weeks. Now it will expend an additional 35 percent for 4 weeks, plus 30 percent for 22 weeks: $4 \times 0.35 + 22 \times 0.30 = 7.8$ weeks, which when halved (half of the workers are unemployed) and then divided by 286, yields an increase of a little less than 1.5 percent. Let us recall that the State already contributes unemployment compensation equivalent to 30 percent of total pay during the first 26 weeks of unemployment.

7. T/E: *Correspondence*, 2 (August 1955); *News and Letters*, 1 (June 24, 1955). (The editor of *Correspondence*, Charles Denby, resigned and began publication of *News and Letters* with this issue.) Most of Castoriadis's article consists of his abridged translation of the *Correspondence* account. We have used the English wording verbatim (except for minor stylistic changes) whenever his translation does not substantially differ from the original.

8. A "serious-minded" illustrated American magazine with a large circulation.

The English Dockers' Strikes

Anon.

"Les grèves des dockers anglais"
Socialisme ou Barbarie, 18 (January–March 1956): 61–74[1]

From October 1954 to July 1955, workers' struggles in England have, one after another, touched the most diverse sectors of the capitalist economy. In October 1954, the dockers conducted a five-week strike. In late March 1955, a strike of electricians and drivers broke out at newspaper printing plants, which left London without dailies for three weeks. In late April, 90,000 Yorkshire miners came out on strike for several weeks. At the very moment when elections were being held in late May, 67,000 locomotive drivers and engineers stopped work for 17 days. At almost the same time, on May 23, 18,000 dockers from the country's main ports (London, Liverpool, Birkenhead, Hull, and Manchester) went back on strike and remained on strike until early July. A few days after the beginning of the dockers' strike, the seamen on transatlantic ocean liners in turn stopped work.

These are but the biggest moments of a mounting wave of struggles, which have been spreading constantly since 1950. They have brought the total number of "working days lost" to strikes in official statistics from 1,600,000 in 1951 to 2,460,000 in 1954 and to almost 3,000,000 for just the first six months of 1955.[2]

The usual interpretation the spokesmen for the English bourgeoisie give for this increasing combativeness is that full employment, achieved practically without interruption since the War, had made the workers lose a sense of what is possible and allowed them to make excessive demands. Some conclude from this that a "little" unemployment crisis would be welcome to bring workers back to a sense of reality and to remind them that they are worth something only so long as there is a demand on the market for labor power. Others, more realistic, knowing that neither from the domestic nor the foreign point of view can English capitalism deliberately afford the luxury of deflation, insist on the need for new regulations on strikes, which would make some categories of them "illegal," with prosecution of the "ringleaders."[3] In thinly-veiled terms, Labour Party leader Mr. Herbert Morrison declared at the time of the Fall 1954 dockers' strike: "The blessings of full employment carry with them the power and the temptation to be selfish and this has to be resisted."[4]

That full employment creates conditions favorable to workers' struggles is one thing; the character, content, and orientation of these struggles are another. This whole literature on full employment, as well as Morrison's imprudent statement about the workers' selfishness, leave the impression that the workers are indulging in overbidding on wage demands. Now, the extraordinary fact is precisely this: the workers are struggling less and less over wage demands. Does that mean that they are satisfied with existing wages? Certainly not. According to the official indexes, from 1947 to 1954 wage rates have increased 42 percent, that is to say, a bit less than the 43 percent cost-of-living increase over the same period. Thanks to overtime, bonuses, and so on, actual pay in real terms had to increase somewhat over those seven years, but certainly much less than the workers' actual productivity, which rose more than 30 percent between 1947 and 1954. And yet, in light of this situation, *barely one-fifth of the workers on strike during the first half of 1955 were on strike for wage demands.*[5]

The first striking fact is precisely that struggles are unfolding more and more around issues concerning labor conditions and the control or organization of production.

The second important fact, closely connected to the first, is that strikes often unfold independently of the trade-union bureaucracy or in direct opposition thereto. Both the newspaper strike and the railwaymen's strike were not recognized by their respective unions. The biggest of those strikes, the two dockers' strikes in the Fall of 1954 and the Summer of 1955, unfolded, so to speak, against the trade-union bureaucracy as such.

This aspect increasingly disturbs the English bourgeoisie, which understands that its situation would be impossible if the protective screen the trade-union bureaucracy interposes between the present-day system and the workers' revolt were to collapse. A *Financial Times* editorial[6] devoted to the ocean-liner seamen's strike is worth quoting at length and needs no commentary. "Beside the rail and dock strikes," writes the organ of the City of London,

> ...the liner strike...may seem to be a minor affair, and it has certainly received less than its share of attention. But as a further example of the structural malaise now apparently endemic in the trade union movement it is worth some explanation.

The circumstances of the strike include a number of features which are now familiar. Wages and working conditions in the Merchant Navy were recently reviewed; the settlement came into force on the day before the strike began. The strike, in fact, is completely unofficial, and the men have been urged by their union to honour their contracts; the shipowners have refused to enter into discussions with the strikers' spokesmen. The strikers, on the other hand, have disclaimed recognition of the union and alleged that it is controlled by the shipowners. They have formed their own local committee, and have sent delegations to other ports.

The strike began in Merseyside, the storm-centre of the stevedore's revolt, and there are indications that special influences are at work in that area. There appears to be a widespread emotional revolt among the men against all official leaderships (including that of the Communist Party), and some disagreement among the strikers' leaders in their attitude to the strike. At the same time, there have been allegations of violence, and men other than seamen have taken a prominent part at strikers' meetings. It would be a facile oversimplification to suggest that any particular outside interest has been entirely responsible.[7] There are special factors at work on Merseyside, and in the ports as a whole, certainly complex and possibly unsavoury.

There is another side to the question, however. The National Union of Seamen is comparatively small. The very fact that its members spend most of their time at sea and are constantly moving from port to port makes branch meetings almost impossible. The executive is out of touch with the men, and trouble has been boiling up for some time. The present dispute centres on working hours, but its fundamental cause is the fact that the union members do not have confidence in their leadership.

Certainly the situation of the seamen is an unusual one, one in which normal trade union organisation is almost impossible. But here again the symptoms are apparent of a conflict between the local group and the central organisation, or a frustration with the existing structure of negotiation which is open to exploitation by outside interests. It is becoming more than ever urgent that the structure of the trade union system should be investigated, discussed, and, if necessary, revised.

But undoubtedly it is the two dockers' strikes that have cast the most intense light on these two aspects (whose historical importance could not be exaggerated) of present-day workers' struggles: the passage from the level of purely economic demands to that of demands that raise the problem of the very structure of capitalist relations of production, on the one hand, and the growing opposition between workers and the trade-union bureaucracy, on the other.

LABOR CONDITIONS AND LABOR ORGANIZATION ON THE ENGLISH DOCKS

The first dockers' strike, which took place in October 1954 and lasted five weeks, unfolded around the issue of overtime. The strikers were demanding that overtime work performed by dockers be "voluntary" and not "compulsory." Behind these words, of apparently minor significance, is implicitly posed the problem of the management of production.

The dockers were not and could not be against overtime. It is not only that those overtime hours are presently indispensable to achieving a living wage. It is that, by the very nature of work on the docks, working hours can be neither regular nor set in advance. The arrival and departure of vessels depends on the tides, and labor inevitably has to adapt to these all the time. So, he who organizes "overtime" in fact organizes all port activity (and no need to be reminded what the ports mean to England).

* * *

Here we must open a parenthesis about labor organization on the English docks.

Traditionally, dockers' labor was "occasional": the dockers were practically at the permanent disposal of the employers; waiting in cattle pens named "waiting halls," they were hired based on the needs of the bosses for such-and-such work during such-and-such a period of time, recruited according to the bosses' criteria; overtime hours to be worked were determined by the employers. These labor conditions created constantly renewed conflicts that culminated in 1945, immediately after the end of the War, in a series of big strikes.

When the Labour Party came to power in 1945, Ernest Bevin, the leader of the Transport and General Workers' Union (TGWU), with which the great majority of dockers are affiliated, and one of the principal ministers in the Labour government, prepared an Act for the "normalization" of labor on the docks that was aimed at "pacifying" labor relations and, at the same time, at letting the TGWU's trade-union bureaucracy participate in the organization of production. This Act, which became law in 1947 under the name "Dock Labour Scheme," contains, among others, the following measures:

a) Dockers who would come twice a day to work would receive, if they found no work, "attendance money" equal to around 40 percent of the minimum wage. This benefit is presently equivalent to 55 shillings (2,750 francs) per week.

b) A National Dock Labor Board was set up, composed of representatives of employers and union representatives. This Board acts in fact as the dockers' employer; it hires for each job and imposes disciplinary sanctions through its Port Commissions.

c) As for overtime, the law limits itself to laying out that each docker must "work for such periods as are reasonable in his particular case."

* * *

Apart from the enormous increase in the trade-union bureaucracy's powers, this new set of regulations changed nothing essential about labor conditions on the docks.

Here, for example, is how a study published in 1954, after some detailed investigations conducted in 1950–1951 by the Department of Social Sciences at the University of Liverpool, expressed itself about the system of individuals' waiting to be called to work:

. . . the system adversely affects relationships between the dockers.

In the first place, the calling-on procedure must be deemed to provoke excessive competition and even conflict between individual dock workers. The struggle between them which arises in this way is, moreover, exacerbated by the physical conditions in which it takes place. These are not likely to encourage orderly or co-operative behaviour, and the dockers showed that they were well aware of this when they were interviewed. Many comments were made by them about the call-stand, the most frequent being that its conditions resembled too closely those which obtained in a cattle market. . . .[8]

The only result of the trade-union representatives' participation in the National Dock Labor Board and in the Port Commissions has been the worsening of the workers' situation; the trade-union bureaucrats, feeling much more independent vis-à-vis their rank and file, have entirely assumed the "responsibilities" inherent in their new roles and have transformed themselves into galley-slave drivers pure and simple. The university study mentioned above reports the following incident concerning a "former full-time official who is said to have told the dock workers at a branch meeting that he did not care what they thought about him; he had himself and his job to think of first, and if he had to choose between being popular with them or standing well with higher officials, he would not hesitate to choose the latter."[9]

The results of this state of affairs for the docker's relations with the trade-union bureaucracy were not long in coming. As the *Observer* wrote:

Evidently the officials have to a great extent lost the confidence of the men.

In the docks, there is one specific reason (among others) for this. The Dock Labour Boards, which are responsible for labour supply at all the docks, include trade union representatives, who are thus acting as employers' agents towards the very men they represent.[10]

Finally, as for the burning issue of overtime, the law has settled nothing and could settle nothing. The general regulations for the whole industry stipulate that the work week is forty-four hours, all work beyond that being voluntary. Dock labor law foresees, as we have seen, that a docker is obliged to accept overtime work "for such periods as are reasonable in his particular case." This intentionally ambiguous phrase resulted from the impossibility of settling the problem in a general formula without provoking an explosion on the part of the dockers. Yet in the same stroke, the conflict was officially transformed into a permanent one. What is a "reasonable period" of time and who determines it? For five years, from October 1948 until October 1953, the employers' and trade-union representatives talked about the meaning of the words *period* and *reasonable*. They were in fact all in agreement that overtime hours had to be considered compulsory: a tiny difference existed between the position of the major union, the TGWU, which thought that *reasonable* could not be determined on a national scale and ought to be defined in each port through an agreement between the union and the employers, and the small National Amalgamated Stevedores and Dockers (NASD) union, which demanded a national agreement.

The negotiations led to nothing and were suspended in late 1953. But before as well as after this suspension, the employers, strengthened by the trade unions' recognition of the fact that overtime hours were voluntary . . . in the sense that they were "reasonably" compulsory, could, through the Port Managers (themselves under the control of the National Dock Labour Board), call upon dockers to perform overtime work and, in case of refusal, punish them (usually, through a three-day suspension with a corresponding loss of wages).

* * *

The issue of overtime obviously includes several aspects. The present system allows employers to maintain a portion of dockers in a state of semi-unemployment and thus to exert pressure on wages, to engage in discriminatory hiring, to create fierce competition among workers, and so on. This is what can be called the *economic* aspect of the issue in the narrow sense. Stalinists as well as other English "Marxists" have wanted to present it as the sole issue involved and the dockers' struggle exclusively as a struggle against the extension of the working day. But this aspect is a subordinate one, because the attempt to resolve the problem thus posed leads to posing a problem of management, the problem of the organization of labor on the docks. The struggle is not purely and simply a struggle against the extension of the working day, for, as has been said, there is no work in the ports without overtime. In struggling for these overtime hours to be "voluntary," the dockers are struggling for the *power to organize their labor themselves*. The compulsory character of overtime signifies that labor is organized by the employers and the trade-union bureaucrats. The voluntary character of overtime signifies that the dockers organize it among themselves. This is what the big trade-union bureaucrat and TGWU leader, the late Mr. Arthur Deakin, understood very well when, in his language, he interpreted the October 1954 strike as "another reckless attempt to involve the ports of the country in chaos."[11]

THE ORGANIZATION OF THE DOCKERS

While the first strike, in October 1954, took place over the issue of overtime, the second one, in May–July 1955, took place for the right of dockers to organize themselves in the union of their choice. A few words must be said about the way in which the dockers are organized.

Traditionally, the dockers belonged to the TGWU, the biggest of British trade unions. The initial core of this trade union had been the dockers' union, formed during the great London docks strike of 1889. But since that time, the TGWU has become a large "amalgamated" trade union (that is to say, one including categories of workers belonging to very diverse branches of industry) comprising around one and a half million members and led by well-paid trade-union officials.[12] Parallel with this expansion in trade-union membership was the members' desertion from meetings and their massive abstention during trade-union elections. In most large British trade unions, but particularly in the TGWU, the ruling bureaucracy forms an irremovable stratum that perpetuates itself through cooptation.

The incarnation of this TGWU bureaucracy, Bevin's successor Arthur Deakin, was, in the view of English workers, the symbol of the trade-union bureaucracy's dictatorship. His lack of contact with the rank and file had become proverbial; when he died, in the Spring of 1955, the newspapers wrote of him that he was "like an American union boss." "Elegant, with an American taste for the color of his ties, Arthur helped to liquidate the class barrier between bosses and workers that continued to exist in British society. He dressed like a boss, spoke like a boss."[13] Under the title "Death of a Statesman," *The Economist* wrote, at the announcement of his death:

> Mr. Deakin was a notable example of the type of trade-union leader that has emerged in the last two decades. . . . He was deeply conscious of the responsibility of a powerful trade-union movement towards the nation. . . . This led him to support the unpopular policy of wage restraint and to oppose wholesale nationalization. . . . He dies at the moment when there may be renewed doubts whether Britain can solve the great economic problem of the post-Keynesian age: the problem of maintaining the fullest possible production

and fullest possible employment, without the inflation and labour irresponsibility that would eventually undermine both production and employment.[14]

In addressing the workers of the TGWU and in particular the dockers, the Labour Left, the Stalinists, and the Trotskyists have long tried to persuade them to be more actively militant in the union in order to expel Deakin from it. They advised dockers to come to trade-union meetings and to struggle for a program of "democratization" of the union. Again quite recently, after the first dockers' strike had shown the way in which the dockers intended to struggle against the bureaucracy, Mr. Harry Pollitt, leader of the Stalinist party, said:

> Let the stevedores, dockers and lightermen now use the proud position they have won to cement a still closer unity, and above all let the transport men see that the fight for real democracy in the T.G.W.U. reaches new heights. In this way they can help to bring about changes in policy and leadership not only in the Transport and General Workers Union but in the whole trade union movement.[15]

As the dockers ignored these repeated calls aimed at replacing the present group of leaders with another one, the "left-wing" organizations concluded from this that the dockers were backwards and did not understand anything about organizational questions.

The dockers, however, had their own methods of organization, concerning which backwards politicians were unable to understand very much.

* * *

In London, as in all other English ports, the dockers are, "on paper," unionized in the TGWU. They are unionized because otherwise they cannot work; the union card is, in practice, equivalent to a clearance card. But they are so only on paper; most of their strikes since 1945 have been "unofficial," that is to say, contrary to the decisions of the trade-union leadership groups and not supported financially by them. They have local shop stewards, elected in each port by the rank-and-file workers, who can be recalled from office at any time, and the meetings of the rank and file, independent of all trade-union convocation or organization, occur with extreme frequency. These shop stewards in fact represent the dockers in the everyday conflicts that arise with employers and are in more or less permanent opposition to the trade-union apparatuses.[16] As a comrade from England writes us,

> the true leaders of the dockers are committees made up of the workers' representatives in the port. These representatives can be recalled at any time, so that, when a critical situation develops, it is difficult for someone from the outside to understand what the dockers are in the process of doing because they recall their representatives and change policy with disconcerting rapidity.[17]

Alongside the major trade union, the TGWU, since 1923 there has been in London a small trade union, the National Amalgamated Stevedores and Dockers (NASD), which is accepted by the employers as representative of a section of dockers. Through their local committees and their grassroots meetings, the dockers succeed in more or less controlling a small trade union like the NASD, something that is out of the question in relation to the enormous apparatus of the TGWU.

This possibility of control does not mean that the NASD's leadership is highly different in nature from that of the TGWU. We saw above that their attitude during the 1948 to 1953 negotiations about overtime did not differ in substance from that of the TGWU. The NASD's leader, [Dickie] Barrett, had declared on several occasions that overtime was "in principle entirely voluntary" and was to be "settled by mutual agreement," but also that "some overtime working is essential and that to that end some measure of direction is required."[18] And, throughout the strikes, Barrett's attitude and that of the other official leaders were oriented toward capitulation.

THE OCTOBER 1954 STRIKE

On January 3, 1954, a number of dockers, including an NASD leader, were punished for refusing to work overtime. In response, the NASD dockers held a meeting on January 16 and decided to ban all work beyond normal hours, rejecting the call for overtime work addressed to them by the Executive Committee of the NASD. This decision took effect starting January 25; the members of another small trade union, the Watermen, Lightermen, Tugmen, and Bargemen's Union (WLTBU), joined in this decision February 9. From January until August, numerous attempts aimed at making the dockers go back on their decision were undertaken, among others an appeal signed by the leadership groups of all the trade unions involved; all of them were of no effect. The employers dared not punish the dockers who refused to work overtime; their only reaction was to refuse to have any discussions with the NASD until its members went back on this decision.

So, when in September 1954, apropos of a trivial incident concerning the unloading of a vessel in London, employers refused to hold discussions with the NASD, the members of that union held a meeting, rejected the proposal by Barrett, who wanted to postpone the strike, and decided to stop work until the employers agreed to discuss "all outstanding matters,"[19] therefore basically the issue of overtime. The strike began October 4; the 7,000 members of the NASD were immediately joined by the 4,500 members of the WLTBU and 15,300 of the 22,000 dockers from the TGWU, these latter "unofficially," their leadership not being simply against the strike but opposed to that of the NASD, its decisions being "final" for the rank-and-file members. Shortly afterward, the majority of the dockers from the TGWU of Hull, Birkenhead, and other ports joined in the strike. In total, 70,000 dockers stopped work, including 27,000 (of 34,000) in London.

The strike lasted five weeks and it ended in a sort of armistice: the dockers resumed work, and overtime would not be compulsory until the issue was definitively settled by negotiations between the trade unions and the employers.

THE DOCKERS AS MR. DEAKIN'S PRIVATE PROPERTY

Shortly before the October 1954 strike, 1,600 dockers from Birkenhead (of the 2,000 from this port) decided to desert the TGWU and to form a local branch of the NASD. The TGWU responded with the threat of a lockout.

Mr. P. J. O'Hare, the Merseyside district secretary of the T. and G.W.U., said this week-end that his union had not been bluffing when it warned its Birkenhead members that any attempt at a breakaway would jeopardize their jobs. The Birkenhead branch, he said, would "open its lists immediately," and approach the labour exchanges if necessary. There would be no difficulty in getting people on the register. Mr. O'Hare said that no other union could issue the clearance card which must be produced at the control point before a docker could obtain his new record book, which he must have to start work.[20]

Faced with this threat, most dockers, while organizing within the NASD, continued to pay their TGWU dues. The TGWU nevertheless excluded the NASD from joint meetings with the employers.

But, following the October strike, the dockers began to join the NASD in large numbers in a series of other major ports, particularly on the banks of the Mersey (Liverpool, Manchester). The TGWU leadership demanded that the supreme ruling organ of English trade unions, the Trades Union Congress,[21] intervene, accusing the NASD of "poaching" on its lands.[22]

The TUC demanded on October 18, 1954 that the NASD give assurance that it would cease to organize the dockers who were leaving the TGWU. As the NASD refused to do so, it was suspended from the federation a few days later. But the creation of new NASD branches continued, particularly in Liverpool, Manchester, and Hull.

The NASD leadership had, from the beginning, adopted a hesitant attitude, trying to sort out its conflict with the TGWU via recourse to official channels. On November 20, 1954, it spoke to the Ministry of Labour, asking that the dockers be allowed to join the trade union of their choice. The Ministry responded with total silence. But the NASD rank and file intended to conduct a serious struggle for the right of dockers to organize themselves as they wished. Upon the initiative of members from London, some of the most combative London dockers were sent to the ports in the north of England and organized NASD branches in several ports with the men who were deserting the TGWU.

The first conflict broke out in April on the date of annual renewal of dockers' clearance cards. The TGWU and its representatives at the National Dock Labour Board refused to renew cards of dockers who had joined the NASD. NASD members then stopped work, and TGWU members joined them through a sense of solidarity. The National Board immediately capitulated and renewed all cards.

THE MAY–JULY 1955 STRIKE

It nevertheless remained the case that, following the NASD's exclusion by the TUC, this trade union was no longer represented in any discussion with the employers, who were treating its members as "unorganized" and were sending their demands to the TGWU for "settlement through the normal channels."[23]

Thus, on May 23, 18,000 NASD dockers in London and in the North began a strike, which was to last seven weeks, demanding that the

NASD union branches be officially recognized everywhere they existed, that they be represented in official commissions, and so on.

The way the strike unfolded testifies to an extraordinary political maturity on the part of the dockers. The strike was conducted despite the constant attempts at capitulation by the NASD leadership and by its general secretary Barrett. Two days before the strike broke out, *The Economist* wrote:

> But the TUC changed its mind about parleying with an outlaw after Mr. Barrett, the NASD leader, had said that he was willing to talk with them. It may be that he is wavering—as he is apt to do—afraid of becoming too notorious as a strike leader, or else afraid that in this strike he will not get dockers outside his union to follow him. But he is not playing the principal part in the present dispute. He is overshadowed by two lieutenants, and is said to be suffering from nervous debility.[24]

Indeed, immediately after the strike broke out, the NASD's Executive Committee met and called upon its men to resume work. But the committee of representatives of the local branches of dockers rejected this appeal, affirmed that the strike would continue . . . and decided to send Barrett on holiday for health reasons!

Eighteen thousand dockers participated in the strike; we have seen that, six months earlier, the NASD had only 7,000 members. The difference represents the dockers who in the meantime joined the NASD but also a number of dockers, still belonging to the TGWU, who struggled for the right of their comrades to organize themselves as they wished.

The real leadership of the strike, from beginning to end, belonged to the strikers' elected representatives, and the main decisions were always made during mass meetings. On the role—or rather the absence of any role—of the Stalinists, *The Economist* put it as follows:

> Fourth—and less comforting—the Communist agitators for once are not at work. Officially the party line is that it is better to work for control of the TGWU, with its vast power and tentacles in every industry, than to disrupt it; unofficially, the Communists may have decided that they would be wise to keep out of a venture that they felt was likely to fail.[25]

That the organ of the English bourgeoisie finds it "less comforting" that the Communists are not participating in the strike is in no way surprising. They are, ultimately, of the same ilk, and there are always some possibilities of getting along with the CP, whereas there is none with the irresponsible mass.

However, even after Barrett was sent on holiday, the NASD Executive Committee continued its attempts at capitulation. "The executive committee," noted *The Economist* of June 4 ["Mediation and Frustration," p. 844], " . . . contemplating the failure of their strike to spread to the dockers of the Transport and General Workers' Union, want to call it off. But their members insist on staying out."

A few days later, the Executive Committee addressed a letter of capitulation to the TUC. "The TUC's . . . inflexible attitude" toward the NASD, writes *The Economist* of June 11 ["Peace at the Ports?", p. 925],

> has now produced results. Mr. Newman of that union has crawled abjectly (!) under another yoke. He has agreed unreservedly to accept whatever judgment the TUC's disputes committee may pass on the NASD's dispute with the Transport and General Workers' Union; and he has accepted two of the TUC's prior conditions before that committee can be set to work. He agrees that no more recruiting should be carried out, and no more contributions received from the members "poached" from the big union; but he asks to be allowed to pursue representation on the local committees by peaceful means. He says, with some truth (!), that the men cannot be handed back as if they were cattle. Mr. Newman himself, indeed, is finding them very far from docile, for they are more enthusiastic than their own leaders, who have tried to call off the strike. . . . But it would take more than a letter from Mr. Newman or a frown from Sir Vincent Tewson[26] to prevent people holding meetings if they want to. The TUC has, therefore, wisely accepted Mr. Newman's offer; and there now seems no reason why the docks should not get fully back to work.

Indeed, from the moment that a small bureaucrat wrote to a big bureaucrat, there no longer was any reason for the dockers to continue the strike! The cattle-dealer mentality common to *The Economist*, the big bureaucrats of the TUC, and the small bureaucrats of the NASD's Executive Committee obviously could not take the will of the dockers themselves into account. Newman's letter to the TUC was publicly repudiated by the strike committees and the strike continued.

After four weeks of striking, the TUC having accepted only the reaffiliation of the NASD and, for the rest, maintaining its intransigence toward the groveling attitude of the NASD bureaucrats, the latter succeeded in winning acceptance, at a meeting of London dockers held on June 21, for a recommendation to resume work on the 27th if the men in the Northern ports also accepted it. Let us recall that the London dockers were on strike for recognition of their Northern comrades' right to organize themselves in the union of their choice. But the dockers from the North absolutely refused to resume work. On June 29, after five weeks of striking, and despite the opposition of a strong minority, the London dockers voted to resume work; but the dockers from the North then declared that they would organize a "march on London" to discuss matters with their comrades and the mere announcement of this march convinced the men from London to go back on their decision.

In late June, the TUC's Disputes Committee rendered its verdict on the dispute between the TGWU and the NASD. As was expected, it declared the latter guilty of "poaching" and ordered it to return to the TGWU the members it had "pinched" from the TGWU.

Work resumed only on July 4, after six weeks of striking, during which the dockers struggled alone, without financial support from anywhere, against the big bureaucracy of the TGWU and while constantly thwarting the maneuvers of their own trade-union leadership group. From the standpoint of the objective it set—recognition of the representativeness of the new NASD branches in the Northern ports—the strike was undoubtedly a failure. But, going far beyond this failure, there remains the historical significance of the first great struggle a section of the English proletariat has conducted head-on against its own bureaucracy as such. What remains is the chasm definitively dug between the workers and the counterfeiters who claim to "represent" them. What remains is the demonstration of the astonishing capacities for self-organization of the most "backward" fraction of English laboring people.

It remains the case that, according to all indications presently available, the English dockers have not finished giving us lessons.

Notes

1. T/E: Reprinted, with additional notes not included here, in *EMO1* and *EP1*.
2. *The Economist*, July 16 and 30 and August 20, 1955.
3. Thus, *The Economist* of June 18, 1955 devoted a three-page editorial [T/E: "Rules for Strikes?", 1011–13] to proposing new legislative

measures in this direction, the emphasis being placed on the need to quell "unofficial" or wildcat strikes. [T/E: Like "wildcat" (translating the French *grèves sauvages*), the word "ringleaders" (translating the French *meneurs*) does not directly appear in this editorial. The editorial refers instead to what were also called at the time in Britain "lightning strikes," while its proposals were aimed at "making those who incited workers into this newly illegal type of strike subject to civil suits for damages." Stating that "the word 'unofficial' when attached to a strike has somehow become a dirty word," the editorialist notes that "the Labour Party, in particular, seems to be devising a new doctrine that 'unofficial' strikes should be treated differently than 'official' strikes even in the present state of the law"; his aim is to transform "unofficial" into "illegal," while noting that one must "tread very carefully," for one could not have "sent to prison . . . all the 140,000 miners."]

4.   *The Observer*, November 7, 1954. [T/E: Quoted—like many other citations used here—in Peter Murray's article, "The British Dock Strike—October 1954," *Contemporary Issues: A Magazine for a Democracy of Content*, 25 (October–November 1955): 67. This magazine, published in London and New York from 1948 to 1970 by the mysteriously secretive post-Trotskyist "Movement for a Democracy of Content," was the sister publication to the German review *Dinge der Zeit: Zeitschrift für inhaltliche Demokratie*. Murray Bookchin was among *Contemporary Issues*' authors in the 1950s.]

5.   [T/E: "Remedies for Strikes,"] *The Economist*, July 30, 1955: 375.

6.   June 7, 1955: 4.

7.   Thus, *The Economist* wrote a few days later apropos of seamen: "These men are striking against the community. Their action has been nicely timed by someone to do the maximum damage to the country's tourist trade" ([T/E: "Striking Back,"] June 25, 1955: 1,114). When it is not the hand of Moscow, it is that of the evil competitor that provokes strikes. That the workers might be able to act on their own obviously is inconceivable for the bourgeois.

8.   *The Dock Worker* (Liverpool: University of Liverpool Press, 1954), 65, quoted in *Contemporary Issues, op. cit.*: 70–71.

9.   *The Dock Worker*, 131 [T/E: quoted in *Contemporary Issues, op. cit.*: 71.]

10. T/E: *Contemporary Issues, op. cit.*: 83, quoting "*Observer* 10/54."

11. T/E: *Daily Herald*, October 4, 1954: 1. Quoted, without reference and missing the word "another," in *Contemporary Issues, op. cit.*: 67; full quotation and reference available in Colin John Davis, *Waterfront Revolts: New York and London Dockworkers, 1946–61* (Urbana:

University of Illinois Press, 2003), 208 and 217, n. 84.

12. According to official reports, the TGWU's total assets in 1953 reached 10 million pounds sterling, or 10 billion francs. The income from this capital (held in the form of Government and municipal bonds and other securities), along with members's dues (more than £2 per member per year), allow it to have annual expenditures of around one and a half billion francs, a billion of which is devoted to salaries for officials and expenditures of the Executive Committee. Report of the Chief Registrar of Friendly Societies, cited by *Contemporary Issues, op. cit.*: 72.

13. T/E: With no exact reference, we have simply retranslated the French into English.

14. May 7, 1955: 457–58.

15. *Daily Worker*, November 1, 1954 [T/E: quoted in *Contemporary Issues, op. cit.*: 81, n. *.].

16. Shop stewards [*délégués d'atelier*] of like character exist in all of English industry.

17. T/E: For lack of the English original, this is a translation of the French translation of this letter.

18. T/E: *Contemporary Issues, op. cit.*: 69, quoting from a London Court of Inquiry.

19. T/E: Ibid.: 68.

20. [T/E: "Stevedores' Union Accepts 'Lock-out' Challenge of T. and G.W.U.,"] *Manchester Guardian*, September [27], 1954: 16. [T/E: In the French, O'Hare is misidentified as "O'Hara" and the date is wrongly provided as "September 13." Slightly modified quotation found in *Contemporary Issues, op. cit.*: 79.]

21. T/E: The French text erroneously says, in English: Trade Union Council.

22. The English term *poaching* is borrowed from the jargon of hunters and means precisely hunting on another's lands.

23. T/E: *The Times*, November 30, 1954, quoted in *Contemporary Issues, op. cit.*: 81.

24. [T/E: "Outlawed Union,"] May 21, 1955: 659.

25. [T/E: "Damp Squib at the Docks?"] May 28, 1955: 749.

26. *S. ou B.* Editor's Note: Ennobled union bureaucrat, President of the Trades Union Council.

Automation Strikes in England

Pierre Chaulieu

"Les Grèves de l'automation en Angleterre"
Socialisme ou Barbarie, 19 (July 1956): 101–15[1]

A year and a half ago, the precarious balance on which British capitalism has rested since the war was again threatened with being upset. Prices were rising, imports were increasing, and exports, under the growing pressure of international—and in particular German and Japanese—competition, were stagnating. Thinking that the roots of this evil were to be found in excessive domestic demand that was absorbing too great a proportion of production and not leaving enough for exports, Eden's conservative government tried to combat "inflationary pressures" by means of tax increases and credit restrictions, especially credit on car sales; through these measures it also hoped to induce a certain increase in unemployment, which English capitalists consider an excellent way of disciplining workers and forcing them to "moderate their wage demands." The government's measures have had, till now, only a slow, limited, and uncertain effect on the balance of foreign payments; on the other hand, they have succeeded in bringing about a halt in the growth of production, which has been practically stagnant now for nearly a year, and in delivering a serious blow to the automobile industry, where the workday has been shortened several times since the beginning of the year.

It is in this climate that the April–May 1956 strike of Standard Motor Company workers in Coventry took place. Already, in the month of March, an industrial dispute had broken out when the workers would not accept the rotating layoff of 250 workers a day, as had been decided by the company. But when, on April 27, Standard's 11,000 workers went on strike, rejecting the dismissal of 3,000 among them, the event had an infinitely greater significance.

Standard, one of the "Big Five" in the English automobile industry, owns two plants in Coventry, the Canley factory, where 6,000 workers manufacture cars, and the Banner Lane factory, where 5,000 turn out 70,000 tractors a year (about half of all English tractors produced). The dismissal of 3,000 workers was the result of a reorganization and complete retooling of the tractor factory; the introduction of "automated" methods in this factory will allow the company to raise annual production to 100,000 tractors while reducing by half the number of personnel employed. This reduction in personnel was presented by the company as "temporary" and was accompanied by promises to rehire them once the company had completed its retooling work. The workers refused to accept this, and their stewards presented counter-proposals aimed at a reduction of work time for all personnel and a reorganization of the company's production plans. These proposals were turned down by management. The ensuing strike lasted fifteen days. It ended on May 11 when management partially backed down and promised to re-examine the problem in consultation with the workers' stewards. On May 25 management accepted some of the workers' proposals, but on May 31 it rejected others and declared that it was going to dismiss 2,600 workers. Since then a conflict has been brewing between the men and their shop stewards, on one side, who want to go on strike, and the official trade unions on the other side, who are trying by all kinds of maneuvers to avoid this sort of struggle.

The Standard workers' strike has had immense repercussions in England. It would not be an exaggeration to say that, since April 26, "automation" has become one of the major preoccupations of the workers, the unions, the capitalists, and the English government. What was for so long only utopia and "science fiction," what yesterday was still on the drawing boards and planning charts of the industry's engineers and top accountants, has become in a few days a predominant factor in the social history of our time and the subject for front-page headlines in the major newspapers. For, the problems raised by automation affect both the "liberal" structure of Western capitalism and the structure of the capitalist factory. At the same time, some of the deep-seated features of the relations existing in the modern factory between the workers, the unions, and management have been brutally brought to light. In the Standard strike, the following features are clearly apparent: the degree of spontaneous organization among the workers, their assertive attitude toward how production is to be organized, and management's inability to have effective control over the factory.

THE ROLE OF THE SHOP STEWARDS

The role played by the shop stewards during the Standard strike makes it necessary for us to give a short explanation of this form of organization among English workers, for it has no equivalent form in France (where the shop delegates have been completely integrated into the apparatus of the trade unions).

English shop stewards are in fact independent of the trade unions. They are elected by each factory department; they can be recalled by a simple meeting of the department's workers through a vote of no confidence, in which case a new steward is elected immediately. These stewards conduct most of the negotiations with management over daily conflicts concerning production, norms, rates, etc. In fact, the unions' role tends to be reduced to that of formulating, once a year, demands on base wage rates. In England, as elsewhere, base wage rates bear little relation to the workers' actual wages, and as time passes this relation is becoming more and more remote.

The shop stewards' movement appeared in England toward the end of the First World War. Between the two wars, it was the constant source of conflict in the struggle between workers and capitalists. The latter refused to recognize the stewards and dismissed them as soon as they could; and since they were forced to meet with them often, they took advantage of the first relaxation in working-class pressure to go back on the offensive. During the Second World War, however, the capitalists were forced to realize that it would be impossible to increase production if they did not recognize the shop stewards; and England's fate depended upon such production increases. In this way, the stewards finally achieved a semilegal status. At present, the workers would consider any attack upon the stewards as an attack upon the trade-union movement and elementary democratic rights.

The trade unions theoretically control the shop stewards' movement since they issue the stewards a certificate testifying to their qualifications. But in fact there is not a single example in which a union has refused to recognize a steward elected by the workers (in France, as is well known, delegates are practically appointed by the unions, and the workers are called upon only to vote for a particular union). The shop stewards' de facto independence is clearly expressed when strikes occur. As the trade unions are opposed most of the time to striking, the stewards get things moving by calling a strike as the men have been asking for; then they go to the union and ask that the strike be "recognized" (which allows the workers to receive strike benefits from the large funds the unions have at their disposal). Then the union almost invariably will say that this is impossible and will ask that the steward persuade the men to go back to work. The steward will call a meeting of the men, for form's sake, and then return to the union to explain that nothing can be done. Most of the time, the union will give in and recognize the strike. If it does not give in, the stewards, as a general rule, will continue their action paying no attention to the union.[2]

But the most characteristic aspect of the shop stewards' movement is that it tends to go beyond the shop level and to be organized on a much vaster scale, at the industry-wide and regional levels. Regular, but completely unofficial, meetings of shop stewards from all four corners of the country take place in most large sectors of industry; on occasion, the stewards of all branches of industry in a given region will hold joint meetings. After many years of not knowing about this or pretending not to know about it, the bourgeois press now has been brought around to taking notice of it. One can read in the English newspapers of March 5 that on Saturday, March 3, an (unofficial) committee meeting of shop stewards in the automobile industry had taken place in Birmingham; these stewards had voted on a resolution blaming the government for being directly responsible for the crisis situation in the automobile industry, calling on the automobile workers to hold meetings and mass demonstrations on March 26, and inviting the representatives of workers in other industries affected by the government's economic policy to join with them; they also decided to call a special conference of automobile industry shop stewards in Birmingham on April 22. Similarly, as soon as the problem of automation was posed on a practical level, the shop stewards, ignoring the grandiloquent and Platonic resolutions voted by the trade unions, set up contacts on a national scale. On May 28, the papers took note of a national conference of shop stewards in the machine-tool and other related industries held in London on Sunday, May 27. This conference demanded:

> full consultation at shop-floor level before the introduction of new technical advances . . . increased production to be reflected in higher earnings. . . . Employers were warned that unless they take account of these demands, they could expect all-out resistance.

The unanimously adopted motion declared:

> We are not opposed to the introduction of new technological advances, but insist that full consultation with the workers should take place at shop-floor level prior to their introduction. We are determined to safeguard the workers involved and to fight for a higher standard of living as a result of automation, full consultation, no redundancy, workers to receive full wages pending satisfactory settlement of the problems in the plant, a shorter work week, and three weeks' annual holiday.[3]

It undoubtedly would be wrong to think that the shop stewards' movement is *entirely* independent of the trade-union bureaucracy. Some of these stewards at the same time are active trade unionists, and among those there are some who try to get the workers to accept the union's line. But the fact that they can be recalled at any moment prevents them from being able to do so systematically or on issues the workers consider important. However that may be, we need only compare the stewards' actual conduct in the great majority of cases, or the automation resolution quoted here, with the general attitude and the constant babbling of the trade unions in order to understand that the shop stewards' movement and the trade-union bureaucracy are in fact divided by a class line.

REAL POWER IN THE FACTORY AND THE WORKERS' SELF-MANAGERIAL ATTITUDE

As soon as such an organizational form comes into being—despite its partial and informal character, the maneuvers of the trade-union bureaucracy, and the enormous weight of the means at capitalism's disposal in the factory and in society—the power of the modern proletariat appears in the fact that capitalist management no longer is the undisputed master in its "own house. "United around the shop stewards, the workers in many cases will refuse to carry out unconditionally the orders from the offices [*bureaux*]; in the conflicts that arise daily within the production process, a perpetually unstable and shifting compromise is achieved at every instant between the management line and the workers' collective resistance. The following two examples show that with a certain level of organization and combativeness on the workers' part and without barricades or soviets, what is more or less in question is the very power of capitalists within the factory.

In 1954, Standard's management enacted a series of regulations concerning the activities and the rights of shop stewards—which by itself shows already the degree of permanent, ongoing tension that has existed in the firm. The stewards paid heed only to the parts they found to their liking. In December 1954, management dismissed three stewards for failing to comply with these regulations. The factory's 11,000 workers went out on strike, and after a few days management capitulated and rehired the stewards.

The second example comes from the series of actions that began at Standard this past March. At the beginning of March, before there were any disputes over automation, Standard decided to cut automobile production, which had surpassed demand, and to introduce a rotation system that involved laying off in turns 250 workers a day. Through a vote by the stewards, the workers responded by proposing an alternative method of achieving the desired reduction in production: a 36-hour work week with the same pay. Under threat of strike, a compromise with management was reached.

Still more characteristic was the attitude of the workers and stewards when the problem of layoffs due to the introduction of automation in the Banner Lane tractor factory came up at the end of April. Management had announced at the outset its intention to lay off 2,500 workers temporarily while the factory was being reorganized through automation; later on, it raised this figure to 2,900 and announced at the same time that it would turn down any plan to reduce the workday. The firm's 11,000 workers then went on strike, and the stewards presented a plan aimed at avoiding the layoff of any workers that in fact amounted to a reorganization of the factory's production plans.

They proposed three basic changes. First, some of the workers would be assigned to produce parts common to both the present and the new model. Some of these parts would be used as spare-part stocks for the old model, and the rest would serve as components that could be used later for the new model. Second, production should also resume right away at full volume on jobs already retooled and those that can quickly be retooled. Third, the rest of the displaced workers in the tractor factory should be absorbed by the automobile factory. Work in the latter factory should be organized around three short shifts in place of the usual combination of one long day shift and one short night shift. To management's claim that this would mean tripling the number of foremen and the rest of the nonproductive personnel, the strike committee responded that the foremen could work on two long shifts against the men's three short shifts; they added that, in any case, "it does not really matter whether the supervisors above charge-hand level are there or not because the incentive bonus scheme stimulates the work."[4]

Beyond these specific proposals, what is important here is the workers' and stewards' self-managerial attitude. They adopt the point of view of how to organize the entire production process in the factory, and they are led to do this by necessity so that they can respond in concrete terms to the capitalist organization of the factory and counter the damages it entails for them.

THE ATTITUDE OF THE TRADE UNIONS

Since April of this year, resolutions "congratulating" the workers for their resistance to layoffs,[5] threatening the employers with strikes, etc.[6], have followed one after another at the various annual Trades Union Congresses and at meetings of their governing bodies. But in point of fact, the trade unions—the official leadership bodies—have done all they could to avoid having the problem placed on the terrain of a real struggle of the workers against the capitalists. After a series of contradictory and evasive statements, at last their attitude was clearly expressed by Mr. J. Crawford, a member of the Trades Union Congress,

> When it comes to laying down union policies in regard to automation the talks must be conducted by men at the top level, not by shop stewards. . . . Otherwise, we will have anarchy creeping in.[7]

During the April–May strike, the trade unions had succeeded, through a series of delaying tactics, in avoiding taking any position on the strike. But they were not able to get by so easily after it was over.

When, on May 31, Standard's management announced the permanent dismissal of 2,600 workers, the trade-union secretary of the Coventry district declared that his union was "greatly shocked" by the news. The same day, the factory's shop stewards decided to demand that the trade unions officially call the workers out on strike. The stewards' prudent attitude may be explained by how the situation had changed since April: Standard was in the process of reducing car production, and a portion of the laid-off workers had been working at the company's automobile factory; the strike might be long, and the workers could not hold on without the financial support of the trade unions. The union leadership was to meet on June 3 to decide its position. This meeting was then postponed until June 6. When the meeting finally took place, the union leaders declared unanimously that they were against striking. "Instead of a strike," the *Manchester Guardian* innocently noted on June 7, "the unions . . . have asked the Minister of Labour to call a meeting of all concerned" to discuss the situation. The Minister of Labour, Mr. MacLeod, actually received these union leaders on June 7, only to declare that "whether or not there was sufficient work in a particular firm to keep on all its workers was for the firm to decide."

No doubt the workers at Standard and elsewhere can appreciate the true value of this tangible outcome of "top-level discussions."

AUTOMATION AND THE CAPITALIST ECONOMY

What is automation and what does it consist of in Standard's case? The word is vague and covers over a complex and confused reality. There is nothing revolutionary about the techniques Standard has introduced, when they are taken separately. As far as we can tell, they involve a battery of "semiautomated" machines (which have already been in use at Renault for years) and a certain degree of automatic control over production through electronic means. There are no absolutely new inventions at the basis of the reorganization of the Banner Lane factory. For years, research has been done on these new "automatic" processes, and there have been some partial applications in a host of industrial sectors. Then suddenly, it became technically possible and economically feasible to reorganize a factory *totally* on the basis of these processes, simply by extending their application as far as possible in each individual sector and by rethinking how they can be incorporated into one production assembly unit through methods that are themselves "automated." The revolutionary aspect of "automation" today consists in its ability to make a tabula rasa of the factory's previous organization and to apply en masse in every department the processes and the machines that were until then utilized only partially and sporadically.

Now, the application of new processes on a hitherto unknown scale not only gives the "automated" factory a qualitatively new structure but poses on a society-wide scale tremendous problems that from the outset put the pseudoliberal organization of Western capitalism into question.

The first of these problems obviously results from the technological unemployment of workers pushed out of "automated" factories.

"Automation" appears to result in enormous savings of labor power. In Standard's case, it seems that production will increase more than 40 percent while personnel will be reduced on the order of 50 percent. That is equivalent to an increase in labor productivity of more than 180 percent and signifies that the past level of production now can be attained with a third of the manpower previously employed.

Obviously, this does not mean that total unemployment will increase exactly in proportion to the number of workers laid off. On the one hand, employment ought to increase in the factories that make this new equipment, that maintain it, replace it at the end of its productive life, etc., and this increase in employment will have secondary repercussions in industries that produce consumer goods for these workers. On the other hand, capitalist accumulation does not immediately take the form of full investment in "automated" factories; it continues, for the most part, to take place in the form in which investments today are made, where each $10 million invested in new equipment creates, let us say, a demand for a thousand new workers. We cannot go here into the complex problems that are posed in this connection. The final net outcome will depend on a number of factors that involve not only the degree of labor-power savings realized by new inventions, the extent of investments required, the rate of accumulation and its distribution among traditional and new investments, but also in the long run all the important features of the capitalist economy. Just as it would be wrong to think that the unemployment resulting from automation will be exactly equivalent to the number of workers initially laid off,[8] it would also be wrong to say that capitalist production automatically will create an equivalent number of new jobs.[9]

Even setting aside the question of what the overall level of unemployment resulting from automation will be, one thing, however, is certain: Unemployment awaits the workers who are directly affected. From the abstract economic point of view, there might be an equal number of workers laid off by Standard and taken in at the same time by the electronic equipment, machine-tool, or even the chemical-products industries. From a real point of view, however, things do not work this way at all. New jobs created elsewhere due to the existence of automation itself or to the general expansion of the capitalist economy will not be in the same locality, nor will they require the same skills. Moreover, only a small proportion of the workers who were there before will fill the jobs remaining in the "automated" factory, since these jobs are now of a different nature. As the *Manchester Guardian* said, paraphrasing Marx (probably without knowing it), "What help is it for a laid-off mechanic from Coventry to know that there are jobs open for bus conductors in Edinburgh?"[10]

The problems the worker will encounter are practically insurmountable. The feat involved for the individual worker to acquire a skill, find lodging, and then move in cannot easily be repeated twice in a lifetime. From the capitalist point of view, these considerations cannot be taken into account; a firm cannot base its equipment and production on the principle of keeping its present workers employed. It is in the autocratic logic of capitalist production to treat the worker as just another commodity, which ought to move about in order to meet demand and transform itself in order to answer the requirements set by economic demand. That the object of this displacement or of this transformation is the very person of the worker does not change the matter one bit. At the limit, if the worker cannot be transformed so as to conform to the exigencies of this mechanical universe, which is in a state of permanent upheaval, his fate cannot and should not be different from that of any other instrument of production that becomes outmoded before becoming completely worn down: He is simply discarded.

In the past, this was the way capitalism "settled" the problem of technological unemployment. But what was possible in the nineteenth century is no longer possible with the proletariat of today. Its actual power within society today prevents one from merely saying that the workers should just pull themselves up by their own bootstraps or else die of hunger. Present-day capitalists know that under such circumstances, the workers might raise themselves up in a completely different manner. The problems posed by the relocation of laid-off workers—lodgings in another locality, new training, paying for all these things—can be faced only on the national level and they call for State action. In Western capitalist societies, this state of affairs can only give new momentum to the efforts of State and trade-union bureaucracies to intervene concretely at specific points in the organization of the economy.

It is only too natural then that the Labour party's daily paper, the *Daily Mirror*, published on May 8 a multicolumn, center-page "10-point plan for the second industrial revolution." Starting from the principle that "unless there is political planning, there will be industrial chaos," the Labour newspaper demanded that the Government provide funds so that laid-off workers can move to other localities, that it furnish them with the necessary housing, that it cover the training expenses of workers who have to learn new skills, that it set up "expert mobile teams" to attack the problems created in various regions by the introduction of automation,[11] etc.

Much more characteristic is the great liberal daily paper, the *Manchester Guardian*, which not only adopts this point of view completely and insists that only the State can assure a solution to the problems created by the introduction of automation, but goes so far as to write,

> We might take a leaf here from the Soviet book. Discussing yesterday how the Russians dealt with the problem of "automation," Mr. S. Babayants, a leader of the Russian engineering unions on a visit to this country, said that new machines meant no loss to the workers, for those replaced were trained on full pay for other jobs before any change took place.

"Individual managements," the paper continues,

> have an obvious responsibility for such training, but clearly they cannot be expected to shoulder full responsibility for it. If we had a national scheme of this sort, there would be far less fear of "redundancy." ... This is the kind of help that the unions should now be demanding from the Government, and it is the kind of help that should be given.

For the time being, the conservative government has restricted itself to launching appeals for calm and to declaring that "the area of manpower is in essence an issue that ought not to be determined by the Government." But this attitude can be maintained only so long as the introduction of new methods remains limited in extent. The inevitable expansion of automation will oblige the Tories to throw their "ideology" overboard (it won't be the first time) or to stand aside.

AUTOMATION AND THE CAPITALIST FACTORY

But the effects automation has on the structure of the capitalist factory, on the concrete relations of production, and on the daily activity of the workers have a still greater impact.

From May 14 to 17 a conference on automation, organized by the European Productivity Agency (EPA), took place in London. We present here the statements of one of the participants, Mr. Serge Colomb, a technician at Renault in Paris, as they were reported by the English newspapers.[12] They take on their full significance when it is remembered that the trade unions brought together by the EPA are anything but "subversive."

After having recalled that Renault had launched its own automation program in 1947 and that since that year the factory's labor force had increased 15 percent and production 300 percent, Mr. Colomb continued, saying,

> It has not been possible to attain a state of equilibrium in the redeployment of the labor force. The number of workers downgraded by automation techniques is higher than that of the new posts created and often requirements for the latter are such that the new men must be recruited from other categories.
>
> The gap between production and training is another key problem of automation. The company's apprenticeship scheme was taken unawares and was unable to foresee three years in advance what the works would need. A few years ago milling machine hands, fitters and turners were required. Now the need is for machine setters and other different sorts of workmen.
>
> Hours worked are not reduced and although somewhat better paid, the workers in sections which have turned over to automation have not received the advantages announced by the automation prophets. The workers' isolation in the midst of complicated machinery may have very serious repercussions and accentuate the dehumanization of the work felt all the more in the absence of hard physical labor.

As for wages, Mr. Colomb said that obviously it was not possible to make use of piece-rate wages or bonuses, since the machines determine the rate of work. The company had to go ahead with an extensive reevaluation of various jobs and to set up a wide range of new wage scales.

This astonishing declaration requires little comment. Here we have a technician in a capitalist factory. We must pay tribute to his honesty, which, in a few sober lines, demolishes the entire mythology of capitalist "progress." We should merely emphasize the significance of the information he provides on wages. Automation removes yet another "objective" basis for wage disparities. Management reacts by going ahead with an "extensive reevaluation of various jobs"—this is the increasingly widespread practice of initiating "job audits"—which obviously cannot help but be arbitrary, for they are designed for one purpose alone: maintaining divisions among the workers.

In order to understand the effects automation has on the concrete structure of the capitalist factory, we must grasp the social function it is called upon to fulfill in an exploitative society and its place in the history of capital-labor relations.

Considered in the abstract, the major technical changes in the field of production in capitalist society appear as the result of a relatively "autonomous" technological evolution, and their employment in production appears as the result of an application of an equally "autonomous" principle of profitability—that is, independent of all social considerations. In fact, the application of these changes en masse to industry takes on an extremely precise social content; bluntly speaking, it almost always constitutes a moment in the class struggle, a capital offensive against labor, considered as the originating force in production. At each stage in the development of capitalist society (which begins by corrupting everything and bringing everything into its service), technical changes are the sole, apparently conclusive means of "disciplining" the workers; this is done by attacking the worker's living productive forces. In each instance a faculty of some sort is wrung from the worker and incorporated into the machinery. Unable to tolerate the workers' ongoing resistance, capital distorts the technique when applying it in the production process and subordinates it to the pursuit of its own utopian goal: the elimination of man *qua* man from the sphere of production. But at every stage, this attempted elimination of the human element again and again proves impossible to achieve: The new technique cannot be applied en masse unless millions of workers adapt themselves to it; this new technique itself opens up new possibilities that cannot be exploited unless the workers collaborate in the process of applying it within the sphere of production. Sooner or later the concrete dialectic of human action in production—of technique and of class struggle—brings to the fore the predominant element in the modern production process: the proletariat.

Thus the technological revolution that took place around the time of the First World War (with the introduction of semiautomatic machinery and assembly lines) appeared to capital as the initial stage in finally ridding itself of skilled workers. The capitalists thought they would be left with a mass of "unskilled brutes" with whom they could do as they pleased. Twenty years later, they had to stop singing this tune: The universal application of these new processes had culminated in the creation of a mass of semiskilled workers, homogeneous and disciplined *on its own behalf*. Now that narrow occupational skills have disappeared, the creation of this well-organized mass of workers is of decisive importance for the evolution of the production process since this mass of workers is all the more ready and able to resolve the problem of workers' management of production. In fact, capitalism proves to be much less capable of disciplining the proletariat of 1955 than that of 1905 *in production as well as in society*. It only succeeds in this thanks to the trade-union and political bureaucracy.

It is within this context that the application of the techniques of automation will acquire its true meaning. We easily could go back and show the links leading from the "economic" and "technical" imperatives imposed upon business firms to the historical signification of this movement tending toward increased automation. But what concerns us here is this historical meaning itself. What the application of automation objectively aims at in the present era is the replacement of every one hundred semiskilled workers with a score of "unskilled brutes" and a score of "salaried professionals." But what we now know about automation in its actual application (at Renault, for example) shows us that, put in contact with semiautomated machinery, unskilled workers and some skilled workers tend to appropriate for themselves the "know-how" that is involved in applying these new methods.[13] In particular, we now know also that what seems to make sense for an individual firm becomes an absurdity on the larger scale of capitalism as a whole.

Applied to production as a whole, this transformation would end up giving a majority of workers a greater technological education [*culture*]. Barring its ability to throw 60 percent of the population out of work, capitalism will then have to face a still more skilled, more conscious, and more intractable proletarian mass than exists at the present time.

Notes

1. T/E: Reprinted in *EMO1* and *EP1* and translated in *PSW2*.
2. This is what happened in several large strikes in 1954 and 1955; see "The English Dockers' Strikes" [T/E: now available above in the present *Anthology*].
3. *Manchester Guardian*, May 28, 1956.
4. *The Times* (London), May 3, 1956.
5. Amalgamated Engineering Union, in *Manchester Guardian*, April 25, 1956.

6. Electrical Trades Union, in *Manchester Guardian*, May 16, 1956.

7. *Manchester Guardian*, May 18, 1956.

8. If that were so, unemployment during the last century and a half would have reached unimaginable proportions.

9. Thus, *The Economist* on May 12 (p. 592), after having rejected the idea "generally being advanced today"—by capitalists and their spokespeople—according to which "the short-term effects of automation must inevitably be painful, but in the long run automation will equally inevitably create more jobs," proposes to replace this idea with a "revised, honest version" (!) which "might run like this, 'One thing is certain, for our comfort: automation cannot occur without the effective demand—probably widely distributed—to buy the extra goods.'" *The Economist*'s sole justification for this idea is that a company will go ahead with costly new investments that involve automation only insofar as it *expects* an increase in sales. But this expectation will not necessarily be fulfilled, and it is far from being the sole reason for introducing automation. Most of the time both production increases and personnel reductions occur; automation can be introduced even in the face of stagnant demand, simply in order to reduce costs. Moreover, within the context of a technological revolution, increases in actual demand have no necessary connection with employment increases; demand can increase and employment can decline precisely because the new technique makes it possible for a given level of production to be attained—and a corresponding level of demand satisfied—with a *different* (lesser) quantity of labor. It is hard to say to what extent *The Economist* wants to deceive others and to what extent it is just deceiving itself.

10. T/E: *Manchester Guardian*, June 7, 1956. We have translated Castoriadis's wording of the *Guardian* editorial. The original editorial says, "The fact that there may be vacancies for fifty bus conductors and fifty dustmen does not necessarily solve the problem of a hundred men who lose their jobs in a tractor plant." It appears Castoriadis has accidentally combined this statement with a paragraph in the *Daily Mirror*'s "10-point plan for the Robot Revolution" (see three paragraphs below), which reads, "It is no use telling a man in Coventry that there is a job waiting for him in Glasgow unless he can be assured that he will be able to get a home, school places for his children, and money to help him move."

11. "Every team should include one trade-union expert . . ." to look into the more specifically working-class aspects of these problems, perhaps? Not at all: " . . . who can iron out the difficulties if a man has to

join a new union." The Labour Party bureaucracy has not forgotten which way is up, nor has it forgotten that it needs to protect its hunting grounds. [T/E: Again, with the "10-point plan for the second industrial revolution," we have translated Castoriadis's translation; the *Mirror* actually calls this plan a "10-point plan for the Robot Revolution," though it mentions the "Second Industrial Revolution" in point six.]

12. *Manchester Guardian*, May 18, 1956.

13. Alain Touraine's recent book, *L'Évolution du travail ouvrier aux usines Renault* (Paris: CNRS, 1955), makes this point clearly.

The Factory and Workers' Management

Daniel Mothé

"L'Usine et la gestion ouvrière"
Socialisme ou Barbarie, 22 (July–September 1957): 75-92
Socialisme ou Barbarie—Anthologie, 88-103

It is difficult to have an overall view of things in our society. It is even more difficult for a worker, from whom the organization of the world remains hidden as a mysterious thing obeying magical laws unknown to him. The worker perceives things at first only within his quite narrow frame; he has to fight to see further. Our horizon is limited to the parcel of labor demanded of us and imposed upon us. Nearby us, we no longer know what is there. We no longer know what becomes of our labor; it is sent off into the organization's machinery. We have done it, yet we no longer see it unless, by some fluke, we might encounter it again and then, most often, it will be a surprise, an astonishment, or a disappointment to note that what we have done serves some purpose or is completely useless. We are not to know anything and the organization of the world seems to be the organization of our ignorance. All our resentments at our being thus partitioned may blow up at any moment. The worker complains six days a week to his comrades while thinking only of the day society will liberate him from his tedious and exhausting task. But these resentments are of no interest to anyone but ourselves. We are free men; we have the right to vote and the right to express ourselves about the general problems of the world, but people refuse to listen to our voices about what we do every day, about the part of the universe that is ours. We know through experience that our ballot changes nothing about this universe. We are able to express ourselves, but such expression remains limited to our comrades. We are alone. No one cares about us, about our resentments, and people strive to prove to us that these cares are alien to the general problems of politics.

The working class has its slums, its low wages, and the whole lot of misery that flows therefrom, everything that moves literature, tourists, and trade-union organizations to pity. But there is another sort of misery upon which an enormous silence weighs, and that is the misery that emanates from one's role in work.

In order to oppose the bosses, union papers rely on phrases like "pauper's wages [*salaires de misère*]," the "furious pace" of work, and "inhuman norms." That does not challenge capitalist society, the system is not attacked, the safety valve still works: if the working class threatens, it suffices to increase wages and decrease the norms and pace of work. That is how world harmony is achieved. The struggle between the bosses and the trade unions will take place around how this misery is evaluated. For both sides, the lie will become the basis for the argument.

Thus can one see, in *La Vie Ouvrière* [the magazine of the Communist-allied *Confédération générale du travail* (CGT, General Labor Confederation)], images representing the starving French worker before an out-of-reach piece of bread, whereas bourgeois newspapers will draw the most optimistic conclusions from the number of cars and television sets the working class owns. The trade unions reproach the bosses for making huge profits, for "going a bit hard."

The bosses respond that the workers have more wealth than fifty years ago. From this controversy is born the codification of the worker's consumption, his "subsistence level." The trade unions try to prove that it is in the boss's interest to feed the working class well.

The worker, like the consumer, is kept to his station as a machine. He has the same needs as the latter: energy supply, maintenance, rest. It is on this essentially bourgeois basis that the trade union places itself. It discusses with the boss while adopting his criteria. On this terrain, interminable discussions can be opened up as to whether the worker's rest and food are sufficient; for that, the technicians of the human machine—doctors, psychologists, neurologists, and so on— will be called upon. The trade unions could thus argue for months to get the employers and the government to admit that the tennis ball has to be replaced by the soccer ball in the 213 articles on the list of subsistence-level items. The worker remains no less society's thing; he has become the 213-articles machine.

The worker may very well eat steak and even have a television set and his own automobile. He remains, in society, a production machine and nothing more, and therein lies his great misery, which is manifested

48 hours a week. It would be wrong to believe that alienation ceases as soon as he has gone beyond the factory walls. We shall limit ourselves here, however, to describing what happens within these walls, and, here, we shall abandon the idea that man is a commodity. We will not gauge his misery and his suffering by the number of pieces and movements he makes in a work hour or a work day or by the salary he receives every two weeks; we shall base ourselves on the simple fact that he is a man, with all the consequences that entails.

His struggle is the permanent demand for this right to be recognized as such and it is this that, at the outset, is contested by the entire social system.

Is this the inevitable price of progress and of modern society, as both the defenders and the detractors of this so-called progress try to make us believe?

It is to this question that we wish to respond in the most concrete way possible. This is why we shall avoid offering a general image of the life of workers in the factory. The lines that are going to follow are the description of a very specific shop, of the contradictions in the way it is organized, of the worker's reactions, and, finally, of the solution a socialist society can bring. In a forthcoming study, we intend to tackle another, much more complex sector, the sector of assembly-line work. For the moment, we will be dealing with a tooling shop at the Renault factory that brings together skilled workers—that is, workers who have learned a trade and who enjoy a certain amount of autonomy and certain privileges. This is what is usually called the *labor aristocracy*. This autonomy is nonetheless counterbalanced by Management's rationalization efforts, which increasingly compartmentalizes [*rend . . . parcellaire*] such labor, and all the more so as, in this shop more than in any other, the worker tends to be unaware of what he is doing since he does not manufacture parts for cars. He manufactures pieces and tools for the machinery that machines or mounts the elements of cars.

Although the critique of shop organization, and the solutions proposed, are related to this shop and nothing more, a series of ideas follows from this example that have a universal value. But first, one must see what happens in this shop.

For the reasons we have indicated above, it is difficult to offer a general view of factory organization. There are, of course, organigrams that are available to the public and that are published in the *Bulletin Mensuel Renault*. But what is the relation between these diagrams and reality, between Management's plan and the fulfillment of this plan by the various services and by laboring people? In order to respond in such an overall way to that question, it would have to be assumed that a person could know in detail all the cogs of this organization. It is precisely this possibility that we are denying. Of course, the factory's "managers" know by heart the organigram, yet their knowledge is but theoretical.

The major part of the reality of production is inaccessible to them, hidden by the minor supervisory staff, by the workers, and by the technical staff for the simple reason that the "managers" not only are people who are to coordinate but also are people who give commands and exercise coercive powers. Such coercion, a formidable weapon that threatens each person, to different degrees, is a phenomenon that paralyzes the whole hierarchy of this organization and makes subordinates as distrustful of their superiors as a child toward adults.

The only way to have an overall view of the industry would be to obtain testimony from those who participate in this industry and especially from those who make these diagrams a reality, much more than from those who design them.

This article is made by only one worker. That is why it will give only a partial view, and it is for this reason, too, that this article's claim is not to respond to all problems of factory organization but to those ones that affect the sector of certain skilled workers: the tool-makers.

RATIONAL ALLOCATION

When Management presents a rational diagram of the factory, anyone is inclined to consider it true. However, what is perceptible to us is entirely different. Our shop appears in the right place on this diagram. Yet at our level, it is difficult for us to speak of rationality. What we perceive is the very negation of any organized plan; in other terms, it is what we call "a goddamned mess" [*le bordel*].

The Rationalization of Manpower

If you ask Management the size of the workforce, that is, the number of metalworkers, milling-machine operators, turners, and so on, the various classifications among these journeymen, P1s [low-grade Position 1], P2s, P3s, the number of OS [semiskilled workers], and if you then check for yourself, you will be astonished not to locate yourself thereon. If you delve deeper into the question, you will be still more astonished to note that some metalworkers are on machines, that turners are on milling machines, that some OS do the same work as professionals, that a large part of the workers do work they never learned at technical school, and that some OS do a job they supposedly do not know. If you believed for a single moment in the rationalization of manpower, this single shop visit will make you lose in an instant all illusions on this topic.

What then is going on?

Were you not steeped in the formula you had learned in industry manuals and reviews or through the explanations of the "managers": "The worker is paid according to his occupational abilities and the work he does"? This formula loses all its meaning as soon as one has entered within the walls of the shop; it has nothing to do with reality.

Why are there OS and P1s, P2s, P3s? Why is a given worker in one classification rather than another? To answer that, you must not only forget the formula you were taught; you must also close your eyes to the labor workers perform; still more is required, for you must know the history of each worker. This is the only way to know why this guy is paid more than another. His labor may indeed be identical to that of a worker in another classification; it is his past alone that counts. But it would take too long to try to report the story of one hundred workers, so we shall limit ourselves to grouping these stories together. Some are skilled workers because they have passed through the factory's technical school. But do not think that they necessarily do the trade they learned. There are metalworkers, for example, who have learned their trade for three years and who have been placed in the shop on machines with which they were previously unfamiliar. They are milling-machine operators, planers, surfacers, because the trade of metalworker is on the way out and because more and more workers are needed on the machine. They went to their new trade with their old classification. So, it is not rare to see a P2 metalworker from one day to the next do the job of a P2 milling-machine operator, but as one can more easily change jobs than occupational classifications, the P2 metalworker will remain his whole life classified as a metalworker, even though he no longer touches a file. On the other hand, the OS who works on a milling machine and who does the same job as a P1 or P2 milling-machine operator will be able to acquire this skill and this salary only after going for a test, and the tests do not depend, as we shall see, on his will but especially on the number of available spots.

Here are a few cases among so many others:

A worker works on a machine as an OS. He wants to go for a test to become a professional. As he learned the trade of metalworker when he was young, he asked to go for a metalworker test. By continuing to ask, he ends up being given the test, which he passes; he thus becomes a P1 metalworker. Will he change his trade? No; he will continue what he has done up till now. He will remain on his machine (a surfacer) but will earn more, because he is capable of plying the trade he does not use, and which the factory does not need. Another OS works on a milling machine, but he prefers to go for a turner's test, for he did his apprenticeship in this occupation. He goes for the test, passes it, and becomes a P1 turner. He certainly will never touch a lathe in his life.

Here one can draw two conclusions:

The first one is on the level of work. Occupational classification is independent of the worker's ability to practice this occupation; it depends on the needs of production, and it depends on "the test."

The second conclusion is situated at the level of wages. It can be said that pay is not a function of the job performed but of the test one passes.

The Test

First of all, it is difficult to give the reasons why certain test requests are accepted while others are explicitly or implicitly rejected. This is a law that has to observe a certain number of factors that are foreign to us and that only the supervisor or the hiring office is likely to know. One thing is sure: it is that acceptance of test requests is independent of the worker's ability to do the job of the occupational classification he is seeking. Moreover, the difficulty of the tests is not commensurate with the job the journeyman will later have to perform. This makes the worker hesitate to request the test. He knows that he is capable of doing the same job as his neighbor, but he doubts he will pass a test whose ratings and required times are extremely difficult to achieve. There are workers who have to start their test over again more than six times (which takes them several years) in order to reach a higher classification, and this even though they might have long been doing the job of this classification.

But passing the test does not depend only on the quality of the test itself. It depends on other, much more important factors. It depends on the shop foreman's assessment, which the workers commonly call the "popularity rating" and which itself depends most often on the worker's relationships with the supervisors. It depends on the "telephone call," the support of an influential person in the factory. It depends on the support of an influential trade union federation at the factory, like, presently, Force Ouvrière (FO) or Syndicat Indépendant Renault (SIR).

The worker who returned to the factory right after the War had much greater opportunities than today. The factory needed skilled workers to get the assembly lines going. It created them from scratch. Many OS became professionals. The tests were less difficult; they were done in the worker's shop on his machine. Everyone (his comrades and the supervisors) was ready to give him advice or to help him if he was having difficulties. Thus, the test would sometimes be the product of collaboration with the whole shop. In certain cases even, if it was deemed too difficult, or for greater safety, it was the best worker around who performed it. Such a test, which seemed to have broken the rules, was in reality a test that corresponded much more precisely to the kind of job now being performed. Many OS became skilled workers and a few skilled workers went over into supervisory roles without much difficulty. Opportunities for promotions within the supervisory staff were also made easier. For several years, those opportunities have been reduced to the point that an OS has few chances of becoming a professional, and, except with exceptional luck, a professional will never go over into a supervisory role or will never become a technician.

Despite this anarchy in the allocation of manpower, the shop operates. The OS who does a P2 job "makes do" through improvisational coping [*se débrouille*]. The metalworker given a new machine makes do. He learns his trade. We shall see later that such improvisational coping has nothing to do with individual improvisational coping. The worker can learn his trade or ply a trade with which he is unfamiliar only because he lives in a collectivity, because his comrades teach him and communicate to him their experience and their technical know-how. Without this contribution from other workers, the irrationality in the use of manpower would bring on catastrophes at the point of production. In a word, if the workers did not fulfill, in addition to their job, this role of technical-school instructors for which they are not paid, it would be impossible for Management to obtain such great mobility and such perfect adaptation from the workers.

The Choice of Organizers
As we have seen, to a great extent the allocation of manpower is subject, directly or indirectly, to the arbitrariness of the supervisory staff,

but the workers react against this arbitrariness. There is the constant pressure of a collective worker-morality that keeps them quite often from bending to the requirements of their supervisors. The worker is continually being judged by his comrades. He is most often judged openly in front of everybody. A brown-nose, a worker who is too respectful of factory discipline, is condemned by his comrades. This condemnation exerts a pressure that is so real that even the most individualistic are quite often obliged to yield. A worker who openly tattles finds himself in such a hostile climate coming from his comrades that his life in the shop becomes extremely painful. The shop is the place where we live the greatest part of our lives. We live in a collectivity and human relations among us have considerable importance and play a primary role in production. Each gesture is judged to such an extent that, if a worker stays to chat amicably more than ten minutes with his foreman, he runs the risk of being hissed at and being treated as a brown-nose.

We all succeed in washing our hands before time's up. We arrived at this result gradually. Although the supervisory staff exerts pressure in the opposite direction, starting from the moment when this habit was introduced, it became almost impossible to stop it. The collective pressure is too strong. Everyone washes their hands early, and yet it is forbidden. But if one of us refuses to commit this infraction, he will be disapproved of by all the workers. Disapprovals of that kind have such great import that there are no exceptions in this domain. Promotion from the working class by brown-nosing is therefore considerably curbed by these tacit morals. But as soon as one passes onto the higher level—that is, into the ranks of the supervisory staff—that morality suddenly vanishes. There is no longer any collective morality in functions involving coercion. One gets into the supervisory camp because one possesses the qualities of "chief," "leader"—that is, what is called in our language the qualities of "galley-slave driver." The choice of organizers obeys this law. Those most devoted to management are chosen. Those are the ones most capable of opposing these collective worker morals, those who are opposed to all infractions of the rules. But here, too, this choice is wholly subject to interpretations and is arbitrary. There is a test that serves as a barrier between the different classifications of workers, and, as was seen, this test is above all symbolic. In the case of supervisory staff, this test, which is called "the errand," is even more symbolic. After having gone for the errand, only those who have demonstrated the qualities indispensable to this role will be admitted into the various supervisory classifications. But that will not suffice; you also have to belong to cliques, have friends in the right places. Here, the race for promotion no longer encounters the barriers of the collective morality we found among the workers. It is the unchecked law of competition that plays out there and supercedes all other laws. In order to climb the hierarchical rungs, one not only has to go on the errand; one not only has to be graded well by Management, not have any strike on one's record, and one not only has to have friends in the right places, for such string-pulling is widespread. One also has to have the best friends in the right places and, as is inevitable in races or rather with stockcars, one has to eliminate dangerous competitors. Here, elimination of competitors is not done through violence. The sole weapon is tattling and denigration. These selective laws for organizers, which appear in no manual, nevertheless play a considerable role in the rationalization of production itself.

Does this kind of competition between organizers make others want to emulate it? Certainly not. The organizers, who are controlled only from above, observe on their own scale the same system we practice—making do—but that kind of improvisational coping has nothing collective about it; it is individual and ruthless. Making do, competition, limited responsibility vis-à-vis Management, no control on the part of the workers; all that provokes a sort of anarchy of which we at our level perceive only the consequences. The enumeration of these consequences could, by itself alone, fill volumes.

—Why do we have the bad job?
—Because our chiefs don't know how to make do.

—Why do we have good machines?
—Because the chief is buddies with the guy who divvies up the machines.

—Etc., etc.

The shop chief and the foremen will try to cope improvisationally for the shop to work well. They will make do at the expense of other shops. The general view of the interest of the whole factory does not exist at the scale of the shop chief. One cannot say where it begins. Does it even exist? The factory is no one's if it is not the workers'. It is not the property of the supervisory staff, which have only compartmentalized responsibilities. All these managers are just captains, often petty despots, sometimes nice fellows obsessed by their own situation, who keep themselves balanced on this hierarchical scaffolding and are tormented by a single idea: Remain at their post; if needs be go higher, but beyond that, NOTHING.

THE FUNCTION OF THE WORKER

In the shop, everything is organized for the worker to have the least contact possible with his comrades. The worker is to remain at his machine and everything is done so that he remains there, so that his time there brings in a return, for, beyond his machine, the worker is supposed not to be producing and, what is more serious, not producing profit for the factory. So, it is even thought that, when we shake the hands of our comrades, we are breaking sacred factory law: we are in a production collectivity, but there is an ongoing effort to isolate us through a whole very complex system of surveillance, as if we were, each of us, an isolated craftsman. We have draftsmen who draw the pieces we have to make, technicians who have indicated the series of machining operations to perform and who have divided them up among the different types of machine tools; we have a store, which is to procure for us the sets of tools [*outillage*] we need; above us, we have team leaders, foremen, and shop chiefs, who are to procure jobs for us to do and watch over us; below us, we have conveyers to bring us the pieces to machine. We have inspectors who check our work and sometimes superinspectors who note, every quarter hour, whether our machine is operating, time-study men who allot us times, security agents who are vigilant about the protection of our bodies; finally, we have union delegates who claim to be looking after our interests. Everyone, down to the sweeper who comes to clean our spots, all of them look after us, so that we have only one thing to do: make the machine operate and not look after the rest.

An Organizer: The Team Leader

We do a quite varied and sometimes very complex job—that is to say, a job that precludes relying on automatic reflexes. There is a purely intellectual job of interpreting the drawing: we have to decide on how to organize the machining operations. However much the lineups [*gammes*][1] have been planned out, whatever mentions are made by the technical staff about what we have to do, spoonfeeding us all the calculations, in some cases we have to personalize our job, that is, find a scheme to do it quicker and easier. But that cannot be an individual effort; it is eminently collective work. Here come into play experience, routine, that is, features that are shared unequally among all the workers and not combined in a single one. To make the piece, we need to see our comrades and discuss it with them. To avoid this heresy, Management has invented the super-man, the super-worker who is to combine all forms of knowledge, who is to accumulate all experiences and know all the schemes. Management makes this man the team leader. The choice of this man did not occur without some difficulties, of course: the functions of team leader require that he be the best worker, but the best worker is not necessarily devoted to Management; on the other hand, the extreme division of labor has also reached the tooling shops, so that, even though the journeyman would have to know how to do everything, one tries more and more to make him specialize, and for this reason it will be all the more difficult to find a worker who would have general experience on the job. In addition, Management hesitates to take a worker with whom it is completely satisfied in order to remove him from his machine and put him behind a desk.[2]

Finally, it is not inevitable for a worker who would have these super-man qualities to possess as well the qualities of overseer, exert his authority, and maintain discipline. For a team leader to acquire those qualities, he is made to leave his machine; this increasingly leads him to lose contact with the work, which is perpetually changing. In giving a coercive role to the team leader, one takes away from him in the same stroke the confidence of the workers. Thus, in wanting to avoid all collaboration among the workers, in wanting to create a super-worker, Management has taken a productive worker away from his machine, confined him to a paperwork job, and practically deprived him of any productive and organizational role. The privileges it has given him are not enough for him to agree to carry out his other role of overseer and coercive agent. Much more importantly, Management has not been able to avoid workers collaborating among themselves, as we are going to see below.

The Problem of Responsibility

The responsibility of the worker tends to be reduced more and more. This is not pushed here to the maximum, as on the assembly line, where the OS is responsible for practically nothing, only the adjusters, the leaders, and the various categories of inspectors being considered responsible people. The worker is responsible for the parcel of labor he accomplishes and nothing more: he is not to worry whether this parcel is worthwhile in relation to the whole. Moreover, how could he do so, since everything is organized to hide this whole from him?

He therefore is to stick to the directives he receives, that is, to the drawing. He is to work blindly and do solely what is necessary to clear his responsibility. But here the man comes into play. What is he going to do, accomplish his role as an automaton or really react?

The worker finds himself placed before an alternative. The first possibility is to clear his responsibility—that is, conform to the drawing and do things such that the piece will be accepted by the inspectors. Factory rules and factory organization are designed in terms of this attitude alone. If, therefore, the worker sticks to this solution, he will work with the sole goal of being paid, that is, to get his piece accepted.

The second possibility is to try to understand what the piece is used for, so that it would be not only good for the inspectors but usable, or else to ease the task of his fellow employee who will take over the operations.[3]

This is the worker's drama of conscience, the tragedy he faces. On the one hand, he can react individually, worrying only about his own material interest, his paycheck, and that is what the rules demand that he do; on the other, his reaction may be deeply social: he will seek to guess at the goal of his job and try to show solidarity with his comrades by facilitating their task.

But then he will have to face off against the regulations, and here, too, he will have to cheat. Here is situated the dialogue between the worker and his conscience (which is the same as the dialogue he has with his comrades). This dialogue has special words, its own slang, and we come across it again every day because it obsesses us:

> Human worker: What's the use of this piece?
> Robot worker: What the fuck is it to you?
> Human worker: Do you believe this dimension is important?
> Robot worker: It's just going into the wall.[4]
> Human worker: Have you already done it?
> Robot worker: You're worrying yourself sick over NOTHING. The important thing is to be paid.
> Human worker: So, you think that'll do?
> Robot worker: You don't buy it? COME ON! . . .

Errors

A craftsman who makes a machine from start to finish, who himself executes all the cogs of the device and who has in his head the idea of the finished object, works in accordance with this ideal object. For this reason, he will be less likely than anyone to make mistakes. He knows what is important and what is not; in addition, if he makes mistakes, he will fix them along the way, for one can compensate for an error on one piece by modifying the piece on which the first is fitted without compromising the mechanism of the object itself.

Things are quite different when each cog of the machine is entrusted not to one but to ten workers of different trades, none of whom know the importance of the job he is performing. Possibilities for error are multiplied by the facts that there is a great number of executants and that none of the executants has the ideal machine in his head, that is, none of them knows what use the piece serves. We are obviously talking here not about the worker having an abstract knowledge of the entire mechanism of the device to whose manufacture he contributes but about him having concrete knowledge of the part of this device where his piece is to fit.

Such knowledge can guide him both in the way he makes his piece and in the care he is to bring to the different parts of this piece. Moreover, each executant is subject to constant pressure from the way the factory is organized, pressure that is also exerted in blind fashion.

To speak only of the most important of these pressures, it suffices to mention that, from the draftsman to the person who finishes the piece, and going by way of the typist who copies the lineups and the times onto the card given to the workers, all are subject more or less directly to the imperative of the planning department: Go ever faster.

A Case Where the Worker's Functions are Universal
It happens in some cases that workers break the rules and try to get over the partitioning of functions and the isolation of laboring people: this is the example of the shop that makes "Widia" tools.

When the milling-machine operator in this shop receives an order to execute, he first has to obtain for himself the drawing, consult the files, and therefore do a job for which he is not paid, for this time is not reckoned on by the time-study men. As an automaton, he should make the piece in conformity with the drawing, but he knows through experience that that is above all not what he ought to do, for he could have a lot of trouble.

That is to say, he will get yelled at if the tools he has made are not usable, even if they faithfully correspond to the drawing. The drawing is the finished reproduction of the tool, but it frequently happens that, in its manufacturing, a slight modification of the drawing might improve how the machining operations will unfold.

Now, the tools are to come out of the shops finished and are to fit not the drawing but the needs of the shops that make use of these tools. In this "Widia"-tool shop, which comprises only a small number of workers (around fifty), the grinders have passed on oral instructions involving modifications in the dimensions and in the original drawing to the surfacers, who have passed oral instructions on to the milling-machine operators, and so on, all this with the aim of facilitating each person's work. These instructions have not been codified, and one suspects a bit why; in order to codify such modifications, which are frequent, they would continually have to be sent back up the chain of offices and that could bring about clashes and difficulties of all sorts and really offend people's sensibilities. That is why the shop works in a rather craftsmanlike mode. It must be said that things would be much too simple if this mode of operation were recognized, if cooperation among workers could be achieved. But it is not recognized; it is tacit. Those who finish pieces are "common OS," whereas those who begin them are, for the most part, skilled workers, and between the two there is a difference in pay of some 15,000 francs per month. That an OS advises a skilled worker how to do his job is already an anomaly that contradicts the factory's hierarchical system, however absurd it might be.

Another obstacle: the worker is considered to be someone deprived of all responsibility, so even the least amount of initiative on his part can turn against him. On the other hand, if he conforms strictly to the drawing, he will get yelled at if, later in the series of operations, difficulties are encountered. Therefore, to clear his responsibility, the worker can ask the team leader what shape he is to give to his piece, and the team leader will speak to the foreman; both will go to the inspector's office to ask him what the workers had asked them; the team leader, the foreman, and the inspector will go, finally, to the grinder to ask the same question. The answer will follow the same path and the worker will finally be able to begin. But as the worker is in a hurry, he often will do without all those go-betweens. He will go directly to the workers who take over the operations after him, which is theoretically forbidden. But he will not yet begin his job at that moment. After having altered the shape of the piece and sometimes the drawing, the time limits will have to be changed: that modification will have to follow the opposite path and go back to its source.

The worker knows the pay rate for operations, but he has no right to alter anything; only the various responsible officials share among themselves the parcels of this right. So, here is the result. The worker adds in pencil the additional time limit on his order, which he then gives to the team leader, who will personally rewrite in ink what the worker has written in pencil and will sign off, and then the time-study man will come to supervise everything by appending his signature. After having been metamorphosed into a time-study man, team leader, inspector, and foreman, our worker resumes his place at his machine, quite happy if he can be forgiven for all the infractions he has just committed. But he knows through experience that everything will be forgiven if it works; otherwise, his initiatives will come back at him, like a boomerang that has missed its target. If it does not work, he can be blamed for two things: either for not having taken initiative or for having taken bad ones. But let us keep from shedding tears: if he knows how to prove that he is not a robot at his job, he knows, too, how to prove it when someone comes to yell at him.

The Rationalization of Our Equipment

The tooling [*outillage*] shop is the big victim of the contradiction that exists between the efforts at rationalization and the limits of such rationalization. One tries to standardize the equipment [*outillage*] and mass produce it, but the equipment is too varied and the production of it too narrow to push these methods to their limit, that is, to transform the tooling shops into equipment assembly lines.

The obstacle we are going to talk about comes from the fact that the shop thus remains a hybrid between a craft shop and a mass-production shop. It is a mixture of a small-shop operation functioning by piece work and via small production series, on the one hand, and a modern manufacturing shop, on the other.

First of all, we would have to have our sets of tools delivered by an escort, but the diversity of our work would then lead to an unacceptable increase in escorts, who in addition would have to know the job—that is, have the same kinds of knowledge as the journeyman they are to service—which is not the case. Consequently, we have to go find our sets of tools ourselves and leave the machine for a rather long time while we have to stand in line at the tool store. If the tools-sets are not available, they have to be ordered in order to obtain them a few days later.

The grinding shop is a separate shop. It receives tool deliveries for next week's grinding. If, therefore, a worker returns a grinding tool with certain contours to his tool store, he can wait for up to fifteen days before receiving it. In reality, it is a grinding job that takes at the very most ten to fifteen minutes of work, but the worker will have to interrupt his job for a dozen days. If we conform to this rule, we have to wait, leave aside our job, start something else, and all the time we spent adjusting our machine is thus lost; in addition, this time will not be counted for us. If we object to the time-study man that his time limit is too short, because we have had tool problems, he answers us that his times cannot take such incidents into account. There is no set of tools, OK, but there should be, and the time-study man can do nothing about that. So as not to lose time, we arrange our tools among ourselves; we prefer losing a bit of time in transforming ourselves into a grinder than waiting. But here again, we have to face the angry response from the storeman who criticizes us, rightly, for having modified a set of tools that thereby end up being unusable by others.

It would have been better to proceed in regular fashion by making our request of the storeman who, himself, would have made out an order form for the central tool store that, in turn, could have looked in its stock, if he did not possess a tool of the kind requested.

Thus, one would have avoided wasting a tool, but one would have wasted time.

It happens that the pieces we make follow a certain rotation, that is, we know that the same orders will come back to the shop after a certain amount of time. For this reason, we manufacture tools or assemblies to go faster. On account of this, each time we receive an order, we try to get information from our comrades; we seek to know whether one of us who has already done such pieces has not invented some scheme to go faster. That is not the path we normally ought to follow; the team leader should be asked, and he would put us in contact with the journeyman, who could provide us the information and help us benefit from his personal tool setup [*outillage*].

As is seen here, the multiplication of go-betweens separating the worker and the tool stock and the grinder is a permanent obstacle we have to surmount. We surmount it by ourselves creating a kind of more or less clandestine tool store wherein we stock for ourselves and our comrades certain tools we have procured. Once again, we have shortcircuited the factory's organization. Once again, we are at fault. But it is only at this price that we can work.

Yet this normal process has a great drawback. It informs the team leader of our schemes and there is a risk that he will inform the time-study man or higher authorities about them, which could lead to lowered time limits. For us, things are clear: each new discovery is to be translated into a lightening of our troubles, whereas for Management, on the contrary, each innovation is to be turned into an increase in our work load. Here again, the robot worker's conception runs up against reality; it induces waste and tends to be a brake on production, that is, it attains the objective that is contrary to the one that had been set.

The Struggle Against the Time Limits

In addition to its shape and to the quality of its metal, each piece has, in the factory, another property: its time limit for machining.

This time limit is written on the order the worker receives. But an output-based labor system has been instituted and each worker can go beyond the allotted times.

Thus, if a piece that has an allotted time of 90 minutes is done in an hour, the worker will receive extra pay. It is said that he settles up at 150 percent. In reality, this possibility has little by little become the rule. Today, the worker who makes his pieces in the allotted time is not only cheated on his wages but runs the risk of being fired. What was at the outset only a possibility has become an obligation.

It must be said that this obligation to work quicker than the allotted times has a limit that is set by Management. Right after the war, this limit was around 138 percent. Union pressure, which at that time vehemently supported accelerated production, gradually raised this ceiling. Today, the worker has the right to settle up at 153 percent, that is, in two weeks of work of 100 hours he will be able to perform 153 hours of time limits, and the time-limit hours above 153 hours will not be paid.

There are two ways of establishing a time limit for the time-study man. If the piece has never been made and the journeyman who has made the piece has accepted the time limit, all the pieces that will follow will have the same time limit. In this way, the time limits are established, and we know it. When a journeyman makes a new piece, he really has to pay attention not to let an overly short time limit get through. For that, he most often is monitored by his comrades, who may soon have to make the same piece. It is at this moment that a sort of farce is acted out by the worker and the time-study man. The worker tries to have the longest time; the time-study man tries to bestow the shortest time limit. But no one is fooled. Each partner thoroughly knows the other's role. He even knows the lines. The time-study man therefore tries at the outset to put in a fake time limit, that is, one below what he deems normally feasible, since he thinks that the worker is very likely to protest. As for the worker, he tries to ask for a time limit above what he can achieve, because he is counting on all the unforeseen conditions the time-study man does not want to take into account. Then comes the haggling from which will ultimately arise the time limit.

The time limit will be the product of this struggle. In addition, it will be distorted by the system's other added effects. In order to avoid wage increases, Management has raised the ceilings of output coefficients. They have thus passed from 138 to 153 percent since the war. But as the worker wants to get top pay, he demands that the allotted time limit in turn be raised 53 percent. If he makes a piece in an hour's time, he will demand that the time limit noted down be 53 percent longer.

The time limits are thus all the more fake. Once established, the time limit will be monitored by the worker, who keeps his own account of the times he has obtained. Each time the piece comes back into the shop, he or his comrades will be able to verify its accuracy. Thus, the time limit noted on a card is much more a function of the worker's combativeness and vigilance, or of the personality of the time-study man, than of the slide rule. It happens, as a matter of fact, that certain workers have been too accommodating to the time-study man and that some pieces are physically impossible to machine in the anticipated times. What happens in this case? As it is no longer a question of affecting the time limit which, once established, has become untouchable, the team leader can compensate for this "bad job" by giving the cheated worker pieces whose time limit is well above what he usually does. This can also be remedied by means that are more or less tolerated, that is, one is lent or given hours to achieve the maximum coefficient. Finally, one can, by illegal means, purely and simply falsify the cards where the time limits are recorded. The worker therefore continually has to stand up for himself in order to earn maximum wages; he also has to stand up for himself if he wants to satisfy his self-esteem as a worker, that is, to do something useful. [. . .]

Notes

1. When a worker asks for a job from his team leader, he receives an order card on whose back is glued the drawing of the piece to machine. On this card is written the whole series of operations to perform, from casting to cutting the metal, and all the way to the mounting of the piece on its mechanical unit. The card's "lineup" is therefore the written record of the series of operations, followed by

the times allotted for the machining, the number of the shop where this machining will take place, and the name of the worker who will carry it out.

2. The team leader earns around 10 to 20 thousand francs more than a journeyman; in principle, he does no manual work. His desk is to be found amid the machinery. He has no glass enclosure; his life is in practice connected with that of the journeymen; his true function is that of dispatcher between the workers and the other services of the factory. Yet it quite often happens that the workers do without this go-between for reasons of efficiency and rapidity. He also has a surveillance and inspection function, but, practically speaking, that function is fulfilled, on the one hand, by the work-time system that in principle forbids the worker from doing anything other than work and, on the other hand, by the inspection office.

In reality, the team leader intervenes when a rag-ball fight threatens to involve everyone in the shop. He spends most of his day chatting. His major misery is boredom.

3. Sometimes, in order to facilitate the job, we make direct contact with those who will take over the operation and there we succeed in reaching among ourselves some genuine secret agreements. Thus, with the machining of lathing tools, some milling-machine operators agree to finish the pieces directly on their machines, so that the metal worker who takes on the following operation has practically no more metal to remove from the tool. It is agreed beforehand that the latter will share the allotted time with the milling-machine operator who has done the work for him.

4. A common saying, meaning that the piece does not need to be more precise than some old piece of iron cemented into the wall.

PART THREE

THE CRISIS OF THE BUREAUCRATIC SYSTEM (1953–1957)

"1953–1957: La Crise du système bureaucratique"
Socialisme ou Barbarie—Anthologie, 105–106

Prior to 1953, the majority of the French working class had been won over to Stalinist Communism. It faithfully followed the Party's marching orders: rebuild French capitalism, which had been damaged by the War; stop one strike; launch another one, and so on. No one publicly questioned the ability of the leaders to guide the movement, to avoid the traps set by an adversary that was opposed, by all means possible, to the march of progress, or to coordinate local economic demands with the fight being led, on an international level, by the socialist camp. While some alleged that the objectives being set were straying from the genuine interests of the working class, the response they received was that nothing of the sort was going on and that one had to take the entire picture into consideration: the constant strengthening of the camp of progress, with victory guaranteed by rallying around the country of socialism and its brilliant guide, Stalin.

Nonetheless, in the shadow of these major maneuvers, the review *Socialisme ou Barbarie* and the limited circle of people surrounding it carried on their efforts at clarification. They observed that capitalism was not rotting on the vine, but, on the contrary, was continuing to develop. They maintained that, in Russia, the bureaucracy constituted a social class of its own that appropriated the surplus value extorted from laboring people by means of a state-run capitalist system and that, in the countries of private capitalism, the officials heading up working-class organizations stood ready to take on for themselves the roles of managers in a reinvigorated State. And finally, they affirmed that, for the workers, social protest was not to be limited to the defense of current wages but had to take on the overall organization of work. And yet, when these militants advanced the idea of workers' directing their own struggles, they were ridiculed by their comrades on the shop floor; when they defended the idea of lodging demands relating to *how* work was organized, union leaders accused them of creating a diversion; and when they supported a strike launched independently of the unions, they were denounced as divisive. So it was that, while being attacked by French Communist Party activists, lacking an audience among the laboring people to whom they were addressing themselves, and boycotted by intellectuals who were admirers of "really existing" socialism, they learned, on March 5, 1953, of the death of the dictator the Revolution had spawned thirty years earlier. Despite their refusal to impute to a single man the monstrosity of an entire system, the good news shook them, as it shook, in jubilation or in bafflement, the entire world. Three months later, the workers of Berlin, who had been subjected to the bureaucracy of the East German State, started an insurrectional strike, thus letting loose the crisis of the bureaucratic system.

Recalling the stages of this crisis, we present, in succession:

- An article by Albert Véga ("The Meaning of the June 1953 Revolt in East Germany") that relates how this crisis was launched in Berlin;
- An excerpt from Claude Lefort's analysis of the new path of Russian policy after the CPSU's 20th Congress ("Totalitarianism Without Stalin");
- Lefort's major substantive article on the Hungarian insurrection ("The Hungarian Insurrection"); and
- A selection of texts written by people directly involved in the Hungarian Revolution.

G.P.

The Meaning of the June 1953 Revolt in East Germany

Albert Véga

"Signification de la révolte de juin 1953 en Allemagne orientale"
Socialisme ou Barbarie, 13 (January–March 1954): 4–8
Socialisme ou Barbarie—Anthologie, 107–11

Giving an account of the Berlin strikes, Véga shows that the German workers, twenty years after the last battles against the Nazis, had rediscovered their full combativeness and knew perfectly well how to identify as new enemies the Communist leaders installed by the Russian troops in their zone of occupation. In issues 7 and 8, Socialisme ou Barbarie *had published, under the name Hugo Bell, an enlightening analysis of Stalinization in East Germany, large excerpts of which are reproduced in Part 1 of the present* Anthology. *He showed there that the harsh exploitation of laboring people, the dismantling of factories, the direct levies, and "reparations" had culminated in the dilapidation of the economy, overall shortages, and famine. The Communist leaders' quest for approval from working-class strata thus was dashed. They then sought to obtain the population's adherence by bestowing various advantages, mainly food benefits; by offering promotions within the hierarchy, which was beginning to settle in; and through reinforcement of control measures. A slight decrease in manifestations of discontent was thus able to be obtained, but the attempt to remedy laboring people's loss of motivation was a failure, and the leaders continued to apply a policy that gradually isolated them from the rest of society. The workers who, till then, had resisted silently, knew perfectly well, when confronted in June 1953 with an abrupt increase in productivity norms, how to reply to this mixture of American Taylorism and Russian Stakhanovism that had been imposed on them. The explosion occurred in Berlin, on the model building site of the Stalinallee, and rapidly spread into the factories of the capital and of other large cities. Committees were set up that pushed aside the state-run trade-union organizations. The insurgents established contacts, federated their struggles from firm to firm and from city to city, and began to free political prisoners. In a few days, they won a general lowering of productivity norms, a revision of the Plan to favor the production of consumer goods, and an immediate improvement in supplies.*

As early as 1949, after the reconstruction period properly speaking, after famine, too, a conflict took shape between the stratum of leaders, made up of former technical staff and former workers promoted to be bureaucrats, and laboring people as a whole.

In the factories, this involved a struggle against the "Stakhanovites" and the time-study men. In factory assemblies and trade-union meetings, the workers opposed the raising of work norms and measures aimed at pushing up output. They even used the organs of the bureaucratic apparatus nearest them—the rank-and-file trade-union bodies—to defend their rights, and they succeeded in getting those rights respected in many cases.

This conflict intensified in early 1953. The policy of rearmament, all-out industrialization, and rapid collectivization of agriculture aggravated the shortage of consumer products and provoked price increases for commodities on the free market. At the same time, the official campaign for the "voluntary" raising of norms spread. The Government demanded increased output from the workers. But it reduced social-insurance benefits and canceled the 75-percent reduction on rail tickets for workers commuting to work. Sporadic strikes broke out in Magdeburg and Chemnitz.

In May, an overall 10-percent increase in norms was decided. It was to be applied in early June.

Now, at the same moment, the Party had decided on a turnaround intended to improve the economic situation and to echo the Russian peace offensive. Measures of detente were taken for peasants, private business and industry, and the Church. But no measure directly concerned the workers.

One knows how this situation provoked the June 16–17 explosion, how the strike, begun on the construction sites of Stalinallee in Berlin, transformed itself into a street demonstration and grew into a vast movement of revolt among all East German workers.[1]

But what must be emphasized is the clear awareness laboring people have manifested of the regime's antiworker character, their dynamism in the struggle, their organizational capacities, and the political import of their initiatives.

The formation of strike committees is an established fact, recognized even by the official press organs. In Berlin, we know of those of the *Kabelwerke* factories, Block 40 on Stalinallee, the Friedrichshein building sites, and the Henningsdorf steelworks. Indeed, it was the Henningsdorf steelworkers who, on the morning of June 17, along with the workers of Oranienburg, traveled 14 kilometers to participate in the demonstrations and occupy the Walter-Ulbricht-Stadion, where discussions took place about replacing the Government, and during which workers launched the idea of a "Steelworker Government."[2]

The character of the strike was quite clear from the outset in Berlin. On the 16th, in front of the seat of government the workers proclaimed the following specific demands: abolition of the 10 percent increase in norms; 40-percent price reduction for supplies and commodities sold in the sector's free shops; resignation of the Government; and free elections. To Minister [of Mines Fritz] Selbmann, who, trying to calm them, cried, "Comrades, I am also a worker, a communist," they responded: "You no longer are. We're the true communists."

In the zone's industrial towns, the workers' actions were clearer still and even more violent.

In Brandenburg, the building workers formed a strike committee with those from the Thälmann shipbuilding sites. They immediately sent cyclists to the main factories. Twenty thousand demonstrators marched through the streets. They liberated political prisoners and attacked the local headquarters of the Socialist Unity Party of Germany (SED). Most of the "VoPos" (People's Police) were disarmed or joined the demonstrators; a minority defended itself.

In Leipzig, more than 30,000 demonstrators attacked the Radio Building and the Party's local party offices. People's Policemen were disarmed.

In Rosslau (Elbe), the strike began at the Rosslauer shipbuilding sites. The workers headed toward City Hall, where the mayor ended up joining them. They used trucks with loudspeakers taken from the VoPos. They entered the prison and liberated twenty political prisoners. Upon encountering a truck full of VoPos, they disarmed them and imprisoned them.

In Jena, the strikers attacked the local offices of the Party and the Communist Youth, destroyed their files, and seized a few weapons. They attacked the prison and liberated political detainees.

In Halle, political prisoners were freed. At six in the evening, thousands of strikers met on the Hallmarkt and the Grossenmarkt. Ad hoc [*improvisés*] speakers gave speeches. Russian tanks stopped in the midst of the protesters. A central strike committee was elected.

At Magdeburg, the law courts and police headquarters were attacked and files were burned. One thousand strikers attacked the Sudenburg-Magdeburg prison. They were able to liberate only some of the detainees, for the People's Police shot at them from rooftops and Russian tanks intervened, with twelve dead.

At Gera, in Thuringia, the strikers occupied police headquarters. In Erfurt, the strike was general and the political prisoners were liberated.

At the Leuna factories, near Merseburg, 20,000 workers went out. They formed a strike committee, and a delegation was sent to Berlin to make contact with the strikers in the capital. The Leuna strike committee used the factory's radio facilities. The workers marched on Merseburg. Around 240 VoPos were disarmed or joined the columns of protesters.

In Merseburg, 30,000 demonstrators marched through the streets, liberated political prisoners, and disarmed the VoPos. Seventy thousand people met on the Uhlandplatz. There were workers there from the Leuna and Buna factories, from the Gross-Kayna mines, from the Königsmühle paper mill, construction workers, streetcar workers, staff workers, VoPos, and housewives. They elected a 25-member central strike committee. Having learned that Russian troops were arresting strikers and holding them, the workers headed toward the prison and got back those detained by the Russians.

At Bitterfeld, in the same region, around 35,000 protesters met on the Platz der Jugend.

The central strike committee ordered the firemen to cleanse the town of Stalinist wall slogans and posters.

This same committee sent a telegram that began:

To the so-called German Democratic Government, we, laboring people of Bitterfeld district, demand:

1. the withdrawal of the so-called German Democratic Government, which came to power through rigged elections;
2. the setting up of a Provisional Government of progressive laboring people . . .

It also sent a telegram to the Soviet High Commissioner demanding the lifting of the state of siege in Berlin and "of all the measures taken against the working class so that, in this way, we Germans might be able to keep believing that you are really the representative of a regime of laboring people."

In all these cities, for a few hours or a day, the workers ruled the streets. Rumors spread: the Government had resigned; the Russians dared not support it. The Russian tanks were finally coming out, the state of siege was proclaimed, gatherings were forbidden. The People's Police regrouped. The workers beat a retreat. But the strike lasted another day or two, longer in certain factories.

The workers' resistance was not broken. The Government sent emissaries into the factories while the Party's Central Committee published, on June 22, a program intended to improve living standards and to help to erase the "acrimony against the Government." It included the following ten points:

1. Return to lower productivity norms and calculation of wages according to the system in effect April 1, 1953.
2. Reduction of transportation fares for workers earning less than 500 marks per month.
3. Upgrading of widow and disabled pensions and of old-age pensions.
4. Sick leave will not be deducted from the normal annual vacation leave.
5. No obligatory enrolment in Social Security.
6. A 3.6-billion-mark increase in budget credits for construction of apartments and private buildings.
7. Allocation of an additional 30 million marks for improvements in sanitary facilities and social services in state factories.
8. Allocation of an additional 40 million marks for a new cultural program intended to construct a greater number of movie houses, theaters, schools, playgrounds, and cultural institutes for leisure time.
9. Improvements in work shoes and clothing distributed by the unions.
10. Reduction in electricity cuts at the expense of heavy industry.

The movement has obliged the bureaucracy to back down. Resistance pays. The lesson of these days will not be forgotten by the workers and it may have deep repercussions in other countries of the Russian "glacis." [...]

Notes

1. See the article by Sarel [Benno Sternberg], "Combats ouvriers sur l'avenue Staline," *Les Temps Modernes*, October 1953.
2. According to the correspondent from *L'Observateur*.

Totalitarianism Without Stalin

Claude Lefort

"Le Totalitarisme sans Staline"[1]
Socialisme ou Barbarie, 19 (July–September 1956): 17–36
Socialisme ou Barbarie—Anthologie, 112–27

In the lead article for issue 19, Claude Lefort analyzes the meaning of the new political course inaugurated by the Khrushchev Report to the Twentieth Congress of the Communist Party of the Soviet Union, held three years after Stalin's death. During that Congress, Khrushchev, recognizing in part the failure of the "construction of socialism" and the crimes of the system, attempted to impute the responsibility for these solely to Stalin and to his "cult of personality." Comparing state bureaucratic capitalism and private capitalism, Lefort shows that, unlike the private capitalist, the bureaucrat has at his disposal neither some power on which he could rely nor a market that would allow him to regulate relationships with other bureaucrats. His power stems from the place he occupies in a hierarchical social organization, and the coordination of his activities with those of other bureaucrats occurs through a cascade of orders descending from the summit to the base. Unveiling the nature of Soviet totalitarianism, he shows that the Party-State heading up this system is obliged to know all, to decide everything. The bureaucracy embodied in the Party-State thus covers the totality of the social and political field. However, by masking its power beneath the illusory affirmation of the power of the working class and by proclaiming its fantastical absence, as a class, in the social game, it is forced to engage constantly in mystificatory propaganda and lying and is subject to permanent insecurity. Denying, furthermore, the existence of divergent interests within the society born of the Revolution, it fails, ultimately, to implement compromise procedures capable of substituting, in a more or less lasting way, for phases of overt struggle, and it thus erects violence as the rule in social relationships.

After having examined how the situation has changed, inasmuch as one could glimpse events close-up, Lefort concludes on the regime's inability to surmount its contradictions in a lasting way.

THE HISTORICAL FUNCTION OF STALINISM

Stalinist totalitarianism came to the fore when the political apparatus forged by the Revolution, after having reduced the old dominant social strata to silence, freed itself from all control by the proletariat. *This political apparatus then directly subordinated the production apparatus to itself.*

Such a formula does not mean that a disproportionate role is being attributed to the Party. If we looked at things from an economic perspective, the central phenomenon would be, in our view, capital concentration, the expulsion of owners and the merger of monopolies into a new production unit, and the proletariat's subordination to a new centralized management of the economy. We would then easily underscore that the transformations that occurred in the USSR simply brought to its ultimate phase a process that is manifest everywhere in the contemporary capitalist world, as illustrated by the very constitution of monopolies, intermonopoly combines, and the growing intervention of States within all sectors of economic life, so that the instauration of the new regime would seem to represent a mere transition from one type of appropriation to another within capitalist management. From such a perspective, the Party could no longer appear to be a *deus ex machina*; it would look, rather, like a historical instrument, that of state capitalism. But besides the fact that we are seeking for the moment to understand Stalinism as such and not Russian society as a whole, if we took up only the economic perspective we would allow ourselves to be taken in by the image of a historical pseudonecessity. While it is indeed true that the concentration of capitalism can be spotted in all contemporary societies, it cannot be concluded therefrom that it would have to, on account of some ideal law, end in its final stage. Nothing allows us, for example, to affirm that, in the absence of a social upheaval that would sweep away the ruling capitalist stratum, a country like the United States or England would necessarily have to subordinate monopolies to state management and abolish private property. One is all the less sure about this (and we will have occasion to return to this point) as the market and competition continue to play a positive role in certain regards in social life and as their ouster through planning creates new kinds of difficulties for the dominant class. In remaining within a strictly economic framework, one must ask, for example, whether the requirements involved in a harmonious integration of different production branches would not be offset by the need to develop labor productivity to the maximum, assisted by the relative autonomy of the capitalist business firm. But whatever the case may be, it must be acknowledged that the tendencies of the economy, however determinant they might be, cannot be separated from overall social life: Capital's "protagonists," as Marx says, are also social groups whose past, way of life, and ideology shape economic conduct itself. In this sense, it would be contrived to see in the transformations the USSR has undergone starting in 1930 merely the transition from one type of capitalist management to another, in short, the advent of state capitalism. Those transformations constitute a *social revolution*. It would therefore be just as contrived to present the Party as the instrument of this state capitalism, leaving the impression that the latter, written in the heavens of History, was, for its incarnation, awaiting the propitious moment Stalinism offered it. Neither demiurge nor instrument, the Party has to be grasped as a social reality—that is, as a milieu within which, simultaneously, the needs of a new form of economic management assert themselves and historical solutions are actively worked out.

If the production apparatus had not allowed, prepared, and been in command of its own unification, the role of the political apparatus would be inconceivable. Conversely, if the executive personnel [*cadres*] of the old society had not been dismantled by the Party, if a new social stratum had not been promoted to take on managerial functions in all sectors, the transformation in the relations of production would have been impossible. It is on the basis of these observations that the extraordinary role Stalinism has played becomes clear. It was the at-first unconscious and then the conscious and self-assured agent of a tremendous social upheaval that ended in the emergence of an entirely new structure. On the one hand, it conquered a new social terrain by simultaneously dispossessing the old masters of production and the proletariat of all power. On the other hand, it gathered into a new formation people snatched from all classes and ruthlessly subordinated them to the task of management the new economy gave to them. In both cases, terror necessarily dominated the effort. Nonetheless, the exercise of such terror all at once against private owners, the proletariat, and the new dominant strata apparently muddled things. For having failed to understand that violence had, despite its multiple expressions, only one function, people, depending on their preferences, strove to prove that it served the proletariat or the bourgeois counterrevolution; some took the argument that it had decimated the ranks of the new leadership stratum to present Stalinism as a small caste, devoid of any class basis and concerned solely with maintaining its own existence at the expense of the classes competing within society. The development of Stalinist policy was nonetheless unambiguous from the start: terror was not a means of defense used by a handful of individuals whose prerogatives were threatened by opposing social forces; it was constitutive of a new social force whose advent presupposed a wrenching by forceps from the womb of the old society and whose survival required new members being sacrificed daily to the unity of the already formed organism. That Stalinism might first be characterized—before 1929 and then in the period of collectivization and initial industrialization—by its struggle against private owners and the proletariat, and later by the massive purges within the dominant strata is obviously not due to chance. Terror followed the path of the new class, which had to recognize its existence against the other classes before "recognizing itself" in the image of its functions and multiple aspirations.

Bureaucratic consciousness also followed this path. It cannot be said that, prior to industrialization, Stalinism had in mind the goals that would later constitute the formation of a new society. Fear of undertaking such industrialization and resistance to the Trotskyist program advocating it testify to Stalinism's uncertainty as to its own function. Stalinism was already behaving empirically along the lines of the model that would later predominate; it feverishly reinforced state power, proceeded to annihilate oppositional forces, and sketched out a still cautious policy of income differentiation. The Bureaucracy is to be defined by something entirely other than a complex of psychological traits. It conquered an existence for itself, which radically differentiates it from the proletariat. Yet it still lived within the horizons of present society. Once having launched into collectivization and planning, new historical horizons arose, a genuine class ideology—and therefore a concerted policy—was elaborated, and solid bases for a new material power—a power that creates itself and recreates itself, maintaining itself daily by sucking up the productive forces of the entire society—were constituted. At this level, however, new tasks arose and Stalinism's awareness of its historical role then proved, in a new way, to be a decisive factor in development. For, the tremendous industrialization that was achieved did not only give an already constituted bureaucracy its bases; it revolutionized this bureaucracy, giving rise—this can never be overstated—to an entirely new society. At the same time that the proletariat was being transformed, with millions of peasants coming, in a few years, to swell its ranks, new social strata *were being manufactured* as they were wrenched from the old classes and from the traditional way of life the former division of labor had reserved for them. Technical staff, intellectuals, bourgeois, soldiers, former feudal lords, peasants, and workers, too, were mixed into a new hierarchy whose common denominator is that it directs, controls, and organizes, at all levels of its operation, the production apparatus and living labor power, that of the exploited classes. The very same people who remained in their old occupational categories saw their way of life and their mindset shaken up, for those old professions were refocused as they were integrated into the new division of labor created by the Plan. Most certainly, the mode of work of these new strata and the statuses granted them on account of their dominant position within society could not but create in the long run a genuine class community. But in the time when this upheaval was occurring, the action of the Party proved decisive. Through the iron discipline it established and through the uncontested unity it embodied, the Party alone could cement together those heterogeneous elements. It anticipated the future, proclaiming before all that particular interests are strictly subordinate to the interests of the bureaucracy taken as a whole.

A key function of Stalinism, one *necessary* within the framework of the new society, appears here. The terror it exerted on the dominant strata was not some accidental trait: terror was inscribed within the very development of the new class, whose mode of domination was no longer guaranteed by private appropriation, whose privileges it was forced to accept through a *collective apparatus of appropriation*, and whose dispersion could, at first, be surmounted only through violence.

Of course, it can very well be said that the purges carried out by Stalinism went so far as to endanger the operation of the production apparatus. The efficiency of acts of repression that at one point wiped out half of all technical staff in place may be doubted. Nonetheless, such reservations do not challenge what we call *the historical function of Stalinism*. They allow one merely to detect, as we have already mentioned, the way in which Stalin's personal behavior diverged from the norm dominating party conduct.[2] To say, in effect, that Stalinism has a function is not to insinuate that it is—from the bureaucracy's standpoint—"useful" at every moment, still less that the policy it follows is at every moment the sole one possible; it is simply to affirm here that, in the absence of Stalinist terror, the bureaucracy's development is inconceivable. In other words, it is to acknowledge that, beyond Stalin's maneuvers, the factional struggles within the leadership team, and the massive purges carried out at all levels of society, the need to fuse all the bureaucracy's strata within the mold of a new managerial class stands out. This requirement is clearly attested to by the behavior of the purged circles: Stalinist terror was able to develop within a society in full economic expansion and the representatives of the bureaucracy were willing to live under the permanent threat of extermination or dismissal, despite their privileges, because the ideal of social transformation the Party embodied prevailed among the victims as well as everyone else. The much-talked-about theme of sacrificing present generations for the benefit of future ones, which Stalinism presented in the travestied form of a program for building socialism, acquires its real content: The Party required the sacrifice of the particular and immediate interests of the rising strata to the general and historical interest of the bureaucracy as a class.

Nonetheless, one could not limit oneself to understanding the role of Stalinism solely within the framework of the Bureaucracy. The terror it exerted on a proletariat in full expansion presupposes that, in certain respects, it came to respond to a specific situation of the working class. It would indeed be shallow to deny that the Party's policy, while it might encounter increasingly firm resistance within the ranks of the proletariat—whom the labor code had chained to production and Stakhanovism had dragged into a mad race to increase production—had at the same time incited people to participate in the ideal of the new regime. Ante Ciliga showed this very well in his otherwise harshly critical works on the USSR. On the one hand, the frenzied exploitation reigning in the factories went hand in hand with an enormous proletarianization of the small peasantry; for the latter, which was used to very harsh living conditions, such exploitation was not as palpable as for the already constituted working class; it represented much more in certain respects a sort of progress: living in cities, becoming accustomed to industrial tools and products really awakened their mindset, made them aware of new social needs, and sensitized them to change. On the other hand, within the proletariat itself a significant stratum of workers found itself promoted to new roles thanks to the Party, to the trade unions, or to Stakhanovism, and thus found ways of escaping the common condition that were unknown under the old regime. Finally, and especially, in everyone's view industrialization—which made thousands of modern factories suddenly appear, increased tenfold the workforce of existing cities or drew entirely new ones out of the ground, and multiplied communication networks—appeared, beyond all dispute, progressive, with poverty and terror constituting the temporary price to pay for tremendous primitive accumulation. Most certainly, Stalinism, with whip in hand, cynically instituted forms of social discrimination inconceivable in the postrevolutionary period, and unequivocally subordinated production to the needs of the dominant class. However, the tension of the energies it required in all sectors, the social mixing it carried out, the chances for promotion it therefore offered to individuals in all classes, and the acceleration of all productive forces it imposed as an ideal, and which it achieved—all these traits provided an excuse for its excessive power and its omnipresent policing.

THE ESSENTIAL CONTRADICTION
OF STALINIST TOTALITARIANISM

If Khrushchev, ungrateful son if ever there was one, had not been obsessed by the snubs Stalin, at the end of his life, was to make him suffer, might he have been able to consider more calmly the path taken? Could not he have reread calmly the chapter [XXXI] of *Capital* Marx devoted to primitive accumulation and repeated after him: "Force is the midwife of every old society pregnant with a new one. It is itself an economic power"? Could not he have explained to the Twentieth Congress, in his usual coarse language: *Stalin did the dirty work for us?* Or else, in terms chosen to paraphrase Marx: "This is what it costs to release the eternal natural laws of planned production"? To read Isaac Deutscher,[3] the well-known English historian of Soviet society, one might almost grieve about such ingratitude. Not that Deutscher is exactly fond of Stalinism, but in his view the necessities of primitive accumulation imposed themselves on socialism like they had on capitalism: Stalinist purgatory was unavoidable. The unfortunate thing is that our author does not see that the idea of socialist primitive accumulation is absurd. For Marx, primitive accumulation signifies mass deportations of peasants into places of forced labor, factories, and the extortion by all means—most often illegal ones—of surplus value. Its aim was to create a mass of means of production such that, by subordinating labor power thereto, it might later on automatically reproduce this mass and increase it for a profit. In its principle and in its aim, it necessarily involves the division of Capital and Labor: capitalism can indulge in its "orgies," to use Marx's term, only because it has, opposite it, totally dispossessed men, and it acts in such a way that their dispossession is daily reproduced at the same time that its might is daily maintained and increased. Of course, one can dispute whether socialism is achievable in a society that has not already built up an economic infrastructure—that is, one that has not passed through a stage of accumulation—but one cannot say that socialism as such would have to pass through that stage, since, whatever the level of productive forces to which it is tied, it presupposes collective management of production—that is, the effectively actual directing of factories by workers assembled in their committees. To recognize primitive accumulation in the USSR is to admit that a capitalist type of production relations reigns there. It is to admit, too, that those relations tend to reproduce themselves and to deepen the opposition they presuppose (the constitution of a stock of machines and raw materials, on the one hand; that of a totally dispossessed workforce, on the other), whose effect could be nothing other than a normalization of exploitation. In this sense, Khrushchev's obstinate silence about the problems of primitive accumulation in the USSR seems quite reasonable. An "original sin" in the view of the bourgeoisie, as Marx said again, primitive accumulation is much more so in the view of the bureaucracy, which has to hide its very existence as a class.

Moreover, it would be contrived to explain Stalinism solely on the basis of the economic difficulties it has had to face. What we have attempted to bring out is the role it has played in the crystallization of a new class and in the revolutionizing of society as a whole. If one wants to retain the Marxist term taken up by Deutscher, its content must be updated and one must speak of *social accumulation*, understanding thereby that the Bureaucracy's present-day traits could have come about only through the Party that brought them out and maintained them through violence until they became stabilized in a new historical figure.

Still, it has to be understood that it is of the essence of the bureaucracy to constitute itself in accordance with the process we have described. For, we will understand, in the same stroke, that this class harbors a permanent contradiction that evolves, certainly, along with its history but could not be resolved with the liquidation of Stalinism.

The Party's "terroristic" dictatorship is not only the sign of the new class's immaturity. It corresponds, we have said, to its mode of domination within society. This class's nature is other than that of the bourgeoisie. It is not composed of groups that, through their ownership of means of production and their private exploitation of labor power, each hold a share of material might and strike up relationships based on their respective strengths. It is a set of individuals who, through their function and the status associated therewith, share in a profit realized through collective exploitation of labor power. The bourgeois class constitutes itself and develops inasmuch as it *results* from the activities of individual capitalists; it is underpinned by an economic determinism that grounds its existence, whatever may be the struggle its agents engage in and whatever may be the current political expression in which that struggle culminates. The intercapitalist division of labor and the market make capitalists strictly dependent upon one another and make them show collective solidarity in the face of labor power. On the other hand, bureaucrats form a class only because their functions and their statuses differentiate them collectively from the exploited classes, only because those functions and statuses bind them to a seat of management that determines production and has Labor Power at its free disposal. In other terms, it is because there are production relations within which are opposed the proletariat, reduced to the function of mere executant, and Capital, embodied by the Person of the State—it is because there is, therefore, a class relation that the activities of bureaucrats link them to the dominant class. Integrated into a class system, their particular functions constitute them as members of the dominant class. Yet, if it can be put thus, it is not as acting individuals that they weave the network of class relationships; it is the bureaucratic class in its generality that, a priori—that is, by virtue of the existing structure of production—converts the particular activities of bureaucrats (privileged activities, among others) into class activities. The unity of the bureaucratic class is therefore given immediately with the collective appropriation of surplus value and dependent immediately upon the collective exploitative apparatus, the State. In other terms, the bureaucratic community is not guaranteed by the mechanism of economic activities; it is established as bureaucrats are integrated around the State and demonstrate their absolute discipline with regard to the directorial apparatus. Without this State, without this apparatus, the bureaucracy is nothing.

We do not mean that the bureaucrats *qua* individuals do not enjoy a stable situation (though this stability was indeed threatened during the Stalinist era), that their status procures for them only ephemeral advantages, in short, that their position in society would remain fortuitous. There is no doubt that the bureaucratic personnel are little by little consolidating their rights, acquiring with time some traditions, a lifestyle, and a mindset that make of them a "world" apart. Nor do we mean that the bureaucrats are undifferentiated within their own class and do not fuel severely competitive relationships among themselves. All that we know of the struggle among clans within the Administration proves, on the contrary, that such competition takes the form of a struggle of all against all, as is characteristic of every exploitative society. We are affirming merely that the bureaucracy cannot do without individual and group cohesion, each person being nothing in himself and the State alone supplying the social cement. Without overly simplifying the operation of bourgeois society, it has to be recognized that, despite the ever increasing extension of state functions, the latter never frees itself from the conflicts engendered by competition among private groups. Civil society[4] is not absorbed into the State. Even when it tends to win acceptance for the general interest of the dominant class at the expense of clashing private interests, it still expresses intercapitalist relations of force. For, private property creates in principle a divorce between capitalists and Capital—each of the terms successively positing itself as *reality* and excluding the other as *imaginary*. The vicissitudes of the modern bourgeois State attest rather well to this *separation* about which Marx had so much to say: separation between the State itself and society and, within society, among all spheres of activity. Within the framework of the bureaucratic regime, such separation is abolished. The State can no longer be defined as an *expression*. It has become consubstantial with civil society, by which we mean the dominant class.

Yet has it? It has and it has not. Paradoxically, a separation in some respects more profound than was the case in any other society is reintroduced. The State is really the soul of the bureaucracy and the latter knows that it is nothing without this supreme power. Yet the State dispossesses each bureaucrat of any effective might. It repudiates the bureaucrat *qua* individual, denying him all creativity in his particular domain of activity, and subjects him, *qua* anonymous member, to the irrevocable decrees of the central authority. The Bureaucratic Spirit hovers [*plane*] above the bureaucrats as a divinity indifferent to particularity. Thus is planning (the kind that claims to assign to each his correct task and to attune it with all the other ones) worked out by a core of leaders [*dirigeants*] who decide everything; functionaries can only translate into numbers the guiding [*directrices*] ideas, deduce consequences from principles, transmit, and apply. The class perceives in its State naught but the impenetrable secret of its own existence. Each functionary can very well say *I am the State* [*l'État c'est moi*], but the State is the Other, and its Rule dominates as an unintelligible Fatality.

This infinite distance between the State and the bureaucrats has another unexpected consequence: the latter are never in a position to criticize the instituted Rule unless they set themselves up as opponents. Formally, such criticism is inscribed within the bureaucracy's mode of existence: since each is the State, each is invited, by right, to direct—that is, to compare his real activity with socially set objectives. Yet in reality, criticizing signifies breaking rank with the bureaucratic community. As the bureaucrat is a member of his class only inasmuch as he is integrated into state policy, every deviation on his part is in effect a threat to the system. Whence, during the entire Stalinist period, the bureaucracy's indulgence in an orgy of petty criticisms while concealing any genuine critique. The bureaucracy solemnly indicts bureaucratic methods but continues to enforce scrupulously the rules that establish and maintain its irresponsibility. It blabs on and keeps silent. Whence also any serious disturbances to the operation of production necessarily being translated into a massive purge of bureaucrats, technical staff, scientists, or trade-union officers whose divergence from the norm (whether willed or not) betrays an opposition to the State.

The contradiction between civil society and the State has been surmounted in one form, only to reappear in another, aggravated one. In the bourgeois era, in effect, the State was linked to civil society by the same ties that distanced it therefrom. For the capitalists, the secret of the State was an open secret, for, despite all its efforts to embody generality in the view of particular persons, the State aligned itself with the positions of the most powerful particular person. Although it profited from crises in order to govern among different currents, its policy still expressed a sort of natural regulation of economic forces. In bureaucratic society, on the other hand, the integration of all spheres of activity is carried through, but society has undergone an unforeseeable metamorphosis: it has produced a monster it contemplates without recognizing its own image, Dictatorship.

This monster was called Stalin. An effort is made to persuade people that he is dead. Perhaps his embalmed corpse will be left in the mausoleum as testimony to a bygone past. It is nonetheless in vain that the bureaucracy would hope to escape its own essence. It may very well bury its dead skin in the basement of the Kremlin and adorn its new body with enticing rags: totalitarian it was; totalitarian it remains.

Before considering the efforts being made by the New Management [*Nouvelle Direction*] to circumvent the unavoidable difficulties to which the structure of state capitalism gives rise, we must gauge the scope of the contradiction that haunts it. This contradiction affects not only interbureaucratic relations; it manifests itself no less strongly in the relationships the dominant class maintains with the exploited classes.

Once again, a comparison must be made between the bureaucratic regime and the bourgeois one, for the ties between the dominant class and the proletariat are of a new type in the USSR. The historical origin of the bureaucracy already attests to this; the latter was in effect formed on the basis of institutions, the Party and the Trade Union, that were forged by the proletariat in its struggle against capitalism. Of course, within the Party the proportion of intellectuals or revolutionary bourgeois elements was undoubtedly high enough to exert a decisive influence on the Organization's political orientation and behavior. It would be no less contrived to deny that the Party was born within the framework of the working class and that, while it ultimately excluded its representatives from all real power, it has not ceased to present itself as the proletariat's Leadership [*Direction*]. Incidentally, the bureaucracy continues to feed upon a portion of the working class to which it opens the doors of its cadre training schools (much more widely than the bourgeoisie ever did), and which it removes from the common condition through the privileges the bureaucracy grants it and the opportunities for social advancement the bureaucracy offers it. In addition, the proletariat's sociological definition, so to speak, finds itself transformed. In bourgeois society, an essential difference is expressed at the level of the relations of production between the owner of the means of production and the owner of labor power. Both are presented as partners in a contract; formally, they are equal, and such equality, moreover, is consecrated in the democratic regime through universal suffrage. However, this equality is apparently fictive; it is clear that being an owner of the means of production and owner of one's labor power do not have the same meaning. In the first case, ownership gives one the power to use the labor of another in order to make a profit and having this labor at hand implies some real freedom. In the other case, ownership gives one the power to submit so as to preserve and reproduce one's life. The partners' equality in the contract therefore should delude no one; the contract is enslavement. State capitalism muddles the terms. The contract then presents itself as a relation between individuals and Society. The worker does not hire out his labor power to the capitalist; he is no longer a commodity. He is supposed to be a parcel of a whole that is called *society's productive forces*. His new status therefore is distinguished in no way from that of the bureaucrat; he has the same relationship with total Society as the factory Manager. Like him, the worker receives a salary for a function that comes to be integrated into the totality of the functions defined by the Plan. In reality, as one knows too well, such a status, which grants each person the benefit of calling his superior "comrade," is the other side of a new enslavement to Capital, and this enslavement is in certain respects more complete since banning collective demands and strikes and chaining the worker to his place of work can flow *naturally* therefrom. How could the proletariat struggle against the State that represents it? The response to demands can always be that they are tied to a particular viewpoint, that the workers' interests may not coincide with those of society as a whole, that their immediate objectives have to be placed back within the framework of the historical objectives of socialism. The mystificatory procedures the State has at its disposal are therefore subtler and more effective within the new system. In the *social thought process* [*raisonnement social*], the structure develops in accordance with its formal articulations, essential links being concealed from the proletariat's view; everywhere, it encounters the signs of its power whereas it is radically dispossessed thereof.

Nonetheless, the exploited classes are not the only ones mystified. On account of this mystification, even the dominant strata are not up to the task of positing themselves as a class apart within society. Of course, the bureaucrats may be distinguished by their privileges and by their statuses. But this situation demands to be justified in the eyes of the proletariat: the bureaucracy has a need, much more than the bourgeoisie, to be "recognized." Thus, a major portion of the activity of the bureaucracy (via the Party and the Trade Unions) is devoted to persuading the proletariat that the State governs society in its name. If, from one perspective, the education of the masses and socialist propaganda appear to be mere instruments for the mystification of the exploited, from another perspective they testify to the illusions the bureaucracy develops about itself. The latter absolutely does not succeed in thinking of itself as a class. Prisoner of its own language, it imagines that it is not so, that it is responding to the needs of the entire collectivity. Of course, this *imagination* yields to the exigencies of exploitation—that is, to the imperative to extort surplus value from the proletariat by the most ruthless means. As Marx said apropos of another bureaucracy, that of the nineteenth-century Prussian State, hypocrisy then gives way to conscious Jesuitry. It remains no less the case that a conflict is haunting the bureaucracy, never leaving it in peace, and exposing it to the permanent torments of self-justification. It has to prove to those whom it dominates and prove to itself that what it does is in no way contrary to what it says. During the Stalinist era, the brutal hierarchization of society, the implacable labor legislation, the furious pursuit of output at the expense of the masses, on the one hand, and the constant affirmation that socialism is being achieved, on the other, constitute the two terms of this cruel antinomy. Now, this antimony engenders, at the same time, a demystification on the part of the masses. While the State calls upon the proletariat to participate actively in production and persuades it of its dominant role in society, the State denies the proletariat all responsibility, all initiative, and maintains it under the conditions of a mere servant of the mechanism to which capitalism has condemned it since its inception. Propaganda therefore teaches daily the opposite of what it is intended to teach.

We will see later on that the way the Russian proletariat evolved, its emancipation from the peasant shackles that confined it during the first five-year plans, and its apprenticeship in the ways of modern technology considerably aggravated this contradiction of bureaucratic exploitation and played a decisive role in the recent political transformation. What we want to underscore is simply that such a contradiction stems from the essence of the bureaucratic regime; its terms may very well evolve, and new artifices may very well be invented to render them "viable," but the bureaucracy as it exists cannot but be torn by a dual requirement: to integrate the proletariat into social life and to have its State "recognized" as that of society as a whole while denying the proletariat such integration by capturing the fruits of its labor and dispossessing it of all social creativity.

In other words, mystification is everywhere, but for this reason it engenders the conditions for its overthrow; it makes a threat weigh everywhere upon the regime. In some respects, the latter proves infinitely more coherent than the bourgeois system, whereas in other respects it exposes a new vulnerability.

THE IDEAL OF THE PARTY AND ITS REAL FUNCTION

The problems the Party faces in bureaucratic society bring us to the heart of the contradictions we have mentioned, and it is not by chance that they are to be found, as we will bring out, at the center of the preoccupations of the Twentieth Congress.

Yet one would search in vain among the critics of the USSR for an understanding of these problems. The Party's originality is never glimpsed. Bourgeois thinkers are often susceptible to the totalitarian enterprise the Party embodies. They denounce the social mystique that dominates it and its effort to integrate all activities that subordinate those activities to a single ideal. Yet this idea is dulled down to the hackneyed theme of *state religion*. Haunted by historical precedents that exempt one from thinking the Present as such, one compares Party rules to those of the Crusading Orders, its ideology to seventh-century Islam;[5] what one ignores, then, is the crucial function it plays in modern social life in the twentieth-century world, which is unified by Capital, dependent for its development upon the development of each of its sectors, and disarticulated by technical specialization while rigorously centered around industry. Moreover, Trotskyism wears itself out unfavorably comparing the present-day Communist Party to the Bolshevik model as if the former were to be defined by wholly negative traits: its distortion of socialist ideology, its absence of democracy, its counterrevolutionary conduct. Trotsky himself, as one knows, long hesitated before recognizing the Party's bankruptcy in the USSR and could only recommend a return to its initial forms. Not only could he not admit that the traits of Stalinism were foretold by Bolshevism and that the adventure of one was tied to that of the other, but he absolutely rejected the idea that the Party might have acquired a new function. The Bolshevik Party was the *real* Party, Stalinism a fantastical and monstrous projection of this party in a world cut off from the revolution.

It would suffice, however, to observe the extent of the tasks assigned to the Party and the extraordinary growth in its numbers (today, it comprises more than seven million members) to persuade oneself that it plays a decisive role in society. In fact, it is something other than a coercive apparatus, something other than a caste of bureaucrats, something other than an ideological movement destined to proclaim the sacred historical mission of the State, although it *also* connotes all those traits. It is the essential agent of modern totalitarianism.

This term must, however, be understood rigorously. Totalitarianism is not the dictatorial regime, as one is given to understand each time one designates under this name a type of absolute domination wherein the separation of powers is abolished. More precisely, it is not a political regime: it is a societal form—the form within which all activities are immediately linked together, deliberately presented as modes of a single world; in which one value system predominates absolutely, such that all individual or collective undertakings must find therein a coefficient of reality; and in which, finally, the dominant model exerts a total physical and spiritual constraint upon the conduct of particular people. In this sense, totalitarianism claims to deny the separation—characteristic of bourgeois capitalism—of the various domains of social life—of the political, the economic, the juridical, the ideological, and so on. It performs a permanent identification among them. It is therefore not so much a monstrous excrescence of the Political Power within society as it is a metamorphosis of society itself through which the political ceases to exist as a separate sphere. As we understand it, totalitarianism has nothing to do with the regime of a Franco or a Syngman Rhee, despite their dictatorships; it is beginning to take shape, on the other hand, in the United States, even though democratic institutions have continued to reign there. For, at the deepest level, it is tied to the structure of modern production and to the corresponding requirements for social integration. At the same time that they create a growing isolation of the producers in their particular sphere, the expansion of industry and the gradual invasion of all domains by its methods effect, as Marx says, a *socialization* of society, make each person dependent upon the other and upon all, and make it necessary to recognize explicitly the ideal unity of society. That such social participation might be repressed at the same time that it is expressed and encouraged, that community is shattered in the face of a new implacable division into Masters and Slaves, that socialization deteriorates into a standardization of beliefs and activities and collective creativity into passivity and conformism, and that the search for universality sinks into the stereotypy of the dominant values—this immense failure could not conceal the positive exigencies to which totalitarianism responds. It is, one may say, the underside of Communism. It is the travesty of the effectively actual totality.

Now, the Party is the typical institution in which the socialization process is carried out and overturned. And it is not by chance that, proceeding from the struggle for the instauration of socialism, it can, without changing form, become the vehicle for totalitarianism. The

Party embodies, within bureaucratic society, a historical function of an absolutely *new* type. It is the agent for civil society's complete penetration by the State. More precisely, it is the setting within which the State changes itself into society or society into the State. The huge network of committees and cells that cover the entire country establishes a novel form of communication between town and country, among all branches of social activity, and among all the business firms of each branch. The division of labor, which tends to isolate individuals utterly, is, in a sense, overcome within the Party: the engineer, the shopkeeper, the worker, and the employee find themselves side by side and alongside them are the philosopher, the scientist, and the artist. All of them find themselves torn from the narrow confines of their speciality and resituated together within the framework of total society and its historical horizons. The life of the State and its objectives are part of their everyday world. Thus, all activity, the most modest as well as the most lofty, finds itself valued, posited as a moment in a collective undertaking. Not only do individuals seem to lose, within the Party, the status that differentiates them within civil life so as to become "comrades," social men, but they also are called upon to exchange their experiences, to expose their activity and that of those around them [*leur milieu*] to a collective judgment opposite which these activities acquire a meaning. The Party tends, therefore, to abolish the mystery of one's occupation by inserting really separate milieus into a new loop. The Party makes it appear that there is one way of managing a factory, of working on a production line, of caring for the sick, of writing a philosophy treatise, and of playing a sport that involves all individuals because it implies a mode of social participation and ultimately integrates itself into a whole whose harmony is regulated by the State. This is to say, in particular, that the Party radically transforms the meaning of the political function. A separate function, the privilege of a ruling minority within bourgeois society, it now spreads out into all branches of activity, thanks to the Party.

Such is the Party's Ideal. Through its *mediation*, the State tends to become immanent to Society. Yet, via a paradox we have already analyzed at length, the Party proves *in reality* to assume a quite opposite signification. As the division of Labor and Capital persists and deepens, and as the strict unification of Capital gives effective omnipotence to a ruling Apparatus, subordinating all productive forces to this Apparatus, the Party cannot but be the simulacrum of socialization. *In reality*, it conducts itself as a particular group that comes to be added to the groups engendered by the division of labor—a group whose function is to mask the implacable partitioning of activities and statuses, to give figure within the imaginary to the transitions reality rejects, and whose speciality is not to have a speciality. In reality, the exchange of experiences deteriorates into control over those who produce, whatever their field of production, by professionals of incompetence. The answer to the ideal of active participation in the social work to be accomplished is blind obedience to the Norm imposed by the Bosses: collective creation becomes collective inhibition. Thus, the Party's penetration into all domains signifies solely that each productive individual finds himself *duplicated* by a political functionary whose role is to assign to his activity an ideological coefficient, as if the official norm, defined as the building of socialism and by whatever might be the current rules that flow therefrom, could allow him to gauge his distance from reality. Reduced to commenting on men's effectively actual conduct, the Party thus reintroduces a radical split within social life. Each has his ideological *double*. The manager or technician acts beneath the gaze of this double who "qualifies" the rise or fall of production or any other quantifiable result in terms of a fixed scale of values provided by the ruling Apparatus. Likewise, the writer is judged according to the criteria of realism determined by the State, the biologist is ordered to adhere to Lysenko's genetics. It matters little, by the way, that the double might be an Other. Each can play the role in relation to himself; the Manager, the writer, and the scientist can also be Party members. Yet however close to the other each may wish to be, the two terms represent no less a permanent social contradiction. Everything happens as if social life in its complete entirety was dominated by a fantastic time study whose norms would be worked out by the most secret Research Department.

The Party's activity thus engenders anew a separation of the political function, whereas it was trying to abolish it, and in a sense, it lays there the blame. Indeed, in each concrete domain of production, however particular it might be, the intrusion of the political makes itself felt. The freedom of work collides everywhere against the Party's norms. Everywhere, the "cell" is the foreign body: not the essential element that links the individual to the life of the organism but the inert core where society's productive forces come to rot.

Finally, the Party is the main victim of this separation. For, in society, the requirements of production create, at least within certain limits, a de facto independence of labor. The Party's exclusive job is, on the other hand, to proclaim, disseminate, and impose ideological norms. It gorges on politics. Its main function becomes justifying its own function by meddling in everything, denying every particular problem, and constantly affirming the leitmotiv of the official ideal. At the same time that it persuades itself that its activity is essential, it finds itself, on account of its behavior, cast out of real society. And this contradiction increases its authoritarianism, its championing of its prerogatives, its claim to universality. For, the Party is effective where it knows not how to be so, inasmuch as it dresses up Society in the cloth of the State, inasmuch as it simulates a social and historical unity beyond real-world divisions and conflicts, or, as Marx would have said, it is real *qua* imaginary. Conversely, it is imaginary inasmuch as it is real, being deprived of all historical effectiveness precisely where it believes that it is enforcing such effectiveness—on the terrain of the productive life of society, which it haunts as a perpetual disrupter.

It is therefore not surprising that the flaws of the Bureaucracy, which we had noted already, are in fact to be found again within the Party, there driven to their point of paroxysm. "Universal" individuals delivered from the narrowness of one situation or one status, promoted to fulfilling the task of building socialism, multiple embodiments of a new humanity—thus could the members of the Party ideally be defined. They are in fact condemned to the abstraction of the Dominant Rule, doomed to servile obedience, fastened to the particularity of their function as militants, drawn into a merciless struggle of chasing after the highest post, servants to self-justifying paperwork, a particular group among others attached to preserving and reproducing the conditions that legitimate its existence. However, they could no more give up on what they would have to be than give up what they are. For, it is through this contradiction that the Party achieves the essence of totalitarianism as the seat of society's "socialization" and of the productive forces' subordination to the domination of Capital. [...]

Notes

1. T/E: The original's subtitle translates as: "The USSR in a New Phase."
2. Stalin's own role should not make us forget that there is in terror a sort of internal logic that leads it to develop to its utmost consequences, independent of the real conditions to which it was responding at the beginning. It would be too simple for a State to use terror as an instrument and reject it once the objective has been attained. Terror is a social phenomenon; it transforms the behavior and the mindset

of individuals and, no doubt, of Stalin himself. It is only after the fact that one can denounce its excesses, as Khrushchev has done. At present, it is not excess; it constitutes social life.

3. We are referring to his studies collected in *Heretics and Renegades* (London: Hamish Hamilton, 1955), particularly "Mid-Century Russia" [T/E: 1951].

4. We are taking back up the classical term *civil society* to designate the whole set of classes and social groups, inasmuch they are shaped by the division of labor and determine themselves independently of the State's political action.

5. Jules Monnerot, *Sociologie du Communisme* (1949) [T/E: *Sociology and Psychology of Communism*, trans. Jane Degras and Richard Rees (Boston: Beacon Press, 1953)].

The Hungarian Insurrection

Claude Lefort

"L'Insurrection hongroise"
Socialisme ou Barbarie, 20 (December 1956–February 1957): 85–104
Socialisme ou Barbarie—Anthologie, 128–44

The third act of the crisis of the bureaucratic system was played out in Budapest. Relying on information from Hungarian radio and the Hungarian press, Claude Lefort recounts and comments the main events that took place between October 23 and November 3, 1956. He refutes the arguments advanced in the left-wing French press that, in order to deny the evidence of an exemplarily proletarian movement, stressed the outbreak of reactionary tendencies (an inevitable risk in the complex unfolding of a revolution). The description he gives of the events establishes definitively this revolutionary content and lays out the difficulties the workers had to surmount in the struggle they conducted against the most thoroughgoing form of capitalism. Finally, he brings out the following valuable lesson for every revolutionary movement to come: The fight for socialism cannot be directed by a party distinct from the working class, and socialism is, essentially, nothing other than workers' management of production.

THE TRUTH ABOUT TWELVE DAYS OF STRUGGLE

As one knows, everything began October 23 with the demonstration in solidarity with the Poles, organized by the Petőfi Circle—that is, by students and intellectuals. Masses of workers and employees who had left factories and offices joined in this demonstration, which was first banned and then authorized by the government at the last moment. On the whole, it developed peacefully. But in the evening, the speech by [Hungarian CP leader Ernő] Gerő set sparks flying. Whereas they were expecting major concessions on the part of the government, the demonstrators heard that the friendship between Hungary and the USSR was unshakeable, that troublemakers who wanted to create unrest would be subdued, and that the Central Committee had no intention of meeting before October 31, or eight days later. After Gerő, Imre Nagy poured out a few nice words and appealed for calm. The demonstrators experienced Gerő's speech as a provocation. A column of demonstrators headed to the radio building and sought entrance in order to have their demands broadcast: "The radio is lying! We want people to know what we want." The security police then fired on the demonstrators and, from that moment on, fighting spread within the city. A few hours later, a panicked Gerő called Nagy to form a Government, but that in no way altered the attitude of the insurgents, who had put forward some basic demands and were not content with a change in personnel.

So, Gerő's speech set sparks flying. Yet it would be risky to think that the demonstrators would have quietly gone home if one had really wanted to announce to them Nagy's immediate return to power. For a very long time, extraordinary turmoil reigned in Budapest. And we are not thinking only of the Petőfi Circle demonstrations, where large meetings had ever more violently denounced governmental policy and the role of the USSR. Neither are we thinking only of the extraordinary climate created by László Rajk's funeral and then those of former party members and former officers, which the masses had sometimes learned about at the same time as their liquidation and rehabilitation. A strong oppositional current had been growing for months within the Party; democratization and limitation of Russia's grip were demanded insistently; the crimes and flaws of the regime were denounced publicly. The events in Poland had brought such agitation to its peak. It is this situation that explains how, later on, the great majority of average party cadres and rank-and-file militants found themselves on the insurgents' side. Yet at the same time, there were major manifestations of agitation within the factories.

As early as last July, the party's organ noted this agitation and demanded emergency reforms to appease the workers. The government thus had to promise, at that time, that the masses' living standards would be raised 25 percent and to announce the abolition of the forced loan (equivalent to a 10 percent withholding on wages). Promises, however, had not sufficed; they were tempered, moreover, by legislation for a 46-hour week (regular hours), whereas a previous bill had foreseen 42 hours. In any case, the workers were determined not to be content with a few crumbs; they no longer wanted the pace of production to be imposed by the government; they no longer wanted orders from the trade union and the Party, agents of the State who were as servile as the factory manager; and they raised their voices all the louder as, opposite them, the trade-union and political leaders were each day being discredited in the press by the parade of the misdeeds of the Rákosi regime, to which they had belonged.

The workers who were in the street October 23 had come not only to demand Nagy's return. They had something else in mind. Their attitude can be summarized in the statement by a worker—a turner from the big Csepel factories—published two days earlier in the organ of the Communist Youth: "So far, we have not said a word. We have learned during these tragic times to be silent and to move stealthily. Be calm; we, too, will speak out."

During the night of the 23rd/24th, the security police continued to fire on demonstrators. But Hungarian soldiers fraternized with the latter, and in the barracks the soldiers themselves furnished the demonstrators with weapons or put up no resistance when the latter seized arms. Workers at arsenals brought weapons and distributed them. The next day a big battle notably took place before Parliament, where, as Radio Budapest announced, Russian tanks and planes intervened. There is no doubt about the role the workers played on Wednesday, the 24th; they fought fiercely. Workers from the Csepel factories were in the vanguard, creating a central insurrection committee. A tract put out by "the revolutionary students and workers" called for a general strike. The same day, the official radio station announced that disturbances had broken out in provincial factories; it constantly broadcast communiques reporting on the demonstrations that arose in the industrial centers of Hungary. That evening, it announced that calm had returned in some provincial firms, and it instantly called upon the workers to resume work the next morning. On Thursday, the government again gave the order for workers and functionaries to resume work, which attests to the fact that the strike continued.

On several occasions, the government thought that it had mastered the situation and said so. It did not understand exactly what was happening in the entire country: workers' committees were being set up almost everywhere, but in most cases they expressed their trust in Nagy; the strike was general, but it was not directed against Nagy. For example, the revolutionary council of Miskolc, which very quickly played a key role, demanded on the 25th "a government in which are placed communists devoted to the principle of proletarian internationalism who would above all be Hungarian and respect our national traditions and our millennial past."

The councils sprung up all over Hungary, and their power became, as early as Thursday, the sole real power beyond the Russian army. On Wednesday, the government alternately brandished threats and offered up prayers. Alternately, it announced that the insurgents would be crushed and proposed that they turn in their arms in exchange for an amnesty. Yet, starting on Thursday afternoon, it proved impossible to do anything at all against the general strike and the Councils. Between three and four in the afternoon, Nagy and János Kádár promised that they were going to negotiate the Russians' departure; in the evening, the Patriotic People's Front declared on the radio: "The government knows that the insurgents are acting in good faith." The organ of the Hungarian CP, *Szabad Nép*, had already recognized on the same day that the movement was not only the work of counter-revolutionaries but that it was also "the expression of the bitterness and discontent of the working class." This partial recognition of the insurrection was, as we saw, outstripped by events in a few hours and the government was forced to legitimate the whole insurrection. The next morning, the commander of the forces of order addressed the insurgents via the radio, calling them "young patriots."

Thus was there, on Thursday, a kind of turnabout. It seemed that the insurrection had won, that the government had yielded. And Nagy sanctioned this change by overhauling the government; he called on former Secretary of the Smallholders Party Béla Kovács, who had been imprisoned by the Russians for "espionage," and Zoltán Tildy, of the same party, a former President of the Republic right after the War, to collaborate with it. This governmental transformation was quite astonishing. It really was aimed at satisfying public opinion since it showed that the Communist Party was now ready to collaborate with other parties; at the same time, Nagy gave proof of his hostility to the Russians, for there was no doubt that his new collaborators, recently persecuted by Moscow, would help him to demand new relations with the USSR. Yet this reform did not satisfy the Workers' Councils: the latter were really demanding national independence and democracy, but they did not want reactionary politicians who, moreover, had already collaborated with the Russians. The return to power of former "Smallholders" leaders probably satisfied, on the other hand, a portion of the peasantry and the petty bourgeoisie of Budapest, but at the same time such reform encouraged these strata to embolden themselves, to formulate their own demands, and to come front stage, whereas, until then, the revolutionary fight had rested mainly on the proletariat.

Let us now place ourselves on Saturday, October 27, and, before looking into how the revolution evolved, let us consider what the workers' insurrection had been during its first four days.

The Miskolc Council shall serve as an example.

This council was formed as early as the 24th. It was elected democratically by all the workers in the Miskolc factories, independent of any political position. It immediately ordered a general strike, except in three sectors: transportation, electrical power, and the hospitals. These measures testify to the Council's concern to govern the region and to ensure for the population the maintenance of public services. Also very soon thereafter (the 24th or the 25th), the Council sent a delegation to Budapest in order to make contact with the insurgents in the capital, bringing them active support from the provinces and acting in concert with them. It published a four-point program:

- immediate withdrawal of all Soviet troops;
- formation of a new government;
- recognition of the right to strike;
- general amnesty for all insurgents.

On the political level, the Council clearly defined its position on Thursday, the 25th. Thanks to radio communications, which it seized, that position was immediately known throughout Hungary. As we have already reported, it was for proletarian internationalism and, at the same time, for national Hungarian socialism. The association of these two ideas may seem confusing from the standpoint of the principles of communism. Under present circumstances, it is perfectly understandable. The council was internationalist—that is, it was ready to struggle with communists and workers of the whole world. But it was national—that is, it rejected all subjection to the USSR and demanded that Hungarian communism be free to develop as it sees fit.

Moreover, the Council was not opposed to Nagy. It proposed a government directed by him. That did not prevent it from doing the opposite of what Nagy asked. At the moment Nagy was begging the insurgents to lay down their arms and, more specifically, the workers to resume work, the Miskolc Council formed workers' militias, maintained and extended the strike, and organized itself as a local government, independent of the central power. This was not only because it wanted to chase away the Russians and believed that Nagy was their prisoner. It was ready to support Nagy only if the latter applied the revolutionary program. Thus, when Nagy brought into the government representatives of the Smallholders Party, it reacted vigorously. In a "special communique" broadcast by its radio on Saturday the 27th at 9:30 PM, the Council declared in particular that it "has assumed power in the entire county of Borsod. It severely condemns all those who describe our fight as a fight against the will and power of the people. We have confidence in Imre Nagy," it added, "but we are not in agreement with the composition of his government. All these politicians who have sold out to the Soviets should have no place in the government. Peace, Freedom, and Independence."

This last declaration also brings out very well the activity of the Council, which, we just said, behaved as an autonomous government. The very day when it took power in Borsod County, it dissolved those bodies that were the mark of the previous regime—that is, all the Communist Party's organizations (this measure was announced Sunday morning by the radio). It also announced that the district's peasantry had chased out the kolkhozes' officials and had proceeded to redistribute land.

The next day, finally, Radio Miskolc broadcast an appeal demanding that the workers' councils in all provincial towns "coordinate their efforts with a view toward creating one and only one powerful movement."

What we have just reported suffices to show that, the day after the insurrection was triggered in Budapest, a proletarian movement had emerged that found its true expression straightaway in the creation of councils and that constituted the sole real power in the provinces. In Győr, in Pécs, and in most of the other large cities, it seems that the situation was the same as in Miskolc. It was the Workers' Council that ran everything; it armed fighters, organized resupply, and presented political and economic demands. During this time, the Budapest government represented nothing; it fidgeted about, sent out contradictory communiques, threatened then begged the workers to lay down their weapons and resume work. Its authority was nil.

Opposite the councils there were only the Russian troops, and yet in some regions it seems that they were not fighting. In the Miskolc district in particular, it was indicated that the troops were holding back and that, on several occasions, Soviet soldiers were fraternizing. Similar facts were reported in the Győr region.

We do not know exactly all the demands formulated by these councils. But we have the example of the Szeged Council. According to a Yugoslavian correspondent (from the Zagreb newspaper *Vjesnik*) who was in that city, a meeting of representatives of the Workers' Councils of Szeged took place on October 28. The demands adopted were: replacement of local Stalinist authorities, implementation of *workers' self-management*, and departure of Russian troops.

It is quite extraordinary to note that the councils that spontaneously sprang up in various regions and that were partially isolated by the Russian army immediately sought to federate. At the end of the first revolutionary week, they were tending to set up a republic of councils.

On the basis of such information, the image the bourgeois press painted of mere worker participation in a national uprising was obviously contrived. Let us repeat: We were face to face with the first phase of a proletarian revolution.

What were the objectives of this revolution?

We know them through a resolution of the Hungarian trade unions published Friday the 26th—that is, three days after the insurrection was triggered. It contains a whole series of demands of immense import.

On the political level, the trade unions demanded:

1. That the struggle stop, that an amnesty be announced, and that negotiations be undertaken with youth delegates.
2. That a broad government be set up, with Mr. Imre Nagy as president, and including representatives of the trade unions and youth. That the country's economic situation be laid out with complete frankness.
3. That assistance be granted to persons injured in the tragic struggles that have just unfolded and to the families of the victims.
4. That the police and the army be reinforced in order to maintain order through a national guard composed of workers and young people.
5. That an organization of working-class youth be set up with the support of the trade unions.
6. That the new government immediately start negotiations for a withdrawal of Soviet troops from Hungarian territory.

On the economic level:

1.   Constitution of workers' councils in all factories.
2.   Instauration of a working-class leadership. Radical transformation of the system of planning and management of the economy practiced by the State. Adjustment of wages, immediate 15-percent increase in salaries below 800 forints and 10 percent for wages less than 1,500 forints. Establishment of a ceiling of 3,500 forints for monthly pay. Abolition of production norms, except in factories where workers' councils would demand keeping them. Abolition of the 4-percent tax paid by unmarried people and families without children. Raising of the lowest pensions. Increase in the rate for family allowances. Accelerated housing construction by the State.
3.   The trade unions demand, in addition, that the promise made by Mr. Imre Nagy be kept to start negotiations with the governments of the USSR and other countries to establish economic relationships that give the parties mutual benefits on the basis of the principle of equality.

It was said in conclusion that the Hungarian trade unions would have to operate as they did before 1948 and would have to change their name and henceforth be called "free Hungarian trade unions."

This list of demands was signed by the presidency of the Hungarian Council of Trade Unions. Yet there is no doubt that it took up and systematized the demands put forth by the various Workers' Councils.

Let us closely consider these demands. Of course, they do not constitute a maximum socialist program. For, such a program would have, as its first point: a government of the representatives of the councils reliant on workers' militias. Perhaps that was what numerous workers, already quite ahead of the declarations from the "summits," were wishing for. Perhaps not. We know nothing about that. At any rate, what can be considered theoretically just is not necessarily what was being thought and said by those who were engaged in a revolution and who were placed in determinate conditions.

As such, the trade unions' program goes quite far. On the one hand, it demanded that Nagy govern with representatives from the youth and trade-union movements. Now, the young were at the vanguard of the revolution. On the other hand, the trade unions had to be transformed and become free trade unions, genuine class representatives, once again; their bodies had to be elected democratically. The demand therefore boiled down to requiring a revolutionary government.

In the second place, the program foresaw the permanent arming of workers and youth who, with the army and the police, would be the mainstay of the government.

In addition, and this point is key, the resolution demanded the constitution of councils in all factories. This proves that the workers saw in their autonomous bodies a power that had a universal meaning. They did not say so; they perhaps had no awareness of what it would be possible for them to do, but they were tending toward a sort of republic of councils. They were not at all disposed to turn back over to the government the responsibility to decide everything in their name. On the contrary, they wanted to consolidate and extend the power they themselves held in society.

Yet what proves the revolutionary maturity of the movement are the demands relating to the organization of production. Those demands obviously elude the intelligence of the bourgeois journalist, for he saw only what was happening on the surface—that is, on the narrowly political level. Now, what *in reality* decides the struggle of social forces are the relationships that exist within production, at the heart of business firms.

The workers could very well have in the government men in whom they have confidence and who are motivated by excellent intentions. They would have won nothing yet, if in their everyday lives, in their work, they would remain mere executants whom the managerial apparatus orders around [*commande*] like it commands the machinery. The councils themselves would ultimately be deprived of effectiveness and destined to wither away if they did not understand that their task is to take over the organization of production.

The Hungarian workers were aware of this. And that is what gives immense import to their program. They were all the more conscious of this as the Stalinist regime, while denying them all participation in the management of the factories, had not stopped proclaiming that the workers were the true owners of their firms. In a way, the Stalinist regime had contributed on this score to its own overthrow, for it had allowed the workers to understand one thing more clearly than anywhere else: Exploitation does not come from the presence of private capitalists but, more generally, from the division within factories between those whose decide on everything and those who have only to obey.

The trade unions' program therefore tackled this fundamentally revolutionary issue: it demanded, in the same paragraph: "Instauration of workers' management" and "*Radical* transformation of the system of planning and management of the economy practiced by the State." How would that radical transformation be effectuated?

How would the workers succeed through their leadership in participating in planning? That is not said. Moreover, that could not be said, three days after the insurrection, still in the heat of the struggle, and in a document that could affirm only some principles. Yet while the demand was still ill-defined, its spirit left no doubt: the workers no longer wanted the production plan to be worked out independently of them; they no longer wanted a state bureaucracy sending orders. What interested them to the utmost was to know what the leadership decides on the national level, how production would be oriented, in which branches one projected to make the greatest efforts and why; what volume was to be attained in various sectors; what were the repercussions of those objectives on their living standards, on the duration of the work week, and on the work pace this would impose.

If one continues to examine attentively the program's "economic" paragraph, one glimpses finally that the workers did not stop at making demands based on principles. They made a very specific demand, one that immediately had a tremendous impact on the organization of production in the factories: they demanded the abolition of production norms, except in factories where the councils demanded their retention. That boiled down to saying that the workers were to be free to organize their labor as they thought best.

They wanted to throw out the whole bureaucracy, from the work-study men to the time-study men who try to bring human work into alignment with the working of the machinery and who increasingly bring the working of the machinery into alignment with the mad pace imposed on human work, even if that means breaking the machinery.

They do not rule out needing, in certain cases, to retain norms. But they specified that the workers alone, through their council, are qualified to decide about that.

Quite obviously, this demand began to pave the way for a managerial program and, if the situation had allowed it to develop, it could only lead to that program. And indeed, one cannot separate the organization of people's labor from that of production in general. Business managers have never tolerated such a dissociation and cannot really do so, for everything holds together in the modern factory.

The day when men decide how to conduct their work, they will be led to envisage all the problems of the business firm.

Finally, let us examine separately the trade-union program's wage demands. What is quite characteristic is that they were aimed at narrowing the range of wages—that is, at combating hierarchy. Fifteen percent below 800 forints, 10 percent between 800 and 1,500, a ceiling of 3,500. Now, hierarchy is the weapon of the Stalinists as well as of the capitalists because it allows them, on the one hand, to set up a privileged stratum, which is a prop for the established regime, and, on the other, to divide laboring people, to isolate them from one another by multiplying the levels of pay. The struggle against hierarchy is fundamental today for workers the world over who work in Budapest, [at the Renault factories of] Billancourt, in Detroit, or Manchester, and we are indeed seeing it come to the forefront each time, in the United States, in England, or in France, that a wildcat strike breaks out, independent of the trade unions. This struggle becomes all the clearer for the workers as technical development tends more and more to level out jobs. The extreme differentiation in wages thus appears absurd from the standpoint of the logic of production and justifiable only through the sociopolitical advantages the managerial apparatus derives therefrom.

In the appeal the National Council of Hungarian Trade Unions would issue a few days later (November 2), *a new system* of wages was demanded—that is, undoubtedly, an overhaul of the previous regime's artificial multiplication of pay classifications.

What is the image these first days of struggle paint? The population as a whole rose up and sought to sweep away the regime, which is based on the dictatorship of the CP. The working class was at the vanguard of this fight. It did not dissolve into the "national movement." It appeared with some specific objectives: (1) the workers spontaneously organized their own power—the Councils—which they sought straightaway to extend as far as possible; (2) they set up, with incredible speed, a *military* power capable, in certain cases, of making Russian troops and their tanks back down and, in other ones, of neutralizing them; and (3) they went on the attack against the very root of exploitation by presenting demands whose effect would be to change completely the workers' situation within the very framework of business firms.

DIVERSITY OF THE SOCIAL FORCES IN STRUGGLE

Democratic and National Slogans

Let us resume examining the end of the events where we had broken off. We said that, starting on Thursday the 25th, a turnabout in the situation had occurred. The government recognized at first the validity of the insurrectional struggle; it promised that it would soon negotiate the departure of Russian troops; it gave portfolios to non-Communists (Smallholders). On this basis, it believed that it was in a position to call for the insurgents to lay down their weapons for good. However, fighting continued. In Budapest, the battle raged in the early afternoon of Friday the 26th against the Soviet tanks. The government did not understand that situation: it thought that its concessions were already quite significant, and above all it was persuaded that the workers' councils were going to support it, for, let us repeat, those councils proclaimed that they had confidence in Nagy. An ultimatum was therefore sent out for weapons to be laid down on Friday the 26th before 10 PM. The next morning, the struggle went on and the official radio maintained that those who continued to fight were "bandits" and would be treated as such. The insurgents were again being regarded as "agents of the West."

Faced with the scope of the fighting that had resumed (it was in particular during the night of Saturday to Sunday that the Budapest prison was attacked and that the two Farkases, who were Rákosi-regime police chiefs responsible for a series of crimes, were executed) and with the spread of revolutionary councils on the increase in the provinces and now encompassing *all strata of the population*, the government was led to yield anew. The situation was, it seems, quite confused Sunday morning.

On the one hand, negotiations with student representatives in Budapest culminated in an armistice; on the other, fighting persisted despite this armistice. Most likely, certain insurgent factions that were short on arms or munitions or found themselves in a bad position agreed to negotiations, whereas other ones, resupplied with weapons by soldiers, carried on or resumed the fight.

Still, Sunday afternoon the 28th, the government retreated a second time as the Russians capitulated. Between noon and 1 PM, Nagy announced that he had ordered his troops to cease fire. At 3 PM, Radio Budapest declared: "Soon, the fighting will come to an end. Weapons are still. The city is silent. Dead silent. We should reflect on the motives for this atrocious murder, *the true causes of which are Stalinism and Rákosi's bloodthirsty insanity."* At 4:30 PM, Nagy declared that the Russian troops would withdraw *"immediately."*

In fact, as one knows, the Russians did not evacuate Budapest. They were waiting, supposedly, for the insurgents to lay down their weapons. The latter, on their side, refused to turn them in and were encouraged by the Councils of Győr and Miskolc: fighting resumed. It was only Tuesday evening that one seemed certain of the departure of the Russians, which was officially confirmed by Radio Moscow.

We no longer need, now, to follow so closely the course of events, and we can skim over the second revolutionary week in order to bring out its main features. Yet in order to understand how the revolutionary movement evolved, we must first note what happened on the governmental level, on the general political level, and on the military level.

- On the governmental level, Nagy made a whole series of concessions that, in a sense, were democratic in character and, in another sense, boosted the petty-bourgeois forces. One after another, he announced the end of single-party rule (Tuesday the 30th) and the return to a national coalition government similar to that of 1946; he promised free elections with universal suffrage; he founded a new party (the Hungarian Socialist Workers' Party); he planned for Hungary to have neutral status and denounced the Warsaw Pact; he created a new government in which the Communists had only two portfolios while the other seats (with the exception of one that was granted to a representative of the new Petőfi Party) were divided up among National Peasants, Smallholders, and Social Democrats.
- On the political level, the old parties quickly reconstituted themselves: in the provinces, local branches of the Peasants, Social Democrat, and Smallholders parties grew in number.

  Nevertheless, a new political formation appeared out of the insurrection, the Revolutionary Youth Party, set on a clearly socialist base. Several new newspapers were published.
- On the "military" level, the situation was dominated by the presence of the Russians. They feigned a willingness to depart Sunday the 28th and, instead of departing, they attacked the insurgents in Budapest. They announced that they would withdraw the evening of Monday the 29th and, for the most part, left the capital. But they regrouped at a distance and, starting Thursday, November 1, large numbers of troops entered onto Hungarian territory.

It was within this climate that the mass movement evolved. This movement now encompassed some new social strata. At first, it was principally a movement in the factories—except, let us recall, in Budapest, where students, employees, and petty bourgeois were to be found alongside the workers. It was expressed through the appearance of councils. But the first governmental retreat (Thursday) and the formation of a coalition government (Friday) encouraged all strata of the population to rise up, for victory appeared at hand to everyone. Both in Miskolc and in Győr, town and country councils were set up and came to the fore. It is quite evident that the non-working-class population and particularly the peasants were appreciative especially of the democratic and national demands. Now, those demands also resonated deeply within the working class, for they constituted a demolition of the old totalitarian State. The workers were for Hungary's independence from Russian exploitation; they were for the abolition of single-party rule, which had merged with Stalinist dictatorship; they were for freedom of the press, which gave opponents the right to express themselves; they were even for free elections, which in their view constituted a way to break the "Communist" party's political monopoly.

In the euphoria of victory, an appreciable unanimity could therefore be reached. It remains no less the case that it went hand in hand with a certain amount of confusion.

This confusion was increased by the threat of the Russian Army, for everyone was obliged to brandish at the same time the flag of national independence.

And this confusion was also kept up by Nagy's policy, which, while recognizing the working class's autonomous bodies and declaring its determination to lean on these, in reality merely made concessions to the Right.

One will have an idea of the fluid political situation by turning once again to the activities of the Miskolc Council. As early as Sunday the 29th, the latter published a program it submitted to the Councils of Győr, Pécs, Debrecen, Székesfehérvár, Nyíregyháza, Szolnok, Magyaróvár, Esztergom, and several other provincial cites:

We demand of the government:

1. The building of a free, sovereign, independent, democratic, and socialist Hungary;
2. A law instituting free elections with universal suffrage;
3. The immediate departure of Soviet troops;

4. The elaboration of a new Constitution;
5. The elimination of the A.V.H. (*Allamvedelmi Hatosagnom*, political police); the government should be based on only two armed forces: the national army and the regular police;
6. Total amnesty for all those who have taken up arms and indictment of Ernő Gerő and his accomplices;
7. Free elections within two months, with the participation of several parties.

Clearly, this program no longer reflects just the will of the workers of the Miskolc factories but also that of population of Borsod County as a whole.

In the second week, it seems that those who were attacking communism (in all its forms) spoke more strongly, whereas those who were struggling for proletarian power did not express themselves as openly on the political level. In Győr, as early as Sunday the 29th, a workers' council communique warned against murky noncommunist elements who were seeking to exploit the situation. On November 2, observers announced that the power of communist elements was being threatened. In Budapest, it seems that reactionary demonstrations took place.

It would be absurd, however, to think that a genuine counterrevolutionary movement was developing. There was no base for such a movement. Nowhere did demands come to light that challenged the working class's gains. The "rightist" elements in the government were careful not to declare that one could in any way go backward. Thus did Tildy, the Smallholders leader, declare November 2: "The agrarian reform is an accomplished fact. Of course, the kolkhozes will disappear, but the land will remain in the peasants' hands. The banks and the mines will stay nationalized; the factories will remain the property of the workers. We have made neither a restoration nor a counterrevolution but, rather, a revolution."

It matters little whether Tildy really believed what he said. The fact is that he could not speak otherwise because the dominant forces were revolutionary.

In Budapest, the insurrection was and remained the work of the workers and students. The first appeal of the Federation of Youth, on November 2, was quite clear: "We do not want the return of the fascism of Admiral Horthy. We will not give the land back to the big landed-property owners or the factories to the capitalists."

In the provinces, the true social force beyond the proletariat was the peasantry. Now, while the peasants' demands and their attitude might have been confused, it is no less obvious that their struggle for the distribution of lands was revolutionary in character and that, for them, chasing out the kolkhoz managers had the same import as chasing away the big landowners.

Indeed, the peasants in Hungary have never had possession of the land. In seizing it, they were not regressing. They were taking a step forward. The immense majority of them under the Horthy regime were agricultural workers, representing at the time more than 40 percent of the population. Having benefitted from the agrarian reform right after the War, they were almost immediately deprived of their new rights and condemned to forced collectivization. Their hatred of the bureaucrats who managed the cooperatives and enriched themselves at their expense substituted almost without hiatus for the hatred they had shown their ancestral exploiters, the landed aristocrats.

In addition, we know that the redistribution of lands after October 23 took place only in certain sectors, whereas, in others, cooperatives taken back over by the peasants continued to operate—which proves that, for certain peasant strata, the advantages of collective labor remained appreciable, despite the exploitation with which they had been associated under the previous regime.

It would therefore be simplistic to claim that the peasants constituted a counterrevolutionary force. Even if a great number of them were prepared to trust the representatives of the "Smallholders" parties, which were attached to religious and family traditions and eager to welcome the return to Cardinal Mindszenty, they remained members of an exploited class liable to join the proletariat in its struggle for socialist objectives.

We just mentioned the 7-point Miskolc program to show that only democratic and national demands appeared therein. We can now mention the Magyaróvár program, which in some way is its counterpart. As the program of a "municipal executive committee" clearly led by peasant elements, it demanded free elections under UN control, the immediate reestablishment of the peasantry's trade organizations, the free exercise of their trades for small craftsmen and small shopkeepers, and the reparation of grave injustices committed against the Church, while formulating a whole series of bourgeois democratic demands, yet *at the same time* it called for the elimination of all class differences (point 13).

Nothing, in our opinion, better shows the ambivalence of the peasant movement, wherein, as the Russian Revolution in particular has shown, conservative and revolutionary elements still coexist.

The Workers' Struggle Continues

Some have tried to make believe that a major counterrevolutionary movement had been triggered at the end of the insurrection's second week and that the workers' gains were about to be liquidated. Kádár later had to retract this lie and declare that reactionary bands posed only a small threat and that the government just had to forestall their action. But that was still a lie. The events that followed proved that. For, the working class fought fiercely throughout Hungary, the strike had again become general, and the factories were once again the bastions of the insurrection. It was the workers' new gains—the councils and the arming of the workers—that the Russians could not tolerate and that they wanted to crush with the help of a puppet government.

During the third week, Radio Budapest could only reissue the program of entreaties it had broadcast under the first Nagy government at the start of the insurrection, beseeching that weapons be laid down and work be resumed.

The truth is that, on the eve of the Soviet tank attack, the situation was open and the future of Hungarian society depended—as in every revolution—on the capacity of the diverse social forces to get across their own objectives and to bring the majority of the population along with them.

What was ruled out in any case was a return to a Horthy-type regime, a restoration of private and big landed-property capitalism. For, there was no significant social stratum likely to support that restoration.

What was possible, on the other hand, was either the rebuilding of a state apparatus that would be based on a parliament, would have used a police force and a regular army, and would have embodied anew the interests of a bureaucratic-type managerial group in production or the victory of workers' democracy, the takeover of the factories by the Councils, the permanent arming of worker and student youth—in short, a movement that would become more and more radicalized.

In the latter case, undoubtedly, a vanguard would have quickly regrouped. It would have opposed to the bourgeois or bureaucratic political program a workers' government program. It would have helped the Councils unify their action and demand the direction of society.

The two paths were open and, undoubtedly, the events that then took place in the other people's democracies would have exerted a strong influence in one direction or the other. On the one hand, it is doubtful that an isolated revolution would have been able to develop and triumph in Hungary. On the other, it is no less doubtful that a proletarian movement would have been able to endure without making its effects felt on the working class in Czechoslovakia, Romania, and Yugoslavia, which continued to varying degrees to undergo exploitation similar to the kind from which the Hungarian workers had liberated themselves, and without giving a huge impetus to the workers' movement in Poland, which for a month imposed unremitting concessions on the Polish as well as Russian bureaucracy.

Of course, when a revolution begins, its outcome is not guaranteed in advance. In the Hungarian Revolution, the proletariat was not alone; alongside it, peasants, intellectuals, and the petty bourgeois had fought the dictatorship of the bureaucracy, which exploited and oppressed the whole population. The democratic and national demands united the whole population during an initial phase; relying thereupon, a process leading to the rebuilding of a separate state apparatus opposed to the Councils, of a parliamentary "democracy" capable of benefitting from the support of the peasants and the petty bourgeoisie, was theoretically conceivable. In a second phase of the revolution, the contradictory content of these demands would have appeared; at that moment, it would have been necessary for one solution to win out brutally at the expense of the other and for a bourgeois-type parliament *or* the Councils, an army and police as a corps specialized in coercion *or* an armed organization of the working class to win out. At the outset, the insurrection bore within itself the seeds of two absolutely different regimes.

Nevertheless, the events that followed showed the strength of the working class. We have deliberately dwelt on the role of the non-proletarian elements that manifested themselves during the second week of the insurrection. Yet their real weight in the situation should not be exaggerated, either. It is inevitable that at the end of a dictatorial regime all political tendencies manifest themselves; that the traditional politicians, barely out of prison, hold meetings, deliver speeches, write articles, and draft programs; that, in the euphoria of shared victory, an audience be ready to applaud all the speechifiers who proclaim their love of freedom. The threat these political tendencies represented did not yet correspond to an organized force within society.

During this time, the Workers' Councils continued to exist. The workers remained armed. *These Councils, these workers were the sole real force, the sole organized force in the country*—outside the Russian army.

It was this force that the Russian bureaucracy absolutely could not tolerate. The Tildys, Kovács, even the Mindszentys—with them, the Russian bureaucracy can make compromises and govern while making concessions. It had already done so in Hungary, in all the people's democracy countries, and in France, where [CP General Secretary and Vice President of the Council of Ministers] Maurice Thorez and Co. were not embarrassed to participate alongside [Christian Democrat Georges] Bidault in several governments from 1945 to 1947. But the organization of Councils by armed workers signified for the bureaucracy a total defeat. That is why, in creating the excuse of the "reactionary peril," it launched on Sunday, November 4 its tanks against the Councils, whose victory risked having huge repercussions and disrupting its own regime.

What happened then is absolutely incredible. For six days, the insurgents resisted an army that had overwhelming firepower. It was only on Friday, November 9, that organized resistance ceased in Budapest. Yet *the end of military resistance absolutely has not put a complete end to the revolution.* The general strike continued, plunging the country into complete paralysis and clearly demonstrating that the Kádár government had strictly no support among the population. Kádár, however, had already accepted in his program most of the insurgents' demands—among others, workers' management of the factories. Yet the Hungarian proletariat obviously could not let itself be duped by a traitor who wanted to establish his power by force of Russian tanks. For a week, from November 9 to 16, Kádár's puppet government made appeal after appeal, by turns threatening, begging, promising, and making—in words—ever greater concessions. Nothing worked. Then, on Friday, November 16, Kádár was obliged to enter into talks with the Councils—with the Central Workers' Council of Budapest. He was thereby recognizing that he himself was a big fat zero, that the sole genuine force in the country was the Councils, and that there was only one way for work to resume—which was for the Councils to give the order. Upon the express condition that a series of their demands would be satisfied immediately, and while declaring that they would not abandon "a single comma" of the rest, the workers' delegates asked on the radio for their comrades to resume work.

These facts do not show only, in a retrospective way, the relative weight of the various forces in the Hungarian Revolution and the extraordinary might of the Workers' Councils. They shed harsh light on the *total defeat* of the Russian bureaucracy, even after its military "victory." The act of resorting to massive repression and mobilizing

20 divisions to put down a popular movement was already in itself an extremely heavy political defeat for the Russian bureaucracy, which is obliged to claim to adhere to socialism. Yet that defeat is nothing in comparison to the one it is now in the process of undergoing: it must, via Kádár, recognize that it has massacred people for no reason, that it has not restored its power in Hungary, that Kádár may well have had 20 Russian divisions yet must still come to terms with the Workers' Councils.

The Hungarian Revolution is not over. In the country, two forces continue to face each other: the Russian tanks and the workers organized in the Councils. Kádár is trying to create support for himself, making extremely broad concessions. But his situation is hopeless. As these lines are being written, on the eve of Monday, November 19, it is not certain whether the order to resume work given by the Council will indeed be followed; it seems that many workers think that the delegates were wrong to grant Kádár this resumption. The latter has just made another misstep (which he was indeed obliged to make): in order to be assured that the resumption of work will actually happen, he has only one means, starving the workers, exactly like a boss or a capitalist government. He has therefore forbidden the peasants to resupply Budapest without the permission of the government and the Russian army, and he has forbidden the workers to receive rationing cards except in the factories. He thereby shows more clearly still to the Hungarian workers who he is—the head of a firing squad coupled with a payer of starvation wages—and deepens the ditch separating him from them. At the same time, the workers continue to demand doggedly and before all else the departure of the Russian troops; with them gone, one can easily imagine what Kádár's fate would be. [...]

Documents, Narratives, and Texts on the Hungarian Revolution

"Documents, récits et textes sur la Révolution hongroise"
Socialisme ou Barbarie, 21 (March–May 1957)
Socialisme ou Barbarie—Anthologie, 145–51

The men who took up arms in Hungary in 1956 carried out the first mass revolutionary act to raise the issue of power against the bureaucracy. After their movement was crushed by Russian tanks, many of them had to go into exile. Socialisme ou Barbarie *opened its columns to them, for they were the living word of the revolution. We offer here three excerpts.*

THE WORKERS' COUNCILS OF THE HUNGARIAN REVOLUTION
by Pannonicus[1]

[. . .]

The existence and nature of these councils were not totally unknown in Hungary. Although one was not exactly familiar in detail with the Yugoslavian workers' councils, the little one knew about them sufficed for the creation of such councils to become one of the demands of the anti-Stalinist struggle that vigorously manifested itself during the year 1956. It is quite understandable that, in a totalitarian state-capitalist dictatorship—where the trade unions and the so-called "party of the working class" have become annexes and executive forces of the exploitative bureaucratic State, which was also betraying the country's interests, as was the case in Hungary—the idea of workers' councils reverberated greatly. That is why, before October 23 and especially in the period preceding the insurrection, the Petőfi Circle and the Union of Writers insisted on the need to create them. One of the main slogans for the large demonstration initiated by the students on October 23 was workers' autonomy; one of its goals was to force the creation of workers' councils. It is even known that the first response of the Gerő clique to the demonstration was rejection and even provocation. Yet, as early as October 24, Gerő and his clique, faced with the growing development of the insurrection and with the near-total collapse of the Party's and trade unions' apparatuses, switched tactics. They accepted the creation of the workers' councils and entrusted the party apparatus with carrying out that task. The way events unfolded shows precisely what their goal was: to curb the revolutionary momentum and, on the other hand, to impress the working class, with a view toward diverting the revolution and regaining control over it. Whereas, earlier, they had denied the need for workers' councils, now they rushed to organize them in order to mobilize the working class—according to their words—against the counterrevolution.

Of course, they organized the workers' councils as they wished— that is, with a view toward being assured "of their loyalty." These councils were therefore composed of the manager, the secretary of the cell, trade-union bosses, and a few domesticated workers.

And yet they were overtaken by events. The working class was already on the side of the revolution. The evening of October 23, the students had demonstrated, calling upon the workers to engage in a general strike. That night, they went from factory to factory with trucks asking the workers to leave work and join the revolution. As early as the morning of October 24, the unity of workers and students became an indisputable fact and remained the revolution's greatest force.

In this way, a strangely contradictory situation appeared: the workers took part in the revolution as much through the general strike as by struggling in armed groups, side by side with the students, and, during this time, the officially formed so-called workers' councils were launching appeals for the cessation of the strike and were declaring themselves against the insurrection. The workers were struggling against Gerő, and Gerő's puppets were speaking in their name.

It was obvious that this situation could not last long. The workers, seeing great possibilities for the councils, became aware of their own forces and could not bear that Gerő's men were clothing themselves in the prestige of the workers' councils and speaking in the name of the working class. They returned to the factories, kicked out the usurpatory bureaucrats, and created the workers' councils through democratic and revolutionary means.

The formation of the Hungarian Revolution's workers' councils was therefore not the product of chance. While these councils were not the result of long preparations, they were born of the direct activity of the working class.

Analysis of the elections and of the constitution of workers' councils is a major problem, though less from a sociological than from a political standpoint. Although we do not have at our disposal complete documentation on the councils, the data we possess do allow us to make some major observations. It can be stated that the election of the councils, even when it occurred under exceptional conditions, unfolded democratically. The date of the elections was announced several times and each worker, each employee in the factories was invited to vote. Thanks to these precautions, 50 to 70 percent of the workforce was involved in the elections. The workers voted despite the continued fighting in the streets and even though communications had been interrupted. It is quite natural that percentages differed from factory to factory.

The elections were carried out in the open. One could speak out quite freely. Each voter could propose candidates and people discussed the competence, attitude, and the past and recent activity of each one.

The unity of the insurrection manifested itself on the occasion of these elections, when the various factories unanimously left aside all the party and trade-union organizations. Each acted not as a delegate of some party but as a worker from this or that factory.

Analysis of the composition of the workers' councils also reflects the unity of the revolution, its popular character, and the working class's political maturity.

This analysis is to be done as much from the social standpoint as from the political standpoint. The councils faithfully reflected the social composition of the factories, their majority being made up of workers who worked near machinery and who, on account of that, had the most right to manage the factories. They especially were the ones who manifested the greatest amount of activity. Despite their feeling of superiority, the workers elected numerous employees and technical staffers, several times even as presidents. This phenomenon expresses the social unity of the revolution, wherein—without taking class differences into account—all honest people participated at least by manifesting their sympathy. Secondly, the election of intellectuals, technicians, and economists proves that the workers had a very clear view of the situation—the councils were not merely to be organizations intended to defend material interests but also organizations capable of managing the factories and representing the workers' opinion and general attitude toward other organizations.

[. . .]

It is very important to analyze the new political phenomena that appeared for the first time within the framework of the workers' councils. First of all, there was the organization of the general strike, stronger than ever before in history. This strike was total; it embraced the whole working class, assured the absolute defense of the factories, and organized the armed struggle of the mass of workers. This political work also had some new traits. It did not have any bureaucratic character, for the workers' meetings were the supreme organs for discussion and deliberation, and these were uniquely popular organs. Thus, the workers' councils were the free expression of the working class in a new and revolutionary mode, a free expression that thus manifested itself, almost without any intermediary organ, both on the local level and on the national level.

Among the economic problems with which the councils had to concern themselves, we must mention, first, the demands formulated on a national scale—which, while being political demands, touched very closely at the same time on the country's economic situation, including, of course, the workers' situation. The councils demanded the abolition of the system of labor norms, wage increases, the right to strike, genuine democratic trade unions, a break with the country's economic colonization, the establishment of trade with the Soviet Union upon an equal footing, and so on, all these demands conforming to the revolution's goals.

The councils organized in the factories the economic bases for the strike. They continued to pay salaries, with an across-the-board 10-percent increase (they had therefore immediately commenced the implementation of demands); they organized resupply through direct trade with peasants with the help of truck convoys; and they concentrated the distribution of food within the factories themselves. For the poorest working families, the councils gave immediate assistance.

During the few days of the revolution, the system of workers' councils organized itself at incredible speed. The councils were first formed in the factories, and the factory delegates designated the local district councils, whose delegates ultimately constituted the Greater Budapest Council [that is, the capital and its suburbs, around two million inhabitants, among whom are found almost half of the Hungarian working class—*French Translator's note*].

The Workers' Council of Greater Budapest acquired immense authority in very little time and appeared to be the country's sole real political force, especially after the second Soviet offensive on November 4. It demanded autonomous representation for the workers' councils in the future national assembly, which means that it made an attempt to transpose its real political force into parliamentary forms. This demand by the Council expressed the opinion of the working class, which tended to express its political views directly, *qua* working class, independent of the parties. This opinion also was expressed by the fact that the workers declared their opposition to the creation of cells in the factories and denied all parties the right to create cells. Numerous organizers were chased out of the factories.

The birth of the workers' councils and their activity prove the popular and socialist character of the Hungarian Revolution and offer some experiences, new acts in the search for the forms of socialism, direct management, workers' self-directing activity [*l'auto-direction ouvrière*].

Among the conclusions to be drawn, one must place at top this one: Workers' revolutionary self-directing activity is the indispensable condition for every uprising, for each popular combat—a fact that, unfortunately, has not been recognized by Hungarian politicians, writers, and intellectuals. Secondly, under any regime, a system that massively excludes workers from direct participation or that is achieved without them is a fraud if it calls itself *socialist*. Thirdly, the experience of the workers' councils has demonstrated that a calm and wise policy, an effort at economic organization, can be achieved only by autonomous and free workers who self-direct themselves [*se dirigent eux-mêmes*]. Fourthly, management of a country can be confided to workers who are equal to the other social strata and are able to collaborate with them. Fifthly, the history of workers' councils is to be studied in detail, because, without knowledge of these general and particular experiences, no one can any longer call himself *socialist*.

I hope that the present article, which is rather an essay for sketching out the history of the Hungarian workers' councils, will encourage all those who are interested in the fate of Hungary and, more broadly, in the fate of world socialism, to undertake a more profound study of the problem.

The Re-Stalinization of Hungary
by Jean Amair[2]

[...]

On November 4, 1956, the Kádár government, in its first declaration, recognized that the Revolution had some just objectives but claimed that it had been transformed, along the way, into a counterrevolution. Thus did it accept all the demands of the Hungarian insurgents, with the exception of five among them: those concerning Hungarian neutrality, the Warsaw Pact, withdrawal of Russian troops, free elections, and publication of the Russo-Hungarian trade agreements. Yet, since January 1957, the entire revolution, en bloc, has become for the government a counterrevolution: even the October 23 student demonstration is not immune from this characterization and, since the publication on March 7 of József Révai's article, the whole ideological preparation of the Revolution (which began after Stalin's death and reached extraordinary intensity throughout the year 1956) has been officially considered a web of counterrevolutionary intrigues. It is only too natural that the concessions granted to the people on the first days were being taken back or adulterated. This began with the dissolution of the revolutionary committees (not to be confused with the Workers' Councils) and ended—for the moment—with the new debasement of the March 15 national holiday. What is surprising in this backward movement is that the measures taken are generally not applicable. The masses were denied the right to participate in the celebration of the national holiday, but the Government was to celebrate it more solemnly than ever. Mandatory teaching of Russian and "Marxism-Leninism" was reintroduced, but the application of this measure had to be postponed indefinitely. Officially, the reconstitution of agricultural cooperatives had begun, but for several weeks already nothing more has been heard about that. The counterrevolution was continually attacked, but the government had to justify itself day after day. One cannot help but recognize, in these retreats on the part of the government, the strength of the people's resistance, even while it remains silent.

[...]

Will the government be able to influence the intellectuals or the masses in this way? That is highly doubtful. One must recall the extraordinary fact that, after the victory of the Russian intervention, the Committee of Revolutionary Intellectuals issued a resolution in which it proclaimed that initiative for the resistance thenceforth belonged to the Workers' Councils and it committed itself to following all their decisions. This resolution was not only a manifestation of the intellectuals' faith in the working class—even though, as such, it constitutes a moving and solemn human document—it is the expression of a political, economic, and social truth. It expresses the political unity that has indeed existed during the Revolution, which is in turn grounded on the social unity that had been created under pressure from the Stalinist regime, and it expresses the current situation, where the key to economic change is to be found in the hands of the working class, without whom technical staffers can accomplish nothing in production. And the workers are working the least possible. Their goal is to live, more exactly to survive, without giving their oppressors more than the bare minimum.

[...]

And what about the Party, one might ask oneself, recalling that the old Party numbered almost a million members? This Party, encompassing a tenth of the population, collapsed at the sight of the first truly popular demonstration. Kádár's party is weaker still, not only from the numbers standpoint but also from the standpoint of quality. It has reached the figure of two hundred thousand members, but the leaders' cynical statements about the superiority of an "elite party" over a "mass party" ill-camouflage the organization's difficulties—all the less so as a few inadvertent expressions betray their resignation about reaching the manpower levels of the Rákosian party. These leaders behave like the fox beneath the grapes that are too high: *True, we are not a big party, but it is bad to be a big party*, they say. Yet they are not only few in number. They are especially weak among the laboring masses: while having had to forbid admission of new members in offices and central organizations, they hardly succeed in forming one factory cell among thousands of workers. The same goes where they are formed: these cells have no strength and do no work. That is why a big factory's cell meeting is triumphantly announced in the main party newspaper. In wanting to proclaim their activity, they are thus only betraying their weakness.

[...]

A Student's Narrative[3]

[. . .]

On November 8, I spoke with a young Soviet tank crew member. He was so bold that he came down from his tank and entered our alleyway. He was looking for weapons; we could easily have killed him, but he was so young, looked so afraid, and he was seeking out friendly looks with his eyes.

The conversation took a rather long time to start up but became more and more personal. We showed him the big store on the neighboring street gutted by fire caused by a Russian tank shell, asking him whether such destruction was necessary to wipe out "fascists." He first avoided answering directly, but then he pulled out of the pocket of his coat one of our bilingual leaflets. The text said: "Soviet soldiers! Leave our country! We are not fascists: we want only to live freely! Go back home: we aren't mad at you and no one wants to attack you." He reread the leaflet, which he clearly knew well and asked us: "Is this true?" To which we responded to him: "Do we look like fascists?" He went on: "We're told that it's a lie, that this leaflet must be thrown away, that we must ask no more questions." Saying these words, he put the leaflet back into his pocket.

We had understood. He knew the truth. And I thought of the piece of poetry we were listening to, which was interrupted by Soviet cannon fire; it ends with these words:

For order is needed in the world
And order is there to ensure
That the child serves some purpose
And that good be not allowed

And if the child remains mouth wide open,
Looks at you or complains
Don't let yourself be conned, don't believe
That it is your lesson that maddens him.
Look at this Russian baby
He screams for one to pity him
But while he is smiling at the breast
His nails and teeth grow.

Notes

1. "Les Conseils ouvriers de la Révolution hongroise," *Socialisme ou Barbarie*, 21 (March–May 1957): 106-12. *Socialisme ou Barbarie—Anthologie*, 145-48.
2. "La restalinisation de la Hongrie," *Socialisme ou Barbarie*, 21 (March–May 1957): 113-18. *Socialisme ou Barbarie—Anthologie*, 149-50.
3. "Récit d'un étudiant," *Socialisme ou Barbarie*, 21 (March–May 1957): 93. *Socialisme ou Barbarie—Anthologie*, 150-51.

PART FOUR

THE CONTENT OF SOCIALISM

"Le Contenu du socialisme"
Socialisme ou Barbarie—Anthologie, 153-56

"On the Content of Socialism," by "Pierre Chaulieu" (Cornelius Castoriadis),[1] from which these pages are drawn, appeared in issue 22 (July–September 1957: 1–74) of the review. In all, Chaulieu addressed this question four times. The first text, "Le programme socialiste" (The socialist program), was published in no. 10 (August 1952: 1–9). Chaulieu insisted there on the fact that the two key elements of the traditional program—nationalization and planning, on the one hand, party dictatorship as the expression of the dictatorship of the proletariat, on the other hand—had become "the programmatic bases for bureaucratic capitalism." Whence the need to define socialism in a positive and concrete way (as workers' management) and not in a negative and abstract way (as abolition of private property and planning in general). As for the second one, "On the Content of Socialism" (no. 17 [July 1955]: 1–25), this initial version of the one presented and reprinted below was headed by a summary of how the group was analyzing bureaucracy at that time. The one we present and reprint in part here is therefore the third of the articles published by Chaulieu on the question of how "socialism" was to be defined. A final "On the Content . . . " was published in the following issue (no. 23 [January–February 1958]: 23–81). When Castoriadis republished his texts in the "Éditions 10/18" collection, he opted to include this final text—the one where he analyzed the connections between the contradictions in the organization of the capitalist business enterprise and the forms working-class organization, consciousness, and struggle take on—in the volume entitled *L'Expérience du mouvement ouvrier, 2: Prolétariat et organisation* (Paris: Union Générale d'Éditions, 1974), 9–88.

"On the Content . . . " (1957) is presented therefore as "a new draft of the entire text" and not as a mere sequel to the 1955 article. The introductory paragraph notes that the text "opens a discussion on programmatic questions" and that "the positions expressed here do not necessarily express the point of view of the entire Socialisme ou Barbarie group." Its particular feature is that it is written as a "balance sheet" or "assessment" [*bilan*], with Chaulieu arranging previously scattered components in a condensed and systematic way. Yet this is one of the most innovative texts he published in the review. It claims to be the theoretical formulation of "the experience of a century of working-class struggles"—and, in large part, it is indeed so. It is also stated there explicitly that the revision of the traditional ideas about the nature of capitalism (some "of which have reached us [with or without distortion] from Marx himself") to which this analysis leads "did not of course start today," for "various strands of the revolutionary movement—and a number of individual revolutionaries—have contributed to it over time." And yet at the same time, this article, through its introduction of new formulations, indisputably marks a turning point in the theoretical development of the author and in that of the group. While he did not underestimate the novelty involved (the need for a "radical revision" is stated on the very first page), it is likely that neither the group nor Castoriadis himself gauged all the consequences thereof, concerned as they were at the time with emphasizing all the points of continuity, rather than the points of rupture, with a certain Marxist tradition.

The originality of the group's "method," and of its relation to theory, is strongly manifested in this text: one approaches reality with certain ideas in mind in order to shed light on this reality (for, "one cannot understand anything about the profound meaning of capitalism and the crisis it is undergoing unless one begins with the most total idea of socialism," as is said in the text), yet one is ever ready to alter one's ideas in terms of what reality lets one perceive. Also to be found there, in a fragmentary way, are some key elements of an Economics textbook, of a general presentation of his positions in this domain that Castoriadis would have liked to write, but, for various reasons, was never able to write: the impossibility of rigorously imputing the product to various "factors" or "units" of production and, therefore, of providing any basis whatsoever for income and wage differentials; the potential for a "socialist" society to instaurate a genuine market grounded on consumer sovereignty; and, finally, a critique of the idea of a neutral "technique" that might be used, as such, for other ends, capitalist technology being a choice made along a "spectrum" of possible technical solutions. The main idea here is that of the possibility of democratically deciding the overall distribution of a society's resources between consumption and investment and between public consumption and private consumption, with the help of a "technical" setup (the "plan factory") subject to the political control of the collectivity, itself organized through forms ("councils") that allow for effective self-government, including at the level of production units. These ideas—which, moreover, Castoriadis maintained until the very end of his life—are obviously in total conflict not only with the basic orientation of contemporary society but also with entire sections of "Marxist" ideology and, ultimately, with the work of Marx himself. They could not help but give rise to reservations among the members of the group who were most attached to the Marxist tradition. "On the Content . . . " (1957) represents an important stage in Castoriadis's gradual break with Marxism, which would culminate in his texts from 1964–1965. But the discussion this article should have "opened" never really took place, undoubtedly because two other questions almost immediately, and one right after the other, drew the group's full attention: the debate over organization, which ended in a split with Claude Lefort, Henri Simon, and some other S. ou B. members in 1958 (see Part 5); and then, beginning in 1959, the debate over "Modern Capitalism and Revolution"—which culminated in the split of 1963 with Véga, Brune, and Lyotard, and which is dealt with in Part 7 of the present *Anthology.*

"On the Content . . . " (1957) probably was the article published in the review that was most widely disseminated in other countries (England, Italy, Spain [T/E: and the United States]), in some cases even before it was reprinted in book form by Castoriadis himself. Some of its ideas (critique of capitalist technology, the idea of possibly "automating" some of the economy's managerial operations) have also had, directly or indirectly, an afterlife we cannot retrace here. There is one major point on which Castoriadis altered (as early as 1963, in "Recommencing the Revolution") his position. The 1957 text takes it to be self-evident that the industrial proletariat has a historically privileged role. This predominant role of the working class means that the business enterprise is not only a unit of production but the basic social unit of the new society to come: "The normal form of working-class representation in the present age undoubtedly is the Workers' Council." Now, it is obvious that, in a society in which the working class is no longer in the majority and no longer has any "historical" privilege, "considerations of geographical proximity" or other such considerations treated in the text would play a much more important role. It is also certain that in no way does the extraordinary degree of political activity on the part of the population in such a society go without saying. Castoriadis nonetheless continued to believe, until the very end, that the Council "form" (the assembly of elected representatives, able to be recalled at any moment, giving an account of their activities before their constituents, and combining the functions of deliberation, decision-making, and execution) was the sole conceivable instrument for the self-governance of society and that what is here called *socialism* (and what he would later call *autonomous society*) "aims at giving a meaning to people's life and work; at enabling their freedom, their creativity, and the most positive aspects of their personality to flourish; at creating organic links between the individual and those around him, and between the group and society; at reconciling people with themselves and with nature."

E.E.

Notes

1. With the title "Sur le contenu du socialisme, II," this article was, with some minor formal corrections, reprinted by the author under his real name, Cornelius Castoriadis, in the volume *Le Contenu du socialisme* (Paris: Union Générale d'Éditions/"10/18", 1979), 103–221. This volume includes, beyond the set of Castoriadis's articles in the review devoted to the question of the "socialist program," several texts from 1974–1978 and a major introduction, "Socialisme et société autonome." [T/E: See *PSW2* and *PSW3*.]

On the Content of Socialism

Pierre Chaulieu

"Sur le contenu du socialisme"
Socialisme ou Barbarie, 22 (July–September 1957): 1–23, 30–47
Socialisme ou Barbarie—Anthologie, 157–95[1]

The development of modern society and what has happened to the working-class movement over the last 100 years (and in particular since 1917) have compelled us to make a radical revision of the ideas on which that movement has been based. Forty years have elapsed since the proletarian revolution seized power in Russia. From that revolution it is not socialism that ultimately emerged but a new and monstrous form of exploitative society and totalitarian oppression that differed from the worst forms of capitalism only in that the bureaucracy replaced the private owners of capital and "the plan" took the place of the "free market." Ten years ago, only a few people like us defended these ideas. Since then, the Hungarian workers have brought them to the world's attention.

Among the raw materials for such a revision are the vast experience of the Russian Revolution and of its degeneration, the Hungarian workers' councils, their actions, and their program. But these are far from being the only elements useful for making such a revision. A look at capitalism and a century of workers' struggles in other countries shows that throughout the world working people are faced with the same fundamental problems, often posed in surprisingly similar terms. These problems call everywhere for the same response. This answer is socialism, a social system that is the very opposite of the bureaucratic capitalism now installed in Russia, China, and elsewhere. The experience of bureaucratic capitalism allows us clearly to perceive what socialism *is not* and *cannot be*. A close look both at past proletarian revolutions and at the everyday life and struggles of the proletariat enables us to say what socialism could and should be. Basing ourselves on a century of experience, we can and must now define the positive content of socialism in a much fuller and more accurate way than was possible for previous revolutionaries. In today's vast disarray, people who call themselves socialists may be heard to say that they "are no longer quite sure what the word means." We hope to show that the very opposite is the case. Today, for the first time, one can begin to spell out in concrete and specific terms what socialism really could be like.

The task we are about to undertake not only leads us to challenge many widely held ideas about socialism, many of which go back to Lenin and some to Marx. It also leads us to question widely held ideas about capitalism, about the way it operates and about the root of its crises, many of which have reached us (with or without distortion) from Marx himself. The two analyses are complementary and in fact the one necessitates the other.

The revision we propose did not of course start today. Various strands of the revolutionary movement—and a number of isolated revolutionaries—have contributed to it over time. From the very first issue of *Socialisme ou Barbarie* we endeavored to resume this effort in a systematic fashion. There we claimed that the fundamental division in contemporary societies was the division into directors and executants. We attempted to show how the working class's own development would lead it to a socialist consciousness. We stated that socialism could only be the product of the autonomous action of the proletariat. We stressed that a socialist society implied the abolition of any separate stratum of directors and that it therefore implied the power of mass organs and workers' management of production.

But in a sense we ourselves have failed to develop the content of our own ideas to the full. It would hardly be worth mentioning this fact were it not that it expressed, at its own level, the influence of factors that have dominated the evolution of Marxism itself for a century, namely, the enormous dead weight of the ideology of exploitative society, the paralyzing weight of traditional concepts, and the difficulty of freeing oneself from inherited modes of thought.

In one sense, our revision consists of making more explicit and precise what was the genuine, initial intention of Marxism and what has always been the deepest content of working-class struggles—whether at their dramatic and culminating moments or in the anonymity of everyday life in the factory. In another sense, our revision consists of eliminating from revolutionary thought the accumulated dross of a century of revolutionary ideology. We want to break the distorting prisms through which we have become accustomed to looking at the life and action of the proletariat. Socialism aims at giving a meaning to people's life and work; at enabling their freedom, their creativity, and the most positive aspects of their personality to flourish; at creating organic links between the individual and those around him, and between the group and society; at reconciling people with themselves and with nature. It thereby rejoins the most basic goals of the working class in its struggles against capitalist alienation. These are not aspirations about some hazy and distant future, but rather the content of tendencies existing and manifesting themselves today, both in revolutionary struggles and in everyday life. To understand this is to understand that, *for the worker, the ultimate problem of history is an everyday problem*. To grasp this is also to perceive that socialism is not "nationalization" or "planning" or even an "increase in the standard of living." It is to understand that the real crisis of capitalism is not due to "the anarchy of the market" or to "overproduction" or to "the falling rate of profit." Indeed, it is to see the tasks of theory and the function of a revolutionary organization in an entirely new way.

Pushed to their ultimate consequences, grasped in their full strength, these ideas transform our vision of society and the world. They modify our conception of theory as well as of revolutionary practice.

The first part of this text is devoted to the positive definition of socialism. The following part[2] concerns the analysis of capitalism and the crisis it is undergoing. This order, which might not appear very logical, may be justified by the fact that the Polish and Hungarian revolutions have made the question of the positive definition of the socialist organization of society an immediate practical question. This order of presentation also stems from another consideration. The very content of our ideas leads us to maintain that, ultimately, one cannot understand anything about the profound meaning of capitalism and the crisis it is undergoing unless one begins with the most total idea of socialism. For, all that we have to say can be reduced, in the last analysis, to this: Socialism is autonomy, people's conscious direction of their own lives. Capitalism—whether private or bureaucratic—is the ultimate negation of this autonomy, and its crisis stems from the fact that the system necessarily creates this drive toward autonomy, while simultaneously being compelled to suppress it.

THE ROOT OF THE CRISIS OF CAPITALISM

The capitalist organization of social life (we are speaking about private capitalism in the West and bureaucratic capitalism in the East) creates a perpetually renewed crisis in every sphere of human activity. This crisis appears most intensely in the realm of production.[3] In its essence, however, the situation is the same in all other fields, whether one is dealing with the family, education, international relations, politics, or culture. Everywhere, the capitalist structure of society consists of organizing people's lives *from the outside*, in the absence of those directly concerned and against their aspirations and interests. This is but another way of saying that capitalism divides society into a narrow stratum of directors (whose function is to decide and organize everyone's lives) and the vast majority of the population, who are reduced to carrying out (executing) the decisions made by these directors. As a result of this very fact, most people experience their own lives as something alien to them.

This pattern of organization is profoundly irrational and full of contradictions. Under it, repeated crises of one kind or another are absolutely inevitable. It is profoundly irrational to seek to organize people, either in production or in politics, as if they were mere objects, deliberately ignoring what they themselves think or wish about how they are to organize themselves. In real life, capitalism is obliged to base itself on people's capacity for self-organization, on the individual and collective creativity of the producers. Without making use of these abilities, the system could not survive for a day. But the whole "official" organization of modern society both ignores and seeks to suppress these abilities to the utmost. The result is not only an enormous waste due to untapped capacity. The system does more: It *necessarily* engenders opposition, a struggle against it by those upon whom it seeks to impose itself. Long before one can speak of revolution or political consciousness, people refuse in their everyday lives in the factory to be treated like objects. The capitalist organization of society is thereby compelled not only to structure itself in the *absence* of those most directly concerned but also *against* the interested parties. The net result is not only waste but perpetual conflict.

If a thousand individuals have among them a given capacity for self-organization, capitalism consists in more or less arbitrarily choosing fifty of these individuals, vesting them with managerial tasks, and deciding that the others should just be cogs. Metaphorically speaking, this is already a 95 percent loss of social initiative and drive. But there is more to it. As the 950 ignored individuals are *not* cogs, and as capitalism is obliged up to a point to base itself on their human capacities and in fact to develop them, these individuals will react and struggle against what the system imposes upon them. The organizational faculties they are not allowed to exercise *on behalf* of a social order that rejects them (and which they reject) are now utilized *against* that social order. A permanent struggle develops at the very heart of social life. It soon becomes the source of further waste. For, the main object of the activities of the narrow stratum of directors is henceforth not so much to organize the activity of the executants but to retaliate against the executants' struggle against the kind of organization imposed on them. The key function of the managerial apparatus ceases to be merely organizational and soon assumes all sorts of *coercive* aspects. Those in authority in a large modern factory in fact spend less of their time organizing production than putting down, directly or indirectly, the resistance of the exploited—whether it be a question of supervision, quality control, determining piece rates, calculating bonuses, "human relations," or discussions with shop stewards or union representatives. On top of all this there is of course the permanent preoccupation of those in power with making sure that everything is measurable, quantifiable, verifiable, and super-visable so as to deal in advance with any inventive counterreaction the workers might launch against new methods of exploitation. The same applies, with all due corrections, to the total overall organization of social life and to all the essential activities of any modern State.

The irrationality and contradictions of capitalism do not show up only in the way social life is organized. They appear even more clearly when one looks at the real *content* of the life this system proposes. More than any other social order, capitalism has put *labor* at the center of human activity—and more than any other regime capitalism makes of work something that is *absurd* (absurd not from the viewpoint of the philosopher or of the moralist, but from the point of view of those who have to perform it). What is challenged today is not only the "human organization" of work but its nature, its content, its methods, the very instruments and purpose of capitalist production. The two aspects are of course inseparable, but it is the second that needs to be stressed. As a result of the nature of work in a capitalist factory, and however it may be organized, the activity of the worker, instead of being the organic expression of his human faculties, turns into an alien and hostile process that dominates the subject of this process.

The proletarian is tied to this activity, to its regulating principles, to its concrete methods, and to its ultimate goals only by a thin (but unbreakable) thread: the need to earn a living. But this ensures that his work, even the day that is about to begin, dawns as something hostile. Work under capitalism therefore implies a permanent mutilation, a perpetual waste of creative capacity, and a constant struggle between the worker and his own activity, between what he would like to do and what he has to do.

From this angle, too, capitalism can survive only to the extent that reality does not yield to its methods and conform to its spirit. The system functions only to the extent that the "official" organization of production and of society is constantly resisted, thwarted, corrected, and completed by the effective self-organization of laboring people. Work processes can be effective under capitalism only to the extent that the real attitudes of workers toward their work differ from what is prescribed. Working people succeed in learning the general principles pertaining to their work—to which, according to the spirit of the system, they should have no access and concerning which the system seeks to keep them in the dark. They then apply these principles to the specific conditions in which they find themselves, whereas in theory this practical application can be spelled out only by the managerial apparatus.

Exploitative societies persist because those whom they exploit help them to survive. Slave-owning and feudal societies perpetuated themselves because ancient slaves and medieval serfs worked according to the norms set by the masters and lords of those societies. The proletariat enables capitalism to continue by acting *against* the system. Here we find the origin of the historical crisis of capitalism. And it is in this respect that capitalism is a society pregnant with revolutionary prospects. Slavery or serf society functioned as far as the exploited did not struggle against the system. But capitalism can function only insofar as those whom it exploits actively oppose everything the system seeks to impose upon them. The final outcome of this struggle is socialism, namely, the elimination of all externally imposed norms, methods, and patterns of organization and the total liberation of the creative and self-organizing capacities of the masses.

THE PRINCIPLES OF SOCIALIST SOCIETY

Socialist society implies people's self-organization of every aspect of their social activities. The instauration of socialism therefore entails the immediate abolition of the fundamental division of society into a class of directors and a class of executants.

The *content* of the socialist reorganization of society is first of all *workers' management*. The working class has repeatedly staked its claim to such management and struggled to achieve it at the high points of its historical actions: in Russia in 1917–1918, in Spain in 1936, in Hungary in 1956.

The *Council* of the enterprise's laboring people is the *form* of workers' management and the institution capable of realizing it. Workers' management means the power of the enterprise Councils and ultimately, at the level of society as a whole, the power of the *Central Assembly and Government of the Councils*. Factory councils or enterprise councils will be composed of representatives who are elected by the workers, responsible for reporting to them at regular intervals, and revocable by them at any time, and will unite the functions of deliberation, decision, and execution. Such councils are historic creations of the working class. They have come to the forefront every time the question of power has been posed in modern society. The Russian Factory Committees of 1917, the German Workers' Councils of 1919, the Hungarian Workers' Councils of 1956 all sought to express (whatever their name) the same original, organic, and characteristic working-class pattern of self-organization.

To define the socialist organization of society in concrete terms is to draw all the possible conclusions from two basic ideas: workers' management and the Government of the Councils, which are themselves the organic creations of the proletarian struggle. But such a definition can come to life and be given flesh and blood only if combined with an account of how the institutions of this society might function in practice.

There is no question for us here of trying to draw up "statutes" for socialist society. Statutes as such mean nothing. The best of statutes can have meaning only to the extent that people are permanently prepared to defend what is best in them, to make up what they lack, and to change whatever they may contain that has become inadequate or outdated. From this point of view, we obviously should condemn any fetishism for the "soviet" or "council" type of organization. The rules of "constant eligibility and revocability" are of themselves quite insufficient to "guarantee" that a council will remain the expression of laboring people. The council will remain such an expression for as long as people are prepared to do whatever may be necessary for it to remain so. The realization of socialism is not a question of better legislation. It depends on the autonomous action of the working class, on this class's capacity to find within itself the necessary awareness of ends and means, the necessary solidarity and determination.

But this autonomous mass action cannot remain amorphous, fragmented, and dispersed. It will find expression in patterns of action and forms of organization: in methods of operation and in institutions that adequately embody and express its purpose. Just as we must avoid the fetishism of "statutes," we should also condemn any sort of "anarchist" or "spontaneist" fetishism that, in the belief that proletarian consciousness ultimately will determine everything, takes little or no interest in the concrete organizational forms such consciousness should take if it wants to be effective in changing society. The council is not a *miraculous* institution. It cannot be a means for the workers to express themselves if the workers have not decided that they will express themselves through this medium. But the council is an *adequate* form of organization: Its whole structure is set up to enable this will to self-expression to come to the fore, when it exists. Parliamentary institutions, on the other hand, whether called the "National Assembly," the "U.S. Congress," or the "Supreme Soviet of the USSR"[4] are by definition types of institutions that cannot be socialist. They are founded on a radical separation between the masses, "consulted" from time to time, and those who are supposed to "represent" them, but who are in fact uncontrollable and irremovable. The Council is designed so as to represent laboring people, but may cease to fulfill this function. Parliament is designed not to represent the masses and so it *never* fulfills that function.

The question of the existence of adequate institutions is basic to socialist society. It is particularly important as socialism can be instaurated only through a revolution, that is to say, as the result of a social crisis in the course of which the consciousness and activity of the masses reach a state of extreme tension. Under these conditions, the masses become capable of sweeping away the ruling class, its armed forces, and its organizations, and of overcoming within themselves the heavy legacy of centuries of servitude. This state of affairs should be thought of not as some kind of paroxysm but, on the contrary, as the prefiguration of the level of both activity and awareness demanded of people in a free society. The "ebbing" of revolutionary activity has nothing inevitable about it. It will always remain a threat, however, given the sheer enormity of the tasks to be accomplished. Everything that adds to the innumerable problems facing revolutionary mass action will enhance the tendency to such a reflux. It is therefore essential that revolutionary society, from its very beginning, furnish itself with a network of institutions and methods of operation that both allow and favor the unfolding of the activity of the masses and that it abolish along the way everything that inhibits or thwarts this activity. It is essential, too, that revolutionary society should create for itself, at each step, those stable forms of organization that can most readily become effective normal mechanisms for the expression of popular will, both in "important matters" and in everyday life (which is, in truth, the *first and foremost* of all "important matters").

The definition of socialist society that we are attempting therefore requires of us some description of how we visualize its institutions and of the way they will function. This endeavor is not "utopian,"[5] for it is but the elaboration and extrapolation of the historical creations of the working class, and in particular of the concept of workers' management.

The guiding principle of our effort to elaborate the content of socialism is as follows: Workers' management will be possible only if individuals' attitudes to social organization alter radically. This in turn will take place only if the institutions embodying this organization become a *meaningful* part of their real daily lives. Just as work will have a meaning only when individuals *understand* and *dominate* it, so will the institutions of socialist society have to become *understandable* and *controllable*.[6]

Modern society is a dark and hidden jungle, a confusion of apparatuses, structures, and institutions whose workings no one, or almost no one, understands, and no one really dominates or takes any interest in. Socialist society will be possible only if it brings about a radical change in this state of affairs and massively simplifies social organization. Socialism implies that the *organization* of a society will have become transparent to its members.

To say that the workings and institutions of socialist society must be easy to understand implies that people must have a maximum of information. This "maximum of information" is something quite different from an enormous mass of data. The problem is not to equip everybody with a portable version of the Bibliothèque nationale or the Library of Congress. On the contrary, *the maximum of information* depends first and foremost on a *reduction of data to their essentials* so that they can readily be handled by everyone. This will be possible because socialism will result in an immediate and enormous simplification of problems and the disappearance, pure and simple, of four-fifths of current rules and regulations, which will have become quite meaningless. It will be facilitated by a systematic effort to gather and disseminate information [*connaissance*] about social reality, and to *present* facts both adequately and simply. Further on, when discussing the functioning of socialist economy, we will give examples of the enormous possibilities that already exist in this field.

Under socialism, people will dominate the workings and institutions of society, instead of being dominated by them. Socialism will therefore have to realize democracy for the first time in human history. Etymologically, the word "democracy" means *domination by the masses*. We are not concerned here with the formal aspects of the word "domination." Real domination must not be confused with voting. A vote, even a free vote, may only be—and often only is—a parody of democracy. Democracy is not the right to vote on secondary issues. It is not the right to appoint rulers who will then decide, without control from below, on all the essential questions. Nor does democracy lie in calling upon people to voice their opinions upon incomprehensible questions or upon questions that have no meaning for them. Real domination lies in one's being able to decide for oneself on all essential questions *in full knowledge of the relevant facts.* "In full knowledge of the relevant facts": in these few words lies the whole problem of democracy.[7] It is meaningless to ask people to voice their opinions if they are not aware of the relevant facts. This has long been stressed by the reactionary or fascist critics of bourgeois "democracy," and even by the most cynical Stalinist.[8] It is obvious that bourgeois democracy is a farce, if only because literally *nobody* in capitalist society can express an opinion in knowledge of the relevant facts, least of all the mass of the people from whom political and economic realities, and the real meaning of the questions asked, are systematically hidden. But the answer is not to vest power in the hands of a few incompetent and uncontrollable bureaucrats. The answer is to transform social reality in such a way that essential data and fundamental problems can be grasped by individuals, enabling everyone to express opinions in full knowledge of the relevant facts.

To decide means to decide for oneself. To decide who is to decide already is not quite deciding for oneself. The only total form of democracy is therefore *direct democracy*. And the enterprise Council exercises authority and replaces the enterprise's General Assembly only when the latter is not in session.[9]

To achieve the widest, the most meaningful direct democracy will require that all the economic, political, and other structures of society be articulated around grassroots cells that are concrete collectivities, organic social units. Direct democracy certainly requires the physical presence of citizens in a given place, when decisions have to be made. But this is not enough. It also requires that these citizens form an organic community, that they live in the same milieu, that they be familiar through their daily experience with the subjects to be discussed and with the problems to be tackled. It is only in such units that the political participation of individuals can become total, that people can know and feel that their involvement will have an effect, and that the real life of the community is, in large part, determined by its own members and not by unknown or external authorities who decide for them. There must therefore be the maximum amount of autonomy and self-administration for the social cells.

Modern social life has already created these collectivities and continues to create them. They are based on medium-sized or large enterprises and are to be found in industry, transportation, commerce, banking, insurance, and public administration, where people by the hundreds, thousands, or tens of thousands spend the main part of their life harnessed to a common task, where they encounter society in its most concrete form. A place of work is not only a unit of production: it has become the primary unit of social life for the vast majority of individuals.[10] Instead of basing itself on territorial units, which economic developments have rendered completely artificial—save precisely when it has maintained an existing unit of production there or endowed them with a new production unit, as with a village, on one end of the spectrum, and a single-company or one-industry town, on the other end—the political structure of socialism will be largely articulated around collectivities of laborers involved in common work. Such collectivities will be the fertile soil on which direct democracy can flourish, as the ancient city or the democratic communities of free farmers in the United States of the nineteenth century were in their times, and for similar reasons.

Direct democracy gives an idea of the amount of *decentralization* socialist society will be able to achieve. But this democratic society will have to find a means of democratically *integrating* these grassroots units into the social fabric as a whole as well as achieving the necessary degree of *centralization*, without which the life of a modern nation would collapse.

It is not centralization as such that has brought about political alienation in modern societies or that has led to the expropriation of the power of the many for the benefit of the few. It comes rather from the constitution of separate, uncontrollable bodies, exclusively and specifically concerned with the task of centralization. As long as centralization is conceived of as the independent function of an independent apparatus, bureaucracy and bureaucratic rule will indeed be inseparable from centralization. But in a socialist society there will be no conflict between centralization and the autonomy of grassroots bodies, insofar as both functions will be exercised by the same bodies. There will be no separate apparatus whose function it will be to reunite what it has itself fragmented; this absurd task (need we recall it) is precisely the "function" of a bureaucracy.

Monstrous centralization is a feature of all modern exploitative societies. The intimate links between centralization and totalitarian bureaucratic rule *in such class societies* provoke a healthy and understandable aversion to centralization among many people. But this response is often confused, and at times it reinforces the very things it seeks to correct. "Centralization, there's the root of all evil" proclaim many honest militants as they break with Stalinism in France as well as in Poland or Hungary. But this formulation, at best ambiguous, becomes positively harmful when it leads—as it often does—either to formal demands for the "fragmentation of power" or to demands for a limitless extension of the powers of local or enterprise organs, neglecting what is happening at the center. When Polish militants, for instance, imagine they have found the way to abolish bureaucracy when they advocate a social life organized and directed by "several centers" (the state administration, a parliamentary assembly, the trade unions, workers' councils, and political parties), they are arguing beside the point. They fail to see that this "polycentrism" is equivalent to the absence of any real and identifiable center, controlled from below. And as modern society has to make certain central decisions, the "constitution" they propose will exist only on paper. It will serve only to hide the reemergence of a real, but this time masked (and therefore all the more formidable), "center" from amid the ranks of the state and political bureaucracy. The reason is obvious: If one fragments any body accomplishing a significant or vital function, one only creates ten times over an enhanced need for some other body to reassemble the fragments. Similarly, if, in principle or in fact, one merely advocates extending the power of local councils to the level of the individual enterprise, one is thereby handing them over to domination by a central bureaucracy that alone would "know" or "understand" how to make the economy function as a whole (and modern economies, whether one likes it or not, *do* function as a whole). To refuse to face up to the question of central power is tantamount to leaving the solution of these problems to some bureaucracy or other.

Socialist society therefore will have to provide a socialist solution to the problem of centralization. This answer can only be the assumption of power by a Federation of Councils and the institution of a Central Assembly of Councils and of a Government of the Councils. We will see further on that such an assembly and such a government do not signify a *delegation* of the masses' power but are, on the contrary, an *expression* of that power. At this stage we only want to discuss the principles that will govern the relationship of such bodies to councils and social communities. These principles affect in several ways the functioning of all institutions in a socialist society.

In a society where the population has been robbed of political power and where this power is in the hands of a centralizing authority, the essential relationship between this authority and its subordinate organs (and ultimately, the population) can be summed up as follows: Channels of communication from the base to the summit transmit only *information*, whereas channels from the summit to the base transmit *decisions* (plus, perhaps, that minimum of information deemed necessary for the understanding and proper execution of the decisions made at the summit). The whole setup expresses not only a monopoly of power by the summit—a monopoly of decision-making authority—but also a monopoly of the *conditions* necessary for the exercise of power. The summit alone has the "sum total" of information needed to evaluate and decide. In modern society it can only be by accident that any individual or body gains access to information other than that relating to his or its immediate milieu. The system seeks to avoid, or at any rate it does not encourage, such "accidents."

When we say that in a socialist society the central power will not constitute a delegation of power but will be the expression of the power of the masses, we are implying a radical change in this way of doing things. Two-way communications will be instaurated between the "base" and the "summit." One of the essential tasks of central bodies, including the council government, will be to collect, transmit, and disseminate information conveyed to them by local groups. In all essential fields, decisions will be made at the grassroots and will be sent back up to the "summit," whose responsibility it will be to ensure their execution or to carry them out itself. A two-way flow of information and decisions thus will be instaurated and this will not only apply to relations between the government and the councils but will also be a model for relations among all institutions and those who participate in them.[11]

SOCIALISM IS THE TRANSFORMATION OF WORK

Socialism can be instaured only by the autonomous action of the working class; it *is* nothing other than this autonomous action. Socialist society is nothing other than the self-organization of this autonomy. Socialism both presupposes this autonomy and helps to develop it.

But if this autonomy is people's conscious domination over what they do and what they produce, clearly it cannot merely be a *political* autonomy. Political autonomy is but a derivative aspect of the inherent content and the basic problem of socialism: the instauration of people's domination over their primary activity, the work process. We deliberately say *instauration* and not *restoration*, for never in history has this kind of domination existed. All comparisons with historical antecedents (for instance, with the situation of the artisan or of the free peasant), however fruitful they may be in some respects, have only a limited scope and risk leading one into a backward-looking type of utopian thinking.

A purely political autonomy would be meaningless. One cannot imagine a society where people would be slaves in production every day of the week and then enjoy Sundays of political freedom.[12] The idea that socialist production or a socialist economy could be run, at any political level, by "technicians" supervised by councils, or by soviets or by any other body "incarnating the political power of the working class" is pure nonsense. *Real* power in any such society would rapidly fall into the hands of those who managed production. The councils or soviets sooner or later would wither away amid the general indifference of the population. People would stop devoting time, interest, or activity to institutions that no longer really determined the pattern of their lives.

Autonomy is therefore meaningless unless it implies *workers' management*, that is, unless it involves organized workers determining the production process themselves at the level of the shop, the plant, entire industries, and the economy as a whole. It cannot remain external to the structure of work itself. It does not mean keeping work as it is and just replacing the bureaucratic apparatus that currently manages production with a council of laboring people—however democratic or revocable such a council might be. It means that, for the whole set of laboring people, new relations will have to be instaurated with their work and about their work. The very *content* of work will immediately have to be altered.

Today the purpose, means, methods, and rhythms of work are determined from the outside by a bureaucratic managerial apparatus. This apparatus can manage only through resort to abstract, universal rules determined "once and for all." Inevitably, though, they are revised periodically with each new "crisis" in the organization of the production process. These rules cover such matters as production norms, technical specifications, rates of pay, bonuses, and the organization of production areas. Once the bureaucratic managerial apparatus has been eliminated, this way of regulating production will be unable to continue, either in its form or its substance.

In accordance with the deepest aspirations of the working class, production "norms" (in their present meaning) will be abolished, and complete equality in wages will be instituted. Taken together, these measures mean the abolition of economic coercion and constraint in production—except in the most general form of "those who do not work do not eat"—as a form of discipline externally imposed by a specific coercive apparatus. *Labor discipline* will be the discipline imposed by each group of workers upon its own members, by each shop upon the groups that make it up, by each enterprise Assembly upon its shops and departments. The *integration* of particular individual activities into a whole will be accomplished basically by the cooperation of various groups of workers or shops. It will be the object of the workers' permanent and ongoing coordinating activity. The essential *universality* of modern production will be freed from the concrete experience of particular jobs and will be formulated by meetings of workers.

Workers' management is therefore not the "supervision" of a bureaucratic managerial apparatus by representatives of the workers. Nor is it the replacement of this apparatus by another, similar one made up of individuals of working-class origin. It is the *abolition* of *any* separate managerial apparatus and the restitution of the functions of such an apparatus to the community of workers. The enterprise council is not a new managerial apparatus. It is but one of the places in which coordination takes place, a "local meeting area [*permanence*]" from which contacts between the enterprise and the outside world are regulated.

If this is achieved, it will imply that the nature and content of work are already beginning to be transformed. Today work consists essentially in obeying instructions initiated elsewhere, the direction of this activity having been removed from the executants' control. Workers' management will mean the reunification of the *functions* of direction and execution.

But even this is insufficient—or rather it does and will immediately lead beyond mere reunification. By restituting to the workers the functions of direction, they necessarily will be led to tackle what is today at the *core* of alienation, namely, the *technological structure* of work, its objects, its tools and methods, which ensure that work dominates the workers instead of being dominated by them. This problem will not be solved by the workers overnight, but its solution will be the task of that historical period we call *socialism*. Socialism is first and foremost the solution to *this problem*. Between capitalism and communism there are not thirty-six different types of "transitional society," as some have sought to make us believe. There is but one: socialist society. And the main characteristic of this society is not "the development of the productive forces" or "the increasing satisfaction of consumer needs" or "an increase in political freedom." The hallmark of socialism is the *transformation it will bring about in the nature and content of work*, through the conscious and deliberate transformation of an inherited technology. For the first time in history, technology will be subordinated to human needs (not only to the people's needs as consumers but also to their needs as *producers*).

The socialist revolution will allow this process to begin. Its realization will mark the entry of humanity into the communist era. All other things—politics, consumption, etc.—are consequences, conditions, implications, and presuppositions that certainly must be looked at in their organic unity, but which can acquire such a unity or meaning only through their relation to this central problem: the transformation of work itself. Human freedom will remain an illusion and a mystification if it doesn't mean freedom in people's fundamental activity: their productive activity. And this freedom will not be a gift bestowed by nature. It will not arise automatically, by increments or out of other developments. People will have to create it consciously. In the last analysis, this is the content of socialism.

Important practical consequences pertaining to the *immediate* tasks of a socialist revolution follow from these considerations. Changing the nature of work will be tackled from both ends. On the one hand, the development of people's human capacities and faculties will have to become the revolution's highest priority. This will imply the systematic dismantling, stone by stone, of what remains of the edifice of the division of labor. On the other hand, people will have to give a whole new orientation to technical developments and to how such developments should be applied in the production process.

These are but two aspects of the same thing: man's relationship to technique. Let us start by looking at the second, more tangible point: technical development as such.

As a first approximation, one could say that capitalist technology (the current application of technique to production) is rotten to the core, not only because it does not help people dominate their work, but also because its main aim is exactly the opposite. Socialists often say that what is basically wrong with capitalist technology is that it seeks to develop production for purposes of profit, or that it develops production for production's sake, independently of human needs (people being conceived of, in these arguments, only as potential consumers of products). The same socialists then tell us that the purpose of socialism is to adapt production to the real consumer needs of society, in relation both to the volume and to the nature of the goods produced.

Of course, all this is true. But the fundamental problem lies elsewhere. Capitalism does not utilize a socially neutral technology for capitalist ends. Capitalism has created capitalist technology, which is by no means neutral. The real intention of capitalist technology is not to develop production for production's sake: It is to subordinate and dominate the producers. Capitalist technology is characterized, essentially, by its drive to eliminate the human element in productive labor and, in the long run, to eliminate man altogether from the productive process. That here, as everywhere else, capitalism fails to fulfill its deepest tendency—and that it would fall to pieces if it achieved its purpose—does not affect the argument. On the contrary, it only highlights another aspect of the crisis of this contradictory system.

Capitalism cannot count on the voluntary cooperation of the producers. On the contrary, it constantly runs up against their hostility (or at best indifference) to the production process. This is why it is *essential* for the machine to impose *its* rhythm on the work process. Where this is not possible capitalism seeks at least to measure the work performed. In every productive process, work *must* therefore be definable, quantifiable, supervisable from the outside—otherwise this process has no meaning for capitalism. As long as capitalism cannot dispense with the producers altogether, it *has to* make them as interchangeable as possible and reduce their work to its simplest expression, that of unskilled labor power. There is no conspiracy or conscious plot behind all this. There is only a process of "natural selection," affecting technical inventions as they are applied to industry. Some are preferred to others and are, on the whole, more widely utilized. These are the ones that fit in with capitalism's basic need to deal with labor power as a measurable, supervisable, and interchangeable commodity.

There is no capitalist chemistry or capitalist physics as such. There is not even a specifically capitalist "technique," in the general sense of the word. There certainly is, however, a capitalist *technology*, if by this one means that of the "spectrum" of techniques available at a given point in time (as determined by the development of science) a given group (or "band") of processes actually will be selected. From the moment the development of science permits a choice of several possible procedures, a society will regularly choose those methods that have a meaning for it, that are "rational" within the framework of its own class logic. But the "rationality" of an exploitative society is not the rationality of socialism.[13] The conscious transformation of technology will therefore be the central task of a society of free workers. Correspondingly, the analysis of alienation and crisis in capitalist society ought to begin with this central core of all social relations, which is found in the concrete relation of production, people's relations in work, as seen in its three indissociable aspects: the relation of the workers to the means and objects of production, workers' relations among themselves, and the relation of the workers to the managerial apparatus of the production process.

Marx, as is well known, was the first to go beyond the surface of the economic phenomena of capitalism (market, competition, distribution) and to tackle the analysis of the central area of capitalist social relations: the concrete relations of production in the capitalist factory. But volume one of *Capital* is still awaiting its sequel. The most striking feature of the degeneration of the Marxist movement is that this particular concern of Marx's, the most fundamental of all, was soon abandoned, even by the best of Marxists, in favor of an analysis of "important" phenomena. Through this very fact, these analyses were either totally distorted, or ended up dealing with very partial aspects of reality, thereby leading to judgments that proved catastrophically wrong.[14] Thus it is striking to see Rosa Luxemburg entitle two large volumes *The Accumulation of Capital*, in which she totally ignores what this process of accumulation really signifies in the concrete relations of production. Her concern in these volumes was solely with the possibility of an overall equilibrium between production and consumption, and she finally came to believe that she had discovered in capitalism a process of automatic collapse (an idea, needless to say, that is concretely false and a priori absurd). It is just as striking to see Lenin, in his *Imperialism*, start from the correct and fundamental observation that the concentration of capital has reached the stage of domination by monopolies—and yet neglect the transformation in the capitalist factory's relations of production that results precisely from such concentration. At the same time, he ignored the crucial phenomenon of the constitution of an enormous apparatus managing production, which was henceforth to incarnate exploitation. He preferred to see the main consequences of the concentration of capital in the transformation of capitalists into "coupon-clipping" rentiers. The workers' movement is still paying the consequences of this way of looking at things. Insofar as ideas play a role in history, Khrushchev is in power in Russia as a by-product of the conception that exploitation can take the form only of coupon clipping.

But we must go back even further. We must go back to Marx himself. Marx shed a great deal of light on the alienation the producer experiences in the course of the capitalist production process and on the enslavement of man by the mechanical universe he has created. But Marx's analysis is at times incomplete in that he sees *only* alienation in all this. In *Capital*—as opposed to Marx's early writings—it is hardly brought out at all that the worker is (and can *only be*) the *positive* vehicle of capitalist production, which is obliged to base itself on him *as such*, and to *develop* him *as such*, while simultaneously seeking to reduce him to an automaton and, at the limit, to drive him out of production altogether. Because of this, the analysis fails to perceive that the primary crisis of capitalism is the crisis at the point of production, due to the simultaneous existence of two contradictory tendencies, neither of which could disappear without the whole system collapsing. Marx shows in capitalism "despotism in the workshop and anarchy in society"—instead of seeing it as *both* despotism *and* anarchy in *both* workshop *and* society. This leads him to look for the crisis of capitalism not in production itself (except insofar as capitalist production develops "oppression, misery, degradation, but also revolt," and the numerical strength and discipline of the proletariat), but in such factors as overproduction and the falling rate of profit. Marx therefore fails to see that as long as *this type of work* persists, this crisis will persist with all it entails, and this not only whatever the system of property but also whatever the nature of the State, and finally whatever even the system of *management* of production.

In certain passages of *Capital*, Marx is thus led to see in modern production *only* the fact that the producer is mutilated and reduced to a "fragment of a man"—which is true, *as much as the contrary*—and, what is more serious, to link this aspect to modern production and finally to *production as such*, instead of linking it to *capitalist technology*. Marx implies that the basis of this state of affairs is modern production as such, a stage in the development of technique about which nothing can be done, the famous "realm of necessity." Thus the takeover of society by the producers—socialism—at times comes to mean for Marx only an external change in political and economic *management*, a change that would leave intact the structure of work and simply reform its more "inhuman" aspects. This idea is clearly expressed in the famous passage of volume three of *Capital*, where Marx, speaking of socialist society, says,

> In fact, the realm of freedom actually begins only where labor which is determined by necessity and mundane consideration ceases; thus, in the very nature of things it lies beyond the sphere of actual material production.... Freedom in this field can only consist in socialized man, the associated producers, rationally regulating their interchange with Nature, bringing it under their common control, instead of being ruled by it ... and achieving this with the least expenditure of energy and under conditions most favorable to, and worthy of their human nature. But it nonetheless still remains a realm of necessity. Beyond it begins ... the true realm of freedom, which, however, can blossom forth only with this realm of necessity as its basis. The shortening of the working day is its basic prerequisite.[15]

If it is true that "the realm of freedom actually begins only where labor which is determined by *necessity* and *mundane considerations* ceases," it is strange to read from the pen of the man who wrote that "industry is the open book of human faculties" that freedom *"thus"* could be found only outside of *labor*. The proper conclusion, which Marx himself draws in certain other places, is that the realm of freedom begins when labor becomes *free activity*, both in what motivates it and in its content. In the current way of looking at things, however, freedom is what is not work, it is what surrounds work, it is either "free time" (reduction of the working day) or "rational regulation" and "common control" of exchanges with Nature, which minimize human effort and preserve human dignity. In this perspective the shortening of the working day certainly becomes a "basic prerequisite," as mankind would be free only in its leisure.

The reduction of the working day is in fact important, not for this reason however, but because it will allow people to achieve a balance between their various types of activity. And, at the limit, the "ideal" (communism) is not the reduction of the working day to zero, but the free determination by each of the nature and extent of his work. Socialist society will be able to reduce the length of the working day, and will have to do so, but this will not be its fundamental preoccupation. Its first task will be to tackle "the realm of necessity" *as such*, to transform the very nature of work. The problem is not to leave more and more "free" time to individuals—which might well be only *empty* time—so that they may fill it at will with "poetry" or the carving of wood. The problem is to make all time a time of liberty and to allow concrete freedom to embody itself in creative activity. The problem is to put poetry into work.[16] Production is not something negative that has to be limited as much as possible for mankind to fulfill itself in its leisure. The instauration of autonomy is also—and in the first place—the instauration of autonomy in work.

Underlying the idea that freedom is to be found "outside the sphere of actual material production" there lies a double error: first, that the very nature of technique and of modern production renders inevitable the domination of the productive process over the producer, *in the course of* his work; second, that technique and in particular modern technique follows an autonomous development, before which one can only bow down. Modern technique would moreover possess the double attribute of, on the one hand, constantly reducing the human role in production and, on the other hand, of constantly increasing the productivity of labor. From these two inexplicably combined attributes would result a miraculous dialectic of technical progress: More and more a slave *in the course of* work, man would be in a position to reduce enormously the *length* of work, if only he could succeed in organizing society rationally.

We have already shown, however, that there is not an autonomous development of technique in its application to the production process, that is, of technology. Of the sum total of technologies that scientific and technical development makes possible at any given point in time, capitalist society brings to fulfillment those ones that correspond most closely to its class structure and that best permit capital to struggle against labor. It is generally believed that the application of this or that invention to production depends on its economic profitability. But there is no such thing as a neutral economic "profitability": The class struggle in the factory is the main factor determining "profitability." A given invention will be preferred to another by a factory management if, other things being equal, it enhances the "independent" progress of production, freeing it from interference by the producers. The increasing enslavement of people in production flows essentially from *this* process, and not from some mysterious curse, inherent in a given phase of technological development. There is, moreover, no magic dialectic of slavery and productivity: Productivity increases as a function of the enormous scientific and technical advancements that are at the basis of modern production—and it increases *despite* the slavery, and not because of it. Slavery implies an *enormous* amount of waste, due to the fact that people only contribute to production an infinitesimal fraction of their potential abilities. (We are passing no a priori judgment on what these faculties might be. However low they may estimate these faculties, [Renault Chief Executive Officer] Mr. [Pierre] Dreyfus and Mr. Khrushchev would have to admit that their own particular ways of organizing production only tap an infinitesimal fraction of their potential.)

Socialist society, therefore, will not be afflicted with any kind of technical curse. Having abolished bureaucratic-capitalist relations, it will tackle at the same time the technological structure of production, which is both the basis of these relationships and their ever-renewed product.

WORKERS' MANAGEMENT OF THE BUSINESS ENTERPRISE

It is well known that workers can organize their own work at the level of a workshop or department. Bourgeois industrial sociologists not only recognize this fact but point out that "primary groups" of workers often get on with their job better if management leaves them alone and doesn't constantly try to "direct" them.[17]

How can the work of these various "primary groups"—or of various shops and sections—be coordinated? Bourgeois theoreticians stress that the present managerial apparatus, whose formal job it is to ensure such coordination, is not really up to the task: It has no real grip on the producers and is itself torn by internal conflicts. But, having "demolished" the present setup by their criticisms, these modern industrial sociologists have nothing to put in its place. And because beyond the "primary" organization of production there has to be a "secondary" organization, they finally fall back on the existing bureaucratic apparatus, exhorting it "to understand," "to improve itself," "to trust people more," and so on.[18] The same can be said, at another level, of "democratically reformed" or "de-Stalinized" Russian leaders.[19] What no one seems prepared to recognize (or even to admit) is the capacity of working people to manage their own affairs outside a very narrow radius. The bureaucratic mind cannot see in the mass of workers employed in an enterprise an active subject, capable of managing and organizing. In the eyes of those in authority, both East and West, as soon as one gets beyond a group of ten, fifteen, or twenty individuals the crowd begins—the mob, the thousand-headed Hydra that cannot act collectively, or that could act collectively only in a display of collective delirium or hysteria. They believe that only a managerial apparatus specifically designed for this purpose, and endowed of course with coercive functions, can master and "organize" this mass.

The inconsistencies and shortcomings of the present managerial apparatus are such that even today individual workers or "primary groups" are obliged to take on quite a number of coordinating tasks.[20] Moreover, historical experience shows that the working class is quite capable of managing whole enterprises. In Spain, in 1936 and 1937, workers had no difficulty running the factories. In Budapest, in 1956, according to the accounts of Hungarian refugees, big bakeries employing hundreds of workers carried on during and immediately after the insurrection. They worked better than ever before, under workers' self-management. Many such examples could be cited.

Summary of pp. 23-30:

After having described the various functions of the capitalist enterprise's managerial apparatus—(a) coercive; (b) "general services" of all sorts; (c) "technical"; (d) "top managerial"—the author examines what aspects will disappear or will be resumed in another form within the framework of workers' management of the enterprise, while looking more particularly into the issue of the relations between workers and technical staff. On this matter, the author does not believe in the possibility of a major conflict between the "workers' power" in the factory and the technical staff. As for truly managerial functions, some are destined to disappear with the change in nature of the economic system. Others, like coordination among the various sectors of the enterprise and proposals "about the present or future role of the enterprise in the overall development of the economy," will revert to two bodies in the enterprise.

All managerial tasks will be carried out by two organs:

a) A Council composed of delegates from the various shops and offices, all of them elected and instantly revocable. In an enterprise of, say, 5,000 to 10,000 workers, such a council might number 30-50 people. The delegates will remain at their jobs. They will meet in full session as often as experience proves it necessary (probably on one or two half-days a week). They will report back each time to their workmates in shop or office—and anyway they already will have discussed with them the agenda. Rotating groups of delegates will ensure continuity. One of the main tasks will be to ensure liaison and to act as a continuous regulating locus between the enterprise and the "outside world."

b) The General Assembly *of all those who work in the plant, whether manual workers, office workers, or technicians. This will be the highest decision-making body for all problems concerning the enterprise as a whole. Differences or conflicts between various sectors of the enterprise will be thrashed out at this level.*

This General Assembly will embody the restoration of direct democracy into what should, in modern society, be its basic unit: the place of work. [. . .] The Assembly will meet regularly, say, one or two days each month. There will, in addition, exist procedures for calling such general assemblies, if this is wanted by a given number of workers, shops, or delegates (p. 28).

As for the tasks workers' management in the enterprise will have to accomplish, one must distinguish between a "static" aspect and a "dynamic" one. First, the "static" aspect. The plan sets for an enterprise, for a given period of time, targets and means. Now, between these targets and these means, there is a "process of concrete elaboration" that "only the workers of the particular enterprise can carry out," for these targets and these means "do not automatically or exhaustively define all the possible methods that could be used." This concrete elaboration is "the first area in which workers will exercise their autonomy," "an important field but a limited one," for it is obvious that the workers can only participate in the determination of targets and means; they cannot determine them fully in autonomous fashion. But there is also a "dynamic aspect" to this question.

Let us now take a look at workers' management in its dynamic aspect, that is, the function of workers' management in *developing and transforming* socialist production. More precisely, let us look at how the development and transformation of socialist production will become the *primary objective* of workers' management. Everything we have suggested so far will now have to be reexamined. In this way we will see how the limits to autonomy will gradually be pushed back.

The change will be most obvious in relation to the *means* of production. As we have said, socialist society will attack the problem of how to consciously transform the technology it has inherited from capitalism. Under capitalism, production equipment—and more generally, the means of production—are planned and manufactured *independently* of the user and of his preferences (manufacturers, of course, pretend to take the user's viewpoint into account, but this has little to do with the real user: the worker on the shop floor). But equipment is made to be used productively. The viewpoint of the "productive consumers" (i.e., those who will *use* the equipment to *produce* the goods) is of primary importance. As the views of those who *make* the equipment are also important, the problem of the structure of the means of production will be solved only by the vital cooperation of these two categories of workers. In an integrated factory, this involves permanent contacts between the corresponding shops. At the level of the economy as a whole, it will have to take place through the instauration of normal, permanent contacts between factories and between sectors of production. (This problem is *distinct* from that of overall planning. General planning is concerned with determining a quantitative framework—so much steel and so many hours of labor at one end, so many consumer goods at the other. It does not have to intervene in the form or the type of intermediate products.) Cooperation necessarily will take two forms. The choice and popularization of the best methods, and the standardization and rationalization of their use, will be achieved through the *horizontal* cooperation of Councils, organized according to branch or sector of industry (for instance, textiles, the chemical industry, engineering, electrical supply, etc.). On the other hand, the integration of the viewpoints of those who make and of those who utilize equipment (or, more generally, of those who make and those who utilize intermediate products) will require the *vertical* cooperation of Councils representing the successive stages of a productive process (the steel industry, and the machine-tool and engineering industries, for instance). In both cases, cooperation will have to be organized on a permanent basis through Committees of enterprise council representatives (or wider Conferences of producers) organized both horizontally and vertically.

Considering the problem from this dynamic angle—which ultimately is the only important one—we see at once that the terrain for exercising autonomy has expanded considerably. Already at the level of individual enterprises (but more significantly at the level of cooperation between enterprises), the producers are beginning to influence the structure of the means of production. They are, thereby, reaching a position where they are beginning to dominate the work process: They are not only determining its methods but are now also modifying its technological structure.

This fact now begins to alter what we have just said about *targets*. Three-quarters of gross modern production consists of intermediate products, of "means of production" in the broadest sense. When producers and users of intermediate products decide together about the means of production, they are participating in a very direct and immediate way in decisions about the objectives of production. The remaining limitation, and it is an important one, flows from the fact that these means of production (whatever their exact nature) are destined, in the last analysis, to produce consumer goods. And the overall volume of these can be determined only in general terms, by the plan.

But here, too, looking at things dynamically radically alters one's vision. Modern consumption is characterized by the constant appearance of new products. Factories producing consumer goods will conceive of, receive suggestions about, study, and finally produce such products.

This raises the broader problem of contact between producers and consumers. Capitalist society rests on a complete separation of these two aspects of human activity and on the exploitation of the consumer *qua* consumer. There isn't just monetary exploitation (through overcharging) and limitations on one's income. Capitalism claims that it can satisfy the masses' needs better than any other system in history. But in fact capitalism, if it does not determine these needs themselves, decides upon the method of satisfying them. Consumer preference is only one of numerous variables that can be manipulated by modern sales techniques. The division between producers and consumers appears most glaringly in relation to the *quality* of goods. This problem is insoluble in any exploitative society as Daniel Mothé's dialogue between the human-worker and the robot-worker shows: "Do you believe this dimension is important?—It's just going into the wall."[21] Those who look only at the surface of things see only a commodity as a commodity. They don't see in it a crystallized moment of the class struggle. They see faults or defects, instead of seeing in them the resultant of the worker's constant struggle with himself. Faults or defects embody the worker's struggles against exploitation. They also embody squabbles between different sections of the bureaucracy managing the plant.

The elimination of exploitation will of itself bring about a change in all this. At work, people will begin to assert their claims as future consumers of what they are producing. In its early phases, however, socialist society will undoubtedly have to instaurate regular forms of contact (other than "the market") between producers and consumers.

We have assumed, as a starting point for all this, the division of labor inherited from present-day capitalism. But we have also pointed out that, from the very beginning, socialist society cannot survive unless it demolishes this division. This is an enormous subject with which we cannot even begin to deal in this text. Nevertheless, the first benchmarks of a solution can be seen even today. Modern production has destroyed many traditional professional qualifications. It has created universal automatic or semiautomatic machines. It has thereby itself demolished on its own the traditional framework for the industrial division of labor. It has given birth to a universal worker who is capable, after a relatively short apprenticeship, of using most existing machines. Once one gets beyond its class aspects, the "posting" of workers to particular jobs in a big modern enterprise corresponds less and less to a genuine division of *labor* and more and more to a simple division of tasks. Workers are not allocated to given areas of the productive process and then riveted to them because their "occupational skills" invariably correspond to the "skills required" by management. They are placed here rather than there because putting a particular worker in a particular place at a particular time happens to suit the personnel officer—or the foreman—or, more prosaically, just because a particular vacancy happened to exist. Under socialism, factories would have no reason to accept the artificially rigid division of labor now prevailing. There will be every reason to encourage a rotation of workers *between shops and departments*—and between production and office areas. Such a rotation will greatly help workers to participate actively in the management of production in full knowledge of the relevant facts as more and more workers develop firsthand familiarity with what goes on in a growing number of shops. The same applies to rotation of workers (*between various enterprises*, and in particular between "producing" and "utilizing" units).

The residues of capitalism's division of labor gradually will have to be eliminated. This overlaps with the general problem of education not only of generations to come but of those adults who were brought up under the previous system. We cannot go into this problem here.

SIMPLIFICATION AND RATIONALIZATION
OF GENERAL ECONOMIC PROBLEMS

The functioning of the socialist economy implies that the producers themselves will consciously manage all economic activity. This management will be exercised at all levels, and in particular at the overall or central level. It is completely illusory to believe that either a central bureaucracy left to itself or even a bureaucracy "controlled" by the workers could guide the economy toward socialism. Such a bureaucracy could only lead society toward new forms of exploitation. It is also wrong to think that "automatic" objective mechanisms could be established that, like the automatic pilot of a modern jet airplane, could at each moment direct the economy in the desired direction. It is just as impossible for an "enlightened" bureaucracy, the mechanisms of a "true market" (supposedly restored to its pristine and original, precapitalist, purity), or the regulatory control afforded by some electronic supercomputer to achieve such an ideal end. Any plan presupposes a fundamental decision on the rate of growth of the economy, and this in turn depends essentially on decisions concerning the distribution of the social product between investment and consumption.[22]

Now, there is no "objective" rational basis for determining how to distribute the social product. A decision to invest zero percent of the social product is neither more nor less objectively rational than a decision to invest 90 percent of it. The only rationality in the matter is the choice people make about their own fate, in full knowledge of the relevant facts. The fixing of plan targets by those who will have to fulfill them is, in the last analysis, the only guarantee of their willing and spontaneous participation and hence of an effective mobilization of individuals around both the management and the expansion of the economy.

But this does not mean that the plan and the management of the economy are "just political matters." Socialist planning will base itself on certain rational technical factors. It is in fact the only type of planning that could integrate such factors into a conscious management of the economy. These factors consist of a number of extremely useful and effective "labor-saving" and "thought-saving" devices that can be used to simplify the representation of the economy and its laws, thereby allowing the problems of central economic management to be made accessible to all. Workers' management of production (this time at the level of the economy as a whole and not just at the level of a particular factory) will be possible only if management tasks have been enormously simplified, so that the producers and their collective organs are in a position to judge the key issues in an informed way. What is needed, in other words, is for the vast chaos of today's economic facts and relations to be boiled down to certain propositions that adequately sum up the real problems and choices. These propositions should be few in number. They should be easy to grasp. They should summarize reality without distortion or mystification. If they can do this, they will form an adequate basis for meaningful judgments. A condensation of this type is *possible*, first, because there is at least a rational outline to the economy; second, because there already exist today certain techniques allowing one to grasp the complexities of economic reality; and finally, because it is now possible to mechanize and to automate all that does not pertain to human decisions in the strict sense.

A discussion of the relevant devices, techniques, and possibilities is therefore indispensable, starting right now. They enable us to carry out a vast clearing of ground. Without them, workers' management would collapse under the weight of the very subject matter it ought to be getting a handle on. The content of such a discussion is in no sense a "purely technical" one, and at each stage we will be guided by the general principles already outlined here.

The "Plan Factory"
A production plan, whether it deals with one factory or the economy as a whole, is a type of reasoning (made up of a great number of secondary arguments). It can be boiled down to two premises and one conclusion. The two premises are the material means initially at one's disposal (equipment, stocks, labor, etc.) and the target one is aiming at (production of so many specified objects and services, within a given period of time). We will refer to these premises as the "*initial conditions*" and the "*ultimate target.*" The "conclusion" is the path to be followed from initial conditions to ultimate target. In practice this means a certain number of intermediate products to be made within a given period. We will call these conclusions the "*intermediate targets.*"

When passing from simple initial conditions to a simple ultimate target, the intermediate targets can be determined right away. As the initial conditions or the ultimate targets (or both) become more complex, or are more spread out in time, the establishment of intermediate targets becomes more difficult. In the case of the economy as a whole (where there are thousands of different products, many of which can be made by several different processes, and where the manufacture of any given category of products directly or indirectly involves most of the others), one might imagine that the level of complexity makes rational planning (in the sense of an a priori determination of the intermediate targets, given the initial conditions and ultimate target) impossible. The apologists for "free enterprise" have been proclaiming this doctrine for ages. But it is false.[23] The problem can be solved and available mathematical techniques in fact allow it to be solved remarkably simply. Once the initial conditions (the economic situation at the start of the planning process) are known and the ultimate target or targets have been consciously set, all planning work (the determination of the intermediate targets) can be reduced to a purely technical task of execution, capable of being mechanized and automated to a very high degree.

The basis of the new methods is the concept of the total interdependence of all sectors of the economy (the fact that everything that one sector utilizes in production is itself the product of one or more other sectors; and the converse fact that every product of a given sector will ultimately be utilized or consumed by one or more other sectors). The idea, which goes back to Quesnay and which formed the basis of Marx's theory of capital accumulation, has been vastly developed in the past twenty years by a group of American economists around Wassily Leontief that has succeeded in giving this idea an increasingly detailed statistical formulation applicable to the real economy.[24] This interdependence is such that at any given moment (for a given level of technique and a given structure of available equipment) the production of each sector is related, in a relatively stable manner, to the quantities of products of other sectors that the first sector utilizes (or: "consumes productively"). It is easy to grasp that a given quantity of coal is needed to produce a ton of steel of a given type. Moreover, one will need so much scrap metal or iron ore, so many hours of labor, such and such an expenditure on upkeep and repairs. The ratio "coal used/steel produced," expressed in terms of value, is known as the "*current technical coefficient*" determining the productive consumption of coal per unit of steel turned out.

If one wants to increase steel production beyond a certain point, it will not help just to go on delivering more coal or more scrap metal to the existing steel mills. New mills will have to be built. Or one will have to increase the productive capacity of existing mills. To increase steel output by a given amount one will have to produce a given amount of specified equipment. The ratio "given amount of specified equipment/ steel-producing capacity per given period," again expressed in terms of value, is known as the *"technical coefficient of capital."* It determines the quantity of *capital* utilized per unit of steel produced in a given period.

All this is perfectly well known and quite trivial. One could stop at this point if one were only dealing with a single enterprise. Every firm bases itself on calculations of this sort (in fact, on much more detailed ones) whenever, in making decisions about how much to produce or how much to increase production, it buys raw materials, orders machinery or recruits labor. But when one looks at the economy as a whole, things change. The interdependence of the various sectors has definite consequences. The *increase* of production in a given sector has repercussions (of varying intensity) on all other sectors and finally on the initial sector itself. For example, an increase in the production of steel immediately requires an increase in the production of coal. But this requires both an increase in certain types of mining equipment and the recruitment of more labor into mining. The increased demand for mining equipment in turn requires *more* steel, and more labor in the steel mills. This in turn leads to a demand for still more coal, and so on and so forth. For their part, newly hired workers get increased wages, and therefore they buy more consumer goods of various kinds. The production of these new goods will require such and such an amount of raw materials, new equipment, and so on (and, again, more coal and steel). The question of how much the demand for nylon stockings will rise in West Virginia or the Basses-Pyrénées if a new blast furnace were to be built in Pennsylvania or the Lorraine is not a joke but one of the central problems to which planners should—and can—respond.

The use of Leontief's matrices, combined with other modern methods such as Koopmans' "activity analysis"[25] (of which "operational research" is a specific instance) would, in the case of a socialist economy, allow theoretically exact answers to be given to questions of this type. A matrix is a table on which the technical coefficients (both "current technical coefficients" and "technical coefficients of capital") expressing the dependence of each sector upon each of the others are laid out systematically. Every ultimate target that might be chosen is presented as a list of material means to be utilized (and therefore manufactured) in specific amounts, within the period in question. As soon as the ultimate target is chosen, the solution of a system of simultaneous equations enables one to define immediately all the intermediate targets and therefore the tasks to be fulfilled by each sector of the economy.

Solving these problems will be the task of a highly mechanized and automated specific *enterprise*, whose main work will consist of a veritable "mass production" of various *plans* (*targets*) and of their various *components* (*implications*). This enterprise is the *plan factory.*

Its central workshop will, to start with, probably consist of a computer whose "memory" will store the technical coefficients and the initial productive capacity of each sector. If "fed" a number of hypothetical targets, the computer will "produce" the productive implication of each target for each sector (including the amount of work to be provided, in each instance, by the "manpower" sector).[26]

Around this central workshop there would be others whose tasks would be to study the distribution and variations of regional production and investment and possible technical optima (given the general interdependence of the various sectors). They would also determine the unit values (equivalences) of different categories of products.

Two departments of the plan factory warrant special mention: the one dealing with stocktaking and the one dealing with the technical coefficients.

The quality of the planning work, when conceived in this way, depends on how much people know about the *real* state of the economy, since such knowledge forms the basis of all planning work. An accurate solution, in other words, depends on adequate information both about the "initial conditions" and the "technical coefficients." Industrial and agricultural censuses are carried out at regular intervals, even today, by a number of advanced capitalist countries, but they offer only a very crude basis because they are extremely inaccurate, fragmented, and based on insufficient data. The taking of an up-to-date and complete inventory will be the first task, once the workers take power, and it will require a great deal of serious preparation. It cannot be achieved "by decree," from one day to the next. Nor, once taken, could such an inventory be considered final. Perfecting it and keeping it up to date will be an ongoing task of the plan factory, working in close cooperation with the departments responsible for industrial stocktaking in their own enterprises. The results of this cooperation will constantly modify and "enrich" the "memory" of the central computer (which indeed will itself take on a large part of the job).

Establishing the "technical coefficients" will pose similar problems. To start with, it could be done very roughly, using certain generally available statistical information ("on average, the textile industry uses so much cotton to produce so much cloth"). But such knowledge soon will have to be made far more precise through information provided by the responsible technical workers in each sector. The data "stores" in the computer will have to be periodically revised as more accurate knowledge about the technical coefficients—and in particular about the *real* changes in these coefficients brought about by new technological developments—is brought to light.

Such in-depth knowledge of the real state of affairs of the economy, combined with the constant revision of basic physical and technical data and with the possibility of drawing *instantaneous* conclusions from them, will result in very considerable, probably enormous gains, though it is difficult at this time to form a precise idea of the extent of these changes. The potentialities of these new computer-assisted techniques have been exploited in particular instances to make considerable improvements upon past practices, thus leading to greater rationality and economic savings. But these potentialities remain untapped in the very area where they could be most usefully applied: that of the economy taken as a whole. Any technical modification, in any sector, could in principle affect the conditions for profitability and the rational choice of production methods in all other sectors. A socialist economy will be able *totally* and *instantaneously* to take advantage of such facts. Capitalist economies take them into account only belatedly and in a very partial way.

It will be immediately possible to actually set up such a plan factory in any moderately industrialized country. The necessary equipment already exists. So do the people capable of operating it. Banks and insurance companies (which will be unnecessary under socialism) already use some of these modern methods in work of this general type. Linking up with mathematicians, statisticians, and econometricians, those who work in such offices could provide the initial personnel of the plan factory. Workers' management of production and the requirements of a rational economy will provide a tremendous impetus to the simultaneously "spontaneous/automatic" and "conscious" development of the logical and mechanical aspects of rational planning techniques.

Let us not be misunderstood; the role of the "plan factory" will not be to decide on the plan. The *targets* of the plan will be determined by society as a whole, in a manner soon to be described. *Before* any proposals are voted upon, however, the plan factory will work out and present to society as a whole the *implications* and consequences of the plan (or plans) suggested. *After* a plan has been adopted, the task of the plan factory will be, if necessary, to constantly *bring up to date* the facts on which the current plan is based *and* to draw conclusions from these modifications, informing both the Central Assembly of Councils and the relevant sectors of any alterations in the intermediate targets (and therefore in production tasks) that might be worth considering. In none of these instances would those actually working in the plan factory decide anything—except, like in every other factory, the organization of their own work.

The Market for Consumer Goods

With a fixed set of techniques, the determination of intermediate targets is, as we have just seen, a purely mechanical matter. With constantly and permanently evolving techniques, other problems arise that we will treat later. But what about consumption? In a socialist society, how could people determine what [*la liste*] and how much is to be produced?

It is obvious that this cannot be based on direct democracy. The plan cannot determine, as an ultimate target, a complete list of consumer goods or suggest in what proportions they should be produced. Such a decision would not be democratic, for two reasons. First, it could never be made "in full knowledge of the relevant facts"; no one can make a sensible decision about lists that include thousands of items in varying quantities. Second, such a decision would be tantamount to a pointless tyranny of the majority over the minority. If 40 percent of the population wish to consume a certain article and are ready to pay for it, there is no reason why they should be deprived of it under the pretext that the other 60 percent prefer something else. No preference or taste is more logical than any other. Moreover, there is no reason at all to cut short the problem in this way, since consumer wishes [*la satisfaction des désirs*] are seldom incompatible with one another. Majority votes in this matter would amount to rationing, an irrational and absurd way of settling this kind of problem anywhere but on the raft of Medusa or in a besieged fortress.

Planning decisions therefore will relate not to particular items but to the general standard of living (the overall volume of consumption), expressed in terms of the disposable income of each person in a socialist society. They will not delve into the detailed composition of this consumption.

Once the overall volume of consumption is defined, one might be tempted to treat its constituent articles of consumption as "intermediate targets." One might say, "When consumers dispose of x amount of income, they will buy y amount of some particular article." But this would be an artificial and ultimately erroneous response. In relation to human consumption, deciding on living standards does not involve the same kind of considerations that go into determining how many tons of coal are needed to produce so many tons of steel. There are no "technical coefficients of the consumer." In actual, material production, such coefficients have an intrinsic meaning, but in the realm of consumption they would represent merely a bookkeeping contrivance. Under capitalism, there is of course some statistical correlation between income and the structure of consumer demand (without such a correlation private capitalism could not function). But this is only a very relative affair. It would be turned upside down under socialism. A massive redistribution of incomes will have taken place; many profound changes will have occurred in every realm of life; the permanent rape of consumers through advertising and capitalist sales techniques will have been abolished; and new tastes will have emerged as the result of an increase in free time. Finally, the statistical regularity of consumer demand cannot solve the problem of *gaps* that might appear within a given period between real demand and that envisaged in the plan. Genuine planning does not mean saying, "Living standards will go up by 5 percent next year, and experience tells us that this will result in a 20 percent increase in the demand for cars, so let's make 20 percent more cars," and stopping at that. One will have to start this way, where other criteria are missing, but there will have to be powerful correcting mechanisms capable of responding to disparities between anticipated and real demand.

Socialist society will have to regulate the pattern of its consumption according to the principle of *consumer sovereignty*, which implies the existence of a real market for consumer goods. The "general decision" embodied in the plan will define: (1) what proportion of its overall product society wishes to devote to the satisfaction of individual consumer needs, (2) what proportion it would like to allocate to collective needs ("public consumption"), and (3) what proportion it wants to apply to the development of the productive forces (i.e., "investment"). But the *structure* of consumption will have to be determined by the demand of consumers themselves.

How would this market operate? How could a mutual adaptation of supply and demand come about?

First, there would have to be an overall equilibrium. The sum total of income distributed in any given period ("wages," retirement funds, and other benefits) will have to be equal to the value of consumer goods (quantities × prices) made available in that period.

An "empirical" initial decision will then have to be made in order to provide at least a skeleton for the structure of consumption. This initial decision will be based on traditionally "known" statistical data, but in full knowledge of the fact that these data will have to be extensively modified by taking into account a whole series of new factors (such as the equalization of wages, for instance). Stocks of various commodities in excess of what might be expected to be consumed in a given period will, initially, have to be scheduled for.

Three "corrective" processes will then come into play, the net result of which will be to show immediately any gap between anticipated and real demand, and then to bridge it:

1. Available stocks will either rise or fall.
2. According to whether the reserve stocks decreased or increased (i.e., according to whether demand had been initially underestimated or overestimated), there will be an initial rise or fall in the price of the various commodities. The reason for these temporary price fluctuations will have to be fully explained to the public.
3. Meanwhile, there will be an immediate readjustment in the structure for producing consumer goods to the level where (the stocks having been replenished) the production of goods equals the demand. At that moment, the sale price would again become equal to the "normal price" of the product.

Given the principle of consumer sovereignty, any differences between actual demand and the amount of production scheduled will have to be corrected by a modification in the structure of production and not by resorting to the instauration of permanent differences between selling prices and normal prices. If such differences were to appear, they would imply ipso facto that the original planning decision was wrong, in this particular field.

Money, Prices, Wages, and Value

Many absurdities have been spoken about money and its abolition in a socialist society. It should be clear, however, that the role of money is radically transformed from the moment it no longer can be used as a means of *accumulation* (no one being able to possess some means of production) or as a means of *exerting social pressure* (all incomes being equal).

Laboring people will receive an *income* [*revenu*]. This "income" will take the form of units [*signes*], allowing people to apportion their expenditures, spreading them out (1) over time, and (2) among various objects, exactly as they wish. As we are seeking here to come to grips with realities and are not fighting against words, we see no objection to calling this income "wages" and these units "money," just as a little earlier we used the words "normal prices" to describe the monetary expression of *labor value.*[27]

Under socialism, labor value will be the only rational basis for any kind of social accountancy and the only yardstick having any real meaning for people. As such, it necessarily will serve as the foundation for calculating profitability in the sphere of socialist production. The main objective of making such calculations will be to reduce both the direct and indirect costs of human labor power. Setting the prices of consumer goods on the basis of their labor value would mean that for each person the cost of consumer objects will clearly appear as the equivalent of the labor he himself would have had to expend to produce them (assuming he had both access to the average prevailing equipment and an average social capacity).

It would both simplify and clarify things if the monetary unit was considered the "net product of an hour of labor" and if this were made the unit of value. It also would be helpful if the hourly wage, equal for all, were a given fraction of this unit, expressing the ratio private consumption/ total net consumption. If these steps were taken and thoroughly explained, they would enable the fundamental planning decision (namely, the distribution of the social product between consumption and investment) to be immediately obvious to everyone, and repeatedly drawn to people's attention, every time anyone bought anything. Equally obvious would be the social cost of every object acquired.

Absolute Wage Equality

Whenever they succeed in expressing themselves independently of the trade-union bureaucracy, working-class aspirations and demands increasingly are directed against hierarchy and wage differentials.[28] Basing itself on this fact, socialist society will introduce absolute equality in the area of wages. There is no justification, other than naked exploitation, for wage differentials,[29] whether these reflect differing professional qualifications or differences in productivity. If an individual himself advanced the costs of his professional training and if society considered him "an enterprise," the recuperation of those costs, spread out over a working lifetime, would at most "justify," at the extremes of the wage spectrum, a differential of 2:1 (between sweeper and neurosurgeon). Under socialism, training costs will be advanced by society (they often are, even today), and the question of their "recovery" will not arise. As for productivity, it depends (already today) much less on bonuses and incentives and much more on the coercions exercised, on the one hand, by machines and supervisors and, on the other hand, by the discipline of production, imposed by primary working groups in the workshop. Socialist society could not increase productivity by economic constraints without resorting again to all the capitalist paraphernalia of norms, supervision, and so on. Labor discipline will flow (as it already does, in part, today) from the self-organization of primary groups in each workshop, from the mutual cooperation and control among the factories' different shops, from gatherings of producers in different enterprises or different sectors of the economy. As a general rule, the primary group in a workshop ensures the discipline of any particular individual. Anyone who proves incorrigible can be made to leave that particular shop. It would then be up to this recalcitrant individual to seek entry into another group of workers and to get accepted by them or else to remain jobless.

Wage equality will give a real meaning to the market in consumer goods, every individual being assured for the first time of an equal vote. It will abolish countless conflicts, both in everyday life and in production, and will enable the development of an extraordinary cohesion among working people. It will destroy at its very roots the whole mercantile monstrosity of capitalism (both private and bureaucratic), the commercialization of individuals, that whole universe where one does not earn what one is worth, but where one is worth what one earns. A few years of wage equality and little will be left of the present-day mentality of individuals.

The Fundamental Decision
The fundamental decision, in a socialist economy, is the one whereby society as a whole determines what it wants (i.e., the ultimate targets of its plan). This decision concerns two basic propositions. Given the "initial conditions" of the economy, how much time does society want to devote to production? And how much of the total product does it want to see devoted respectively to private consumption, public consumption, and investment?

In both private and bureaucratic capitalist societies, the amount of time one has to work is determined by the ruling class by means of direct physical constraints (as was the case until quite recently in Russian factories) or economic ones. No one is consulted about the matter. Socialist society, taken as a whole, will not escape the impact of certain economic constraints (in the sense that any decision to modify labor time will—other things being equal—have a bearing on production). But it will differ from all previous societies in that for the first time in history people will be able to decide about work in full knowledge of the relevant facts, with the basic elements of the problem clearly presented to them.

Socialist society will also be the first society capable of rationally deciding how society's product should be divided between consumption and investment.[30] Under private capitalism, this distribution takes place in an absolutely blind fashion and one would seek in vain any "rationality" underlying what determines investment.[31] In bureaucratic societies, the volume of investment is also decided quite arbitrarily, and the central bureaucracy in these societies has never been able to justify its choices except through monotonous recitations of litanies about the "priority of heavy industry."[32] Even if there were a rational, "objective" basis for making a central decision on this matter, the decision arrived at would be ipso facto irrational if it were reached in the absence of those primarily concerned, namely, the members of society. Any decision made in this way would reproduce the basic contradiction of all exploitative regimes. It would treat people in the plan as just one variable of predictable behavior among others and as theoretical "objects." It would soon lead to treating them as objects in real life, too. Such a policy would contain the seeds of its own failure: Instead of encouraging the participation of the producers in the carrying out of the plan, it would irrevocably alienate them from a plan that was not of their choosing. There is no "objective" rationality allowing one to decide, by means of mathematical formulas, about the future of society, work, consumption, and accumulation. The only rationality in these realms is the living reason of mankind, the decisions of ordinary people concerning their own fate.

But these decisions will not come from a toss of the dice. They will be based upon a complete clarification of the problem and they will be made in full knowledge of the relevant facts.

This will be possible because there exists, for any given level of technique, a definite relation between a given amount of investment and the resulting increase in production. This relation is nothing other than the application to the economy as a whole of the "technical coefficients of capital" we spoke of earlier. A given investment in steelworks will result in such and such an increase in what steelworks turn out—and a given *overall* investment in production will result in such and such a net increase in the overall social product.[33] Therefore, a certain *rate* of accumulation will allow a certain *rate* of increase of the social product (and therefore of the standard of living or of the amount of leisure). Finally, a particular *fraction* of the product devoted to accumulation will also result in a particular *rate* of increase of living standards. The overall problem can therefore be posed in the following terms. A large immediate increase in consumption is possible—but it would imply a significant cutback on further increases in the years to come. On the other hand, people might prefer to choose a more limited immediate increase in living standards, which would allow the social product (and hence living standards) to increase at the rate of *x* percent per annum in the years to come. And so on. "The antinomy between the present and the future," to which the apologists of private capitalism and of the bureaucracy are constantly referring, would still be with us. But it would be *laid out clearly*. And society itself would settle the matter, fully aware of the setting and of the implications of its decision.

In conclusion, and to sum up, one could say that any overall plan submitted to the people for discussion would have to specify:

1. The amount of work involved.
2. The level of consumption during the initial period.
3. The amount of resources to be devoted to investment and to public consumption.
4. The rate of increase of future consumption.
5. The production tasks incumbent upon each enterprise.

To simplify things, we have at times presented the decisions about ultimate and intermediate targets (i.e., the implications of the plan concerning specific areas of production) as two separate and consecutive acts. In practice there would be a continuous give-and-take between these two phases, and a plurality of proposals. The producers will be in no position to decide on ultimate targets unless they know what the implications of particular targets are for themselves, not only as consumers but as *producers*, working in a specific enterprise. Moreover, there is no such thing as a decision made in full knowledge of the relevant facts if that decision is not founded on a *spectrum* of choices, each with its particular implications. The fundamental process of decision therefore will take the following form. Starting from below, there would be discussions in the General Assemblies. Initial incomplete or partial proposals would emanate from the Councils of various enterprises and would deal with their own targets and productive possibilities in the period to come. The plan factory would then regroup these various proposals, pointing out which ones were mutually incompatible or entailed undesirable effects on other sectors. It would elaborate a series of achievable targets, grouping them as far as possible in terms of their concrete implications. (Proposal A implies that factory X will increase production by r percent next year with the help of additional equipment Y. Proposal B, on the other hand, implies . . .) There would then be a full discussion of the various overall proposals, throughout the General Assemblies and by all the Councils, possibly with counterproposals and a repetition of the procedure described. A final discussion would then lead to a simple majority vote in the General Assemblies of each enterprise.

Summary of pp. 47-74:

The final pages of the text are devoted, first, to a resumption of certain themes concerning the "form" of management of the economy, followed by a few considerations concerning the "content" of the latter. One accepts

> *as self-evident that the ideal economy is one that allows the most rapid possible expansion of material production and, as a corollary, the greatest possible reduction of the working day. This idea, considered in absolute terms, is absolutely absurd. It epitomizes the whole mentality, psychology, logic, and metaphysics of capitalism, its reality as well as its schizophrenia. [. . .] This "acquisitive" mentality that capitalism engenders, which engenders capitalism, without which capitalism could not operate, and which capitalism pushes to the point of paroxysm might just conceivably have been a useful aberration during a certain phase of human development. But this way of thinking will die along with capitalism (p. 49).*

Yet what the rest of the text (pp. 50-74) is devoted to is "The Management of Society." The "network of General Assemblies and Councils is all that is left of the State or of power in a socialist society. It is the whole State and the only embodiment of power. There are no other institutions that could manage, direct, or make binding decisions about people's lives." The councils are the "Exclusive and Exhaustive Form of Organization for the Whole Population" (pp. 50-54). The problems this type of organization may pose in agriculture and in services are in no way insurmountable, even if the representation of some strata (shopkeepers, artisans, the "liberal professions") may pose particular problems. "To start with, and up to a point, they will doubtless remain 'attached to property.' But up to what point? All that we know is how they reacted when Stalinism sought forcibly to drive them into a concentration camp instead of into a socialist society" (p. 54). The councils are also the "Universal Form of Organization for Social Activities" (pp. 54-56), since they are not only organs managing production but also organs of local self-administration and the sole articulations of the central power—which does not rule out the existence of "local" councils in the cases where production and one's locality do not overlap. Yet what about the "central" functions of the State?

> The modern State has become a gigantic enterprise—by far the most important enterprise in modern society. It can exercise its managerial functions only to the extent that it has created a whole constellation of apparatuses of execution, within which work has become collective, subject to a division of labor, and specialized.

These "administrations" can therefore become enterprises, with the same status as the other enterprises, managed by those who work there. What remain are the functions of the State that are in no way "technical" but are political, and the body that carries out those functions is really a central power: "The Assembly and the Government of the Councils." On pp. 58-65, Chaulieu discusses the various arguments advanced in the past against the very possibility of direct democracy and affirms, in particular, that it is possible to put the modern techniques of telecommunication in the service of democracy. But he insists especially on the following key point:

> But if the Central Assembly allowed its Governmental Council to exceed its rights—or if members of local assemblies allowed their delegates to the Central Assembly to exceed their authority—nothing could be done. The population can exercise political power only if it wants to. The organization proposed merely ensures that the population could exercise such power, if it wanted to (p. 61).

In the final three parts, "The 'State,' 'Parties,' and 'Politics'" (pp. 66-68), "Freedom and the Dictatorship of the Proletariat" (pp. 68-70), and "Problems of the 'Transition'" (pp. 71-74), Chaulieu draws attention to the fact that there is, in the end, a contradiction between the existence of strong parties and the system of Councils.

> The parallel existence of both Councils and political parties will imply that a part of real political life will be taking place outside the Councils. People will then tend to act in the Councils according to decisions already made

elsewhere. Should this tendency predominate, it would bring about the rapid atrophy and finally the disappearance of the Councils. Conversely, real socialist development would be characterized by the progressive atrophy of parties (p. 67).

Finally, he denounces the mystification contained in the Trotskyists' idea of "transitional societies"

fitting more or less comfortably next to each other. Between communism and capitalism there was socialism. But between socialism and capitalism there was the workers' State. And between the workers' State and capitalism there was the "degenerated workers' State" (degeneration being a process, there were gradations: degenerated, very degenerated, monstrously degenerated, etc.). [. . .] All these gymnastics were performed so as to avoid having to admit that Russia had become again an exploitative society without a shred of socialism about it, and so as to avoid drawing the conclusion that the fate of the Russian Revolution made it imperative to reexamine all the problems relating to the program and content of socialism, to the role of the proletariat, to the role of the party, etc. (pp. 71-72).

And he concludes by insisting on the fact that the program presented in the text is "a program for the present, capable of being realized."

Notes

1. The text was preceded by the following note:

    The first part of this text was published in Socialisme ou Barbarie, *17: 1-22. The following pages represent a new draft of the entire text and a reading of the previously published part is not presupposed. This text opens a discussion on programmatic questions. The positions expressed here do not necessarily express the point of view of the entire Socialisme ou Barbarie group.*

    [T/E: This text was originally translated by Maurice Brinton under the title *Workers' Councils and the Economics of a Self-Managed Society* (London: Solidarity, 1972), with "Our Preface." It was reprinted by Philadelphia Solidarity in 1974 (with forewords by Philadelphia Solidarity and the League for Economic Democracy) and in 1984 as a Wooden Shoe Pamphlet (with a statement about the group,

Philadelphia Solidarity, entitled "About Ourselves," and a new introduction by Peter Dorman, "Workers Councils . . . 25 Years Later"). An adaptation of Brinton's translation later appeared in *PSW2* and was excerpted in *CR*.]

2. This following part will be published in the next issue of *S. ou B.* [no. 23 (January 1958). Reprinted in *EMO2*; T/E: and in *EP2*; trans. as "On the Content of Socialism, III: The Workers' Struggle against the Organization of the Capitalist Enterprise," in *PSW3*].

3. "Production" meaning here the shop floor, not "the economy" or "the market."

4. The *present* "Supreme Soviet," of course.

5. At the risk of reinforcing the "utopian" features of this text, we have always used the future tense when speaking of socialist society. The use of the conditional throughout the text would have been tedious and tiresome. It goes without saying that this manner of speaking does not affect in any way our examination of the problems raised here; the reader may easily replace "The socialist society will be . . ." with "The author thinks that the socialist society will be . . ."

   As for the substance of the text, we have deliberately reduced historical and literary references to a minimum. The ideas we propose to develop, however, are only the theoretical formulation of the experience of a century of working-class struggles. They embody real experiences (both positive and negative), conclusions (both direct and indirect) that have already been drawn, answers given to problems actually posed or answers that would have had to be given if such and such a revolution had developed a little further. Thus every sentence in this text is linked to questions that have already been met implicitly or explicitly in the course of working-class struggles. This should put a stop once and for all to allegations of "utopianism."

   In the first chapter of his book *The Workers' Councils* (Melbourne, 1950), Anton Pannekoek develops a similar analysis of the problems confronting socialist society. On fundamental issues, our points of view are very close.

6. Bakunin once described the problem of socialism as being one of "integrating individuals into structures they can understand and control."

7. The expression is to be found in Part 3 of Engels's *Anti-Dühring*.

8. A few years ago a certain "philosopher" could seriously ask how one could even discuss Stalin's decisions, since one did not know the real facts upon which he alone could base them. (J.-P. Sartre, "Les Communistes et la Paix," in *Les Temps Modernes*, 81, 84–85, and

101 [July and October–November 1952, April 1954]; trans. Martha H. Fletcher, *The Communists and the Peace* [New York: George Braziller, 1968].)

9. Lenin took the opportunity, in *State and Revolution*, to defend the idea of direct democracy against the reformists of his day who contemptuously called it "primitive democracy."

10. On this feature of working life, see Paul Romano, "L'Ouvrier américain," in *S. ou B.*, 5–6 (March 1950): 129–32 [T/E: "Life in the Factory," in *The American Worker* (1947; reprinted, Detroit: Bewick Editions, 1972), 37–39, and above in Part 2 of the present *Anthology*, 104–107], and R. Berthier, "Une expérience d'organisation ouvrière," in *S. ou B.*, 20 (December 1956): 29–31.

11. We must stress once again that we are not trying to draw up perfect blueprints. It is obvious, for instance, that to collect and disseminate information is not a socially neutral function. Not all information can be disseminated—that would be the surest way of smothering what is relevant and rendering it incomprehensible and therefore uncontrollable. The role of the Government is therefore *political*, even in this respect. This is why we call it "government" and not the "central press service." But more important is its explicit function of informing people, which shall be its responsibility. The explicit function of government today is to *hide* what's going on from the people.

12. Yet this is what Lenin's definition of socialism as "soviets plus electrification" boiled down to.

13. Academic economists have analyzed the fact that of several technically feasible possibilities certain ones are chosen, and that these choices lead to a particular pattern of technology applied in real life, giving concrete expression to the technique (understood in the general sense of "know-how") of a given period. See, for instance, Joan Robinson's *The Accumulation of Capital*, 3rd ed. (New York: St. Martin's Press, 1969), 101–78. But in these analyses the choice is always presented as flowing from considerations of "profitability" and in particular from the "relative costs of capital and labor." This abstract viewpoint has little grasp of the reality of industrial evolution. Marx, on the other hand, underlines the social content of machine-dominated industry, its enslaving function.

14. The great contribution of the American group that publishes *Correspondence* has been to resume the analysis *of the crisis of society from the standpoint of production* and to apply it to the conditions of our age. See their texts, translated and published in *S. ou B.*:

Paul Romano's "L'Ouvrier américain" (nos. 1 to 5–6 [March 1949 to March 1950]) and "La Reconstruction de la société" (nos. 7–8 [August 1951 and January 1952]) [T/E: see "Life in the Factory" and "The Reconstruction of Society," in *The American Worker*, with an excerpt above in the present *Anthology*].

In France, it is Philippe Guillaume who has revived this way of looking at things (see his article, "Machinisme et proletariat," in no. 7 [August 1951] of this review). I am indebted to him, directly or indirectly, for several ideas used in the present text.

15. Karl Marx, *Capital* (New York: International Publishers, 1967), vol. 3, 820.

16. Strictly speaking, poetry means creation.

17. Daniel Mothé's text, "L'Usine et la gestion ouvrière," also in this issue [*S. ou B.*, 22 (July 1957), 75ff.; "The Factory and Workers Management" is partially reproduced in Part 2 of the present *Anthology*] already is one de facto response—coming from the factory itself—to the concrete problem of shop-floor workers' management and that of how to organize work. In referring to this text, we are considering here only the problems of the factory *as a whole*.

18. In J. A. C. Brown's *The Social Psychology of Industry* (London: Penguin, 1954), there is a striking contrast between the devastating analysis the author makes of present capitalist production and the only "conclusions" he can draw, which are pious exhortations to management that it should "understand," "do better," "democratize itself," etc. Let it not be said, however, that an "industrial sociologist" takes no position, that he merely describes facts and does not suggest norms. Advising the managerial apparatus to "do better" is itself a taking of a position, one that has been shown here to be completely utopian.

19. See the Twentieth Congress texts analyzed by Claude Lefort in "Le Totalitarisme sans Staline," *S. ou B.*, 19 (July 1956), in particular, 59–62 [now in *Éléments d'une critique de la bureacratie* (Geneva: Droz, 1971), 166ff.; [T/E: 1979 ed., 203ff.; those particular pages are not included in the excerpts from "Totalitarianism Without Stalin" appearing in Part 3 of the present *Anthology*].

20. T/E: See Mothé, "The Factory and Workers Management," partially reproduced in Part 2 of the present *Anthology*.

21. T/E: Ibid., 181 in the present *Anthology*; see the article's fourth note for an explanation of this phrase.

22. One might add that the rate of economic growth also depends: (1) *on technical progress* (but such technical progress is itself critically dependent on the amounts of investment put, directly or indirectly,

into research); and (2) on the evolution of *labor productivity*. But this hinges on the amount of capital invested per worker and on the level of technique—and these two factors again bring us back to the larger question of investment. More significantly, the productivity of labor depends on the producers' attitude toward the economy. This, in turn, would center on people's attitude toward the plan, on how its targets were established, on their own involvement and sense of identification with the decisions reached, and in general on factors discussed in this text.

23. Bureaucratic "planning" as carried out in Russia and the Eastern European countries proves nothing, one way or the other. It is just as irrational and just as anarchic and wasteful as the capitalist "market"—though in different ways. The waste is both "external" (the wrong decisions being made) and "internal" (brought about by the resistance of the workers) to the production process, as we have described in issue 20 of this review (see "The Proletarian Revolution against the Bureaucracy" [T/E: in *PSW2*]).

24. The field is in constant expansion. The starting points remain, however, Leontief's *The Structure of American Economy, 1919-1939: An Empirical Application of Equilibrium Analysis* (1951; reprinted, Armonk, NY: Sharpe, 1976), and the essays by Leontief et al., *Studies in the Structure of the American Economy: Theoretical and Empirical Explorations in Input-Output Analysis* (1953; reprinted, Armonk, NY: Sharpe, 1976).

25. Tjalling Koopmans, *Activity Analysis of Production and Allocation* (1951; reprinted, New Haven, CT: Yale University Press, 1972).

26. The division of the economy into some 100 sectors, which roughly corresponds to *present* [1957] computer capacity, is about "halfway" between its division (by Marx) into two sectors (consumer goods and means of production) and the few thousand sectors that would be required to ensure a perfectly exact representation. Present computer capabilities would probably be sufficient in practice, and could be made more precise, even now, by tackling the problem in several stages.

27. Labor value includes, of course, the *actual* social cost of the equipment utilized in the period considered. For the working out of labor values by the matrix method, see the article "Sur la dynamique du capitalisme," in *S. ou B.*, 12 (August 1953), 7–22. The adoption of labor value as a yardstick is equivalent to what academic economists call "normal long-term costs." The viewpoint expressed in this text corresponds to Marx's, which is, in general, violently attacked by

academic economists, even "socialist" ones. For them, "marginal costs" should determine prices; see, for instance, Joan Robinson's *An Essay on Marxian Economics*, 2nd ed. (New York: St. Martin's Press, 1966), 23–28. We cannot go into this discussion here. All we can say is that the application of the principle of marginal costs would mean that the price of a plane ticket between Paris and New York would at times be zero and at other times equivalent to that of the whole aircraft.

28. The 1955 Nantes strikes took place around an antihierarchical demand for a uniform increase for everyone. The Hungarian workers' councils demanded the abolition of norms and severe limitations on hierarchy. What inadvertently is said in official Russian proclamations indicates that a permanent struggle against hierarchy is taking place in the factories of that country. See "The Proletarian Revolution against the Bureaucracy" [T/E: in *PSW2*].

29. For a detailed discussion of the problem of hierarchy, see the "Simple Labor and Skilled Labor" section of "The Relations of Production in Russia" [T/E: *PSW1*, 144–54; partially reprinted in Part 1 of the present *Anthology*, 79–83], and "Sur la dynamique du capitalisme," in *S. ou B.*, 13 (January 1954): 67–69.

30. We leave aside for now the problem of public consumption.

31. In his major work, which is devoted to this theme—and after a moderate use of differential equations—Keynes comes up with the conclusion that the main determinants of investment are the "animal spirits" of entrepreneurs. *The General Theory of Employment, Interest and Money* (1936), 161–62. The idea that the volume of investment is primarily determined by the rate of interest (and that the latter results from the interplay of the "real forces of productivity and thrift") was long ago demolished by academic economists themselves. See, for example, Joan Robinson's *The Rate of Interest and Other Essays* (1952; reprinted, London: Hyperion, 1981).

32. One would seek in vain through the voluminous writings of Mr. Charles Bettelheim for any attempt to justify rationally the rate of accumulation "chosen" by the Russian bureaucracy. The "socialism" of such "theoreticians" not only implies that Stalin (or Khrushchev) alone can know. It also implies that such knowledge, by its very nature, cannot be communicated to the rest of humanity. In another country, and in other times, this was known as the *Führerprinzip*.

33. This net increase in the social product of which we have spoken obviously is not just the sum of the increases in each sector. Several elements must be added up or be subtracted before one can pass

from one to the other. For instance, there would be the "intermediate utilizations" of the products of each sector and the "external economies" (investment in a given sector, by abolishing a bottleneck, could allow the better use of the productive capacities of other sectors that, although already established, were being wasted hitherto). Working out these net increases presents no particular difficulties. They are calculated automatically, at the same time as one works out the "intermediate objectives" (mathematically, the solution to one problem immediately provides the solution to the other).

We have discussed the problem of how to determine the overall *volume* of investments. We can only touch on the problem of the *choice* of particular investments. Let us limit ourselves to a few brief indications. Allocation of investment *by sectors* is automatic once the final investment is determined (a given level of final consumption directly or indirectly implies such and such an amount of productive capacity in each sector). The choice of a given type of investment from among several producing the same result could depend only on such considerations as the effect that a given type of equipment would have on those who would have to use it—and here, from all we have said, their own viewpoint would be decisive.

From this point of view, when two comparable types of machinery are examined (thermal and hydroelectric power stations, for example), the criterion of profitability still applies. Here, where an "accounting-book" interest rate is used to make one's calculations, socialist society will still be superior to a capitalist economy: For this "rate of interest," the former will use the rate of expansion of its own economy; it can be shown—Von Neumann did it in 1937—that these two rates ought necessarily to be identical in a rational economy.

PART FIVE

ORGANIZATION

"L'Organisation"
Socialisme ou Barbarie—Anthologie, 197–98

The organization question troubled the group from its founding in 1948 until its self-dissolution in 1967. For a collective of such a limited size, that might seem frivolous. The reason for this concern was that at no moment was S. ou B. content with treating organization solely in empirical or pragmatic terms; on the contrary, it always endeavored to ground its principles of operation and action on considerations that were theoretical in nature. In 1948, it was a matter of determining in what way and up to what point the new givens of historical experience—namely, the appearance and the growing power, on the world scale, of workers' bureaucracies—required one to redefine the content and forms of action undertaken by revolutionaries and to draw out therefrom the implications for practice here and now. On these two levels—theoretical and practical—profound divergences became apparent early on, particularly between the two main initiators of the group, Lefort and Castoriadis, and those divergences persisted, even as their respective positions evolved.

The texts we reprint in this section allow one to make out the tenor of this debate. That debate displays two somewhat contradictory characteristics. On the one hand, however robustly the conflicts were expressed, the responses given to the problem of organization converge on major points, profoundly refreshing the views that had hitherto held sway within the workers' movement. On the other hand, and despite that, these responses would continue for a long time to be formulated with the help of notions marked by the legacy of Marxism-Leninism. This may be judged by the way in which S. ou B. announced its organizational project in the first issue of the review: It "represents the ideological and political leadership of the class under the conditions of the present system of exploitation, but a leadership that is preparing its own elimination via its merger with autonomous organs of the class as soon as the class's entry into revolutionary struggle reveals on the historical stage the true leadership of humanity, which is the whole of the proletarian class itself." The nonspecialist reader will undoubtedly be left with an impression not only of the unwieldiness of this passage but also of its obscureness.

Another cause of obscurity resides in things left unsaid that shroud the debate. This is not the place to state, in place of the authors, the things about which they remained silent. Yet as the controversy deepened, from 1948 to 1958, one is more and more inclined to think that the true stakes in this debate involved the nature of revolution, its very legitimacy, the place of the political in a self-managed society, the nature of democracy in such a society, and so on.

Finally, the exacting reader will perhaps be surprised to note that some key problems remain as blind spots and therefore do not facilitate the reading of these texts. As these problems are not posed, answers that are taken for granted are given to them by default, implicitly. Vertiginous problems indeed, such as: What is political consciousness? What roles do affect and passion play? What does it mean to act on political consciousness? Can one do so? And by what means?

Despite these limits, the texts reprinted below raise the question of organization and militant action in terms sufficiently profound so as to remain wholly pertinent today.

The texts we have retained are spread over three periods of the group's history.

I: 1948–1952

From as early as the group's foundation, the organization question and even the question of the revolutionary party (the phrase still being employed) was at the center of its discussions. But in April 1949, circumstances came to crystallize the divergences in relatively concrete terms: it was a matter of defining the relations of the group's members with the "Struggle Committees." The latter had just arisen as autonomous, anti-bureaucratic bodies, and they appeared to be the site where an authentic class consciousness was manifesting itself and wherein, therefore, it was important to intervene. But on what basis? As members of the group? Within the framework of collective discipline? Some rejected that, thus challenging the very existence of the group as bearer of a collective project, as an embryonic organization.

A resolution elaborated by Chaulieu, a few points of which we give here, was ultimately adopted; it defined the conception the group had of itself as a revolutionary party and of its relations with autonomous bodies of the working class, such as the Struggle Committees.

D.B. and D.F.

The Revolutionary Party (Resolution)

"Le Parti révolutionnaire (Résolution)"
Socialisme ou Barbarie, 2 (May–June 1949): 100–102, 106
Socialisme ou Barbarie—Anthologie, 199–202

[. . .]

7. The need for the revolutionary party flows simply from the fact that there exists no other body [*organisme*] of the class capable of accomplishing these tasks of coordination and leadership [*direction*] in an ongoing [*permanente*] way before the revolution and that it is impossible for any other one to exist. The tasks of coordination and leadership of the revolutionary struggle on all levels are permanent, universal, and immediate tasks. Bodies capable of fulfilling these tasks, encompassing the majority of the class or recognized by the latter, and created on a factory base appear only at the moment of revolution. Still, such bodies (soviet-type organs) rise to the height of the historical tasks only as a function of the party's constant action during the revolutionary period. Other bodies, created on a factory base and bringing together only some vanguard elements (Struggle Committees), to the extent that they envisage the achievement of these tasks in an ongoing way and on a national and international level, will be party-type bodies. Yet we have already explained that the Struggle Committees, because they do not have strict boundaries and a clearly defined program, are embryos of soviet bodies and not embryos of party-type bodies.

8. The enormous value of Struggle Committees in the coming period comes not from the fact that they would replace the revolutionary party—which they cannot do and which they do not have to do—but from the fact that they represent the permanent form for grouping

together workers who are becoming aware of the character and role of the bureaucracy. As an ongoing form—not in the sense that a Struggle Committee, once created, will persist until the revolution, but in the sense that workers want to group together around antibureaucratic positions—they will be able to do so only in the form of a Struggle Committee. Indeed, the ongoing problems class struggle poses in its most immediate and most everyday forms make it indispensable to have a workers' organization, the need for which the workers are cruelly aware of. The fact that, on the other hand, the classic mass organization created to respond to these problems, the trade union, has become, and can only increasingly be, the instrument of the bureaucracy and state capitalism will oblige the workers to organize themselves independently of the bureaucracy and of the trade-union form itself. The Struggle Committees have traced out the form of this vanguard organization.

While the Struggle Committees do not resolve the question of revolutionary leadership, of the party, they are nonetheless the basic material for the construction of the party in the present period. Indeed, not only can they be for the party a vital medium for its development both from the standpoint of recruitment possibilities and from that of the audience they offer for its ideology, not only are the experiences of their fight indispensable material for the elaboration and concretization of the revolutionary program, but they also will be the key manifestations of the class's historical presence even in a period when any positive immediate prospects are lacking, as in the present period. Through them, the class will launch partial, yet extremely important assaults against the bureaucratic and capitalist slab, assaults that will be indispensable for it to retain an awareness of its possibilities for action.

Conversely, the party's existence and activity are an indispensable condition for the propagation, generalization, and completion of the Struggle Committees experiment, for the party alone can elaborate and propagate the conclusions of their action.

9. The fact that, before the revolution, in order to accomplish its historical tasks, the class cannot create another body than the party not only is not the fruit of chance but responds to deep-seated traits of the social and historical situation of decaying capitalism. In an exploitative system, the class has its concrete consciousness determined by a series of powerful factors (temporal fluctuations, various local and national corporative allegiances, economic stratification), which ensure that, in its real existence, its social and historical unity is veiled

by a set of particular determinations. On the other hand, the alienation it undergoes under the capitalist system renders it incapable of tackling immediately the endless tasks that preparation for revolution renders necessary. It is only at the moment of revolution that the class overcomes its alienation and concretely affirms its social and historical unity. Before the revolution, there is only a strictly selective body, built upon a clearly defined ideology and program, that might defend the program of the revolution as a whole and collectively envisage preparation for the revolution.

10. The need for the Revolutionary Party does not cease with the appearance of autonomous mass bodies (soviet bodies). Both the experience of the past and analysis of present-day conditions show that these bodies have been and will be, at the outset, just formally autonomous while in fact dominated or influenced by ideologies and political currents historically hostile to proletarian power. These bodies become effectively autonomous only when their majority adopts and assimilates the revolutionary program, which, until then, the party alone uncompromisingly defended. But such adoption is never done, and never will be done, automatically; the class vanguard's constant struggle against hostile currents is an indispensable condition thereof. This struggle requires more intensive coordination and organization when the social situation is more critical, and the party is the sole possible framework for such coordination and organization.

11. The need for the revolutionary party is eliminated only with the worldwide victory of the revolution. It is only when the revolutionary program and socialism have won over the majority of the world proletariat that a body defending this program, which is other than the organization of this majority of the worldwide class itself, becomes superfluous and that the party can carry out its own suppression.

12. The critique we make of Lenin's conception of "the introduction from without of political consciousness into the proletariat by the party"[1] in no way entails for us abandonment of the idea of the party. Such abandonment is equally alien to Rosa Luxemburg's position, which is nonetheless so often invoked. Here is how Rosa expressed herself on this issue:

> The task of social democracy does not consist in the technical preparation and direction of mass strikes, but, first and foremost, in the political leadership of the whole movement. The social democrats are the most enlightened, most class-conscious vanguard of the proletariat. They cannot and dare not wait, in a fatalist fashion, with folded

arms for the advent of the "revolutionary situation," to wait for that which in every spontaneous peoples' movement, falls from the clouds. On the contrary, they must now, as always, hasten the development of things and endeavor to accelerate events.[2]

In fact, the conception of spontaneity that today frequently underlies critiques of the idea of the party is much more the anarchosyndicalist conception than Rosa's.

13. Historical analysis shows that, in the class's development, organized political currents have always played a preponderant and indispensable role. In all the decisive moments of the history of the workers' movement, forward progress has been expressed by the fact that the class, under pressure from objective conditions, has arrived at the level of the ideology and program of the most advanced political fraction and either merged with the latter—as in the Commune—or lined up behind it—as during the Russian Revolution. These organized fractions have certainly not instilled the era's highest degree of consciousness from without into the class—and that suffices to refute Lenin's conception; the class arrives there through the action of objective factors and through its own experience. Yet, without the action of these fractions, the action would never have been pushed so far; it would not have taken the form it took.

[. . .]

20. Our attitude on this fundamental question can be summarized in the following way:

a) We categorically dismiss the confusion-making and eclecticism that are presently the trend in anarchistic circles. For us, there is, each time, but a single program, a single ideology that expresses the class's interests; we recognize as autonomous only the bodies that stand on this program, and those alone can be recognized as the class's rightful leadership. We consider it our fundamental task to struggle for the majority of the class to accept this program and this ideology. We are certain that if that does not happen, every body, however formally "autonomous" it might be, will unavoidably become an instrument of the counterrevolution.

b) Yet this does not settle the problem of the relations between the organization that represents the program and ideology of the revolution and the other organizations claiming to represent the working class, nor does it settle that of the relations between this organization and the class's soviet bodies. The struggle for the ascendency of the revolutionary program within mass bodies can be carried out only through means that flow directly from the goal to be attained, which is the exercise of power by the working class; consequently, these means are directed essentially toward the development of the class's consciousness and its capacities, at each moment and on the occasion of each concrete act the party undertakes before the class. Whence flows not only proletarian democracy as indispensable means for the building of socialism but also the fact that the party can never exercise power as such and that power is always exercised by mass soviet bodies.

Notes

1. T/E: In *What is To Be Done* (1901), Lenin, quoting Karl Kautsky's statement that "socialist consciousness is something introduced into the proletarian class struggle from without" by the Social-Democratic Party, says that these words are "profoundly true and important."
2. T/E: Rosa Luxemburg, *The Mass Strike* (London, Chicago, and Melbourne: Bookmarks, 1986), 69.

The Proletariat and the Problem of Revolutionary Leadership

Claude Montal

"Le Prolétariat et le problème de la direction révolutionnaire"
Socialisme ou Barbarie, 10 (July–August 1952): 22–27
Socialisme ou Barbarie—Anthologie, 203–208

In May 1950, a Bordigist group, the French Federation of the Communist Left, decided to merge with S. ou B. on the basis of a text signed by Véga (no. 7, 82-94) in which the role of the party in the theory of revolution was again reinforced. Let us note, however, that later on Véga would always defend, on the organization question, positions close to Castoriadis's. This orientation, and its practical implications, appeared to some as bearing the seeds of bureaucratization. It was challenged in particular by Lefort in 1951. He expounded his position in a text published in no. 10 of the review under the title "The Proletariat and the Problem of Revolutionary Leadership," of which we reproduce below some major passages.

Lefort broaches the problem in a new way, discussing the responses brought to bear on it no longer in terms of doctrine but as expressions of historical moments of the "proletarian experience." It is under this heading, taken as outdated, that he objects to the Leninist viewpoint and its variants (let us recall that, summarized to the extreme, this thesis states that the proletariat is rationally obliged to aim for an overall change of society, but that, on account of its present alienation, it cannot become aware of this necessity or act accordingly; the party's role is therefore to inculcate in it "from without" what it would necessarily think were it able to acquire an adequate awareness of its condition and of its historical role . . .). Put schematically, Lefort's argument is as follows: Until just after World War II, proletarian consciousness was dominated by an abstract conception of revolution that consisted essentially in overthrowing the bourgeoisie and abolishing capitalism. The party could then appear, in the view of the proletariat itself, as the necessary instrument of this struggle. But the experience of the bureaucracy as exploitative stratum, in the

USSR and elsewhere, leads the proletariat to set for itself a much more radical objective, one of universal import: taking into hand the total management of society. Thus, as he summarizes in a startling formula, "the proletariat is its own theory." And the party, as an organ separated from the class that sets itself up as the class's leadership [direction], reveals itself to be an obstacle.

Here are sections III and IV of this article.

[. . .]

III. THERE IS ONLY ONE FORM OF PROLETARIAN POWER

If the party is defined as the most perfected expression of the proletariat, its conscious or most conscious leadership, it necessarily tends to silence all other expressions of the class and to subordinate to itself all other forms of power. It is not an accident that, in 1905, the Bolshevik Party held that the soviet formed in Petrograd was useless and ordered it to dissolve itself. Nor that, in 1917, the Party dominated the soviets and reduced them to a fictive role. Nor is this the fruit of some Machiavellianism on the part of leaders. If the party possesses the truth, it is logical that it try to impose it; if it functions as the proletariat's leadership before the revolution, it is logical that it continue to behave as such afterward. It is, finally, logical that the class bow down before the party, even if it senses in the revolution the need for its total power, since it itself has felt that a leadership separate from it is required to lead it.

Rosa Luxemburg's critique of the Bolshevik Party expresses the vanguard's anxious reaction when faced with working-class division. It does not challenge the existence of the party, which corresponds to a profound necessity for the proletariat's progress. Such a questioning in that era can be expressed only in an abstract position, that of anarchism, which denies history. In criticizing the extreme traits the separation of the party from the class takes on in Bolshevism, Rosa is indicating only that the truth of the party can never replace the experience of the masses: "Historically, the errors committed by a truly revolutionary movement are infinitely more fruitful than the infallibility of the cleverest Central Committee."[1] She shows, on the other hand, that there is a permanent danger of the class being reduced to the role of raw material for the action of a group of petty-bourgeois intellectuals.

If, like Lenin, we define opportunism as the tendency that paralyzes the independent revolutionary movement of the working class and transforms it into an instrument of ambitious bourgeois intellectuals, we must also recognize that in the initial stage of a labor movement this end is more easily attained as a result of rigorous centralization rather than by decentralization. It is by extreme centralization that a young, uneducated proletarian movement can be most completely handed over to the intellectual leaders staffing a Central Committee.[2]

Rosa's position is surpassingly precious, for it testifies to a more acute sense of revolutionary reality than Lenin's. Yet one cannot say, of these two positions, that one is true. They both express an authentic vanguard tendency: Make the revolution and organize oneself to that end, whatever the mode of that organization, in the first case; in the other, above all do not separate oneself from the class and, within the organization, reflect already the proletariat's revolutionary character. One can go beyond the opposition between Lenin and Rosa only by linking that opposition to a determinate historical period and critiquing that period.

Such a critique is possible only when history carries it out itself, when the overtly counterrevolutionary character of the post-1917 party is revealed. Only then is it possible to see that the contradiction resides not in the strictness of centralism but in the very fact of the party; that the class cannot alienate itself into any form of stable and structured representation without such representation becoming autonomized. Then, the working class can turn back around on itself and conceive its nature, which differentiates it radically from every other class. Until that time, it becomes aware of itself only in its struggle against the bourgeoisie and it undergoes, in the very conception of this struggle, the pressures of exploitative society. It required the party because it had to set against the State, against the concentration of power of the exploiters, one and the same kind of unified leadership. Yet its failure reveals to it that it cannot *divide itself*, alienate itself in stable forms of representation, as the bourgeoisie does. The latter can do so only because it has an economic nature of its own in relation to which political parties are but superstructures. Yet, as we have said, the proletariat has nothing objective about it; it is a class in which the economic and the political no longer have any separate reality; it is one that defines itself only as *experience*. This is precisely what constitutes its revolutionary character, though it is also what indicates its extreme vulnerability. It is *qua* total class that it has to resolve its historical tasks, and it cannot hand over its interests to a part detached from it, for it has no interests separate from that of the management of society.

Shying away from this key critique, the group sticks to points of detail. It says that one must avoid training professional revolutionaries, that one must strive toward abolishing the opposition between directors and executants within the party, as if intentions could have the power to transform the objective meaning of the party, which is inscribed within its structure. The group recommends that the party not behave as an organ of power. Yet, less than anyone else, Lenin never claimed such a role. It is on the factual level that the party behaves as the sole form of power; it is not a point in its program. If one conceives the party as the truest creation of the class, its perfected expression (that is Socialisme ou Barbarie's theory), if one thinks that the party has to head up the proletariat before, during, and after the revolution, it is only too clear that it is the sole form of power. It is only tactically (giving the proletariat time to assimilate experientially the party's truths) that the party will tolerate other forms of class representation. The soviets, for example, will be considered by it as auxiliaries, but always *less true* than the party in their expression of the class because less capable of obtaining cohesiveness and ideological homogeneity and because it would be the theater of all the tendencies of the workers' movement. It is then inevitable that the party tends to impose itself as the sole leadership and to eliminate the soviets, as was the case in 1917.

On the most palpable revolutionary terrain, that of the forms of proletarian struggle, the group, despite its analysis of the bureaucracy, never gets anywhere. In this sense, it can be said that it is far behind the vanguard, which is offering a critique not of Lenin but of a historical period. Today it rejects the party-idea with the same obstinacy as it required that idea in the past because the idea has no meaning in the present period. It is incomprehensible, moreover, to affirm that the vanguard has radically progressed in its understanding of its historical tasks, that it apprehends for the first time the truth of exploitation in its full scope and no longer in its partial form as private property, that it turns its attention toward the positive form of proletarian power and no longer toward the immediate task of overthrowing the bourgeoisie, and to affirm at the same time that this same vanguard has regressed completely in its understanding of organizational problems.

It can in no way be known whether the proletariat in the present period would have the capacity to overthrow the exploitative power. Alienation in work, its exclusion from the cultural process, and the unequalness of its development are traits that are as negative today as they were thirty years ago; the constitution of a workers' bureaucracy that is becoming aware of its own ends and the antagonism it has developed with the bourgeoisie has hampered the proletariat's own struggle and has enslaved it to other exploiters. Nevertheless, its unification has not ceased to continue in parallel with the concentration of capitalism, and the class has behind it an experience of struggles that furnishes it with a total awareness of its tasks. What alone can be affirmed is that the proletariat can now inaugurate a revolutionary struggle only by manifesting its historical consciousness from the beginning. This signifies that the class, at the very stage its vanguard is regrouping, will announce its ultimate objective—that is, it will be led to prefigure the future form of its power. The vanguard will not be able to join any party, for its program will be the leadership of the class by itself.

Undoubtedly, the vanguard will be led through the logic of its struggle against the concentrated power of the exploiter to gather together in a minoritarian form before the revolution. Yet it would be sterile to call *party* such a regrouping that would not have the same function. In the first place, this regrouping will not be able to occur except spontaneously in the course of struggle and within the production process, not in response to a nonproletarian group providing a political program. In the second place and in essence, it will have from the beginning no other end than to permit the class to take power. It will not set itself up as a historical leadership but only as an instrument of the revolution, not as a body functioning according to its own laws but as a purely present and provisional [*conjoncturel*] detachment of the proletariat. Its goal will be able to be, from the beginning, only its self-abolition within the representative power of the class.

We are affirming, in effect, that there can be only one class power: its representative power. To say that such a power is unviable without the party's assistance precisely because it represents all the class's tendencies—the opportunist and bureaucratic tendencies as well as the revolutionary ones—would boil down to saying that the class is incapable of itself ensuring its historical role and that it has to be protected against itself by a specialized revolutionary body—that is, it would boil down to reintroducing the main thesis of bureaucratism we are fighting. Nothing can protect the class against itself. No artifice can make it resolve problems it is not mature enough to resolve.

IV. SITUATION OF THE VANGUARD
AND ROLE OF A REVOLUTIONARY GROUP

The first conditions for present-day experience have been laid down by the failure of the Russian Revolution. Yet this experience was first perceptible only in an abstract form and for a tiny proletarian minority. The degeneration of Bolshevism became clear only with the development of bureaucracy. The vanguard could not draw a partial lesson concerning the problem of its organization before drawing an overall lesson concerning the evolution of society, the true nature of its exploitation. The form within which it conceives the class's power is gradually perceived only in opposition to the form in which the power of the bureaucracy is achieved. The universality of the proletariat's tasks is revealed only when exploitation appears with its statist character and its own universal signification. That is why the last war raised only a new awareness: the economic regime that seemed tied to the USSR spread over part of the world, thus revealing its historical tendency, and the Stalinist parties in Western Europe manifested their exploitative character within the production process. During this period, a fraction of the class acquired an overall awareness of the bureaucracy (signs of which we had at the time seen in the Struggle Committees set up on an antibureaucratic basis). The development of the USSR-USA antagonism, the race toward war, the diversion of every workers' struggle to the benefit of one of the two imperialist powers, the incapacity, where the proletariat finds itself, to act revolutionarily without that action immediately taking on worldwide import—all these factors were opposed and are still opposed to an autonomous manifestation of the class. They also oppose a regrouping of the vanguard, for there is no real separation of the one from the other. The vanguard can act only when conditions objectively permit the total struggle of the class. It no less remains the case that the vanguard has deepened its experience considerably: the very reasons that prevent it from acting indicate its maturity.

It is therefore not only erroneous but impossible in the present period to set up any organization. History justly refutes these illusory edifices called *revolutionary leadership* by periodically shaking them. The Socialisme ou Barbarie group has not escaped such treatment. It is only by comprehending what the situation and the tasks of the vanguard are and what connection is to unite the vanguard to that situation that a collectivity of revolutionaries can work and develop. The only goal such a collectivity can set for itself is to express to the vanguard what is in it in the form of experience and implicit knowledge and to clarify present-day economic and social problems. In no way can it set as its task to contribute to the vanguard a program of action to follow, still less an organization to join. The sole imperatives of such a group have to be those of critique and revolutionary orientation. The review *Socialisme ou Barbarie* is not to present itself as the expression of an established truth or as an already constituted organization but as a site of discussion and elaboration within the framework of a shared ideology whose main lines are easily determined. In a revolutionary period, the group's task will be to merge with the regrouped vanguard and to crystallize its elements by explaining nonstop what are the class's historical goals. A group like Socialisme ou Barbarie is *for* the vanguard, and it is the latter's action that will give a meaning to what it elaborates, just as the vanguard is *for* the class and can never tend toward having a separate existence.

In the same issue, under the title "Proletarian Leadership," Castoriadis distances himself a bit from the position defined in the "Resolution" published in no. 2, which was quoted above. He brings to light the "antinomies" and the "contradictions" connected with revolutionary activity, which has to hold together, on the one hand, "a scientific analysis of society, . . . a conscious perspective on future development, and consequently . . . a partial planning of its attitude toward reality" and, on the other, "the creative activity" of the masses, whose "content will be original and unforeseeable."³ These antinomies cannot be "surpassed" by theory but only through the dynamic of revolution itself. Yet in the meantime, one cannot simply stick to the "implicit knowledge" of the workers' vanguard, for it is presently in the main negative. While the most conscious workers reject the traditional solutions, Stalinism and bureaucracy, they also contest that there would be a general solution and they no longer believe in the proletariat's capacity to become the dominant class.

> *[O]nly the group can . . . carry on with the elaboration of a revolutionary ideology, define a program, and do the work of propagating ideas and educating. These are quite valuable activities even if the results do not appear immediately. The accomplishment of these tasks is a basic presupposition for the constitution of a leadership, once the latter becomes objectively possible . . . [that is, once] the pressure of objective conditions [will] put again before the most conscious workers the necessity of acting.⁴*

The split with Lefort nonetheless remained deep enough that the latter, as well as a few other people, no longer considered themselves members of the group while continuing to participate in its debates and to collaborate in the review (June 1951).

Notes

1. T/E: Rosa Luxemburg, "Organizational Question of Social Democracy" (1904), in *Rosa Luxemburg Speaks*, ed. Mary-Alice Waters (New York: Pathfinder Press, 1970), 130.
2. T/E: Ibid., 126.
3. T/E: Pierre Chaulieu, "Proletarian Leadership" (1952), now in *PSW1*; see 198.
4. T/E: Ibid., 205.

II: 1953–1958

At the margins of this internal debate, issue 14 (April–June 1954) brought an interesting contribution in the form of an exchange of letters between Anton Pannekoek and Chaulieu/Castoriadis. An eminent personality from the left opposition within the Second International, an intransigent critic of the Leninist party and of the Bolshevization of the Russian Revolution, and author of a major work on *Workers' Councils* (published in English after World War II), Pannekoek insisted in his letter on the harmfulness of a party that claimed to assume the revolutionary leadership of the proletariat and on the necessity of conferring upon Workers' Councils alone the driving role both during the revolution and afterward. In his response, Chaulieu reckons that the Workers' Councils could not be the exclusive agents of the revolutionary struggle. The most conscious and determined militants, grouped in an organization, also have a role to play, a role of ideological clarification and, eventually, practical initiative, but assuredly not that of a revolutionary leadership.

The revolutionary movements that broke out in the People's Democracies during the years 1953–1958 proved the pertinence of S. ou B.'s analyses on bureaucracy while the Workers' Councils created in Poland and Hungary began to achieve in reality the central point of the socialist program as redefined by the group. The verification thus given to its theses and then the events of Spring 1958 in France led some militants to draw closer to the group. Its numbers went from around twenty members to about one hundred. Grafted onto the theoretical debate about the revolutionary party were some concrete operational problems. For these new sympathizers who often came from other groupings—the Union of the Socialist Left (UGS), the Internationalist Communist Party (PCI), and anarchist movements—the question was posed whether or not formally to join S. ou B. Those who, in the group, thought it essential to build an organization pushed them to do so; they insisted, at least, on the need to collaborate on "clear platforms." Others, on the contrary, centered around Lefort and Simon, deemed that this question of formal belonging risked turning workers away from the group. The debate picked up again on the basic issues and culminated in a split, Lefort, Simon, and a few others this time definitively leaving the group.

Lefort set out anew his point of view in no. 26 of the review under the title "Organization and Party." Below, one may read some major excerpts from this text.

Organization and Party

Claude Lefort

"Organisation et parti"
Socialisme ou Barbarie, 26 (November–December 1958): 120–24, 129–32
Socialisme ou Barbarie—Anthologie, 211–17

There is no solitary revolutionary action: such action, which strives to transform society, can be carried out only within a collective framework and that framework naturally tends to spread. Thus, revolutionary activity, being collective and seeking ever more to be so, necessarily implies a certain amount of organization. No one has ever denied or is denying this. What has been contested from the time we began elaborating our theses is not the proletariat's need for an organization; it is that of *revolutionary leadership* [direction révolutionnaire], that of the constitution of a party. The core of our main divergences lies there. The true question, whose terms have sometimes been distorted on both sides, is as follows: Does the proletariat's struggle require or not require the building of a leadership or a party?

That this question would be the permanent source of our theoretical conflict is most certainly not accidental. *Socialisme ou Barbarie*'s theses were developed on the basis of a critique of bureaucracy in all its forms: we therefore could not help but confront the problem of revolutionary organization in a critical way. Now, that problem could not help but take on an explosive character, for it challenged our ideological consistency. One can very well grant that there are some gaps in the way one forms a representation of society and set aside some problems for which one does not have a solution; one cannot, within our general ideological conceptions, grant the existence of a contradiction that tends to place thought in opposition to action. Each of us has to see and to show the connection he establishes between the forms of revolutionary action and the ideas he displays.

FROM PAST TO PRESENT

What then, for me, is it to be consistent? At the head of our theses were placed analyses of the bureaucratic phenomenon. We broached that phenomenon simultaneously from various angles before forming for ourselves an overall representation thereof. The first angle was the critique of workers' organizations in France. We discovered in these something other than bad leadership groups whose errors would have to be corrected or whose betrayals would have to be denounced; we discovered that they were part of the exploitative system, forms for the enrollment of labor power within that system. We therefore began by trying to find the material bases of Stalinism in France. We thereby discerned at once the current privileges that ensured the stability of a stratum of political and trade-union cadres and the general historical conditions that favored the crystallization of numerous elements in society by offering them the prospect of a dominant-class status.

The second angle involved the critique of the Russian bureaucratic regime. We showed the economic mechanisms that underlie the domination of a new class.

The third angle involved the discovery of bureaucratic tendencies on a worldwide scale, of the growing concentration of capital, of increasingly extensive state interventions within economic and social life, which were offering a new status to strata whose fate was no longer tied to private capital.

For my part, this deepening on the theoretical level went hand in hand with an experiment I had conducted within the Trotskyist party, the lessons of which seemed clear to me.

The Parti Communiste Internationaliste (PCI), where I had been a militant until 1948, was in no way part of the system of exploitation. Its cadres drew no privilege from their activity within the Party.

Found within it were only elements animated by obvious "revolutionary good will" and conscious of the counterrevolutionary character of the traditional large organizations. Formally, great democracy reigned. The leadership bodies were regularly elected during general assemblies. Such assemblies were held frequently. Comrades had full freedom to assemble in tendencies and to defend their ideas in meetings and congresses (they were even able to express themselves in party publications). However, the PCI behaved as a microbureaucracy and appeared to us as such. No doubt, it yielded to reprehensible practices (rigging of electoral mandates during congresses, maneuvers by the current majority to ensure maximum diffusion of its ideas and to reduce the spread of the minority's, various calumnies employed to discredit adversaries, blackmail evoking the prospect of the Party's destruction each time a militant disagreed with certain major points in the program, cult of Trotsky's personality, etc.).

Yet the key does not lie there. The PCI considered itself the party of the proletariat, its irreplaceable *leadership*. It deemed the coming revolution to be the mere fulfillment of its program. With regard to workers' struggles, the organization's viewpoint prevailed absolutely. Consequently, those struggles were always interpreted in accordance with the following criterion: Under what conditions will they favor the strengthening of the Party? Having identified itself once and for all with World Revolution, the Party was ready to undertake many maneuvers, so long as they were useful to its development.

Although such a comparison could be made only with much care—for, it is valid only from a certain perspective—the PCI, like the Communist Party, saw in the proletariat a mass to be directed. It claimed merely to direct it *well*. Now, this relationship the Party maintained with laboring people—or, rather, that it would have wished to maintain, for in fact it was directing nothing at all—was to be found again, transposed within the organization, between the ruling [*de direction*] apparatus and the base. The division between directors and mere militants was a norm. The former expected of the latter that they listen, discuss proposals, vote, distribute the paper, and stick up posters. The latter, persuaded that *competent comrades* were needed at the head of the party, did what was expected of them. Democracy was grounded on the principle of ratification. Consequently, just as the organization's viewpoint prevailed in the class struggle, the viewpoint of organizational control was decisive in the Party's internal struggle. Just as the revolutionary struggle became confused with the struggle of the Party, the latter struggle became confused with the struggle conducted by the right team. The result was that the militants decided on each issue in accordance with the following criterion: Does the vote strengthen or, on the contrary, risk to weaken the right team? Thus, each abiding by a concern for immediate effectiveness, the law of inertia reigned as in every bureaucracy. Trotskyism was one of the forms of ideological conservatism.

The critique I am making of Trotskyism is not psychological: it is sociological. It does not bear on individual conduct; it concerns a model of social organization whose bureaucratic character is all the more remarkable as it is not determined directly by the material conditions of exploitation. No doubt, this model is but a byproduct of the dominant social model; the Trotskyist microbureaucracy is not the expression of a social stratum but only the echo, within the workers' movement, of the bureaucracies reigning on the level of overall society. Yet Trotskyism's failure shows us how extraordinarily difficult it is to escape the dominant social norms, to institute at the very level of revolutionary organization a mode of grouping people together, of working, and of taking action that would be effectively revolutionary and not marked by the bourgeois or bureaucratic spirit.

Socialisme ou Barbarie's analyses and the experience some, like me, drew from their former intraparty activity naturally brought one to see class struggle and socialism in a new light. No need to summarize the positions the review was led to take. It will suffice to say that autonomy became in our view the criterion of revolutionary struggle and organization. The review has not stopped affirming that the workers had to take their own fate into their hands and to organize themselves on their own, independently of parties and trade unions claiming to be the depositories of their interests and their will. In our judgment, the objective of the struggle could not but be laboring people's management of production, for every other solution would only have consecrated the power of a new bureaucracy. Consequently, we were seeking to determine which demands testified, in the short term, to an antibureaucratic awareness. We were granting a central place to the analysis of the relations of production and of how they evolved so as to show that workers' management was achievable and that it was tending to manifest itself spontaneously, already, within the system of exploitation. Finally, we were led to define socialism as a democracy of councils.

These positions, about which it cannot be said that they have today been sufficiently elaborated, but which have already occasioned some major work, were stated especially when we removed the Trotskyist obstructions weighing upon our ideas. But, of course, they can take on their full meaning only if, simultaneously, we forge a new way of representing revolutionary activity itself. That is a necessity inherent in *Socialisme ou Barbarie*'s theses. In wanting to elude that necessity, we have multiplied conflicts among ourselves without bringing out its import and sometimes without understanding it ourselves. Indeed, it is evident that a divergency on the problem of revolutionary organization little by little affects the entire content of the review: analyses of the political situation and of movements of struggle, the prospects we are trying to sketch out, and especially the language we employ when we address ourselves to workers who read us. Now, on this point, it has proved and it does prove impossible to harmonize our ideas and to offer a common response to the problem.

A certain number of the review's collaborators can do no better than define revolutionary activity within the framework of a party of a new type—which, in fact, boils down to amending the Leninist model Trotskyism had attempted to reproduce in full. Why this failure? And first of all, why must one speak of a failure? [...]

Lefort then endeavors to show that, within the group, those advocating the construction of a party that assumes the revolutionary leadership of the proletariat merely reproduce this model while believing that they are amending it through rules of formal democracy. But, he objects:

Democracy is not perverted by the existence of bad organizational rules. It is so on account of the very existence of the party. Democracy cannot be achieved within it because it is not itself a democratic body [*organisme*]—that is, a body *representative* of the social classes on whose behalf it claims to be acting.

All our ideological work should lead us to this conclusion. Not only do some of us reject it but, in my opinion, in seeking to reconcile the affirmation of the necessity of a party with our basic principles, they collapse into a new contradiction. They want to effect this reconciliation by taking as a model a party in which characteristically soviet-type rules of operation would be introduced and, thereby, they go against their critique of Leninism.

Indeed, Lenin had understood perfectly well that the party was an *artificial* organism—that is, one fabricated outside the proletariat. Considering it an absolutely necessary instrument of struggle, he did not trouble himself with setting soviet-like statutes for it. The party would be good if the proletariat supported it, bad if the proletariat did not do so: his concerns stopped there. So, in *State and Revolution*, the problem of the party's operation is not even broached: the revolutionary power is the people in arms and its councils which exercise that power. In Lenin's view, the party has existence only through its program, which is precisely power to the Soviets. Once taught by historical experience, one discovers in the party a special instrument for the training and selection of bureaucracy, and one can only set out to destroy that type of organization. To seek to confer upon it democratic attributes incompatible with its essence is to collapse into a mystification of which Lenin was not a victim; it is to present it as a *legitimate* body of the exploited classes and to grant to it a power greater than had ever been dreamed of in the past.

THE IDEA OF REVOLUTIONARY LEADERSHIP: GEOMETRICAL PROOF

But if one cannot, at least on the basis of our principles, welcome the idea of the revolutionary party without collapsing into contradiction, is there not, however, a motive that leads us incessantly to postulate its necessity?

I already formulated this motive by quoting from the review's second issue. Let us summarize it anew: The proletariat will be able to triumph only if it has at its disposal an organization and a knowledge of economic and social reality that are superior to those of its class adversary.

If this proposition were true, it would have to be said both that we are summoned to set up a party and that this party, given the criticisms we have just mentioned, cannot but become the instrument of a new bureaucracy. In short, one would have to conclude that revolutionary activity necessarily is doomed to failure. Yet that proposition—which I believe is to be found at the origin of all justifications of the party—is only deceptively self-evident. It is a geometrical proof, which has no social content. Opposite the centralized power of the bourgeoisie, opposite the scientific knowledge [*science*] the dominant classes possess, one *symmetrically* builds up an adversary that, in order to triumph, has to acquire a *superior* power and a *higher* science. This power and this science can then not help but be combined in an organization that, before the revolution, outclasses the bourgeois State. In reality, the paths along which laboring people's experience (and the tendencies of socialism) are enriched do not match this schema. It is utopian to imagine that an organized minority might appropriate for itself a knowledge of society and history that would allow it to forge in advance a scientific representation of socialism. However commendable and necessary might be the efforts of militants to assimilate and themselves advance knowledge of social reality, it must be understood that such knowledge follows a process that exceeds the forces of a definite group. Whether it is a matter of political economy, social history, technology, the sociology of work, collective psychology, or, in general, all the branches of knowledge that are of interest to the transformation of society, one must be persuaded that the current of culture eludes all strict centralization. Discoveries—whether known or unknown to us—that, according to our own criteria, are revolutionary exist in all domains; they raise culture "to the level of the universal tasks of the revolution" and answer to the requirements of a socialist society. Undoubtedly, such discoveries always coexist with conservative or retrograde modes of thinking, so that their gradual synthesis and their development cannot be carried out spontaneously. Yet such a synthesis (which we can conceive only in dynamic form) could not occur without the struggle of the revolutionary class, in giving a glimpse of an upheaval in all traditional relations, becoming a powerful agent for ideological crystallization. Under such conditions, and only then, could one speak in sensible terms of a merger between the proletarian organization and the culture. Let us repeat, this does not mean that the militants do not have a key role to play, that they are not to bring revolutionary theory forward with the help of their own forms of knowledge, but their effort can be considered only as a contribution to a *social* cultural effort always carried out along an irreducible variety of paths.

It is also utopian to imagine that the party might be able to ensure strict coordination of struggles and centralized decision-making. Workers' struggles as they have occurred over the past twelve years—and such as the review has interpreted them—have not suffered from the absence of a party-type organ that would have succeeded in coordinating the strikes. They have not suffered from a lack of politicization (in the sense intended by Lenin). They have been dominated by the problem of the autonomous organization of the struggle. No party can make the proletariat resolve this problem. It will be resolved, on the contrary, only in opposition to the parties, whichever ones they might be—by which I mean also antibureaucratic ones—and whatever their programs. The requirement of a concerted preparation of struggles within the working class and of revolutionary forecasting certainly cannot be ignored (though it does not present itself at every moment, as some would have us believe), but it is inseparable today from this other requirement: that struggles be decided and controlled by those who conduct them. *The function of coordination and centralization therefore does not justify the existence of the party; it falls to minoritarian groups of workers or employees who, while multiplying contacts among themselves, do not stop being a part of the production settings in which they act.*

In the end, the proletariat arrives at an awareness of the universal tasks of the revolution only when it accomplishes those tasks itself, only at the moment when the class struggle embraces society as a whole and when the formation and proliferation of councils of laboring people yield appreciable signs of a possible new society. That militant minorities might do some revolutionary work in no way signifies that a body [*organisme*] might be able, within exploitative society, to embody [*incarner*] opposite bourgeois power, in anticipatory form and thanks to the centralization and rationalization of its activities, the power of laboring people. Unlike the bourgeoisie, the proletariat has, within exploitative society, no representative institution; it has at its disposal only its experience, whose complicated and never-guaranteed course cannot be deposited in any objective form. Its institution is the revolution itself.

MILITANT ACTIVITY

What then is the conception of revolutionary activity that a few comrades and myself have been led to defend? It flows from what militants are not, cannot, and do not have to be: a Leadership Group [*une Direction*]. They are a minority of active elements coming from varying social strata, gathered together because of a deep ideological agreement, and they apply themselves to helping laboring people in their class struggle, to contributing to the development of this struggle, to dissipating mystifications maintained by the dominant classes and bureaucracies, and to spreading the idea that laboring people, if they want to defend themselves, will be summoned to take their fate into their hands, to organize themselves on a society-wide scale, and that that is socialism. [...]

And two pages later, Lefort concludes:

> *The workers' movement will clear a revolutionary path only by breaking with the mythology of the party, so as to seek its forms of action in multiple nuclei of militants freely organizing their activity and providing, through their contacts, their information, and their connections* [liaisons], *not only the confrontation between, but also the unity of, workers' experiences.*

It is in that spirit that Lefort, Simon, and their comrades created in 1958 the group Informations et Liaisons Ouvrières (ILO), which would later become Informations et Correspondance Ouvrières (ICO).

Proletariat and Organization

Paul Cardan

"Prolétariat et organisation"
Socialisme ou Barbarie, 27 (April–May 1959): 72–83
Socialisme ou Barbarie—Anthologie, 218–28[1]

In the following two issues of the review (27 and 28, both appearing in 1959), Castoriadis published—under the pseudonym Cardan—a long text, "Proletariat and Organization," whose second part is a response to Lefort but whose first part has a more general import, as is shown by the titles of its various sections, which we reproduce in order to give an idea of its overall arrangement:

I. SOCIALISM: MANAGEMENT OF SOCIETY BY THE WORKERS
The Autonomy of the Proletariat
The Development of the Proletariat toward Socialism
The Contradictory Character of the Proletariat's Development

II. THE DEGENERATION OF WORKING-CLASS ORGANIZATIONS
The Decline of Revolutionary Theory
The Debasement of the Party Program and of the Function of the Party
The Revolutionary Party Organized on a Capitalist Model
The Objective Conditions for Bureaucratization
The Role of the Proletariat in the Degeneration of Working-Class Organizations

III: A NEW PERIOD BEGINS FOR THE LABOR MOVEMENT
Proletariat and Bureaucracy in the Present Period
The Need for a New Organization
Revolutionary Politics
Revolutionary Theory
Revolutionary Action
The Structure of the Organization

One sees that this study sets the question of the "organization of revolutionaries" back into the perspective of the historical experience the proletariat has of organization at the point of production as well as in the parties and trade unions it has created: as social form, the bureaucracy is tied to an ideology that attempts everywhere to justify the separation between directors and executants. This ideology is also at the origin of the degeneration of workers' organizations. Finally, it permeates the proletariat by perverting the consciousness it can have of itself. Consequently, "the proletariat gets only the organizations it is capable of having." This alienation, however, is also, for the workers' movement, an experience of bureaucratization and therefore a condition for an awareness of and struggle against it. Yet this possibility is not a necessity, and it is here that an organization can and has to intervene. The long excerpt we give below reproduces the conclusion of the second part and almost all of the third part of the text in no. 27.

[. . .]

The Role of the Proletariat in the Degeneration of Working-Class Organizations

Degeneration means that the working-class organization tends to become separate from the working class and a body apart, its de facto and de jure leadership [*direction*]. But this does not come about *because* of defects in the structure of these organizations or their mistaken ideas or some sort of an evil spell cast on organization as such. These negative features express the failure of these organizations, which in turn is only an aspect of the failure of the proletariat itself. When a director/executant relation is set up between the trade union or party and the proletariat, it means that the proletariat is allowing a relation of the capitalist type to be instaurated within itself.

Hence degeneration is not a phenomenon peculiar to working-class organizations. It is just one of the expressions of the way capitalism survives within the proletariat; capitalism expresses itself not in the corruption of leaders by money, but as an ideology, as a type of social structuring and as a set of relations between people. It is a manifestation of the immaturity of the proletariat vis-à-vis socialism. It corresponds to a phase in the labor movement and, even more generally, to a constant tendency toward integration into the system of exploitation or toward aiming for power for its own sake, which is expressed in the proletariat in symmetrical fashion as a tendency toward relying, explicitly or passively, on the organization for a solution to its problems.

In the same way, the Party's claim that in possessing theory it possesses the truth and thereby should direct everything would not have any real appeal if it did not make use of the conviction shared by the proletariat—and daily reproduced by life under capitalism—that general questions are the department of specialists and that its own experience of production and society is "unimportant." These two tendencies express one and the same sense of frustration and failure; they originate in the same facts and the same ideas and are impossible and inconceivable one without the other. Of course, we should judge differently the politician who wants to impose his point of view by all possible means and the worker who is totally incapable of finding a reply to his flow of words or of matching his cunning, and even more differently the leader who "betrays" and the worker who is "betrayed." But we must not forget that the notion of treason has no meaning in such social relations. No one can indefinitely betray people who do not want to be betrayed and who do what is necessary to prevent their being betrayed any longer. Understanding this allows us to appreciate what all this proletarian fetishism and all these antiorganizational obsessions that recently have taken hold of certain people are really all about. When trade-union leaders carry through reformist policies, they succeed only because of the apathy, the acquiescence, and the insufficient response of the working masses. When, for four years, the French proletariat allows the Algerians to be massacred and tortured and feebly stirs only when the question of its being mobilized by the military or of its wages becomes involved, it is very superficial to say that it is all a crime of [French Socialist Party leader Guy] Mollet's or of [French Communist Party leader Maurice] Thorez's or of organizational bureaucratization in general.

The enormous role played by organizations themselves in this question does not mean that the working class plays no part at all. The working class is neither a totally irresponsible entity nor the absolute subject of history; and those who see in the class's evolution only the problem of the degeneration of its organizations paradoxically want to make it both at once. To hear them tell it, the proletariat draws everything from itself—and plays no part in the degeneration of workers' organizations. No, as a first approximation we should say that the proletariat gets only the organizations it is capable of having.

The situation of the proletariat forces it always to undertake and continuously recommence its struggle against capitalist society. In the course of this struggle, it produces new contents and new forms—socialist contents and forms; for, to fight capitalism means to put forward objectives, principles, standards, and forms of organization radically opposed to established society. But as long as capitalism endures, the proletariat will remain partly under its hold.

The effect of this hold can be seen particularly clearly in workers' organizations. When capitalism takes hold of them, these organizations degenerate—which goes hand in hand with their bureaucratization. As long as capitalism lasts, there will always be "objective conditions" making this degeneration possible. But this does not mean that bureaucratization is fated. People make their own history. Objective conditions simply allow a result that is the product of man's actions and attitudes to happen. When they have occurred, these actions have taken a very well-defined path. On the one hand, revolutionary militants have partly remained or have returned to being prisoners of capitalist social relations and ideology. On the other, the proletariat has remained just as much under this hold and has agreed to act as the executant of its organizations.

A NEW PERIOD BEGINS FOR THE LABOR MOVEMENT

Under what conditions can this situation change in the future? First, the experience of the preceding period will have to allow revolutionary militants and workers alike to become aware of the contradictory and, basically, reactionary elements in their own and the other's conceptions and attitudes. Militants will have to overthrow these traditional ideas and come around to viewing revolutionary theory, program, politics, activity, and organization in a new way, in a socialist way. On the other hand, the proletariat will have to come around to seeing its struggle as an autonomous struggle and the revolutionary organization not as a leadership responsible for its fate but as one moment and one instrument in its struggle.

Do these conditions exist now? Is this overthrow of traditional ideas an effort of will, an inspiration, or a new, more correct theory? No, this overthrow is made possible from now on by one great *objective* fact, specifically, the bureaucratization of the labor movement. The action of the proletariat has produced a bureaucracy. This bureaucracy has become integrated into the system of exploitation. If the proletariat's struggle against the bureaucracy continues, it will be turned not only against bureaucrats as persons but against bureaucracy as a system, as a type of social relations, as a reality and an ideology corresponding to this reality.

This is an essential corollary to what was said earlier about the role of objective factors. There are no economic or other laws making bureaucratization henceforth impossible, but there is a development that has become objective, for society has become bureaucratized and so the proletariat's struggle against this society can only be a struggle against bureaucracy. The destruction of the bureaucracy is not "predestined," just as the victory of the proletariat in its struggle is not "predestined" either. But the conditions for this victory are from now on satisfied by social reality, for awareness of the problems of bureaucracy no longer depends upon any theoretical arguments or upon any exceptional amount of lucidity; it can result from the daily experience of laboring people who encounter bureaucracy not as a potential threat in the distant future but as an enemy of flesh and bone, born of their very own activity.

Proletariat and Bureaucracy in the Present Period
The events of recent years show that the proletariat is gaining experience of bureaucratic organizations not as leadership groups that are "mistaken" or that "betray," but in an infinitely more profound way.

Where these organizations are in power, as in Eastern Europe, the proletariat sees them of necessity as purely and simply the incarnation of the system of exploitation. When it manages to break the totalitarian yoke, its revolutionary struggle is not just directed *against* bureaucracy; it puts forward aims that express in positive terms the experience of bureaucratization. In 1953 the workers of East Berlin asked for a "metalworkers' government" and later the Hungarian workers' councils demanded workers' management of production.[2]

In the majority of Western countries, the workers' attitude toward bureaucratic organizations shows that they see them as foreign and alien institutions. In contrast to what was still happening at the end of World War II, in no industrialized country do workers still believe that "their" parties or trade unions are willing or able to bring about a fundamental change in their situation. They may "support" them by voting for them as a lesser evil; they may use them—this is often still the case as far as trade unions are concerned—as one uses a lawyer or the fire brigade. But rarely do they *mobilize* themselves for them or at their call, and never do they actively *participate* in them. Membership in trade unions may rise or fall, but no one attends trade-union meetings. Parties can rely less and less on the active militancy of workers who are party members; they now function mainly through paid permanent staff made up of "left-wing" members of the petty bourgeoisie and intellectuals. In the eyes of the workers, these parties and trade unions are part of the established order—more or less rotten than the rest—but basically the same as them. When workers' struggles erupt, they often do so outside the bureaucratic organizations and sometimes directly *against* them.[3]

We therefore have entered a new phase in the development of the proletariat that can be dated, if you like, from 1953; this is the beginning of a historical period during which the proletariat will try to rid itself of the remnants of its creations of 1890 and 1917. Henceforth, when the workers put forward their own aims and seriously struggle to achieve them, they will be able to do so only outside, and most often in conflict with, bureaucratic organizations. This does not mean that the latter will disappear. For, as long as the proletariat accepts the system of exploitation, organizations expressing this state of affairs will exist and will continue to serve as instruments for the integration of the proletariat into capitalist society. Without them, capitalist society can no longer function. But because of this very fact, each struggle will tend to set the workers against these bureaucratized organizations; and if these struggles develop, new organizations will rise up from the proletariat itself, for sections of wage laborers, salaried workers, and intellectuals will feel the need to act in a systematic and permanent fashion to help the proletariat achieve its new objectives.

The Need for a New Organization
If the working class is to enter a new phase of activity and development, immense practical and ideological needs will arise.

The proletariat will need organs that will allow it to express its experiences and opinions beyond the shop and the office where the capitalist structure of society at present confines them and that will enable it to smash the bourgeois and bureaucratic monopoly over the means of expression. It will need information centers to tell it about what is happening among various strata of workers, within the ruling classes, in society in general, and in other countries. It will need organs for ideological struggle against capitalism and the bureaucracy capable of drawing out a positive socialist conception of the problems of society. It will feel the need for a socialist perspective to be defined, for the problems faced by a working class in power to be brought out and worked out, and for the experience of past revolutions to be drawn out and put at the disposal of present generations. It will need material means and instruments to carry out these tasks as well as interoccupational, interregional, and international liaisons to bring people and ideas together. It will need to attract office workers, technicians, and intellectuals into its camp and to integrate them into its struggle.

The working class cannot directly satisfy these needs itself except in a period of revolution. The working class can bring about a revolution "spontaneously," make the most far-reaching demands, invent forms of struggle of incomparable effectiveness, and create bodies to express its power. But the working class as such, in a totally undifferentiated state, will not, for example, produce a national workers' newspaper, the absence of which is sorely felt today; it will be workers and militants who will produce it, and who will of necessity organize to produce it. It will not be the working class as a whole that spreads the news of a particular struggle fought in a particular place; if organized workers and militants don't do it, then this example will be lost, for it will remain unknown. In periods of normalcy, the working class as such will not absorb within itself the technicians and intellectuals whom capitalist society tends to separate from the workers all their lives; and without this sort of integration a host of problems facing the revolutionary movement in a modern society will remain insoluble. Neither will the working class as such nor intellectuals as such solve the problem of how to carry on a continuous elaboration of revolutionary theory and ideology, for such a resolution can come about only through a fusion of the experience of workers and the positive elements of modern culture. Now, the only place in contemporary society in which this fusion can take place is a revolutionary organization.

To work toward answering these needs therefore necessarily implies building an organization as large, as strong, and as effective as possible. We believe this organization can exist only under two conditions.

The first condition is that the working class recognize it as an indispensable tool in its struggle. Without substantial support from the working class, the organization could not develop for better or for worse. The phobia about bureaucratization certain people are developing at the moment fails to recognize a basic fact: There is very little room for a new bureaucracy, objectively (the existing bureaucracies cover the needs of the system of exploitation) as well as, and above all, in the consciousness of the proletariat. Or else, if the proletariat again allowed a bureaucratic organization to develop and once more fell under its hold, the conclusion would have to be that all the ideas to which we adhere are false, at any rate as far as the present historical period and probably as far as socialist prospects are concerned. For, this would mean that the proletariat was incapable of establishing a socialist relation with a political organization, that it cannot solve the problem of its relationships with the sphere of ideology, with intellectuals, and with other social strata on a healthy and fruitful basis, and therefore, ultimately, that it would find the problem of the "State" an insoluble one.

But such an organization will be recognized by the proletariat as an indispensable tool in its struggle only if—and this is the second condition—it draws out all the lessons of the previous historical period and if it puts itself at the level of the proletariat's present experience and needs. Such an organization will be able to develop and indeed exist only if its activity, structure, ideas, and methods correspond to the antibureaucratic consciousness of laboring people and express it and only if it is able to define revolutionary politics, theory, action, and work on new bases.

Revolutionary Politics
The end, and at the same time the means, of revolutionary politics is to contribute to the development of the consciousness of the proletariat in every sphere and especially where the obstacles to this development are greatest: with respect to the problem of society taken as a whole. But awareness is not recording and playing back, learning ideas brought in from the outside, or contemplating ready-made truths. It is activity, creation, the capacity to produce. It is therefore not a matter of "raising consciousness" through lessons, no matter how high the quality of the contents or of the teacher; it is rather to contribute to the development of the consciousness of the proletariat as a creative faculty.

Not only then is it not a question of revolutionary politics imposing itself on the proletariat or of manipulating it, but also it cannot be a question of preaching to the proletariat or of teaching it a "correct theory." The task of revolutionary politics is to contribute to the formation of the consciousness of the proletariat by contributing those elements of which it is dispossessed. But the proletariat can come to exert control over these elements, and, what is more important, it can effectively integrate them into its own experience and therefore render them fertile, only if they are organically connected with it. This is completely the opposite of "simplification" or popularization, and implies rather a continual deepening of the questions asked. Revolutionary politics must constantly show how society's most general problems are contained in the daily life and activity of the workers, and inversely, how the conflicts tearing apart their lives are, in the last analysis, of the same nature as those that divide society. It must show the connection between the solutions laboring people offer to problems they face at work and those that are applicable to society as a whole. In short, it must extract the socialist contents in what is constantly being created by the proletariat (whether it is a matter of a strike or of a revolution), formulate them coherently, propagate them, and show their universal import.

This is not to suggest that revolutionary politics is anything like a passive expression or reflection of working-class consciousness. This consciousness contains something of everything, both socialist elements and capitalist ones, as we have shown at great length. There is Budapest and there are also large numbers of French workers who treat Algerians like *bougnoules* [a racially derogatory term]; there are strikes against hierarchy and there are interunion jurisdictional disputes. Revolutionary politics can and must combat capitalism's continuous penetration into the proletariat, for revolutionary politics is merely one aspect of the struggle of the working class against itself. It necessarily implies making a *choice* among the things the working class produces, asks for, and accepts. The basis for this choice is ideology and revolutionary theory.

Revolutionary Theory

The long-prevalent conception of revolutionary theory—the science of society and revolution, as elaborated by specialists and introduced into the proletariat by the party—is in direct contradiction to the very idea of a socialist revolution being the autonomous activity of the masses. But it is just as erroneous on the theoretical plane. There is no "proof" of the inevitable collapse of the system of exploitation.[4] There is even less "truth" in the possibility of socialism being established by a theoretical elaboration operating outside the concrete content created by the historic and everyday activity of the proletariat. The proletariat develops on its own toward socialism—otherwise there would be no prospect for socialism. The objective conditions for this development are given by capitalist society itself. But these conditions only establish the context and define the problems the proletariat will encounter in its struggle; they are a long way from determining the content of its answers to these problems. Its responses are a creation of the proletariat, for this class takes up the objective elements of the situation and at the same time transforms them, thereby opening up a previously unknown and unsuspected field of action and objective possibilities. The content of socialism is precisely this creative activity on the part of the masses that no theory ever could or ever will be able to anticipate. Marx could not have anticipated the Commune (not as an event but as a form of social organization) nor Lenin the Soviets, nor could either of them have anticipated workers' management. Marx could only draw conclusions from and sift out the significance of the action of the Parisian proletariat during the Commune—and he merits the great distinction of having shattered his own previously held views to do so. But it would be just as false to say that once these conclusions have been sifted out, the theory possesses the truth and can rigidify it in formulations that will remain valid indefinitely. These formulations will be valid only until the next phase of activity by the masses; for, each time they again enter into action, the masses tend to go beyond their previous level of action, and thereby beyond the conclusions of previous theoretical elaborations.

Socialism is not a correct theory as opposed to false theories; it is the possibility of a new world rising out of the depths of society that will bring into question the very notion of "theory." Socialism is not a correct idea. It is a project for the transformation of history. Its content is that those who half the time are the objects of history will become wholly its subjects—which would be inconceivable if the meaning of this transformation were possessed by a particular category of individuals.

Consequently, the conception of revolutionary theory must be changed. It must be modified, in the first place, with respect to the ultimate source for its ideas and principles—which can be nothing else but the historic as well as day-to-day experience and action of the proletariat. All of economic theory has to be reconstructed around what is contained in embryo in the tendency of workers toward equality in pay; the entire theory of production around the informal organization of workers in the firm; all of political theory around the principles embodied in the soviets and the councils. It is only with the help of these landmarks that theory can illuminate and make use of what is of revolutionary value among the general cultural creations of contemporary society.

The conception of theory must be modified, in the second place, with respect to both its objective and function. This cannot be to churn out the eternal truths of socialism, but to assist in the struggle for the liberation of the proletariat and humanity. This does not mean that theory is a utilitarian appendage of revolutionary struggle or that its value is to be measured by the degree of effectiveness of propaganda.

Revolutionary theory is itself an essential moment in the struggle for socialism and is such to the degree that it contains the truth. Not speculative or contemplative truth, but truth bound up with practice, truth that casts light upon a project for the transformation of the world. Its function, then, is to state explicitly, and on every occasion, the meaning of the revolutionary venture and of the workers' struggle; to shed light on the context in which this action is set, to situate the various elements in it, and to provide an overall explanatory schema for understanding these elements and for relating them to each other; and to maintain the vital link between the past and the future of the movement. But above all, it is to elaborate the prospects for socialism. For revolutionary theory, the ultimate guarantor for the critique of capitalism and for the prospect of a new society is to be found in the activity of the proletariat, its opposition to established forms of social organization, and its tendency to instaurate new relations among people. But theory can and must bring out the truths that spring from this activity by showing their universal validity. It must show that the proletariat's challenge to capitalist society expresses the deepest contradiction within that society; it must show the objective possibility of a socialist society. It therefore must define the socialist outlook as completely as possible at any given moment according to the experience and activity of the proletariat—and in return interpret this experience according to this outlook.

Finally, the conception of theory must be modified with respect to the way it is elaborated. As an expression of what is universally valid in the experience of the proletariat and as a fusion of that experience with the revolutionary elements in contemporary culture, revolutionary theory cannot be elaborated, as was done in the past, by a particular stratum of intellectuals. It will have no value, no consistency with what it elsewhere proclaims to be its essential principles unless it is constantly being replenished, in practice, by the experience of laboring people as it takes shape in their day-to-day lives. This implies a radical break with the practice of traditional organizations. The intellectuals' monopoly over theory is not broken by the fact that a tiny stratum of workers are "educated" by the organization—and thus transformed into second-string intellectuals; on the contrary, this simply perpetuates the problem. The task the organization is up against in this sphere is to have intellectuals and laboring people *as laboring people* link up in the effort to elaborate its views. This means that the questions asked, and the methods for discussing and working out these problems, must be changed so that it will be possible for laboring people to take part. This is not a case of "the teacher making allowances," but rather the primary condition to be fulfilled if revolutionary theory is to remain adequate to its principles, its object, and its content.[5]

These considerations show that it is vain to talk of revolutionary theory outside a revolutionary organization. Only an organization formed as a revolutionary workers' organization, in which workers numerically predominate and dominate it on fundamental questions, and which creates broad avenues of exchange with the proletariat, thus allowing it to draw upon the widest possible experience of contemporary society—only an organization of this kind can produce a theory that will be anything other than the isolated work of specialists.

Revolutionary Action

The task of the organization is not just to arrive at a conception—the clearest possible—of the revolutionary struggle and then keep it to itself. This conception has no meaning unless it is a moment in this struggle; it has no value unless it can aid in the workers' struggle and assist in the formation of their experience. These two aspects are inseparable. Unlike the intellectual, whose experiences are formed by reading, writing, and speculative thinking, workers can form their experiences only through their actions. The organization therefore can contribute to the formation of worker experience only if (a) it itself acts in an exemplary fashion, and (b) it helps laboring people to act in an effective and fruitful way.

Unless it wants to renounce its existence completely, the organization cannot renounce acting, nor can it give up trying to influence actions and events in a particular direction. No form of action considered in itself can be ruled out in advance. These forms of action can be judged only by their effectiveness in achieving the aim of the organization—which continues to be the lasting development of the consciousness of the proletariat. These forms range from the publication of journals and pamphlets to the issuing of leaflets calling for such and such an action and the promulgation of slogans that in a given historic situation can allow a rapid crystallization of the awareness of the proletariat's own aims and will to act. The organization can carry through this action coherently and consciously only if it has a point of view on the immediate as well as the historical problems confronting the working class and only if it defends this point of view before the working class—in other words, only if it acts according to a *program* that condenses and expresses the experience of the workers' movement up to that point.

Summary of pp. 83-85:

"Three tasks facing the organization at present are highly urgent and require a more precise definition. The first is to bring to expression the experience of the workers and to help them become aware of the awareness they already possess." The second is "to place before the proletariat an overall conception of the problems of present-day society and, in particular, the problem of socialism." And the organization's third task is "to help the workers defend their immediate interests and position" (pp. 83-84).

Finally, as concerns the organization's structure, its "inspiration can come only from the socialist structures created by the proletariat in the course of its history. . . . This means":

a. *that in deciding their own activities, grassroots organs enjoy as much autonomy as is compatible with the general unity of action of the organization;*
b. *that direct democracy, that is, collective decision-making by all those involved, be applied wherever it is materially possible; and*
c. *that the central organs empowered to make decisions be composed of delegates elected from the grassroots organs who are liable to recall at any time (p. 85).*

Notes

1. T/E: Reprinted in *EMO2* and *EP1*. The translation included here is an edited version of Maurice Brinton's "Working Class Consciousness," *Solidarity Pamphlets* 22 and 23. An edited version of the entire first part appeared in *PSW2*.
2. See issues 13 and 20 (January 1954 and December 1956) of this review.
3. See the texts on the French strikes of 1953 and 1955 and on the strikes in England and the United States in nos. 13, 18, 19, and 26 (January 1954, January and July 1956, and November 1958) of *S. ou B.* On the meaning of the French population's attitude toward Gaullism, see the text entitled "Bilan" in no. 26 of the review. [T/E: See, in Part 2 of the present *Anthology*: "Wildcat Strikes in the American Automobile Industry," "The English Dockers' Strikes," and "Automation Strikes in England."]
4. Whatever the severity of the crisis—the events in Poland have demonstrated this again recently—an exploitative society can be overthrown only if the masses are not merely stirred into action but

raise this action up to the level needed for a new social organization to take the place of the old one. If this does not happen, social life must continue and it will continue following the old model, though perhaps superficially changed to a greater or lesser degree. Now, no theory can "prove" that the masses will inevitably reach this requisite level of activity; such a "proof' would be a contradiction in terms.

5. There obviously cannot be equal participation on all subjects; the important thing is that there be equal participation on the basic ones. Now, for revolutionaries, the first change to bring about concerns the question of what is a basic subject. It is clear that laboring people could not participate as laboring people and on the basis of their experience in a discussion on the falling rate of profit. It so happens, as if by accident, that this problem is, strictly speaking, unimportant (even scientifically). More generally, nonparticipation in traditional organizations has gone along with a conception of revolutionary theory as a "science" that has no connection with people's experiences except in its most remote consequences. What we are saying here leads us to adopt a diametrically opposed position; by definition, nothing can be of basic concern to revolutionary theory if there is no way of linking it up organically with laboring people's own experience. It is also obvious that this connection is not always simple and direct and that the experience involved here is not experience reduced to pure immediacy. The mystification that there is some kind of "spontaneous process" through which laboring people can, through an effortless and magic operation, find everything they need to make a socialist revolution in the here and now of their own experience is the exact counterpart to the bureaucratic mystification it is trying to combat, and it is just as dangerous.

III: 1959–1967

During this final period, Castoriadis, followed by a part of the members of the group, worked out an analysis of modern capitalism that led to a deep break with Marxism—and culminated in 1963 in a new split (see Part 7 of the present *Anthology*). The conception of organization was not affected by these theoretical developments. It will be noted, however, if one compares "Proletariat and Organization" to the "Resolution" published in no. 2, that it was no longer a question of a party or of the proletariat's revolutionary leadership. Yet in the new analysis of capitalism Castoriadis was proposing, this proletariat, precisely, was no longer but one of the agents for society's revolutionary transformation. From this perspective, bureaucratic alienation extends to almost all aspects of social life. Yet this alienation is not and cannot be total, otherwise society would collapse and the life of each person would become purely absurd. Constantly, individuals as well as collectivities sketch out autonomous and creative approaches—and sometimes go even further. Revolutionaries therefore have to seek to base their action on the multiple forms of resistance to bureaucratization. The role of the organization becomes that of giving some meaning to all the conflicts to which the bureaucratic project gives rise—giving some meaning, that is to say, first of all making them appear as possible seeds [*germes*] of autonomous collective activity and, in the last analysis, of a radically different society. These ideas were expounded upon in particular in the text entitled "Recommencing the Revolution" (no. 35, early 1964), large excerpts of which we reprint in Part 7 of this *Anthology.*

The group succeeded only to a small extent in implementing this revolutionary politics, thus redefined on totally new bases: by enlarging the field of subjects broached in the review (see chapter 7). On the other hand, what appeared to the group to be going on was that French society was then traversing a phase in which people seemed to be giving up on intervening in political, social, and cultural life and to be withdrawing into the private sphere ("privatization"). Under these conditions, the activity of a collectivity of revolutionaries could only run in neutral. So, in 1967 the group decided to disband and suspend publication of the review. That is what is explained in a circular sent to the review's subscribers. Even though it does not appear in *S. ou B.*'s tables of contents, it constitutes a sort of final extension thereof. We reproduce it below for the clarifications it offers about the conception the group then had of revolutionary organization and politics.

The Suspension of Publication of *Socialisme ou Barbarie*

Circular addressed to the subscribers and readers of
Socialisme ou Barbarie in June 1967. Reprinted in *EMO2*[1]
Socialisme ou Barbarie—Anthologie, 231–35[2]

The first issue of *Socialisme ou Barbarie* appeared in March 1949, the fortieth in June 1965. Contrary to what we thought when we published it, this fortieth issue will be, at least for the time being, the last.

In suspending the publication of the review for an indeterminate period of time, which we decided after a considerable amount of reflection and not without some pain, we are not motivated by difficulties of a financial nature. Such difficulties have existed for our group from the very first day. And they have never ceased. Also, they have always been overcome, and would have continued to be overcome, had we decided to go on publishing the review. If we suspend its publication today, it is because the meaning of our enterprise, under its present form, has become for us problematic. This is what we wish to set forth briefly to those who, as subscribers and readers of the review, have followed our efforts for a long time.

Socialisme ou Barbarie was never a review of pure theoretical research. While the elaboration of ideas has always occupied a central place in its pages, it has always been guided by a political aim. Already, the subtitle of the review, "organ of critique and revolutionary orientation," adequately indicates the status of the theoretical labor expressed therein these last eighteen years. Nourishing itself upon revolutionary activity both individual and collective, it derived its value from the fact that it was—or could, foreseeably, become—pertinent for such activity. This activity was one of interpreting and elucidating what is real and what is possible from the standpoint of the transformation of society. The review made sense for us and in itself only as a moment and as a tool of a revolutionary political project.

Now, from this standpoint, the real social conditions—in any case, what we perceive of them—have changed to a greater and greater extent. We have already noted this since 1959—as can be seen in the series of articles entitled "Modern Capitalism and Revolution"—and the subsequent changes have served only to confirm this diagnosis: in the societies of modern capitalism, political activity properly called is tending to disappear. Those who have read us know that this is not some simple statement of fact, but the product of an analysis of what in our opinion are the most profound characteristics of modern societies.

What appeared to us to be a compensating factor for this negative diagnosis, that which balanced, in our view, the growing privatization of the mass of the population, were struggles at the point of production, which we have concretely noted and analyzed in the cases of American and English industry. These struggles called into question the work relations extant under the system of capitalism and express, in an embryonic form, the self-directing [*gestionnaire*] tendencies of working people. We thought that these struggles would develop in France, too, and, above all, that they would be able—though certainly not without an intervention and introduction of the genuine political element—to go beyond the immediate sphere of work relations and to progress toward an attempt to call explicitly into question social relations in general.

In this we were wrong. Such a development did not take place in France, except on a minute scale (the strikes of late, which rapidly were taken over by the trade unions, do not change our judgment on this matter). In England, where these strikes continue (with their inevitable ups and downs), their character has not changed, neither on their own nor in terms of the activity of our comrades in the Solidarity group.

Certainly, a different evolution in the future is not ruled out, although it appears to us improbable for reasons we will mention below. That, however, is not the key question. We believe that we have adequately shown that we are not impatient, and we never have thought, let us repeat it, that the transformation of this type of workers' struggles—or of any other kind—could occur without a parallel development of a new political organization, which it has always been our intention to construct.

Now, the construction of such a political organization under the conditions in which we live—and in which, no doubt, we take part—was and remains impossible due to a series of factors that are in no way accidental in character and that are in fact closely interconnected.

In a society where radical political conflict is more and more masked, stifled, deflected, and sometimes even nonexistent, a political organization, should one be built, could only falter and degenerate rapidly. For, we may ask, first of all, where and in what stratum of the population could such a political organization find that immediate setting necessary for its survival? We have had a negative experience, regarding both a working-class membership and an intellectual membership. As to the former, even when they view a political group sympathetically and recognize in its ideas the expression of their own experience, it is not their habit to maintain permanent contact with it, still less active association, for its political views, insofar as these go beyond their own immediate preoccupations, seem to them obscure, gratuitous, and excessive. For the others—the intellectuals—what in particular they seem capable of satisfying when they come into contact with a political group are their curiosity and their "need for information." We should state here clearly that we have never had, on the part of the public readership of the review, the kind of response we had hoped for, which could have aided us in our work; the attitude of this public has remained, save for the rarest of exceptions, that of passive consumers of ideas. Such an attitude coming from the public, which is perfectly compatible with the role and the aims of a review presented in a traditional style, in the long run renders the existence of a review such as *Socialisme ou Barbarie* impossible.

And who, under these circumstances, will join a revolutionary political organization? Our experience has been that those who came to us—basically young people—often did so based, if not on a misunderstanding, at least on motivations that derived much more from an emotional [*affective*] revolt and from a need to break with the isolation to which society today condemns individuals than from a lucid and firm adherence to a revolutionary project. This initial motivation perhaps is as good as any other; what really matters is that the same conditions for the absence of properly political activity also prevent this motivation from being transformed into something more solid.

Finally, in this context how can such a political organization, supposing it existed, check what it says and what it proposes to do? How can it develop new organizational means and new means of action? How can it enrich, in a living dialectic of praxis with society as a whole, what it draws from its own substance? Above all, how, in the present phase of history, after the colossal and complete bankruptcy of the instruments, methods, and practices of the movement of former times, could it reconstruct a new political practice, faced as it is with the total silence of society? At best it could maintain an abstract theoretical discourse; at worst, it might produce one of these strange mixtures of sectarian obsessiveness, pseudoactivist hysteria, and interpretive delirium of which, by the dozens, "extreme left-wing" groups throughout the world still offer today all conceivable sorts of specimens.

Nothing allows one to count on a rapid change in this situation. Here is not the place to show this through a long and involved analysis (the basic elements of which are to be found already formulated in the last ten issues of *Socialisme ou Barbarie*). What must be emphasized, however, is the tremendous burden weighing down upon reality and upon present prospects: the profound depoliticization and privatization of modern society; the accelerated transformation of workers into mere employees, with the consequences that follow at the level of struggles at the point of production; the blurring of the contours of class boundaries, which renders the coincidence of economic and political objectives more and more problematic.

This overall situation—which acts as an obstacle on another terrain, that of the crisis of culture and of daily life, as has been emphasized in the review for a number of years—may develop and take the form of a positive collective reaction against alienation in modern society. Because any form of political activity, even in embryo, is impossible today, this reaction does not succeed in taking form. It is condemned to remain individual in character, or else is quickly diverted toward a delirious set of folkloric practices that no longer succeed even in shocking people. Deviance never has been revolutionary; today it is no longer even deviance, but serves merely as the indispensable negative complement of "cultural" publicity.

As one knows, for the past ten years these phenomena, more or less clearly perceived and analyzed, have pushed certain people to transfer their hopes onto the underdeveloped countries. We have said for a long time in the review why this transfer is illusory: If the modern part of the world were irremediably rotten, it would be absurd to think that a revolutionary destiny for humanity could be fulfilled in the other part. In fact, in all these underdeveloped countries, either a social movement of the masses has not succeeded in getting off the ground, or else it can do so only in becoming bureaucratized.

Whether it be a matter of its modern half or its starving half, the same question hangs suspended over the contemporary world: Has people's immense capacity for deluding themselves about what they are and what they want changed in any way over the past century? Marx thought that reality would force man to "face with sober senses his real conditions of life, and his relations with his kind." We know that reality has revealed itself not to be up to the task the great thinker thus conferred upon it. Freud believed that progress in the field of knowledge and what he called "our god *logos*" would permit man to modify gradually his relation to the obscure forces he bears within him. We have relearned since then that the relation between knowledge and the way people effectively act—both as individuals and as collectivities—is anything but simple and that the Marxian and Freudian forms of knowledge also have been able to become the source of new mystifications. And they become so again and again with each new day. Over a century of historical experience—and at all levels, from the most abstract to the most empirical—prohibits us from believing in a positive automatic functioning of history or in man's cumulative conquest of himself by himself in terms of any kind of sedimentation of knowledge. We draw from this no skeptical or "pessimistic" conclusion. Nevertheless, the relation of people to their theoretical and practical creations; the relation between knowledge, or better lucidity, and real activity; the possibility of constituting an autonomous society; the fate of the revolutionary project and its potential for laying down roots in an evolving society such as ours—these questions, and the many others they call forth, must thoroughly be rethought. Revolutionary activity will again become possible only when a radical ideological reconstruction will become capable of meeting up with a real social movement.

We thought that this reconstruction—the elements for which have already been laid down in *Socialisme ou Barbarie*—could be carried out at the same time that a revolutionary political organization was being constructed. This today proves to be impossible, and we ought to draw from it the appropriate conclusions. The theoretical work—more necessary than ever, though it henceforth presents other exigencies and involves another rhythm—cannot serve as the axis upon which the existence of an organized group and a periodical review revolves. We would be the last to fail to appreciate the risks immanent in a theoretical enterprise separated from real activity. Present circumstances, however, would permit us to maintain at best only a useless and sterile simulacrum of this activity.

We will continue, each in our own area, to reflect and to act in terms of the certainties and of the interrogations that *Socialisme ou Barbarie* has permitted us to sift out. If we do it well, and if social conditions are propitious, we are certain that we will one day be able to recommence our enterprise upon more solid grounds and in a different relation to those who have followed our work.

Notes

1. T/E: and *EP3*
2. T/E: Translated in *PSW3*.
3. With the exception of four comrades from the group, who, for their part, plan to undertake a publication claiming its kinship with the ideas of *Socialisme ou Barbarie* and who will send to subscribers and readers of the review a text setting forth their intentions.

PART SIX

THE THIRD WORLD (ALGERIA AND CHINA)

"Le Tiers-Monde: L'Algérie et la Chine"
Socialisme ou Barbarie—Anthologie, 237–39

The struggle against colonialism was not at the center of S. ou B.'s concerns, since the group was more concentrated on the analysis of modern bureaucratic-capitalist society and on the struggle against that society. From the Marxist point of view, which was at the time the viewpoint of the entire group, only the struggle of the proletariat in the developed countries of the world could lead to a socialist, revolutionary transformation: the struggles of the underdeveloped world served as an additional aid, in that they weakened capitalism. Yet on the one hand, the uprising of the Algerian people and its ferocious repression by the French State as well as the decolonization of Africa, another subject regularly broached in the review, and, on the other, the rise, within the Left, of Third Worldism obliged the group to ask itself about what was happening in the Third World. The presence of two men—Jean-François Lyotard and Pierre Souyri—who applied all their intelligence and their passion to responding to these questions greatly contributed to the group's reflections on these matters.

Lyotard (Laborde), who came to politics through his engagement in support of the Algerians and his encounter with Souyri (Brune), was a passionate observer of Algeria. He offered detailed analyses, which nourished a debate that, starting from clear positions—anti-imperialism and firm anticolonialism, but also a rejection of nationalism and of the party and state bureaucracy—nonetheless failed to culminate in a complete theoretical analysis accepted by the entire group, in particular as regards the nature of the bureaucracy in an underdeveloped country.

Yet there is one key question that, while of great concern to S. ou B., was in no way reflected in the pages of the review. Should one have aided or not the Front de Libération Nationale (FLN), whose bureaucratic nature and future role as ruling party were clear to those who said "Yes" as well as to those who said "No"? One side refused to endanger the group's overall project for the sake of a conflict whose outcome—a new bureaucratic/bourgeois State—was a foregone conclusion, whereas the other side maintained that one could not hope to influence the most radically critical combatants without being concretely in solidarity with their struggle. In the end, the decision was left to the free will of each member, upon the condition that the group itself not be put in danger. Lyotard, whose texts one will read below, was an ardent defender of giving aid to the FLN, which he actively practiced.

In reality, this war raised questions on several levels, many of which related to the situation in France. During the period around May 1958, with the revolt of the "Ultras" and de Gaulle's seizure of power, the question of the fate of the French State was posed: Was one heading toward fascism, as the Left as a whole maintained, or toward the liquidation of the colonial empire and the modernization of capitalism? S. ou B.'s response distinguished itself by its refusal to believe in the hypothesis that fascism was on the horizon and by its conviction that the most modern branch of capitalism would be able to come out on top and put an end to the anachronism of colonialism.

Other questions concerning the French domestic situation meshed with the group's key concerns: the critique, on the one hand, of the equivocations and reformism of the Communist Party, and, on the other, of the dogmatic way in which the Trotskyists, cut off from reality, tried to apply a rigid Marxist framework to the Algerian situation; and questions about the French working class's lack of solidarity with Algerian immigrants in France and with the fighters in Algeria itself. The role played by the unions and the Left in this process of depoliticization was denounced, yet the basic issue of depoliticization remained a nagging one.

The analysis also followed the situation within Algerian society step by step: it denounced the process whereby a new bureaucratic class was forming within the organs fighting the war and it detected ruptures within everyday life created by years of struggle (changes in relations within the family and in education, activity on the part of women) as well as indications that peasants and workers themselves were, in a concrete way, taking their affairs into their own hands.

We give here some excerpts drawn from three articles that appeared between 1958 and 1961. The first, "Algerian Contradictions Exposed," offers above all a thoroughgoing critique of the Trotskyist and Communist position, whereas the second one ("The Social Content of the Algerian

Struggle") contains an intensive analysis of the social processes then underway—a heightened raising of consciousness concomitant with the bureaucratization of the apparatuses—as well as of their revolutionary potential. The last one ("In Algeria, A New Wave"), which was full of hope after the monster demonstrations of December 1960, analyzes the meaning and importance of the arrival on the scene of urban youth. These texts reflect some of the most important themes that appeared at key moments during the Algerian conflict without following the twists and turns in the positions adopted and the analyses published throughout the war. It is impossible for us, within the framework of the present work, to enter into the details of the historical background and of the various Algerian groups whose politics are discussed by Lyotard. It seems to us that the general direction of his argument is comprehensible, even for an uninitiated reader. Those who wish to have more complete documentation are referred to the specialized works on the subject.

H.A.

Notes

1. For a detailed discussion of the debates and analyses of the S. ou B. group around the Algerian War, the reader is referred to the excellent master's thesis by Aurélien Moreau, *Intellectuels révolutionnaires en guerre d'Algérie: Socialisme ou Barbarie* (History Department, Université du Maine, 1998–1999).

Algerian Contradictions Exposed

François Laborde

"Mise à nu des contradictions algériennes"
Socialisme ou Barbarie, 24 (May–June 1958): 26–30, 33
Socialisme ou Barbarie—Anthologie, 240–44

[. . .]

ALGERIA AND THE "LEFT"

The situation is presently such that the Algerian War is a war that does not seem of concern to the French proletariat. It follows that the few intellectuals who feel that this war is their affair are isolated amid general indifference and that they cannot find in the dynamic of a nonexistent workers' struggle the lessons, the directives for reflection, and, finally, the concepts that would allow them to grasp precisely the historical significance of the Algerian fight and, more generally, of the emancipatory movement of the colonial countries. Reflection on the Algerian question and the positions through which such reflection arrives at conclusions are stricken with sterility on account of the fact that these theories are being elaborated outside all practice. Of course, the leaders and intellectuals of "left-wing" organizations have no difficulty continuing to apply to the Algerian National Liberal Front's (FLN) fight the officially checked labels of provenance affixed by the reformist and revolutionary tradition when it comes to the colonial question, but it happens that those labels have not had a reality check for forty years.

Moved by FLN's accusations in its organs that the "democratic and anticolonialist Left" is "unfit for (anticolonialist) combat," "unfit to handle all the problems posed to its country," and "opportunistic and chauvinistic," this Left sends out to the *Frontistes'* urgent appeals to their political realism, anxiously enquiring about their sectarianism and beseeching them to make its task easier. In this way, it is no doubt manifesting its "political sophistication," an awareness of its "responsibility," and finally, its reformism, slightly less soft than Guy Mollet's.[1] And above all, this confirms the very appreciation the Front has of this Left and, still more, its powerlessness to situate the Algerian resistance correctly within a historical schema.

This may well be seen in the solution the Left does not cease to advocate—something like negotiation, as quickly as possible—and also in the role it has reserved for itself—to put pressure upon both parties, in order to get them to come to terms. Now, it is quite obvious that neither this objective nor this function has anything revolutionary about it: immediate negotiations can be meaningful under the conditions in which the Russian Revolution found itself at Brest-Litovsk for example, but what would have been the meaning, politically, of a roundtable between the Yugoslavian resistance fighters and German generals in 1942? The FLN's situation is undoubtedly not the same, but one does not see that it justifies the *defeatism* the French Left is suggesting that it adopt. Everyone agrees that a straight-out military defeat of the Algerian National Liberation Army (ALN) is ruled out. And this Left offers it a political defeat! It is placing itself "above the fray"; it is claiming to embody the "general interest"; it wants to put an end to the massacre. We do not doubt the excellency of its sentiments, and yet those sentiments objectively aim at making the Algerian Resistance accept a perfectly rotten compromise with Algiers—that is, with the extreme reactionaries [*ultras*]—about which it knows that it will soon be sorry. Heard from where the resistance fighters are, it must be admitted that the Left's appeals for moderation, their "Put yourself in our place," have to ring like the cracked sound of the old social-traitor cookpot.

And the arguments this same "Left" directs toward the French bourgeoisie cannot convince the FLN of the authenticity of its internationalist zeal. For, in the end, what does it keep on repeating to the FLN ad nauseam? That the grandeur of France is suffering from the continuation of this war, that France's prestige abroad is collapsing, that France's self-interest requires negotiations, that one cannot safeguard the legitimate interests of France in Algiers and in the Sahara by continuing to fight, and so on. What is more chauvinistic, after all, than such rhetoric? Its constant compromises with the spokesmen of enlightened capitalism plainly show that in actuality the Left is expending a treasure of understanding to maintain the interests of

French capital, whereas it has never succeeded in taking the colonial proletariat's interest in and for itself as the *sole legitimate reference axis* for grounding its position. The fear of the Right, of its censorship, and so on cannot constitute an adequate excuse; the truth is wholly other.

For its part, the [Trotskyist] Parti Communiste Internationaliste (PCI) occupies on the Left a position that clearly delimits it and that rests on a massive application of the theory of Permanent Revolution to the Algerian problem. As the Parti du Peuple Algérien (PPA, Algerian people's party), which came out of the Étoile Nord-Africaine (ENA, North-African star), indisputably had a working-class base in France and a peasant base in Algeria and as, on the other hand, the leaders of the Mouvement pour le Triomphe des Libertés Démocratiques (MTLD, Movement for the triumph of democratic freedoms), which rallied to the FLN, were leaning, on the eve of the insurrection, toward participation in Algerian municipal elections, the PCI concluded that the FLN was reformist and the Mouvement National Algérien (MNA, Algerian national movement), issuing from the *Méssalistes* [supporters of Messali Hadj], revolutionary. As, finally, the PCI had learned in *The Permanent Revolution* that a colonial bourgeoisie is incapable of achieving independence by its own means and that a proletarian revolution has to come in to extend the democratic revolution in order that the bourgeois objectives that are compatible with socialism might in addition be achieved, the PCI concluded that it is good politics to support Messali, that is to say, the proletarian revolution. The FLN's "sectarianism" and the conciliatory spirit of *Méssaliste* declarations seemed to contradict that interpretation, so the Trotskyists explained that, in reality, the intransigence of the *Frontistes*' objective—independence—had no other goal but to preclude the presence of the MNA in future negotiations and to nip in the bud the possibilities of a revolutionary development in the Algeria of tomorrow. In this way, the murders of *Méssaliste* militants perpetrated by the *Frontistes* would be explained. The Algerian bourgeoisie would profit from terrorism, a weapon absent from the workers' traditional arsenal, in order to destroy physically the vanguard of its proletariat. The PCI therefore concluded, paradoxically, that the sole authentic revolutionary attitude consisted in struggling for "a ceasefire, the convening of a roundtable conference bringing together representatives of all political and religious currents and of all Algeria's ethnic groups, and the organization of free elections under the control of international authorities" (*La Vérité*, February 6, 1958).

Here we have an astounding example of the degree of false abstraction political reflection can attain when it has sunk into dogmatism. First of all, the very sinews of this position are false: the schema of Permanent Revolution is inapplicable in North Africa.[2] At bottom, it presupposes a combined development of colonial society wholly other than the one noted in the countries of the Maghreb. Trotsky writes that,

> in the Russian revolution the industrial proletariat has conquered the very same ground as was occupied by the semi-proletarian artisan democracy of the *sansculottes* at the end of the eighteenth century. . . . Foreign capital . . . gathered around itself the army of the industrial proletariat and prevented the rise and development of crafts. As a result of this process there appeared among us as *the main force in the towns*, at the moment of the bourgeois revolution, *an industrial proletariat of an extremely highly developed social type.*[3]

Before generalizing this schema, it would be advisable therefore to make sure that capitalist penetration in AFN [French North Africa] and especially in Algeria has taken the same forms as in Russia during the imperialist phase and that it produces there the same effects: everything proves the opposite.

It is therefore ridiculous to imagine the MNA, heir to the MTLD and the PPA, as the Algerian proletariat's revolutionary vanguard and Messali as its Lenin. Let the editors of *Vérité* reread the report of the MTLD's Second National Congress (April 1953). They will find therein not one line authorizing such an interpretation, but they will find in the final resolution this principle: "Economic prosperity and social justice," which is declared to be achievable in particular through "the creation of a genuinely national economy, the reorganization of agriculture in the interest of the Algerians, particularly agrarian reform . . . the fair distribution of national income so as to attain social justice, trade-union freedom." Yet this same Congress "assures Messali of its unshakeable attachment to this idea he represents." The MTLD decidedly was not and the MNA decidedly is not Algerian Bolshevism quite simply because there can be no Algerian Bolshevism under present conditions of industrial development. And just because 400,000 North African laborers work in the shops of French factories and on French building sites, it does not follow that they constitute a proletarian vanguard: that would be to forget that here they are emigrants, that they are not integrated, that they cannot be integrated into the French working class, that they always return home, no doubt transformed by factory life but above all confirmed in their calling as Algerians. Finally, even if everything we have just said was false, it would remain the case that these 400,000 laborers are not on the actual sites of the struggle, whereas a revolutionary thrust toward socialism, if it is to be exerted within the actual movement of the bourgeois revolution, requires that the proletariat in arms participate directly in the struggle and be capable of defeating on the spot the national bourgeoisie's counteroffensive. What is the permanent revolution when the working class is separated from its bourgeoisie by 850 miles of land and water?

That does not mean, it will have been understood, that the FLN would be any more the embodiment of the Algerian proletariat. It is a national front—that is, a "sacred union" of peasants, workers, employees, and petty bourgeois elements with bourgeois leadership. The CCE [Conseillers combattants de l'extérieur, Fighting advisors from abroad] is the Committee of Public Safety, all other things being equal: it exercises over all Algerian classes an energetic dictatorship that does not hesitate to employ terror. For an explanation of the Front's murder of Ahmed Bekhat, a *Méssaliste* trade-union leader, no need to go seek it in the pernicious influence of a Stalinism said to be infiltrating the *Frontistes*' leadership: the hypothesis is at the very most worthy of the insight of our Minister for Algeria and his moderate cronies. There is no collusion between the FLN and the Communist Party—no more the French CP than the Algerian one.

On the contrary, the CP's spinelessness [*mollesse*] on the Algerian question is now legendary, on the Right as well as on the Left. The official line justified this attitude through the prospects held out of a Popular Front. It is likely that the Stalinist leadership has lost enough of its sense of political analysis that one might suspect it of having really dreamed of outflanking Mollet "by the base." In any case, it is certain that it has never stopped wanting to infiltrate the State, as the [Socialist] SFIO does. It is generally agreed that still another intention can be credited to it: as Moscow's outpost on Western Mediterranean shores, it prefers to help French imperialism maintain its position in Algeria for better or worse (the worst case being the best, though with one proviso: maintenance of a French presence) rather than see it dislodged by American imperialism.

[. . .]

NATION AND CLASS IN ALGERIA

True, in itself the Algerian struggle has not found in the formulation the Front has given it a manifest class content. Is that because the Front, as a bourgeois leadership, wants to stifle this content? No doubt. Yet this is also because it *can* do so. And if it so easily succeeds in doing so that the French Left loses its ability to speak in Marxist terms, or what for it substitutes for Marxism, that is because Algerian colonial society proper resides in effect in the following: that class boundaries are buried there deeply beneath *national* boundaries. And it is in an entirely *abstract* (that is, exclusively *economistic*) way that one can speak of a proletariat, of *a* middle class, of *a* bourgeoisie in Algeria. If there is *a* peasantry, that is because it is wholly and exclusively Algerian, and it is *that* class that constitutes, obviously, the social base of the national movement at the same time that it is the clearest expression of the radical expropriation Algerian laboring people suffer *qua* Algerians. We will analyze its historical movement and its objectives later on. Yet it is not, by definition, at the level of the peasantry that a uniting of classes can, despite national antagonisms, occur, since, on the contrary, it is in the peasant class, the sole exclusively Algerian class, that national consciousness could obviously find its most favorable terrain. No European from Algeria shares the fate of the fellah, none of them suffer exploitation in the same manner as he: the position in the relations of production is here specifically Algerian. Where the problem begins is when, the position in the relations of production being apparently the same for Algerians and Europeans, neither the ones nor the others group together on the basis of this position but, rather, on that of their respective nationality.

[. . .]

If the solidarity of the French in Algeria has never seriously been broken in such a way that social forces would group together around class positions, that signifies that, through their behaviors, the French of Algeria, though they may be exploited wage-earners in the same way the Algerians are, have not succeeded in thinking of themselves as anything other than Frenchmen occupying Algeria. And then it must be stated clearly: The Algerian nation that was forming itself despite them could assert itself only against them. There is in this hostility no mystique of holy war, no resurgence of barbarism, but instead *a people* (and we employ this so un-Marxist term intentionally)—that is, the strange mixture of antagonistic social classes, which is plunged back into the consciousness of that elementary solidarity without which there would not even be a society, into the awareness that it forms a total organism wherein the development of intrinsic contradictions assumes first the complementarity of that which is in contradiction; colonization both creates the conditions for this complementarity and blocks its development; awareness of being expropriated from oneself can then be only national.

Let us go further: in the very forms in which it is being conducted by the FLN, the national struggle is not just liberatory for Algerian laboring people. It is only through its success that the European laboring people of Algeria can be torn away from the rottenness of society and of colonial consciousness: in an independent Algeria, under whatever form you like, class relations will emerge from the swamp in which the present relations of domination have engulfed them. That in no way means that the new ruling class or the state apparatus of that Algeria will not quickly engage the fight to put down laboring people. But all laboring people will be together, Algerians and Europeans, in order to support the class struggle. [. . .]

Notes

1. T/E: Mollet, which in French also means "soft," was the leader of the Socialists (SFIO) and France's equivalent of a prime minister in 1956–1957. Though he ran on a platform of restoring peace in Algeria, in office he conducted a counterinsurgency campaign there.

2. See "La Bourgeoisie Nord-Africaine," *S. ou B.*, 20, 191ff.

3. Leon Trotsky, Speech at the London Congress of 1907 [T/E: Fifth Congress of the Russian Social Democratic Labor Party, quoted in *The Permanent Revolution & Results and Prospects*, intro. Luma Nichol (Seattle: Red Letter Press, 2010), 243], emphasis added.

The Social Content of the Algerian Struggle

Jean-François Lyotard

"Le Contenu social de la lutte algérienne"
Socialisme ou Barbarie, 29 (December 1959–February 1960): 5–7, 34–38
Socialisme ou Barbarie—Anthologie, 245–51

[. . .]

2. PERSISTENCE OF THE REVOLUTIONARY SITUATION

We have the proof that the war goes on, more violent than ever, in the fact that the slightest decrease in the number of conscripts suffices to undermine the disposition of French troops and justifies the elimination of deferments. If one calls *pacification* the set of operations that make possible the rebuilding of a *nonmilitary* society, no progress has been made toward pacification. It is still ruled out, on an Algeria-wide scale, that the simplest social activities might be performed outside this artificial incubator of 500,000 French soldiers. It does not suffice to hunt down bands, a general said; one must *stay*. It is no secret to anyone that the present-day local organization of the tiniest Algerian village could not long survive were French troops withdrawn. This fact means that the institutions that ought in principle to govern present-day relations in Algeria have lost all social reality; those institutions are alive only within submachine-gun range. From the sociological standpoint, and taking the nature of the Algerian War into account, the fact that the War endures is nothing else but the fact of the permanent discrepancy between social reality and the organizational models supposedly overseeing it for the past five years.

It is known that none of the legal garments that have been tried on Algerian society—neither "assimilation" nor the "Algerian personality" nor integration nor "special place"—has been able to clothe it. De Gaulle has implicitly acknowledged this by offering the choice between three different statuses. Yet this formal impossibility merely reveals, on the legal level, a remarkable sociological situation: to this day, French imperialism has not succeeded in endowing this society with any other organization than terror because, at present, no institution can respond satisfactorily to the needs of the Algerians, because the latter conduct themselves in such a way that the prior social order no longer coincides with that conduct, on the one hand, and that, on the other, such conduct still has not succeeded in becoming stabilized into a set of habits that would form a new order. This situation can be summarized by saying that Algerian society is "destructured."

When the Comité Révolutionnaire d'Unité et d'Action (CRUA, Revolutionary unity and action committee) opened hostilities, one might have believed that the activists of the MTLD [Mouvement pour le Triomphe des Libertés Démocratiques (Movement for the triumph of democratic freedoms)] were pursuing through violence what Messali [Hadj], nay even Ferhat Abbas, had begun in word. When all is said and done, "war is the continuation of politics by other means." Yet, while such a description, borrowed from the most classic reflection on war, applies quite correctly to twentieth-century imperialist conflicts, it does not conform at all to the reality of every anticolonialist war. When a colonized people abandons the arm of criticism for the criticism of arms, it is not content just to change strategy. It itself, immediately, destroys the society in which it was living, in the sense that its rebellion annihilates the social relations constitutive of that society. Those relations exist only insofar as they are tolerated by the people who live there. As soon as those people act collectively outside that framework and produce types of conduct that no longer find a place within traditional relationships among individuals and among groups, the whole structure of society is, by that fact alone, dislocated. The models of behavior belonging to the various classes and social categories that allow all individuals to conduct themselves in a fitting way—that is, to respond to social-typical situations—these models immediately become obsolete because the corresponding situations no longer present themselves.

Thus, within the family, the relations between young and old, men and women, children and parents find themselves profoundly transformed. The authority the father exercises over his son does not withstand the latter's political activity, his departure for the maquis.

The young man takes the initiative, with or without the father's consent, and that suffices to prove that the situation as it is lived by the son not only is at variance with his traditional subordinate relation to paternal authority but that the situation triumphs over it. In a still highly patriarchal family, this is already a remarkable fact. Yet it is still more so when the daughters escape their parents' supervision. No doubt, the Muslim bourgeois females of Algiers had begun to become "emancipated" before 1954, but even in that stratum, the one most permeable to the influence of capitalist civilization, if one consented to show one's legs, one still did not unveil one's face. This in fact offers a rather faithful image of what "our" civilization intends to emancipate among women. Now, women's participation in political and military activity is attested to by the sentencing of female *Frontiste* militants, of whom Djamila Bouhired has become the embodiment for all Algeria.

On another level, the cultural one, the types of conduct involved in the present war go completely beyond the traditions of colonial Algeria. Circa 1950, schooling barely touched 7 percent of the rural Muslim childhood population, which yielded a ratio of 93 percent illiterates (in French) among peasant youth. The Koranic schools inculcated them with some notions of literal Arabic—which, for what use can be made of it, is pretty much what Latin is to French. The small peasant farmers from this era are presently in the maquis. It is hard to conceive how they might take on certain tasks without knowing at least how to read, and possibly write. In learning these elementary techniques, they are, implicitly or explicitly, making a critique of both the French culture sparingly allotted and Muslim culture, which is absolutely useless in their real lives. In struggling against oppression, they are taking back possession of the most basic instruments of thought that colonial Algeria had taken away from them for generations. The revolutionary content of this new relation to culture is so obvious that the French command has had to respond thereto more and more by offering improvised schools on its side. Undoubtedly, the schooling of the members of the Resistance remains as rudimentary as that of the "protected" populations and is limited to future cadres. Yet the idea that such cadres might be drawn from the peasant mass in itself absolutely contradicts the subaltern roles colonization had reserved for the fellaheen. Just as illiteracy simply expressed, on the cultural level, the same prohibition of all initiative that was weighing on rural labor, so the development of initiative and responsibility in the maquis inevitably leads to the learning of written language.

Whether one is talking about religious, economic, or sexual values, one could show that, in all categories of everyday activity, present-day Algeria, inasmuch as it is actively engaged in the war, shatters those types of conduct that local tradition, Islam, and colonization had forged, through their combination, into a "basic personality" for Algerians.

It can be said that a revolutionary situation exists in the sense that people no longer are living in accordance with the formally dominant institutions, and this is very much the case in Algeria. That does not mean that the revolution is accomplished: the latter presupposes that people who thus break with traditional relations would go to the end of their critique, would destroy the class that was dominating society by means of those relations, and would, finally, institute new relations. It remains the case that the lasting and open break, on the part of a class or set of classes, with society's structure necessarily takes on a revolutionary signification.

In Algeria, not only does this situation manifestly exist but it takes on an intensity, and takes up a duration, which, in combination, can set us on the path toward understanding the real sociological content of the Algerian War.

[...]

FORMATION OF THE DEMOCRATIC EMBRYO

Everything that has just been said, as much about the revolutionary process itself as about its class content, can, in a sense, be summarized as follows: The Algerian national struggle could develop only in the maquis form. Members of the Resistance contain within themselves both the revolutionary meaning of the struggle and its social signification. Its *revolutionary meaning*; for, the people who come together in the maquis are consciously and almost geographically abandoning their traditional society in order to take up arms against it. The maquis is the society wanted by them, as distinguished from the society they no longer want, and already present within it. This break with everyday life indicates the depth of the social crisis: Algerian society offering no legal opportunity for its own transformation, one has to place oneself outside the law in order to change it.

Yet the maquis's class signification is much richer. The social base for the maquis is, by definition, the peasantry. While it is true that the FLN's present cadres come, in good part, from the middle classes, which makes of the maquis the meeting point between the Jacobin bourgeoisie and the peasants, the same did not go for the movement's initiators.

[. . .]

In short, there already are, in the relations between cadres and peasants, the signs—those we have just stated, and many others—of an antagonism that ultimately bears on the overall meaning it is fitting to give to political action, and that is revelatory, in a still faint but already identifiable fashion, of a conflict of classes.

Examination of the contradictory relations that connect the members of the *Frontiste* apparatus to petty bourgeois elements and the laboring masses proves, indeed, that the permanent cadres coming from the old MTLD core and increased in numbers by the war itself do not faithfully represent either the middle classes or the proletariat or the peasantry and that they constitute a state apparatus distinct, in fact, from the classes they bring together, under various headings, in the shared struggle. This original stratum embodies the political interests of no particular category within Algerian society; within itself it recapitulates, rather, Algerian society overall: the history of its formation is the unfolding of all Algerian contradictions. At the outset, there was the absence of a bourgeois and petty-bourgeois nationalism that would have been sufficiently strong to crystalize the malaise of all Algerian classes around the idea of independence. Then, the birth of the nationalist movement among emigre workers in France expressed one of the fundamental contradictions imperialism creates in the colony: the tremendous breakdown of the peasantry finds no counterbalance in a complementary industrialization. The peasants became workers, but in France, and the Algerian political movement then overlapped with the French and worldwide workers' movement at the moment when the latter was bringing out into the open, for the first time in the West, the gangrene of Stalinism. The impossibility of finding a way out of colonial exploitation and oppression either from the side of the local middle classes or from that of the French left-wing parties kept a core [*noyau*] of "professional nationalists" isolated during a whole phase. The latter would finally find in the crisis shaking imperialism in Indochina, in Tunisia, and in Morocco the occasion to break this isolation through overt violence.

The form of their struggle and its length—that is to say, what we have called *the intensity and duration of the revolutionary situation*—becomes clearer if that situation is viewed on the basis of this sociohistorical content. No Algerian social stratum had the strength to put an end to the war (which would have been premature, from the cadres' viewpoint) by entering into talks with French imperialism. On the contrary, the continuation of the war was of such a nature as to transform the kernels [*noyaux*] of the Resistance into elements of an apparatus, then to beef up this apparatus itself at the expense of the social strata that were suffering most harshly from the colonial situation. Quantities of young peasants broke away from their villages to swell the ranks of the ALN [National Liberation Army] and to become paid politico-military officials; for their part, the intellectuals left the University or the Bar to be transformed into political commissars or into foreign delegates, breaking fully with their initial material class ties. The Front, drawing, on the one hand, from the peasantry their main forces and breaking down, on the other, the intellectual petty bourgeoisie, began to fill the social void of which we have spoken. Thus, the apparatus tended, through its function in the war and thanks to this war's duration, to set itself up as a distinct stratum. What had at the start been a political bureaucracy in the classic sense—that is, a set of individuals occupying hierarchical roles within a party—began to become a bureaucracy in the sociological sense—that is, a social stratum issuing from the profound breakdown of prior social classes and bearing solutions that none of those classes could have envisaged.

The fact that this bureaucracy was born not out of the production process itself but of this process of destruction that is war changes absolutely nothing in its class nature, since this destruction also directly expresses colonial Algeria's inability to keep the production process going within the framework of prior relations. Destruction is here merely the form the contradiction between the productive forces and the relations of production takes, and as one knew already, violence is, after all, an economic category. That this violence finally gives the class gestating in the maquis the form of a bureaucracy is easily conceivable since all the relations among the members of this class are nothing other and nothing more than all the relations among the cadres of the politico-military apparatus constituted by the war itself: hierarchically organized wage earners administering in common the destruction of traditional Algeria, as perhaps tomorrow they will administer in common the construction of the Algerian Republic.

The process underway within a revolutionary situation now going on for five years is that of the formation of a new class, and the totality of the facts constituting this situation necessarily goes to make of this class a bureaucracy.

Yet, in order for an Algerian bureaucracy to consolidate itself as a class, it would first be necessary for the revolutionary situation, which maintains wide open the social void within which it takes its place, to continue for a rather long time so that the bureaucratic apparatus might be able to unite notable fractions of the peasantry and the middle classes; it would therefore be necessary for the war to last, and that does not depend on it alone but also, among other things, on imperialism. Once this first hypothesis is granted, it would still be necessary for the apparatus to snatch from imperialism a decisive military victory on the scale of Dien Bien Phu: only then would the bureaucracy have acquired the capacity to eliminate its political competition, the French bourgeoisie, and to take up the country's reorganization without making compromises.

Now, it is obvious that French imperialism weighs much too heavily upon Algerian society for those two hypotheses reasonably to be retained. A tenth of the population—equal to half of Algerian proceeds[1]—claiming allegiance to metropolitan France, two-fifths of the land belonging to the French—that is, more than half of agricultural production—with Saharan subsoil allowing billions of francs in profits—none of that is to be given away, especially when imperialism is exiting in a consolidated way from the crisis the rebellion itself had indirectly made it undergo. On the other hand, all that can be negotiated, and surely will be negotiated, because, whether one likes it or not, the Gaullist regime, if it wants to stabilize, even temporarily, the Algerian situation and abort the bureaucratization process, will have to take into account the fact that, for five years, some very serious applicants have shown up to take leadership of Algerian affairs.

In orienting itself in that direction, de Gaulle's declaration, however abrupt its tone, was attempting to bring out, from within the Front and also outside it, an interlocutor who would be ready to negotiate a sharing of wealth and power with imperialism. And the response of the GPRA [Provisional Government of the Algerian Republic] signifies that the apparatus's bureaucrats are now ready to engage in talks from a democratic national perspective. Under present circumstances— that is, if no serious reversal occurs in the relations between de Gaulle and Algeria's European fraction—this prospect is the most likely one.

Its political and social signification is quite clear: it is this *very same overwhelming weight* of imperialism that has produced the void within which the new class has begun to constitute itself and that now prevents it from developing in full. Since 1957, *Frontiste* cadres have known quite well both that they will not be beaten and that they cannot win: for its part, the French command has acquired the same certainty. This balance cannot be upset from within. It will really have to be resolved in a compromise between the two parties. Whatever might be the date, form, and content of that compromise, the result, at least during a transitional phase, will be that the bureaucracy cannot continue to consolidate itself as it was doing with the help of war. The mere fact that there might be compromise signifies, in effect, that it will have to accept, for example in the form of elections, a new type of relation to the Algerian population. The really democratic character of such elections obviously cannot fool one; but, beyond the liberal comedy, the problem posed will be that of the real implantation of politico-military cadres within the peasant strata, who will, by their numbers, be decisive.

What can still be counted on in the meantime is, first of all, that the Algerian War offers us an additional example of the formation of the bureaucracy in a colonial country (with the specific characteristic that, here, the class in question does not succeed for the time being in developing fully), but also that the emancipatory struggle in the trust territories—in that such a struggle requires that the masses enter onto the political stage—is the bearer of a revolutionary meaning that it is important to underscore. We know very well that the prospects offered to the Algerian Revolution as well as to all colonial revolutions are not and cannot be socialist ones, and we are not supporting the Algerian movement because it will end up modernizing social relations in a backward country: in that case, one would have to applaud the Chinese bureaucracy, nay even an "intelligent" imperialism, if it is true—as we think—that no "objective necessity" is opposed to it proceeding on its own toward decolonization (as one is seeing for Black Africa).

Yet what no ruling class, locally or back home, can allow, or even wish for, is that colonial laboring people might *themselves intervene, practically and directly*, in the transformation of their society, that they might actually smash, without asking anyone for permission, the relations that were crushing them and give, to all the exploited and all the exploiters, the example of socialist activity in person: in short, the recovery of social man by himself. In particular, the Algerian peasants, workers, and intellectuals will no longer be able to forget—and this is of immense import for the future of their country—that, over these years, they have mastered their fate, willed what happened to them, and that what man wills *might* happen to him.

Notes

1. Algeria's overall annual income could be calculated in 1955 at 537 billion francs (on the basis of figures given by [Professor Jacques] Peyréga). According to the 1953 Maspetiol Report, the total income of all Muslim Algerians amounted to 271 billion francs. The French of Algeria therefore received approximately half of the overall product.

In Algeria, A New Wave

Jean-François Lyotard

"En Algérie, une vague nouvelle"
Socialisme ou Barbarie, 32 (April–June 1961): 62–72
Socialisme ou Barbarie—Anthologie, 252–56

In December 1960, Algerians in all towns took possession of their streets. The war had been going on for six years, the forces of order were reinforced everywhere because of de Gaulle's trip, in Algiers the police-administrative network installed since the "battle" of 1957 had become tighter than ever, wilaya organization was "dismantled" four or five times, the Algerians had practically no weapons, all the Europeans were armed, and in the large towns they even took the initiative to demonstrate, seeking to occupy key neighborhoods and to tip the army to their side.

Despite all that, the Algerians "came out." Immediately, the Ultras [extreme reactionaries] fainted, shooting here and there into the crowds of Algerian demonstrators and calling on the paratroopers for help. The true problem has been posed. All those who spoke in the name of Algeria—that is, in the place of the Algerians—kept silent. The Algerians "demonstrated [*manifestent*]," that is, manifested themselves, in flesh and blood, collectively. The object of dispute intervened in the dispute, taking the floor away from everyone who was speaking.

Of course, this intervention of urban masses profoundly alters the relations of force: the Ultras disappear from the front of the political stage, "pacification" and the "winning hearts and minds [*l'intégration des âmes*]" fall entirely by the wayside, the policy of the "third way" and of the "setting up of a provisional executive power" is restored to its rightful size, that of a mere daydream, the GPRA [Provisional Government of the Algerian Republic] officially rises up as the Algerians' representative, and so on. Yet it is not in this sense alone that these demonstrations are important; it is not only because they shift the forces around on the Algerian chessboard; it is, on the contrary, because they contain the destruction of the very idea of a "political chessboard," because they bring outside a new meaning—in Algeria—of politics. Everything has happened suddenly as if the Algerian War was no longer first of all a war: the guns of Order have not fired on the demonstrators like they shoot automatically on combatants. Military relations have gone into the background: between the riot police [*CRS*] and the demonstrators the relation no longer was that of pure violence but, rather, midway between force and speech. Everyone (except the paratroopers) has begun to understand that military repression had no connection with the problem posed by these demonstrations, that there was not a "rebellion to pacify," but that the revolution was winning over the masses. That is why all press outlets, both left and right, French and foreign, all the political "specialists," including de Gaulle, have concluded that one had to hurry up and negotiate; indeed, negotiation alone, it is thought, can halt the "peril." That is not certain, but what is so is that in this way the meaning of negotiation shines forth: it is aimed, first of all and above all, at eliminating the danger of a revolutionary development.

Now, there is a key correlation between the new signification the Algerian question takes on and the political intervention of a new stratum of the population. It is the young from the shop floors, from offices, the university, the high schools and middle schools who were at the movement's forefront: urban youth. If one wants to explain what is happening now in Algeria, it is these young people who are to be understood.

[...]

THE NEW POLITICS

Yet this new social stratum, which is also a new age class, is not just the product of the situation. It is at the same time its most sensitive and most conscious center. Indeed, it is in relation to these young people raised in the revolution, subject to repression and, more profoundly, divided between hatred of the West and a break with tradition that the problem of Algeria is posed in its totality—that is, as the problem of their lives, of what they are going to become. The content they give to politics is incommensurable with all that has been done and thought on this topic in Algeria for decades.

Young Algerians want to be done with their traditional culture, which they sense at once as a curb on their emancipation and also as something hypocritically maintained by the colonizer. Yet at the same time, they respect that culture; they defend it in themselves against the European culture assailing them. On the other hand, they are tempted to value the "European" (that is, capitalist) organization of society because it seems to be able to resolve Algeria's key problem: poverty. Yet at the same time, they know that it is the organization of exploitation, at least theirs. It is within this sort of to-and-fro that the youth of the new working-class suburbs live. For them, the city is no longer the medina [old Arab quarter], with its relatively coherent cultural content, or simply the strange asocial mixture of miserable conditions at the shanty-town fringes. Their urban life contracts into a single experience all the aspects of the colonial situation: the destruction of customary culture with the correlative attraction of European culture; the rejection of the latter, along with the temptation to defend the old values—that is to say, in sum: anxiety and availability.

This situation calls for the response of intensified activity, a thirst for experience and knowledge: communication of information, hypotheses, testing out "solutions" in continual discussions, perception of the tiniest details of life as significant in relation to Algeria's general problems. Social reality is not smothered in the wadding of institutions, which render it unrecognizable; rather, the individual continually encounters it "in the raw." This really political life is quite the opposite of an activity apart, a specialized occupation, a profession. It presupposes, on the contrary, an awareness that general problems are not separate problems, something other than everyday problems, but that everyday problems are the most important, the only real ones. In this regard again, the administration's integrationist initiatives backfire: in wanting to detach the masses from "rebellious separatism" by convincing them (via psychological action), the SAS [Specialized Administrative Sections] merely fuel such ferment; they have been swept away in demonstrations like wisps of straw. And overt repression can itself do nothing: political life is even more intense in the prisons and camps than in the medinas.

For these young Algerians, politics signifies something that exists in practically no social class in France at this moment: discussion and implementation of the future, collectively assumed by each and all. Everyone should really be aware that someone from Algiers, from Oran, a boy or a girl of 15 has no predetermined future. Nothing awaits him; everything is possible. In a modern capitalist country, a 15-year-old individual already has, whatever class he belongs to, a way of being integrated into society that defines rather narrowly the scope of his future. It is, moreover, against this present prefiguration of his whole future, against this premature death, that he protests through, for example, the apparently absurd violence of the "greasers [*blousons noirs*]." The young Algerians who live in "modern housing projects" in working-class suburbs are "leather-jacketed gang members [*blousons noirs*]," if you will—with the difference that their violence is effective because it is that violence, and it alone, that sculpts the shape of their lives. When the Ultras from Algiers said that the FLN was only a "band of greasers," they were expressing quite well their idle dream: that society as it exists would win out over some "young hooligans" who do not want to accept their fate. Yet at the same time, they were expressing this on the basis of the fact, quite obvious on the spot, that a new mentality, comparable to that in modern cities, was arising within the Algerian community.

What young Algerians have manifested in cities in December 1960 and January 1961 is the appearance of this new collectivity, with the intensity of its political life (no quotation marks added).

THE FRONT AND THE DEMONSTRATIONS

They have not demonstrated in order to bring [the GPRA's figurehead President] Ferhat Abbas to power—even if it is true that Abbas will come to power by being borne along by their demonstration. They have demonstrated for the meaning of their lives, and that goes enormously beyond the GPRA: a government cannot be the meaning of one's life. None of them, excepting those who already see themselves as governmental ministers, can tell themselves: My problems will be resolved the day when Algeria will become an independent republic. In fact, the political discussions, hypotheses, and solutions that are circulating concern much more the content of life in independent Algeria than the formal problem of independence. Independence is not a problem for them, if the constitutional form of a future Algeria and the "ties" with France or lack thereof are what is being talked about. For them, the problem of independence is that of what to do when one no longer depends on what dominated you. From this standpoint, they are already independent, already ahead of the negotiations, and in the process of asking themselves what is to be done with the land, with Islam, with relations between men and women, with Europeans who work, with European and non-European bosses—thus catching up with the preoccupations of the most highly developed workers, in France and in Algeria.

[...]

Though not "politicized" in the same sense cadres are, the majority of the new stratum made up of wage-earning youth in the towns has a much richer and much more radical experience of the situation, therefore a much more elevated political level, than cadres do.

Consequently, beneath some tendencies that were beginning to find expression within some organizations—particularly the tendency of UGTA [General Union of Algerian Workers] trade unionists—and that, when the time comes, will be led to express more clearly than they have done so far the solutions they are recommending for the problems of an independent Algeria, a revolutionary current within the masses themselves, especially within the new stratum of urban youth, is starting to take shape.

No doubt, the GPRA is already preparing to bring that current back to order—to its order. It can capture a portion of this force by harnessing the young to the task of constructing the new society. It can repress what resists.[1] Yet in all cases it is really going to have to alienate a major fraction of youth: the awareness these young people have acquired, their participation in the shaping of their own lives, the expectations they are beginning to manifest as to the meaning of the revolution—all that will not easily allow itself to be appeased.

Nonetheless, the subsequent development of this current depends on its current consolidation. In particular, if Algerian youth, which has grown up within the revolution, does not succeed in expressing in the clearest and most complete way possible its experience and its demands, it will more easily be put down by the national bureaucracy. Such a consolidation has to constitute the immediate objective of its most conscious elements in relation to the Algerian problem. That does not mean that the objective of Algeria's unconditional independence is to be placed in the background. In fact, the question posed by this new current, which must be developed, is none other than the question of independence, but envisaged in its real content. Independence is only a form, and the current about which we are speaking has already carried out a critique of this form from the standpoint of the social reality of independent Algeria.

The effort to discuss and clarify that can already now be undertaken with Algerian comrades must be set at the level of the consciousness they have attained and not at the level of the lack of awareness and bureaucratic complicity wherein the French "Left" is stagnating. It has to end in the elaboration of a program for the Algerian Revolution. Without wanting in any way to prejudge the content of this program, it is possible right now to indicate its main chapter headings:

- land question (expropriation of the big companies; land reform and collectivization; farmers, small landowners, agricultural workers);
- industrialization question (problem of the Chinese or Cuban "solution" and of the bureaucracy in underdeveloped countries);
- problem of the trade unions, of their nature, of their role in these countries;
- relations with Tunisia and Morocco (criticism of the Tunisian and Moroccan "solutions"; possibility of creating a revolutionary front in the Maghreb; significance of Morocco's National Union of Popular Forces [UNFP]);
- internationalism and relations with revolutionary currents in modern bureaucratic and capitalist countries;
- meaning and fate of the traditional structures in Algeria: family, communities, religion;
- the Europeans in Algeria;
- problem of languages, of education, and, more generally, of culture.

These questions are not questions for specialists; they are the ones being debated every day among the Algerians when they reflect on the meaning of their revolution. Even when there is a "technical" aspect to them, as with the land question, their solution is necessarily political; technicians can define the possible choices, but it is up to the Algerians alone to know what they want and to impose solutions. Each has had and continues to have a particular experience of the revolutionary situation, has encountered in a concrete form one or another of these problems, and has given to it or dreamed of giving to it this or that solution. It is this wealth of experience accumulated by the youth of the towns, by the peasants in the maquis and the detention centers, and by the workers in France and in Algeria that is to crystallize the revolutionary program; it is from that wealth of experience that this program is to draw lessons. Then, and only then, will the real signification of the Algerians' struggle not be lost.

Notes

1.   A very well informed comrade, to whom we owe a better understanding of the situation in Algeria, suggests to us that such would be the function in store for the two armies on foreign soil (on the Tunisian and Moroccan borders); disciplined like any bourgeois army, trained and supervised by career soldiers who have come from the French army, armed with heavy, modern equipment, and kept under the direct control of GPRA officers, they appear to be the ruling class's future police force.

China

"La Chine"
Socialisme ou Barbarie—Anthologie, 257

The analyses bearing on China are basically due to Pierre Souyri (Brune), whose contributions to the review were limited in number, yet sizeable. They constitute an extremely detailed, marathon study on the evolution of so-called Communist China that demonstrates, with the help of both statistics and a description of struggles, the deeply bureaucratic and anti-revolutionary nature of the regime and of the way it evolved since Mao took power. This was "The Class Struggle in Bureaucratic China," whose extremely innovative analyses preceded by far those of, say, Simon Leys.

After an introduction, a long description of the transformation of Chinese society arrives at the following conclusion:

At the end of this tremendous transformation process, a new China was born, one characterized by an extraordinary simplification of social antagonisms. The old oppositions between the bourgeoisie and the proletariat, rich peasants and agricultural workers, speculating merchants and usurers and workers and the poor in towns and the countryside are now no longer but memories. In the factories, shops, and villages, there remain but two classes face to face: laboring people in their totality, stripped of their means of production, and the bureaucracy, which has become the personification of capital at the outer limits of concentration. Under its bureaucratic form, the capitalist relation has thus become generalized as it had never been in China during the bourgeois stage of its historical development.

We offer here his introduction, a diatribe against Jean-Paul Sartre and Simone de Beauvoir, which tells rather well the context into which this text was dropped, as well as its objective: to demystify rising Third Worldism and its most prestigious French representatives. This introduction is followed by a number of the most significant pages of this detailed study (a scrupulously documented study carried out by reading, day after day, the official Chinese newspapers, whose references we have taken the liberty of eliminating).

The Class Struggle in Bureaucratic China

Pierre Brune

"La Lutte des classes en Chine bureaucratique"
Socialisme ou Barbarie, 24 (May–June 1958): 35–37, 57–75
Socialisme ou Barbarie—Anthologie, 258–73

"These errors have no bearing on the main point, namely, that
fraternity has become the main engine of production."

—Jean-Paul Sartre, in "My Impressions of the
New China," *Jen-min Jih-pao* (November 2, 1955).

MISADVENTURE OF MADAME DE BEAUVOIR & CO.

In France, Mao Tse-tung's China occupies a place somewhat apart in the preoccupations of all avant-garde thinkers who undertook to come to the aid of Stalinism with the whole arsenal of their philosophy just around the time when the masters of the Kremlin themselves were preparing to reveal to the world that Stalinism was but a rather stale and sinister thing, good for being put in the dustbin. It is not like the intellectuals of *Les Temps Modernes* did not sometimes feel some dread concerning the style of Stalinist politics. But tossed about by the century's contradictions, they had been filled with revulsion for the bourgeoisie from which they came in an era when thirty years of victorious Stalinist counterrevolution had persuaded them that, despite all, the forward march of Stalinism was merging with the very movement of history. Noting that the decadent bourgeoisie could no longer yield anything but the spectacle of an ignoble and bloody farce, they had decided to opt for the Stalinist tragedy, persuaded that they were, through this bitter yet virile choice, throwing themselves right into the center of the historical current of the century.

Alas! Hardly had the prophets of *Les Temps Modernes* finished demonstrating that all criticism of the USSR could be placed only under the heading of a sterile moralism that would never have a grasp of history when, in Eastern Europe, the workers began to undertake, with arms, a critique of Stalinism and the USSR. Almost one right after the other, the revolt of Berlin and of East Germany, then the Poznan riots, the October people's movement in Poland and the Revolution of the Workers' Councils in Hungary cascaded down upon the heads of our philosophers, making them look endlessly ridiculous. These unlucky souls had leaped to their rendezvous with history too late, just at the moment when history was changing direction [*sens*] and, suddenly, their philosophy of the meaning [*sens*] of history had developed against the grain [*à contre-sens*] of history.

At least China offered them a final bit of consolation. There, no trials of the old leaders of the Revolution, no insurgent working-class masses, no factories taken back from laboring people by cannon fire, no Workers' Council delegates hanged by the Red Army. In succession, Sartre then Simone de Beauvoir went to visit China. They did not come back disappointed. It was not in vain that they had faced the strains of such a long voyage. They had really seen, with their own eyes, the Land of Economic and Social Harmonies. With measured words and contained emotion, Sartre shared with the readers of *France-Observateur* the enthusiasm he had felt visiting a country in which all governmental acts testify to a "deep humanitarianism." More prolix, de Beauvoir in turn used up nearly five hundred pages to persuade her readers that China was quite close to becoming, despite its virtuous poverty, the achieved philosopher's State. *The Long March* came at the right time in the Spring of 1957. That work was going to allow one, within the mythology on which the French Left nourishes itself, to substitute China for the USSR, whose "progressivist" prestige had been somewhat damaged by the successive waves of revolts of Eastern Europe's proletariat against the Bureaucracy.

And yet History is a cruel goddess. Even before the last pages of *The Long March* had been printed, it was learned from the mouth of Mao Tse-tung himself that not everything was going as well in China as de Beauvoir had thought. Contradictions had appeared in the Land of Social Harmonies. Strikes and demonstrations had broken out in the cities; troubles had perturbed the countryside; discontent had spread to the universities. While the author of *The Long March* was laboring to explain how perfect concord had been able to be established in China between the will of the people and that of the government, the specter of the Hungarian Revolution was hovering over the dingy, impoverished neighborhoods of working-class China, lurking within villages enslaved by the Bureaucracy, and forcing Mao Tse-tung to sound a first cry of alarm.

It is now no longer necessary to busy oneself with the fables de Beauvoir tells us. The Chinese workers' and peasants' class struggle has suddenly appeared in the open and slapped down this lady's impudent lies. Once again, the spreading of political confusion has turned into the confusion of those spreading confusion.

Brune then comes to the heart of the matter.

[. . .] While the granting of major privileges creates the objective conditions for a reinforcement of the bureaucracy's social cohesion opposite the exploited, the various strata capitalist concentration integrates into the ruling [*dirigeant*] apparatus are not, for all that, spontaneously capable of surmounting the diversity of their origins and of tearing themselves away from the grip of their past. The "eight-story pagoda" is in reality a Tower of Babel. Without the Party, which labors to give them a hierarchical structure, imposes ideological unity on them, and inculcates in them the awareness of their historical destiny, those who find themselves promoted by bureaucratic capitalism to the rank of new ruling class would form only a crush of people pulling the State in all directions. The bureaucracy becomes a ruling class only by subordinating itself to the dictatorship of the Party. Supreme incarnation of its ideological truth and guardian of its historical interests, the Party is at once the organ of bureaucratic domination and the all-powerful and fearsome master of the bureaucracy. It raises the bureaucracy to the rank of ruling class only by treating it harshly and terrifying it so as to "remold" it ideologically.

In China, this process of "ideological remolding" has taken on a seriousness and a brutality that are all the greater as the "bureaucratic revolution" was much more a metamorphosis of a part of the old dominant classes than a subversion of those classes by new ruling strata issuing from the laboring classes. Now, given the rapidity with which the process of revolutionary transformation has occurred, a lag has developed between the social change the former bourgeois strata were undergoing and the much slower transformation of their mindset and their ideology. Hundreds of thousands of people had found themselves abruptly projected by the Revolution into bureaucratic posts, whereas subjectively they remained bourgeois retaining a thousand ties of participation with the various forms of the old ideology.

When one thinks about it, all revolutions proceed in their own way to an "ideological remolding," inasmuch as they substitute a new system of social values and social rules for the one that has just crumbled. Yet, whereas the classes they bring to power have generally had entire centuries to differentiate themselves from the old social order and to come to terms with being new classes, the majority of the Chinese bureaucratic apparatus has found itself, in only a few years and sometimes in a few months, torn from the mold of the former society and cast into a new universe. That is why its subjective readjustment to the new social state that has taken effect beneath the baton of the Party—which itself had had a quarter century to ripen its ideology—has taken place in a spectacular way in the form of "brainwashing."

Everything began with an apparently insignificant literary quarrel. In 1952, a scholar, Professor Yu Pingbo republished, with a few additions, his thesis, which had appeared in 1923 and which concerned the classic eighteenth-century novel *Dream of the Red Chamber*. In September 1954, two young students attacked Yu Pingbo in the review of Shandong University, accusing him of doing "idealist" literary criticism. On October 23, the *JMJP* [*People's Daily*] outdid their attacks: Yu Pingbo was highly guilty for not having shown that *Dream of the Red Chamber* has an antifeudal class content. In the Fall, Kuo Mo-jo (the Louis Aragon of China) broadened these attacks. Criticism of the novel became a state affair. In a November 8 interview, Kuo Mo-jo explained, indeed, that the affair in reality went beyond the personality of Yu Pingbo and that it involved a settling of accounts between materialism and idealism. In fact, what was being prepared was the establishment of ideological totalitarianism.

And yet suddenly, a Marxist writer, Hu Feng, a party member since 1937 and one of the best poets of Red China during the Yenan period, stood up against the threat of Zhdanovism. Hu Feng riddled "the great Kuo Mo-jo" with sarcasm and denounced the Zhdanovist dogmas as "the five daggers planted in the skull of Chinese writers." From then on, things proceeded quickly. The literary quarrel turned into political battle, then purges. The press denounced Hu Feng as a deviationist and accused him of having organized a counterrevolutionary network. Kuo Mo-jo and the big shots of Socialist Realism demanded the arrest of Hu Feng and his accomplices. They obtained it immediately. In the first months of the Summer of 1955, the hunt for "Hu Fengists" and "counterrevolutionaries hidden in ruling bodies" was at its height.

One by one, the intellectuals, writers, professors, journalists, and then judges and magistrates, technicians, and, finally, "intellectual workers" of all kinds were imperatively invited to scrutinize their souls in order to detect therein any trace of "Hu Fengism" or "hidden counterrevolutionary sentiment" and to make things right with "Marxism." They first had to compare their thoughts with the texts that were dispatched to them on all the ideological problems that concerned them. Then, they had to appear in public in "self-criticism sessions," during which their whole public and private life—including the most intimate and most shocking details—was closely examined, while they were egged on by those present who posed questions and demanded that nothing be hidden.

Of course, the Chinese intelligentsia did not agree to engage in such sordid displays with joyful hearts. Yet from the outset, recalcitrants were arrested, brought before accusatory gatherings, and sometimes executed as examples. Very quickly, the intellectuals understood that "frank and total self-criticism"—some had to start over several times—was the best way to have peace and quiet, and, with sinking hearts, they came to proclaim publicly their revulsion with their own past and their enthusiastic adherence to materialist principles. Indeed, from month to month, the concept of "Hu Fengism" revealed itself to be infinitely extendable, and it came to encompass all shades of Liberals, Catholics, Buddhists, and Taoists. In reality, what occurred was the total liquidation of all currents of thought alien to Stalinism. Throughout the year 1955, the Party cut into the raw flesh of the bureaucracy. As in the USSR, the bureaucracy became a ruling class only by undergoing a terrible process of self-mutilation.

Yet, while they trembled before the Party and often paid dearly for their privileges, the bureaucrats were no less, in the masses' view, all-powerful lords "enclosed in their litters" and in every respect similar to the mandarins of ancient China. In reality, a world separates the bureaucracy from the lower classes.

As in all bureaucratic States, the Chinese peasants and workers were indeed, despite the fiction that the Party and the State represent the laboring people, radically deprived of all participation in the direction of social life and, in the first place, in the direction of their own laboring activity. That is wholly clear for the workers, to whom the State did not even bother to give a semblance of representation in the central planning organs that unilaterally decide both the orientation of production and the rate of accumulation as well as the division of the social product. Even within each enterprise, the workers are nothing but a mere element in the production process, like the machinery and raw materials. At the very most, the law foresees that a committee, where trade-union representatives sit, will assist the Director who is named by the State and is responsible to it alone for the tasks the Planning Commission assigns his enterprise. Yet the legislative texts allow no uncertainty to remain about the functions "workers' representatives" are to fulfill in relation to management. Their task is to help it to "reinforce labor discipline, organize the mass of workers, so that this mass might adopt a new attitude toward work," and "instigate competition campaigns in production." Entirely in the hands of officials named by the Party who are specially appointed for this task, the trade-union apparatus is merely an instrument for the State's direction of the workforce. "It constitutes," as Li Li-san (the then-Deputy Chairman of the All-China Federation of Trade Unions) said, "the best guarantee for administrators in the fulfillment of their task."

Despite appearances, the situation of peasants in the production process does not differ from that of workers. If one sticks to the letter of the legislative texts, agricultural cooperatives might appear to be genuine peasant communes sovereignly managing [*dirigeant*] their affairs. In principle, it is indeed the general assembly of villagers that elects its ruling [*dirigeants*] organs, approves the cooperative's budget, and shares out profits among all its members. But in reality the cooperative is strictly subordinate to the central bureaucracy. It is the State that sets for it the nature and volume of production it is to carry out, in terms of the needs of the Five-Year Plan. It is the State that unilaterally fixes the prices at which it buys agricultural produce as well as, moreover, the annual percentage of profit the cooperative is to accumulate in order to modernize its means of farming. From the very fact of this integration of the cooperative into the overall operation of the bureaucratic economy, the peasant's economic sovereignty would already be extremely limited. Yet, even within the cooperative, such sovereignty is only a legal fiction. First of all, that is because it is not true that the "cadres are elected" by the peasants; these are "specialists" who have been trained by the Party and are named, recalled, and transferred by it at will. At the very most, countryfolk are sometimes asked to ratify decisions that have been made without them. On the other hand, the system of managing the cooperatives is far too complex for the peasants to be able to use their right of control effectively. Paid work is not in effect the day of work actually performed but an "abstract" day of work established as a function of a complicated system of norms, points, and productivity bonuses whose calculation eludes these peasants, nine-tenths of whom are illiterate. During general assemblies, countryfolk get lost in the maze of figures that are multiplied, added up, and subtracted in the financial report. The boldest demand explanations. Not understanding, they repeat the same questions. The cadres become impatient, and the peasants intimidated, finally falling silent while pondering their discontent. The managerial system does not correspond to the cultural level of the villages, and, later on, it opens the door to all the fraudulent practices of the rural bureaucracy which, in practice, fiddles with the accounts at will in order to increase its privileges. In reality, social relations in the collectivized village as well as in the towns rest on a clear-cut division between directors and mere laborers, and the relations that are established between cadres and peasants are far from idyllic. Denouncing the excesses of the "rural cadres," the editorialist for the *People's Daily* wrote on June 27, 1956:

> The local cadres have at their disposal not only political means, but also economic means, to terrorize people. They declare: "From the moment the land belongs to the cooperatives, we hold the peasants by the throat and they do what we want." He who does not obey the cadres is going to see his wages reduced or his right to work suspended. They employ this dual method of pressure during meetings and even during cultural events.

As we can see, one is quite far from socialist democracy in the village.

Opposite the all-powerful State, which has cemented its apparatus of domination through terror and ideological monolithism, the peasants and workers of "socialist China" are nothing but raw material to produce the surplus value necessary for industrialization.

Yet for the neo-Stalinists themselves, all that constitutes nothing but terrible and sad necessities that will find retrospective justification on the scale of history through the miracle of the industrialization of the largest backward country on Earth. So, let us see now what really are these marvels of the Chinese Five-Year Plan and the "historical superiority" the bureaucracy gladly attributes to itself in the task of developing the forces of production.

ECONOMIC GROWTH AND ITS PHYSIOGNOMY

Since 1952, the first postwar year when Chinese production can be thought to have returned to normal and when the first Five-Year Plan began to be organized, national income has gone from 83 to 125 billion yuan, or an overall increase of 52 percent, a bit more than 10 percent per annum.

The pace of growth is especially remarkable for industry, where production went from a value of 27 billion yuan to 53.5 billion in 1957, almost doubling. For a whole series of staple commodities, the rate of increase in production is at first sight impressive.

During the first five years, production of coal increased 78 percent, that of steel 205 percent, that of electricity 118 percent. The absolute figures, however, give a more realistic idea of the results achieved by Chinese industry. With 113 million tons of coal, 15 billion kWh of electricity, and 4.1 million tons of steel, China is still far from being a great industrial power. If one were to classify it among nations, China would be ranked just before Poland for basic industrial products and, except for coal, markedly below Belgium. After five years of efforts, China is still quite below the level of 1928 Russia. True, factories built since 1952, furnished for the most part by the USSR, meet the latest levels of technical progress, particularly in Manchuria. Despite this, growth in industrial production has been markedly slower than it had been in the USSR during the first five-year plan, when it was 19.3 percent per annum, whereas in China it was only 14.7 percent.

On account of its extreme poverty, China cannot indeed invest as high a percentage of its national income as the USSR did at the outset of its industrialization. Whereas the USSR then invested 33 percent of its national income, China has never succeeded in investing more than 23 percent. Per capita, the rate of investments is laughable. It went from US $6.00 in 1953 to US $8.00 in 1957, as against US $45.00 in Europe's Russian satellites in the years that followed World War II. Yet in none of these States was per capita income as weak as in China and, despite the limited results it has obtained, industrialization weighs enormously on Chinese laboring people. At the Eighth Party Congress, Po I-po recognized that it was impossible to maintain the growth rate for investments without exposing the country to great dangers, and he proposed to plateau them at around 20 percent of national income.

The burden of industrialization is indeed all the heavier for the laboring masses as, more so than in the USSR, economic development in China is characterized by an increasing disproportion between the production sector that manufactures the means of capital goods and the sector producing the means of consumption. Since 1952, 88.8 percent of investments have been in Sector 1 production, a higher proportion than in Russia where, at the time of the first Plan, this sector absorbed only 85.9 percent of total investments. Investments in the sector producing the means of consumption represent in China, during the first Five-Year Plan, only 11.2 percent of the total, whereas they were 14.1 percent in Russia during the corresponding period. If one takes into account the wear upon equipment dating from the prewar period, one comes to the conclusion that the investments made in Sector II must allow barely more than very weak growth in the potential that existed before the Revolution.

This outlook is not contradicted by the fact that the production of a whole series of consumer merchandise has increased, though in weaker proportions than that of Sector I industries. The production of sugar is indeed said to have gone up 108 percent, that of flour 56 percent, that of cotton 47 percent. Yet this increase was achieved much more by a better utilization of existing enterprises than by the construction of new factories. Starting in 1930, and for the entire duration of the world crisis, Chinese factories were indeed working in slow motion or periodically even came to a halt. Revolution and bureaucratic capitalism have eliminated in China the problems of imperialist competition and relative overproduction, thus allowing a better use of the potential of the national production apparatus. Yet the absolute priority granted to the development of Sector I has given rise to other problems. While the factories working at the manufacture of the means of consumption have increased their production, they are not utilizing all their capacities, for they now lack raw materials. Oil and sugar refineries, flour mills, and spinning mills continue to utilize only 70 to 80 percent of their potential. Here, too, the percentages of growth create illusions. In increasing by 108 percent these refineries' production, China has nonetheless succeeded in manufacturing only 520,000 tons of sugar. With a population of more than 600,000,000 inhabitants, that is only a third of French production. In increasing cotton production 47 percent, China—if it did not export cotton fabrics—would not succeed in furnishing nine meters of cotton cloth per year to its inhabitants. That would, however, be only the strict minimum, for cotton suits wear out quite quickly, and each laborer would need several per year.

This disproportion between the two production sectors becomes apparent in its full breadth if one compares the development of industries and agriculture for the last five years. For lack of sufficient investments, agriculture has not been able to meet the demands of economic construction, and this lag has wiped out the growth in production of consumer goods. Of course, the State has employed millions of people—peasants required and condemned to perform corrective labor—in order to repair the dikes and irrigation works. On the Yellow River and its tributaries, a whole system of dams has been built up that furnish hydroelectric power, regulate the flow of rivers, and allow land irrigation. In most villages, the time left free by agricultural labor in the off-season has been used to clear and irrigate new lands. These various works have allowed an increase of 5,000,000 hectares of cultivated surface area. Between 1952 and 1957, the most optimistic figures bring out only a 23-percent increase in the value of agriculture production, whereas, at the same time, the value of industrial production has doubled. In reality, the peasants are quite far from being liberated from those age-old calamities in China: floods and droughts. Since 1950, almost every year vast regions of China have experienced genuine food shortages. The number of ministries, administrative buildings, and dazzlingly luxurious cultural centers has multiplied, and yet one did not have enough money, or enough cement, to master natural disasters. Too much steel has been used for armaments and war factories—national defense eats up 15 percent of national income—for one to be able to produce a decent quantity of metal plows and irrigation pumps. The streets of the large cities of Manchuria are witnessing an increase in the number of American cars, but the peasants continue to hitch themselves to plows and the amount of manure at their disposal—2kg per hectare—remains laughable.

The strenuous labor imposed on countryfolk—on the whole, the annual number of working days is said to have doubled in the cooperatives—has nonetheless allowed a rise in the production of the main agricultural foodstuffs. In 1957, China produced 193 million tons of food products as against 164 in 1952, 1,635,000 tons of raw cotton, as against 1,175,000 in 1952. Yet this growth in rural production itself has been determined less by the concern to increase the masses' consumption than by that of accelerating the pace of construction for heavy industry. A growing proportion of the surplus in produce taken from Chinese soil has indeed been exported in order to pay for importations of raw materials, machinery, and capital equipment, which represent 88.5 percent of the purchases China makes abroad. It is true, if one is to believe the official figures, that these exports of agricultural produce (grains, tea, silk, plant oils) or industrial consumer products (cotton) represent only a small percentage of annual production, 1.2 percent in 1953, 1.6 percent in 1957. Yet if one takes into account the facts that 42 percent of prewar Chinese imports were made up of consumer products and that, on the other hand, the population has grown 12 percent since 1952, one comes to the conclusion that the amount of products available per inhabitant has remained entirely stationary or that, more likely still, it has decreased as industrialization has gotten underway. All the official figures the "friends" of bureaucratic China can invoke could not prevail against the following brutal fact: in 1954, rationing of grain produce had to be instituted, and in 1955 and 1956 the authorities have been compelled to reduce again these rations. Peking had to end up letting the truth come out: the first Five-Year Plan came to an end in an extremely tense atmosphere brought about by a catastrophic shortage of provisions and clothing both in the countryside and in the towns. The flip side of the multiplication of mines of all sorts, of blast furnaces, of factories, and of ultramodern steelworks was chronic underproduction of consumer goods and therefore permanent underconsumption on the part of laboring people.

The physiognomy of economic growth thus reflects quite precisely the class structure of Chinese society and the motives of bureaucratic industrialization. Determined solely by the bureaucracy's need to strengthen its might opposite the imperialist world and to increase the overproduction necessary for the consolidation of its apparatus, accumulation is achieved independently of the masses' consumption or, more exactly, as an inverse function of the development of such consumption. Whereas, in the previous stage of the historical process of capitalism, maximum accumulation and the maximum exploitation on which the former fed itself inevitably entered into contradiction as a result of the difficulties and ultimately the impossibility of realizing surplus value as laboring people's real income decreased, the suppression of the market and of its traditional functions in principle allows bureaucratic capitalism indefinitely to push to the full and in parallel accumulation and overexploitation. In bureaucratic capitalism, disproportions are also naturally produced between the sectors and different branches of production, if only on account of the anarchy of bureaucratic management. Yet while serious disturbances can result therefrom, the production cycle can never be interrupted by the impossibility of valuing products, since, by definition, the substitution of state planning for the market eliminates the problem. It is something else if, after a certain amount of time, the proletariat's resistance obliges the bureaucrats to "concede" a rise in living standards, as has been seen in the USSR for a few years and as one will see further on in the case of China. That is why, much more still than in the previous forms of capitalism, bureaucratic production is "production for production's sake, expansion of production without a corresponding expansion of consumption."[1] The whole alleged historical superiority of the bureaucratic system of planning and its capacity to develop very quickly the forces of production ensues in fact only from the freedom the elimination of the market confers upon it to drain additional capital in enormous proportions toward heavy industries without there ever being a situation where "the more productiveness develops, the more it finds itself at variance with the narrow basis on which the conditions of consumption rest."[2] If progress there be, it is solely from the standpoint of exploitative strata delivered from the contradictions that, through periodic crises, compelled traditional capitalism from time to time to readjust consumption and production.

In the race to achieve might, bureaucratic capitalism has an advantage of prime importance at its disposal: it is not constrained, as bourgeois States are, by the need to realize surplus value, to "waste" a portion of capital it extorts from laboring people in developing the manufacture of means of consumption to the detriment of war industries or enterprises eventually capable of being used for war. On this point at least, Chinese bureaucratic capitalism is in no way special in relation to the other Eastern-Bloc States, except perhaps the exceptional relentlessness it deploys, on account of China's backwardness, in order to impose on the masses ever more uncompensated labor.

THE CONTRADICTIONS OF THE PROCESS OF BUREAUCRATIC ACCUMULATION

Nonetheless, while in bureaucratic capitalism the possibility of crises in the classical sense of the term no longer exists, it does not result from this that state planning brings about the disappearance of all the contradictions that can slow the expansion of the productive forces. It is only in the fantastical constructions of the bureaucracy's theoreticians that economic growth occurs in accordance with a faultless rationality. In reality, the bureaucratic economy, which remains based on alienation and exploitation, outstrips the contradictions that stem from the laws of the market only to see those rooted in alienation and exploitation itself rise up again more fiercely. Just as in other historical forms of capitalism, the development of productive forces is achieved in bureaucratic States only through immense waste of human forces and wealth.

Of course, in itself the existence of a largely privileged and, more-over, in great part idle bureaucratic stratum—the Chinese press would reveal that, in certain administrative offices, a third of the personnel is surplus and that some kill time reading newspapers and playing cards—entails a considerable squandering of wealth that could other-wise be devoted to productive investments. Even in a State like China, where the bureaucracy has still not attained its ultimate social density and where privileges, those of seven million rural cadres in particular, are presently less developed than elsewhere, the maintenance cost of the ruling apparatus absorbs an outrageous portion of the national income. In 1954, the construction of administrative buildings by itself alone soaked up 21.6 percent of investments made by six industrial ministries. At that date, 18 percent of the State's revenues were swallowed up by administrative expenses. That represents 8 percent of the national income. This constitutes, moreover, but a slight portion of the bureaucratic apparatus's maintenance cost, for that apparatus is not limited to administration, properly speaking. In particular, the salaries and bonuses paid to engineers, technicians, trade-union officials, and Stakhanovites who indubitably are part of the exploitative apparatus are not counted under the heading of administrative expenses but, rather, of wages paid to laborers. On the other hand, the cadres and managers of all sorts from cooperatives are not, in principle, salaried employees but coowners of the enterprises they manage and they soak up a portion of the profits. Altogether, these various elements must include no less than 15 million persons. In allocating to these various strata (which include the least privileged elements of the bureaucracy—the rural cadres have salaries certainly lower than those of elite workers) incomes equivalent to only twice workers' average income, and in taking into account the administrative bureaucracy, one comes to the conclusion that the Chinese ruling stratum soaks up 20 to 25 percent of the national income.

One sees the true worth of the argument of these enlightened Stalinists who, without denying the development of a heavily privileged bureaucracy in the "socialist" countries, try to justify "historically" its existence and its privileges during the "transitional period" by the need to "keep high the pace of socialist accumulation." While it is correct that the growth of the bureaucracy's increasingly numerous privileges allows one to make laboring people sweat out more surplus value destined to be capitalized, the development of this apparatus in itself absorbs an increasing proportion of surplus value that is subtracted from the accumulation fund. Now, the overexploitation of the masses rendered possible by the differentiation of the bureaucracy does not compensate for the correlative increase in incidental expenses that is involved in the extraction of surplus value occasioned by the maintenance of the ruling apparatus. This may be seen quite well in the case of a country like China, where labor productivity and national income are still weak: in order to accumulate, at best, 23 percent of national income, one first has to set up an apparatus that soaks up 20 to 25 percent of it—and that is certainly an underestimation. Yet it is true that this astonishing absurdity of the system is destined to abate with time. The bureaucracy is indeed not destined to endless proliferation and the apparatus's cost will therefore end up hitting a ceiling or at the very least registering a slowdown. On the other hand, even if the rate of accumulation is maintained at approximately the same level, the growth of national income will bring with it, in absolute terms, a continual increase in investments. The ratio between the volume of accumulation and that of the bureaucracy's "unproductive consumption" will therefore not remain identical to what it presently is during the implementation period for the apparatus of domination and exploitation.

However considerable it might be, the "social cost" of the ruling apparatus is nonetheless only one of the aspects of the deep-seated irrationality of bureaucratic capitalism. The bureaucracy is not content to levy a huge part of the social product for its own consumption; it directs the economy in a way that is ultimately just as anarchic as private capitalism.

Unlike what happens in the bourgeois economy, where the way in which enterprises are managed may be penalized by the market, and eventually by the entrepreneur's bankruptcy, in the bureaucratic system the directors' incomes are in principle independent of the real economic situation of the enterprises of which they are in charge. Those directors are functionaries remunerated according to their positions in the administrative hierarchy and their incomes do not depend, like those of the capitalists, on the laws of competition. The substitution of planning for the market no less necessitates rigorous control of production, and, for lack of competition, there will be administrative measures that penalize the mistakes or errors committed in the management of the enterprise. Each enterprise is subject to a plan and norms, and the directorial organs are given bonuses or, on the contrary, fines and even legal punishments according to whether they have or have not accomplished the task conferred upon them. Bonuses replace big profits and the threat of prison that of bankruptcy.

Now, this system that provides livelihoods for these directors under permanent threat of dismissal or arrest gives rise to defense reactions that ensure that administrative terror, far from rationalizing the management of the economy, sows incredible disorder therein. In order to protect oneself, cadres organize themselves into cliques and into syndicates of particular interests whose members cover for one another and find jobs for one another in all major departments. Whence not only the overinflation of certain departments but also the inability of the central apparatus to assign posts according to real competencies. The Chinese press continually deplores the mistakes and errors due to the incompetency of cadres, from which both machinery and workers, falling victim to an exceptional number of work accidents, suffer. To this is added the fact that members of different cliques whose interests are interdependent close their eyes about the tamperings and the false statements concerning the real state of production to which they all are led in order not to lose bonuses or suffer sanctions. The proportion of product defects is indeed unbelievable. If the factories deliver the quantities of products they are obligated to manufacture, it is quite often to the detriment of their quality or even because defective products are actually mixed in with the others.

So, the mines deliver coal that has not had the stones removed and that is unusable, while ironworks deliver parts that do not have the requisite qualities and have to be sent back for remelting. Chemical factories send to commercial cooperatives rubber footwear whose soles have holes "the size of beans," the peasants say. Sometimes, up to 40 or 50 percent of the products delivered are defective.

Consequently, enterprises operate from month to month with enormous irregularity, sometimes being forced to reduce their activities to an extreme when they receive consignments of unusable raw materials. Mills and mines fulfill 10 percent of their plan in January, 360 percent in March, 14 percent in April, and 249 percent in June. Such irregularity in the operation of factories is accentuated by the stocking of raw materials and machinery. Knowing that delays in delivery of raw material refills or the sudden delivery of defective products can prevent them from fulfilling their plan and will garner them lost bonuses and penalties, the directors of enterprises take precautions. In 1954, it was discovered, for example, that the Kailan mines had the good sense to buy enough steel springs to cover their needs for 60 years and brushed electric motors for 20 years. Often, raw materials, machinery, and replacement parts that are stocked to prepare for any eventuality are stored outdoors and are ruined.

During this time, other factories reduce their production or even grind to a halt because they are unable to repair their machinery or because they exhausted their raw materials. Elsewhere, factories have been equipped with huge capacities and the production of raw materials does not allow them to utilize their full potential. Latest-model soviet steelworks grind to a halt because not enough iron with low phosphorous content is produced. Gypsum extraction does not correspond to the capacities of cement factories. Costly machines have been installed but they cannot be used profitably for lack of the means to supply them at a satisfactory pace. Not only industries that manufacture the means of consumption but in reality industry as a whole operates by using only 70 or 80 percent of its potential.

Thus, over five years, the bureaucracy, setting above all else the need to industrialize rapidly, has made workers and peasants sweat blood and water in order to equip factories it is incapable of operating at full output. We must once again resign ourselves to displeasing the advocates of the bureaucracy: Development of the forces of production offers no justification for the hardships Chinese laborers undergo, for a huge proportion of the surplus value extorted from them serves to feed not accumulation but exploitation and bureaucratic waste. Even more, the negative effects of exploitation and bureaucratic anarchy on the growth of the productive forces develop cumulatively, the hardships of the masses grow inordinately and thus give rise, by ricochet, to a new obstacle to accumulation, the crisis of labor productivity.

Overworked and exasperated by the permanent underconsumption imposed upon them, the workers quickly discover that "the triumphal march of socialism" changes nothing about their situation in the production process. And they react by refusing to collaborate and, ultimately, by objecting more and more openly. Defects, absenteeism, feigned illnesses, struggles against the pace of production, slowdowns, and, finally, work stoppages and street demonstrations constitute the series of worker ripostes to the intensification of exploitation. For five years, a sly and hidden and then overt and violent struggle has played out in the mines and factories between laboring people and the bureaucracy. Since "collectivization," this struggle has spread in turn to the village level, where the peasants are no longer but proletarians. Far from being an indispensable condition for alleged socialist accumulation, the differentiation of the bureaucracy into a privileged and exploitative class results in the deepening of new social antagonisms whose effect is to undermine and continually slow down the rate of expansion of production and accumulation.

THE WORKING CLASS CONFRONTS
BUREAUCRATIC EXPLOITATION

As soon as power was won, the Chinese bureaucracy cast away its workerist mask and revealed its true face as a new exploitative class. One after another, the traditional demands of the Chinese workers' movement were cynically disowned amid a blaze of propaganda; the bureaucracy endeavored to convince the proletariat that the practices that had been denounced under the Kuomintang as the expression of capitalist rapacity were becoming, under the new regime, the cornerstone for the edification of socialism.

As early as 1950, the party and the trade unions mounted campaign after campaign, endeavoring to persuade the workers that their self-interest required of them a complete change in their attitude toward production. At the rhythm of several times a week, meetings followed one upon another; during them, the trade-union bureaucrats undertook to reeducate laboring people and to convince them that, when they arrived late to work, left without reason, and took breaks in the factory, they were only harming themselves.

Yet this orchestration of productivity ended in partial failure. At the very most, a few hundreds of thousands of workers participated in the campaigns to develop production. Complete state control [*étatisation*] left intact within the bureaucratic enterprise the contradiction between the capitalist relation that tends to deny the human role of the worker in production and the impossibility of making the modern factory, with its complex and fragile technology, operate without the workers deploying in their labor some qualities that belong only to man. After two years of unsuccessful attempts to obtain the active collaboration of workers as a whole within production, the bureaucracy instituted piece rates in 1952. This was meant to break the apathy the Chinese working class continued to manifest as a whole toward bureaucratic production by giving laborers an individual interest in the smooth running of the enterprise, despite social relations that, in depriving the workers of the direction of their own laboring activity by enslaving them to the machinery and through the machinery to the outside will of the exploitative ruling class, made them feel that their own labor was an activity that is foreign and inimical to them. Without a doubt, the bureaucracy succeeded for a time, through piece rates, to impose its will on laboring people. The latter were classed into five categories in turn subdivided into eight pay grades with different base salaries established in terms of the outputs of model workers. Under penalty of being remunerated below the norm with starvation wages, a growing number of workers were obliged to "act productively." The bureaucracy proclaimed its victories. Between 1953 and 1956, labor productivity increased 69 percent. As early as 1953, 80 percent of workers were participating in production campaigns.

The system of norms and piece rates broke up the unity of the working class. Whereas a majority of laboring people attained the norms with difficulty, a minority of shock laborers split off, beat records, and accumulated privileges (bonuses, new lodgings, paid leave in convalescent homes, etc.). True, the exploits of the Chinese Stakhanovites often brought out some uproariously tall stories—like the record broken by the miner Chew Wen-Tsin, who, stronger than Stakhanov in person, on March 19, 1951 mined 242 tons of coal in seven hours and twenty minutes. (Let us point out, in order to underscore the outrageous howler such figures represent, that in the mines of Pennsylvania in the USA, where however the extraction and removal of coal are entirely electrified, the output of the American miner does not exceed four and a half tons per day. And that is, however, three times the output of French miners.)

Yet the "tricks" to which shock workers resorted mattered little to the dictators of the Plan. The key thing was that, in exchange for privileges with which they were stuffed, the Stakhanovites fulfilled the role expected of them: smash the norms to show that they are too low and that, consequently, it is possible and legitimate to speed up the work pace. As in the USSR, Stakhanovism in China is but a huge mystification intended to detach from the proletariat a labor aristocracy that becomes an auxiliary to the bureaucracy in its struggle to step up exploitation.

As early as 1953, however, the bureaucracy was to become a bit disillusioned. The struggle of overexploited laboring people was reborn in the factories. The system of norms and piece rates had not been totally effective. Absenteeism, work slowdowns, breaks during the day, and premature labor stoppages were reappearing. Sick leaves taken as a pretext began to multiply, sometimes touching 15 or even 20 percent of workers in certain enterprises. Discontented with labor conditions, workers left certain factories to go look for work elsewhere. This movement took on exceptional breadth in the mines, threatening to sow disorder in the bureaucracy's plans. The bureaucracy's riposte to the workers' growing indiscipline was then to take coercive measures. In 1954, it promulgated the Labor Law. Workers were henceforth riveted to the factory or the mine. Each of them was provided with a labor passport and could not change jobs without obtaining a visa from the authorities. To struggle against absenteeism, laxness of effort in work, and damage to machinery and raw materials, an entire catalog of sanctions was established: fines, suspensions, demotions, or outright dismissals. Industrial tribunals were created in all working-class cities in order to apply these new regulations. As early as 1954, they operated at full capacity. Two months after its creation, the industrial tribunal of Tientsin passed 61 sentences for this city's railroad workers alone. The penalties were heavy: at Harbin, workers had 92 percent of their wages held back as a fine. The year 1954 marked a turning point: thenceforth, a relentless struggle, each month more bitter, played out in enterprises between the bureaucracy and the proletariat. Portents of the crisis of 1956–1957 began to shine through.

After four years of experience, the illusions the proletariat could have held about the genuine nature of the regime that came out of the Revolution rapidly vanished. All propaganda ruses are impotent against the experience the workers have of the reality of everyday life. […]

The analysis continues in the same vein through the following years, with the development of a privileged workers' aristocracy and the intensification of the working class's struggles, then the description of the peasant condition and the loss of all illusions as to the ability of the Maoist bureaucracy to resolve the problems of the peasant world, ending on the effects of the quite recent Hungarian Revolution, which served as a model for the most revolutionary elements of the movement of struggle in China, without for all that nourishing any illusions about the objective possibility of those struggles from 1957 leading to a genuine revolutionary situation.

Two years later, in "China in the Time of Totalitarian Perfection" (no. 29), Brune continued his denunciation of the properly totalitarian measures adopted to enroll and supervise the population following the struggles of 1957—the same measures Western Maoists extolled so much. He demonstrated at the same time, through an analytical assessment of totalitarian language, how the Chinese, and their emulators, have tried, through a subtle transformation, to pass off as "communism" what Marx denounced as the worst excesses of capitalism. The facts described are now perfectly well known, and have been denounced many times since Maoism has gone out of fashion, which would make a reading of this text a bit tedious, but those facts have rarely been connected, in detail, with the resistance of the Chinese people. In 1960, in any case, such a denunciation contrasted radically with the excited discourses of Mao's adulators.

Notes

1. T/E: The first part of this quotation originally comes from Karl Marx, *Capital* (New York: International Publishers, 1967), vol. 1, pt. 7, ch. 24, 595; the second part, with a quotation of the first, comes from "The Development of Capitalism in Russia" (1899), in V. I. Lenin, *Collected Works* (Moscow: Progress Publishers, 1977) vol. 3, 56.
2. T/E: *Capital*, vol. 3, pt. 3, ch. 15 , 245.

PART SEVEN

MODERN CAPITALISM AND THE BREAK WITH MARXISM

"Le Capitalisme moderne et la rupture avec le marxisme"
Socialisme ou Barbarie—Anthologie, 275-77

From 1956 to 1958, a change in the life of the S. ou B. group began to take place. Having remained, during the nearly ten years since its formation, an almost clandestine, or in any case universally ignored, observer of contemporary societies, starting in the Fall of 1956 the group made its (certainly very discreet) arrival on the public scene. The popular and remarkably proletarian uprisings in Eastern Europe had brilliantly confirmed its analysis of bureaucratic regimes. In May 1958, a coup d'État brought Charles de Gaulle back to power. France then entered into a period of profound institutional, political, and social upheavals. The analyses the group gave of these upheavals, which it delivered to the public via the review but also by actively intervening in the circles it could reach—basically, the University and a few factories—garnered for it a certain amount of influence, at least among students. The group once again radically distinguished itself from the Left and the Far Left: it demonstrated the reactionary character and the decay of the defunct French Fourth Republic and denounced the mystifications the French CP, in particular, was using to try to convince people to think that the Gaullist regime was fascist and to group them against it in an "antifascist front."

A turning point in the group's activities then took place. On the theoretical level, the main axis of its work shifted from the bureaucratic societies of the East toward the liberal capitalism of the West. On the political level, the task it had assigned to itself since its origin—namely, to set up a revolutionary organization of a new kind—appeared to the group to be both more urgent than ever and more achievable than had been the case in the past. This reorientation laid bare a number of problems that had remained more or less latent until that time: that of organization, first of all, the theoretical terms of which are laid out in Part 5 of the present collection; and, especially, that of updating the critique of modern capitalism and the definition of a corresponding revolutionary politics.

In responding to these problems, the group was unable to avoid rifts. The organization question—an object of recurrent debate within the group since its foundation, particularly between Chaulieu (Castoriadis) and Montal (Lefort)—was settled in 1958 by a split. The other debate, which bore on the very content of critique and revolutionary politics, continued in an often very bitter way until 1963 and ended, in turn, with another split. For several years running, it had already underpinned many internal discussions, and particularly in Castoriadis's case, the need for a thorough review of Marxist analysis was expressed on numerous occasions.

In the view of Castoriadis and of a number of other members of the group, the new situation created in France by the Gaullist coup d'état rendered this need an urgent one and intensified it in a radical way: it was now the very basis of Marxist theory that was to be called back into question. On the spot, the Gaullist effort was interpreted—quite rightly, as was shown afterwards—as a modernization and rationalization of French capitalism. That effort, it was foreseen, would be carried out not just at the expense of outdated sectors—*Pieds-Noirs* [Algerian-born French colonials], "beet growers" [taken by de Gaulle in exasperation to be the epitome of a subsidized special interest], shopkeepers, and so on—but especially at the expense of laboring people. And, in fact, the measures undertaken by the new regime translated into a drastic cutback in wage earners' income that could be calculated at around 15 percent. The logic of class struggle therefore allowed one to foresee the rise of major social movements in which Socialisme ou Barbarie would be able to intervene and to pose in concrete terms the question of workers' autonomy. Yet, against all expectations, the working class did not react. No reaction, either, among the population—except among students—to the intensification of the war in Algeria, which had been going on since 1954. What, then, was the meaning of this massive abstentionism? What explanations might be found for this phenomenon in the structure and functioning of a capitalist system that had changed profoundly since its "classical" age had been analyzed by Marx and the Marxists? What implications were revolutionaries to draw so as to orient their action? To what extent did Marxism remain valid? Such were the vast questions that were going to feed the theoretical discussion until 1963.

Castoriadis's theses are contained in a long text, "Modern Capitalism and Revolution," which was published in three installments in issues 31, 32, and 33 of the review. This text includes both an original analysis of what the author called *modern capitalism* and a detailed refutation of the points in Marxist theory that this analysis challenged. For this very reason, each of the points developed takes on such a breadth that excerpts could not be provided here without blurring the overall view that ensures its coherence. It happens, however, that Castoriadis gave a condensed summary of his new theory in a text published in January 1964 under the title "Recommencing the Revolution." As this text constituted the Editorial for issue 35, that means that he had received the approval of the group—now amputated of the numerous opponents of those theses. It is from this text that we publish below some large excerpts.

D.B.

Recommencing the Revolution

"Recommencer la revolution"
Socialisme ou Barbarie, 35 (January 1964): 1–36
Socialisme ou Barbarie—Anthologie, 278-96[1]

I. THE END OF CLASSICAL MARXISM

I. Three massive facts today confront revolutionaries who still wish to claim that they are acting in such a way that they understand what they are doing, that is, in full knowledge of the relevant facts:

- The way capitalism functions has been fundamentally altered in relation to the reality of the pre-1939 era. It has altered even more in relation to the analysis of it Marxism had provided.
- As an organized class movement explicitly and permanently contesting capitalist domination, the workers' movement has disappeared.
- Colonial or semicolonial domination by advanced countries over backward countries has been abolished without this abolition being accompanied anywhere by a revolutionary mutation [*transcroissance*] within the movement of the masses, nor have the foundations of capitalism in the ruling countries been shaken by this process.

2. For those who refuse to mystify themselves, it is clear that, in practice, the establishment of these facts means the ruination of classical Marxism as a *system* of thought and action as it was formulated, developed, and maintained between 1847 and 1939. For, these findings signify that Marx's analysis of capitalism in his masterwork

(the analysis of the economy), Lenin's analysis of imperialism, and Marx-Trotsky's conception of the permanent revolution as applied to backward countries have been refuted or outstripped, and that virtually all traditional forms of organization and action in the workers' movement (save for those of revolutionary periods) are irreversibly bankrupt. They signify the ruination of classical Marxism as a *concrete system of thought* having some grasp on reality. Apart from a few abstract ideas, nothing that is essential in *Capital* is to be found in the reality of today. Conversely, what is essential in reality today (the changes in and the crisis of the nature of work, the scission and opposition between the formal organization and the real organization of production and between the formal and the real functioning of institutions, the phenomenon of bureaucratization, the consumer society, working-class apathy, the nature of Eastern-bloc countries, the changes in backward countries and their relations with the advanced countries, the crisis of all aspects of life and the increasing importance of phenomena previously considered peripheral, people's attempts to find a way out of this crisis) can be understood only in light of different analyses. The best in Marx's work can serve as a source of inspiration for these analyses, but set in front of these analyses is instead a vulgar and bastardized Marxism, the only kind practiced today by his self-proclaimed "defenders" of every ilk, which acts as a screen blocking one's view. The findings also signify the ruination of classical Marxism (and of Leninism-Trotskyism-Bordigism, etc.) as a *program of action* in which what was to be done by revolutionaries at any given moment was coherently linked (at least on the level of intentions) with the real actions of the working class and with an overall theoretical viewpoint. When, for instance, a Marxist organization supported or led a working-class strike for higher wages, it did so (a) with a strong likelihood of receiving a real hearing from the workers, (b) as the only instituted organization fighting on their side, and (c) in the belief that each working-class victory on the wages front was a blow delivered to the objective structure of the capitalist edifice. None of the measures advocated in the classical Marxist programs can today fulfill these three requirements.

3. Certainly, society today still remains profoundly divided. It functions against the immense majority of laboring people. In their everyday lives, these people express their opposition to this society with half of each one of their gestures. The present crisis of humanity will be able to be resolved only through a socialist revolution. But these ideas run the risk of remaining empty abstractions, pretexts for

sermons or for a blind and spasmodic activism, if we do not strive to understand how society's divisions are concretely being realized at the present hour, how this society functions, what forms of reaction and struggle laboring people adopt against the ruling strata and their system, what new kinds of revolutionary activity related to people's concrete existence and struggle in society and to a coherent and lucid view of the world are possible under these conditions. For all of this, what is needed is nothing less than a radical theoretical and practical renewal. It is this effort at renewal and the specific *new* ideas through which this effort has taken on concrete form at each stage that have characterized the Socialisme ou Barbarie group from the outset, not simple-minded rigid adherence to the idea of class struggle, of the proletariat as revolutionary force, or of revolution. Such blind adherence would have sterilized us, as it did the Trotskyists, Bordigists, and nearly all communists and "left" socialists.

[. . .]

7. Indeed, the time has arrived to attain a clear awareness that contemporary reality no longer can be grasped simply at the cost of a low-budget revision of classical Marxism, or even through any kind of revision at all. In order to be understood, contemporary reality requires a new whole in which breaks with the classical ideas are just as important as (and much more significant than) the ties of kinship. This fact was able to be hidden even from our own eyes by the gradual character of our theoretical elaboration and, undoubtedly, also by a desire to maintain the greatest possible degree of historical continuity. Nevertheless, it becomes strikingly apparent when we look back over the path traveled and as we gauge the distance separating the ideas that appear essential to us today from those of classical Marxism. A few examples will suffice to demonstrate this point.[2]

a. For classical Marxism, the division of society was between capitalists who own the means of production and propertyless proletarians. Today it should be seen as a division between directors and executants.
b. Society was seen as dominated by the abstract power of impersonal capital. Today, we see it as dominated by a hierarchical bureaucratic structure.
c. For Marx, the central category for understanding capitalist social relations was that of *reification*. Reification was the result of the

transformation of all human relations into *market* relations.[3] For us, the central structuring moment of contemporary society is not the market but its bureaucratic-hierarchical "organization." The basic category to be used in grasping social relations is that of the *scission* between the processes of direction and execution of collective activities.

d. In Marx, the category of reification found its natural continuation in the analysis of labor power as a commodity, in the literal and full sense of this term. As a commodity, labor power had an exchange value defined by "objective" factors (costs of production and reproduction of labor power) and a use value the purchaser was able to extract at will. The worker was seen as a passive object of the economy and of capitalist production. For us, this abstraction is halfway a mystification. Labor power can never become purely and simply a commodity (despite capitalism's best efforts). Labor power has no exchange value determined by "objective" factors, for wage levels are determined essentially by formal and informal working-class struggles. Labor power has no predefined use value, for productivity levels are the stake in an incessant struggle at the point of production and the worker is an active as much as a passive subject in this struggle.

e. For Marx, the inherent "contradiction" of capitalism was that the development of the forces of production was becoming, beyond a certain point, incompatible with capitalist forms of property ownership and of private appropriation of the social product, and would have to "break them asunder." For us, the inherent contradiction of capitalism is to be found in the type of scission between direction and execution that capitalism brings about, and in its consequent need simultaneously to seek the exclusion and to solicit the participation of individuals in their activities.

f. For the classical revolutionary way of thinking, the proletariat suffers its history until the day it explodes its situation. For us, the proletariat makes its history, under given conditions, and its struggles are constantly transforming capitalist society at the same time that these struggles transform the proletariat itself.

g. For the classical revolutionary way of thinking, capitalist culture produces mystifications pure and simple, which are then denounced as such, or it produces scientific truths and valid works, in which case one denounces the fact that they have been appropriated exclusively by the privileged strata of society. For us, this culture, in all its manifestations, both participates in the general crisis of society *and* helps to prepare the way for a new form of human life.

h. For Marx, production will always remain the "realm of necessity." Whence comes the Marxist movement's implicit idea that socialism is essentially a matter of rearranging the economic and social consequences of a technical infrastructure that is at the same time both neutral and inevitable. For us, production must become the realm of creativity for the associated producers. And the conscious transformation of technology, aimed at putting it at the service of *homo faber*, must be a central task of postrevolutionary society.

i. Already for Marx, and much more so for the Marxist movement, the development of the forces of production was at the center of everything, and its incompatibility with capitalist forms brought history's condemnation down upon these forms. Whence the quite natural identification of socialism with nationalization and economic planning. For us, the essence of socialism is people's domination over all aspects of their lives and in the first place over their labor. Whence the idea that socialism is inconceivable outside of the management of production by the associated producers, and without the power of councils of laboring people.

j. For Marx, "bourgeois right" and therefore wage inequality would still have to prevail during a period of transition. For us, a revolutionary society could not survive and develop if it did not immediately instaurate absolute wage equality.

k. Finally, and to stick to fundamentals, the traditional movement has always been dominated by the twin concepts of economic determinism and the leading role of the Party. For us, at the center of everything is the autonomy of laboring people, the masses' capacity for self-direction, without which every idea of socialism immediately turns into a mystification. This entails a new conception of the revolutionary process, as well as of revolutionary organization and politics.

It is not difficult to see that these ideas—whether they are true or false matters little for the moment—represent neither "additions" nor partial revisions, but constitute rather the elements for an all-around theoretical reconstruction.

8. One must also grasp that this reconstruction affects not only the content of the ideas, but also the very type of theoretical conception we are attempting to make. Just as it is vain to search today for a type of organization that would be able to be, in the new period

to come, a "substitute" for trade unions, resuming somehow its previously positive role but without the negative traits now associated with unions—in short, to seek to invent a type of organization that would be a union without being one, while all the time remaining one—so it is illusory to believe that it will be possible for "another Marxism" to exist henceforth that would not be Marxism. The ruination of Marxism is not only the ruination of a certain number of specific ideas (though we should point out, if need be, that through this process of ruination a number of fundamental discoveries and a way of envisaging history and society remain that no one can any longer ignore). It is also the ruination of a certain type of connection among ideas, as well as between ideas and reality or action. In brief, it is the ruination of the conception of a closed theory (and, even more, of a closed theoretico-practical system) that thought it could enclose the truth, the whole truth, and nothing but the truth of the historical period presently occurring within a certain number of allegedly scientific schemata.

With this ruination, a phase in the history of the workers' movement—and, we should add, in the history of humanity—is drawing to a close. We can call it the theological phase, with the understanding that there can be and there is a theology of "science" that is not better, but rather worse, than the other type of theology (inasmuch as it gives those who share in this belief the false conviction that their faith is "rational"). It is the phase of faith, be it faith in a Supreme Being, be it in an "exceptional" man or a group of "exceptional" men, be it in an impersonal truth established once and for all and written up as a doctrine. It is the phase during which man became alienated in his own creations, whether imaginary or real, theoretical or practical. Never again will there be a complete theory that would need merely to be "updated." Incidentally, in real life there never was any theory of this sort, for all great theoretical discoveries have veered off into the imaginary as soon as one tried to convert them into systems, Marxism no less than the others.

What there has been, and what there will continue to be, is a living theoretical process, from whose womb emerge moments of truth destined to be outstripped (were it only through their integration into another whole within which they no longer have the same meaning). This does not entail some sort of skepticism: at each instant and for a given state of our experience, *there are* truths and errors, and there is always the need to carry out a provisional totalization, ever changing and ever open, of what is true. The idea of a complete and definitive theory, however, is today only a bureaucrat's phantasm helping him to manipulate the oppressed; for the oppressed, it can only be the equivalent, in modern-day terms, of an essentially irrational faith.

At each stage in our development, we ought therefore to assert positively those elements about which we are certain, but we also must recognize—and not just by paying lip service—that at the frontiers of our reflection and our practice we necessarily encounter problems whose solution we do not know in advance, and perhaps we will not know for a good while; we may not even know whether the solution will oblige us to abandon positions we would have died defending the day before. Whether we like it or not, whether we know it or not, each of us is obliged in our personal lives to deploy this lucidity and this courage in the face of the unknownness of the perpetually renewed creation into which we are advancing. Revolutionary politics cannot be the last refuge for neurotic rigidity and the neurotic need for security.

9. More than ever before, the problem of the fate of human society is now posed in global terms. The fate of the two-thirds of humanity that lives in nonindustrialized countries; the relations these countries maintain with the industrialized countries; more profound still, the structure and the dynamic of a world society that is gradually emerging—these questions not only are starting to take on central importance, they are being raised, in one form or another, day after day. For us, however, we who live in a modern capitalist society, the primary task is to analyze this society, the fate of the workers' movement born therein, the orientation revolutionaries should adopt for themselves. This task is *objectively* the primary one, since it is in fact the forms of life of modern capitalism that dominate the world and shape the evolution of other countries. This task is also the primary one *for us*, for we are nothing if we cannot define ourselves, both theoretically and practically, in relation to our own society. It is to this definition that the present text is devoted.[4]

II. MODERN BUREAUCRATIC CAPITALISM

10. In no way can it be said that capitalism, whether in its "private" or in its totally bureaucratic form, is unable to continue to develop the forces of production. Nor is there any insurmountable economic contradiction to be found in its mode of operation. More generally speaking, there is no contradiction between the development of the forces of production and capitalist economic forms or capitalist production relations. To state that a socialist regime would be able to

develop the forces of production infinitely faster is not to point out a contradiction. And to state that there is a contradiction between capitalist forms and the development of human beings is a sophism, for to speak of the development of human beings has meaning only to the exact extent that they are considered as something other than "productive forces." Capitalism is engaged in a movement of expanding the forces of production, and it itself constantly creates the conditions for this expansion.

Classical economic crises of overproduction correspond to a historically obsolete phase characterized by the capitalist class's lack of organization. Such crises are completely unknown in totally bureaucratic capitalism (as exists in Eastern-bloc countries). And they have only a minor equivalent in the economic fluctuations of modern industrial countries, where state control over the economy can and actually does maintain such fluctuations within narrow limits.

11. There is neither a growing "reserve army of the unemployed" nor a relative or absolute "pauperization" of the working class that would prevent the system from selling off its products or would render its long-term operation impossible. "Full employment" (in the capitalist sense and within capitalist limits) and the rise in mass consumption (a type of consumption that is capitalist in its form and in its content) are both the prerequisite for and the result of the expansion of production, which capitalism in actual fact achieves. Within its current limits, the continuous rise in workers' real wages not only does not undermine the foundations of capitalism as a system but is the condition for its survival. The same will go, to an increasing degree, for the shortening of the work week.

12. None of this prevents the capitalist economy from being full of irrationalities and antinomies in all its manifestations. Still less does it prevent capitalism from being immensely wasteful as compared with the possibilities of a socialist form of production. These irrationalities, however, do not come to our attention because of some analysis of the kind found in *Capital*. They are the irrationalities found in the bureaucratic management of the economy, which exists in its pure and unadulterated form in the Eastern-bloc countries. In the Western countries they are mixed with residues from the private-anarchic phase of capitalism.

These irrationalities express the incapacity of a separate ruling stratum to manage rationally any field of activity in an alienated society, not the autonomous functioning of "economic laws" independent of the action of individuals, groups, and classes. This is the reason why they are irrationalities, and never absolute impossibilities, except at the moment when the dominated classes refuse to make the system work any longer.

13. Under capitalism, changes in labor and in the way it is organized are dominated by two profoundly related tendencies: bureaucratization on the one hand, mechanization-automation on the other. Taken together, these tendencies constitute the directors' basic response to the executants' struggle against their exploitation and their alienation. But this fact does not lead to a simple, straightforward, and uniform evolution of labor, of its structure, of the skills it requires, of its relationship to the object of labor and to work machinery; nor does it entail a simple evolution of relations among laboring people themselves. If the reduction of all tasks to compartmentalized tasks has long been and remains the central phenomenon of capitalist production, this process of reducing labor to compartmentalized tasks is beginning to attain its limits in the sectors most characteristic of modern production, where it is becoming impossible to divide up tasks any further without making work itself impossible. Similarly, the reduction of tasks to simple jobs requiring no special qualifications (the destruction of skilled jobs) encounters its limits in modern production, too, and even tends to be reversed by the growing need for greater skills that the most modern industries require. Mechanization and automation are leading to a compartmentalization of tasks, but tasks that have been sufficiently compartmentalized and simplified are taken over at the next stage by "totally" automated units, which entail a restructuring of manpower that involves a division between a group of "passive," isolated, and unskilled attendants, on the one hand, and highly skilled and specialized technicians working in teams, on the other hand.

Side by side with all this, and still the largest segment of the work force in numerical terms, traditionally structured production sectors continue to exist. In these sectors are found all the historically sedimented strata of previous eras in the evolution of work, along with completely new sectors (notably office work) where traditional concepts and distinctions lose in this regard almost all their meaning. We therefore must consider as hasty and unverified extrapolations both the traditional idea (from Marx's *Capital*) that capitalism entails the pure and simple destruction of skills and the creation of an undifferentiated mass of automaton-workers, slaves to their machines, as well as the more recent idea (of Romano and Ria Stone [Grace (Lee) Boggs] in *The American Worker*)[5] of the growing importance of a category of universal workers working on universal machines. Both these tendencies exist as partial tendencies, together with a third tendency toward the proliferation of new categories both skilled and specialized at the same time, but it is neither possible nor necessary to decide in some arbitrary fashion that a single one of these categories represents the future.

14. It follows that neither the problem of uniting laboring people in the struggle against the present system nor that of management of the business enterprise by laboring people after the revolution has a guaranteed solution that relies on some automatic process incorporated into the evolution of technique itself. These problems remain, rather, political problems in the highest meaning of the term: their solution depends on a thoroughgoing raising of people's consciousnesses concerning the totality of society's problems.

Under capitalism, there will always be a problem of uniting the struggles of different categories of laborers who are not in immediately identical situations and who never will be. And during the revolution, and even afterward, workers' management will not consist in the laboring people taking charge of a production process that has become materialized in the form of mechanization and whose objective logic is watertight and beyond argument. Nor will it consist in the deployment of the aptitudes, somehow fully formed, of a collectivity of virtually universal producers, ready-made by capitalism. Workers' management will have to face up to an extraordinarily complex internal differentiation among the various strata of the laboring population; it will have to resolve the problem of how to integrate individuals, various categories of laborers, and different types of activity, for this will be its fundamental problem. Not in any foreseeable future will capitalism produce, through its own workings, a class of laborers that would already be, in itself, a concrete universal. Unless we stick to a sociological concept, actual laboring-class unity can be achieved only through the struggle by laboring people and against capitalism. (Let it be said, parenthetically, that to speak today of the proletariat as a class is merely to indulge in descriptive sociology, pure and simple; what unites laboring people as identical members of a group is simply the set of passively shared traits capitalism imposes upon them, and not their attempt to assert themselves as a class that unites itself and opposes itself to the rest of society through their activity, even if fragmentary in character, or through their organization, even if that of a minority.)

The two problems mentioned above [uniting workers in struggle and workers' management] can be resolved only by the association of all the nonexploitative categories of workers at the workplace, manual workers as well as intellectual workers or office workers and technicians. Any attempt at achieving workers' management that would eliminate a category of workers essential to the modern production process would lead to the collapse of this production process—which could be built back up again only through renewed bureaucratization and the use of coercion.

15. The changes in the structuring of society that have taken place over the past century were not those foreseen by classical Marxism. This has had important consequences. Certainly there has been a "proletarianization" of society in the sense that the old "petty-bourgeois" classes have practically disappeared, and in the sense that the overwhelming majority of the population has been transformed into a population of wage and salary earners and has been integrated into the capitalist division of labor found in the business enterprise. But this "proletarianization" differs essentially from the classical image, where society was supposed to have evolved in two opposite directions, toward an enormous pole of industrial workers and toward an infinitesimal one of capitalists. On the contrary, as it has become bureaucratized, and in accordance with the underlying logic of bureaucratization, society has been transformed into a pyramid, or rather a complex set of pyramids.

The transformation of virtually the whole population into a population of wage and salary earners does not signify that there no longer exists anyone but pure and simple executants on the bottom rungs of the ladder. The population absorbed by the bureaucratic-capitalist structure has come to inhabit all tiers of the bureaucratic pyramid. It will continue to do so. And in this pyramid one can detect no tendency toward a reduction of the intermediate layers. Quite the contrary. Although it is difficult to delimit clearly this concept and although it is impossible to make it coincide with the extant statistical categories of analysis, we can with certainty state that in no modern industrial country do the number of "simple executants" (manual workers in industry and their counterparts in other branches: typists, sales personnel, etc.) exceed 50 percent of the laboring population. Moreover, the previously nonproletarianized population has not been absorbed into the industrial sectors of the economy. Except for countries that have not "completed" their industrialization process (Italy, for example), the percentage of the population in industry stopped growing after reaching a ceiling of between 30 percent and (rarely) 50 percent of the active population. The rest are employed in the "service" sectors of the economy (the proportion of the population employed in agriculture is declining rapidly all over and is already negligible in England and the United States).

Even if the increase in the percentages employed in the service sectors were to stop (due to the mechanization and automation now encroaching upon these sectors in their turn), it would be very difficult to *reverse* this tendency, given the increasingly rapid productivity increases occurring in the industrial sector and the consequent rapid decrease in demand for industrial manpower. The combined result of these two factors is that the industrial proletariat in the classical and strict sense (i.e., defined in terms of manual workers or as hourly paid workers, categories that are roughly overlapping) is in the process of declining in relative and sometimes even absolute size. Thus, in the United States, the percentage of the industrial proletariat ("production and allied workers" and "unskilled workers other than those in agriculture and mining," statistics that *include the unemployed*, as listed according to their last job) has fallen from 28 percent in 1947 to 24 percent in 1961, this decline moreover having accelerated appreciably since 1955.

16. In no way do these observations signify that the industrial proletariat has lost its importance, or that it does not have a central role to play in the unfolding of a revolutionary process, as has been confirmed both by the Hungarian Revolution (though in that case not under conditions of modern capitalism) and by the Belgian General Strike. However, our observations clearly show that the revolutionary movement could no longer claim to represent the interests of the immense majority of the population against a small minority if it did not address itself to all categories of the wage-earning and laboring population, excluding the small minority of capitalists and ruling bureaucrats, and if it did not seek to associate the strata of simple executants with intermediary strata of the pyramid, which are nearly as important numerically speaking.

17. Apart from the transformations in the nature of the capitalist State and of capitalist policy that we have analyzed elsewhere,[6] we must understand what the new form of capitalist totalitarianism exactly signifies and what its methods of domination are in present-day society. In present-day totalitarianism, the State, as the central expression of domination of society by a minority, or the State's appendages and ultimately the ruling strata seize hold of all spheres of social activity and try to model them explicitly after their interests and their outlook. This in no way implies, however, a continuous use of violence

or direct coercion, or the suppression of freedoms and formal rights. Violence of course remains the ultimate guarantor of the system, but the system need not have recourse to it every day. It need not resort to violence precisely to the extent that the extension of its grip into almost all domains of activity assures it a more "economical" exercise of its authority, to the extent that its control over the economy and the continuous expansion of the latter allow it most of the time to appease economic demands without major conflict, and to the extent, finally, that rises in the material standard of living and the degeneration of the traditional organizations and ideas of the workers' movement serve as the constant condition for individual privatization, which, though contradictory and transitory, nonetheless signifies that the domination of the system is not explicitly contested by anyone in society.

We must reject the traditional idea that bourgeois democracy is a worm-eaten edifice doomed to give way to fascism in the absence of revolution. First, this "democracy," even as bourgeois democracy, already has effectively disappeared, *not* through the reign of the Gestapo, but through the bureaucratization of all political and state institutions and the concomitant rise of apathy among the population. Second, this new pseudodemocracy (pseudo to the second degree) *is* precisely the adequate form of domination for modern capitalism, which could not do without parties (including socialist and communist ones) and unions, nowadays essential cogs of the system, whatever point of view you might adopt. This has been confirmed by what has happened over the last five years in France, where, despite the decomposition of the state apparatus and the Algerian crisis, there never was a serious chance of a fascist takeover and establishment of a dictatorship. It also has been confirmed by Khrushchevism in Russia, which expresses precisely the bureaucracy's attempt to move on to new methods of domination, the old ones (totalitarian in the traditional sense) having become incompatible with modern society (it is another thing that there are chances that everything might break apart *during* the passage to these new methods of domination). With the monopoly over violence as its last resort, capitalist domination presently rests on the bureaucratic manipulation of people in their work life, in their consumer life, and everywhere else in their lives.

18. Thus, modern capitalism is essentially a bureaucratized society with a pyramidal, hierarchal structure. In it are not opposed, as in two clearly separate tiers, a small class of exploiters and a large class of producers. The division of society is much more complex and stratified, and no simple criterion is available to sum it up.

The traditional concept of class corresponded to the relationship of individuals and social groups to the ownership of the means of production. We have gone beyond this concept under that form, and rightly so, when we insisted upon looking at how individuals and groups are situated in the real relations of production, and when we introduced the concepts of directors and executants. These concepts remain valid for shedding light on the situation of contemporary capitalism, but they cannot be applied in a mechanical fashion. In their pure state, they can be concretely applied only at the very top and the very bottom of the pyramid, thus leaving aside all the intermediate strata, namely, almost half of the population, the half whose tasks involve both execution (with regard to their superiors) and direction (toward those "below"). Certainly, within these intermediate strata one can encounter again some practically "pure" cases. Thus a part of the hierarchal network basically fulfills the functions of coercion and authority, while another part basically fulfills technical functions and includes those who could be called "executants with status" (for example, well-paid technicians or scientists who carry out only the studies or research they are asked to perform). But the collectivization of production has made it such that these pure cases, increasingly rare nowadays, leave out the great majority of the intermediate strata. While a business enterprise's service personnel may have considerably expanded, it is clear that not only the typists but a good number of employees placed higher up in these departments play no role of their own in the system of coercion and constraints that their departments help to impose upon the company. Conversely, when a research department or a department that performs "studies" or research for the company is developed, a chain of command is set up there, too, for a good number of people in such departments will have as their function the management of the other people's work.

More generally, it is impossible for the bureaucracy—and here is one more expression of the contradiction it experiences—to separate entirely the two work requirements, of "knowledge" or "technical expertise," on the one hand, and of "managerial ability," on the other. True, the logic of the system would want only those capable of "handling the men" to participate in the managerial chain of command, but the logic of reality requires that those who do a job know something about it—and the system can never become entirely unstuck from reality. This is why the intermediate strata are populated with people who combine a professional qualification with the exercise of managerial functions. For some of these people, the problem of how to manage in a way other than through manipulation and coercion crops up daily. Ambiguity vanishes when one reaches the layer of those who really are directors. These are the people for whose interests everything ultimately functions. They make the important decisions. They reactivate and stimulate the workings of the system, which would otherwise tend to become bogged down in its own inertia. They take the initiative for plugging the leaks [*brèches*] during moments of crisis.

This definition is not of the same nature as the simple criteria previously adopted to characterize classes. The question today, however, is not to get wrapped up in how to define the concept of class: it is to understand and to show that bureaucratization does not diminish society's divisions but on the contrary aggravates them (by complicating them), that the system functions in the interests of a small minority at the top, that hierarchization does not suppress and never will suppress people's struggle against the ruling minority and its rules, that laboring people (whether they be workers, clerical staff, or engineers) will not be able to free themselves from oppression, from alienation, and from exploitation unless they overthrow this system by eliminating hierarchy and by instaurating their collective and egalitarian management of production. The revolution will come into being the day the immense majority of the laboring people who populate the bureaucratic pyramid will attack this pyramid and the small minority who rule it. And it will not occur a day sooner. In the meantime, the only differentiation of genuinely practical importance is the one that exists at almost all levels of the pyramid (save at the very top, obviously) between those who *accept* the system and those who, in the everyday reality of production, *combat* it.

19. We already have defined elsewhere the profound contradiction of this society.[7] Briefly speaking, it resides in the fact that capitalism (and this reaches its point of paroxysm under bureaucratic capitalism) is obliged to try to achieve simultaneously the exclusion and the participation of people in their activities, that people are forced to make the system run half the time *against* its rules and therefore in struggle against it. This fundamental contradiction is constantly appearing at the junction of the process of direction with the process of execution, this being, as a matter of fact, the *social* moment of production par excellence. And it is to be found again, in an indefinite number of refracted forms, within the process of direction itself, where it renders the bureaucracy's functioning irrational from the root up. If this contradiction can be analyzed in a particularly clear-cut fashion in the

labor process, that central manifestation of human activity found in modern Western societies, it is to be found again under other forms, transposed to a greater or lesser degree, in all spheres of social activity, whether one is dealing with political life, sexual and family life (where people are more or less obliged to conform to norms they no longer interiorize), or cultural life.

20. The crisis of capitalist production, which is only the flip side of this contradiction, already has been analyzed in *S. ou B.*,[8] along with the crises of political and other kinds of organizations and institutions. These analyses must be complemented by an analysis of the crisis in values and in social life as such, and ultimately by an analysis of the crisis in the very personality of modern man, a result of the contradictory situations with which he must constantly grapple in his work and in his private life. This personality crisis also results from the collapse of values in the most profound sense of the term, namely, the fact that without values no culture is able to structure personalities adequate to it (i.e., to make the culture function, if only as the exploited).

Yet, our analysis of the crisis of production did not show that in this system of production there was only alienation. On the contrary, it has made clear that production occurred only to the extent that the producers constantly have struggled against this alienation. Likewise, our analysis of the crisis of capitalist culture in the broadest sense, and of the corresponding human personality, will take as its starting point the quite obvious fact that society is not and cannot be simply a "society without culture." Alongside the debris of the old culture are to be found positive (but ever ambiguous) elements created through the evolution of history. Above all, we find the permanent effort of people to live their lives, to give their lives a meaning in an era where nothing is certain any longer and where, in any case, nothing from without is accepted at face value. In the course of this effort there tends to be realized, for the first time in the history of humanity, people's aspiration for autonomy. For that very reason, this effort is just as important for the preparation of the socialist revolution as are the analogous manifestations in the domain of production.

21. The fundamental contradiction of capitalism and the multiple processes of conflict and irrationality in which its ramifications are brought out express themselves, and will express themselves so long as this society exists, through "crises" of one kind or another, break-downs in the regular functioning of the system. These crises can open the way to revolutionary periods if the laboring masses are combative

enough to call the capitalist system into question and conscious enough to be able to knock it down and to organize on its ruins a new society. The very functioning of capitalism therefore guarantees that there always will be "revolutionary opportunities." It does not, however, guarantee their outcome, which can depend upon nothing other than the masses' level of consciousness and their degree of autonomy. There is no "objective" dynamic guaranteeing socialism, and to say that one can exist is a contradiction in terms. All objective dynamics that can be detected in contemporary society are thoroughly ambiguous, as we have shown elsewhere.[9]

The only dynamic to which one can, and should, give the meaning of a dialectical progression toward revolution is the *historical* dialectic of the struggle of social groups, first of the proletariat in the strict sense of the term, and today more generally laboring people earning wages or salaries. The signification of this dialectic is that, through their struggle, those who are exploited transform reality as well as themselves, so that when the struggle resumes it can occur only at a higher level. This alone is the revolutionary perspective, and the search for another type of revolutionary perspective, even by those who condemn a mechanistic approach, proves that the true signification of their condemnation of such an approach has not really been understood. The ripening [*maturation*] of the conditions for socialism can never be an objective ripening (because no fact has signification outside human activity of one sort or another, and the will to read the certainty of the revolution in simple facts is no less absurd than the will to read it in the stars). Nor can it be a subjective ripening in a psychological sense (laboring people today do not have history and its lessons explicitly present in their minds, far from it; the main lesson of history is, as Hegel said, that there are no lessons of history, since history is always new). It is a historical process of maturation, that is, the accumulation of objective conditions for an adequate consciousness. This accumulation is itself the product of class action and the action of social groups. It cannot acquire its meaning, however, except through its resumption in a new consciousness and in new activity, which is not governed by "laws" and which, while being probable, never is *fated*.

22. The present era remains within this perspective. The victory of reformism as well as of bureaucratism signifies that if laboring people are to undertake large-scale struggles, they will be able to do so only by combating reformism and bureaucracy. The bureaucratization of society poses in an explicit way the social problem as one of the

management of society: management by whom, to what ends, by what means? The rise in standards of consumption will tend to lessen the effectiveness of consumption as a substitute in people's lives, as motive and as justification for what is already called in the United States the "rat race." Inasmuch as "economic" problems in the narrow sense are diminishing in importance, the interests and preoccupations of laboring people will be able to turn toward the real problems of life in modern society: toward working conditions and the organization of the workplace, toward the very *meaning* of work under present conditions, toward the other aspects of social organization and of people's lives.

To these points[10] we must add another that is just as important. The crisis of culture and of traditional values increasingly raises for individuals the problem of how to orient their concrete life both in the workplace and in all its other manifestations (relations between man and woman, between adults and children, with other social groups, with their neighborhood and immediate surroundings, even with "disinterested" activities), of its modes of being [*modalités*], but also, in the end, of its very *meaning*. Less and less can individuals resolve these problems simply by conforming to traditional and inherited ideas and roles—and even when they do conform, they no longer internalize them, that is, they no longer accept them as valid and unchallenge-able—because these ideas and these roles, which are incompatible with present-day social reality as well as with the needs of individuals, are collapsing from within. The ruling bureaucracy tries to replace them by means of manipulation, mystification, and propaganda—but these synthetic products cannot, any more than any other ones, resist next year's fashions; they can serve only as the basis for fleeting, external types of conformism. To an increasing degree, individuals are obliged to invent new responses to their problems. In doing so, not only do they manifest their tendency toward autonomy, but at the same time they tend to embody this autonomy, in their behavior and in their relations with others. More and more, one's actions are set on the idea that a relationship between human beings can be founded only on the recognition by each of the freedom and responsibility of the other in the conduct of his life. If one takes seriously the character of the revolution as total, if one understands that workers' management does not signify only a certain type of machinery but also a certain type of people, then it also must be recognized that this tendency is just as important as an index of the revolution as the workers' tendency to combat the bureaucratic management of the business enterprise—even if we do not yet see the collective manifestations of this former tendency, nor how it could lead to organized activities.

III. THE END OF THE TRADITIONAL
WORKERS' MOVEMENT: A BALANCE SHEET

23. Today one cannot act or think as a revolutionary without becoming deeply and totally conscious of this fact: The result of the transformations of capitalism and of the degeneration of the organized workers' movement has been that its traditional organizational forms, its traditional forms of action, its traditional preoccupations, ideas, and very vocabulary no longer have any value, or even have only a negative value. As [Daniel] Mothé has written, when discussing the actual reality of this movement for workers, " . . . even the Roman Empire, when it disappeared, left behind it ruins; the workers' movement is leaving behind only refuse."[11]

To become aware of this fact means to be done once and for all with the idea that, consciously or unconsciously, still dominates many people's attitudes, namely, that today's parties and trade unions—and all that goes with them (ideas, demands, etc.)—represent merely a screen interposed between a proletariat, ever and inalterably revolutionary in itself, and its class objectives, or a casting mold that distorts the form of workers' activities but does not modify their substance. The degeneration of the workers' movement has not only entailed the appearance of a bureaucratic stratum at the summit of these organizations, it has affected *all* its manifestations. This process of degeneration is due neither to chance nor simply to the "outside" influence of capitalism, but expresses just as much the proletariat's reality during an entire historic phase, for the proletariat is not and cannot be unfamiliar with what happens to it, let alone what it does.[12]

To speak of the demise of the traditional workers' movement means to understand that a historical period is coming to a close, dragging with it into the nothingness of the past the near-totality of forms and contents it had produced to embody laboring people's struggle for liberation. Just as there will be a renewal of struggles against capitalist society only to the extent that laboring people will make a tabula rasa of the residues of their own past activity that hinder the rebirth of these struggles, so there can be a renewal of the activity of revolutionaries only to the extent that the corpses have been properly and definitively buried.

[. . .]

28. At the same time that we are witnessing the irreversible bankruptcy of the forms that are characteristic of the traditional movement, we have witnessed, we are witnessing, and we will continue to witness the birth, rebirth, or resumption of new forms that, to the best of our ability to judge at the present time, are pointing to the direction the revolutionary process will take in the future. These new forms should guide us in our present thinking and action. The Hungarian Workers' Councils, their demands concerning the management of production, the abolition of [externally prescribed work] norms, and so on; the shop stewards' movement in England and wildcat strikes in the United States; demands concerning working conditions in the most general sense and those directed *against* hierarchy, which various categories of workers in several countries are putting forward, almost always *against* the unions: these are the new forms that ought to be the certain and positive points of departure in our effort to reconstruct a revolutionary movement. We have made an extensive analysis of these movements in *S. ou B.*, and this analysis remains valid (even if it must be reexamined and developed further). These insights, however, will not allow our reflections and our action to become truly fruitful unless we fully come to understand how they represent a *rupture*, certainly not with the high points of past revolutions, but with the everyday historical reality of the traditional movement today, and unless we take them not as amendments or additions to past forms, but as new bases upon which we must continue to reflect and to act, together with what our analysis and our renewed critique of established society teach us.

29. Present conditions allow us, therefore, to deepen and to enlarge both the idea of socialism and its bases in social reality. This claim seems to be in direct conflict with the total disappearance of the revolutionary socialist movement and of all political activity on the part of laboring people. And this opposition is not merely apparent. It is real, and it constitutes the central problem of our age. The workers' movement has been integrated into official society; its institutions (parties, unions) have become those of official society. Moreover, laboring people have in fact abandoned all political and sometimes even trade-union activity. This privatization of the working class and even of all other social strata is the combined result of two factors: on the one hand, the bureaucratization of parties and unions distances these organizations from the mass of laboring people; on the other,

rising living standards and the massive proliferation of new types of consumer objects and new consumer lifestyles provide them with the substitute for and the simulacrum of reasons for living. This phase is neither superficial nor accidental. It expresses one possible destiny of present-day society. If the term *barbarism* has a meaning today, it is neither fascism nor poverty nor a return to the Stone Age. It is precisely this "air-conditioned nightmare," consumption for the sake of consumption in private life, organization for the sake of organization in collective life, as well as their corollaries: privatization, withdrawal, and apathy as regards matters shared in common, and dehumanization of social relationships. This process is well under way in industrialized countries, but it also engenders its own opposites. People have abandoned bureaucratized institutions, and ultimately they enter into opposition against them. The race after "ever higher" levels of consumption and "ever newer" consumer objects sooner or later condemns itself by its very absurdity. Those elements that may allow a raising of consciousness, socialist activity, and, in the last analysis, revolution have not disappeared, but on the contrary are proliferating in contemporary society. Each laboring person can observe the anarchy and incoherencies that characterize the ruling classes and their system in their management of the grand affairs of society. And in his daily existence—and in the first place, in his work—he lives the absurdity of a system that tries to reduce him to the status of an automaton but is obliged to call upon his inventiveness and his initiative to correct its own mistakes.

Here lies the fundamental contradiction we have analyzed, the decrepitude and the crisis of all traditional forms of organization and life. Here, too, we find people's aspirations for autonomy, such as these are manifested in their concrete existence. Here, finally, we discover laboring people constantly struggling in an informal way against the bureaucratic management of production, the movements and just demands we mentioned in point 28. Thus the elements of a socialist solution continue being produced, even if they are hidden underground, deformed, or mutilated by the functioning of bureaucratic society.

Moreover, this society does not succeed in rationalizing its operation (not even from its own point of view). It is doomed to go on producing "crises," which, as accidental as they may appear to be each time they occur, are nonetheless inevitable, and never fail to raise before humanity the totality of its problems. These two elements provide the necessary and sufficient basis upon which a revolutionary perspective and project can be founded. It is a vain mystification to seek another perspective, to try to deduce the revolution, to provide a "proof" for it, or to describe the way in which the conjunction of these two elements (the conscious revolt of the masses and the temporary inability of the established system to go on functioning) will take place and lead to revolution. Besides, no description of this kind ever existed in classical Marxism, except for the passage at the end of the chapter entitled "Historical Tendency of Capitalist Accumulation" in *Capital*. Moreover, this passage is theoretically false, for no revolution that ever has actually taken place in history took place in this way. Every revolution that has occurred began as an unforeseeable "accident" of the system, setting off an explosion of mass activity. (Later on, the historians—whether Marxist or not—who never have been able to foresee anything, but are always very wise after the fact, furnish us with a posteriori explanations for such explosions, explanations that explain nothing at all.)

A long time ago we wrote that it is not a matter of deducing the revolution, but of making it. And the only factor making a connection between these two elements about which *we*, as revolutionaries, can speak is our own activity, the activity of a revolutionary organization. Of course, such activity does not constitute a "guarantee" of any sort, but it is the only factor dependent on us that can increase the likelihood that the innumerable individual and collective revolts taking place throughout society will be able to respond to each other and unite among themselves, take on the same meaning, explicitly aim at the radical reconstruction of society, and finally transform what is at the beginning never anything other than "just another crisis of the system" into a revolutionary crisis. In this sense, the unification of the two elements of the revolutionary perspective can take place only through our activity and by means of the concrete content of our orientation.

IV. ELEMENTS FOR A NEW ORIENTATION[13]

30. As an organized movement, the revolutionary movement must be rebuilt totally. This reconstruction will find a solid base in the development of working-class experience, but it presupposes a radical rupture with present-day organizations, their ideology, their mentality, their methods, and their actions. Everything that has existed and exists today in instituted form in the labor movement— parties, unions, etc.—is irremediably and irrevocably finished, rotten,

integrated into exploitative society. There can be no miraculous solutions. Everything must be remade at the cost of a long and patient labor. Everything must be started over again [*recommencer*], but starting from the immense experience of a century of working-class struggles and with laboring people, who find themselves closer than ever to genuine solutions.

[. . .]

32. Revolutionary criticism of society must switch its axis. In the first place, it should denounce in all its forms the inhuman and absurd character of work today. It should unveil the arbitrariness and monstrosity of hierarchy in production and in society, its lack of justification, the tremendous wastefulness and strife it generates, the incompetency of those who rule, the contradictions and irrationality of bureaucratic management of each enterprise, of the economy, of the State, and of society. It ought to show that, whatever the rise in the "standard of living," the problem of people's needs is not resolved even in the richest of societies, that consumption in the capitalist mode is full of contradictions and ultimately absurd. Finally, it ought to broaden itself to encompass all aspects of life, to denounce the disintegration of communities, the dehumanization of relations between individuals, the content and methods of capitalist education, the monstrousness of modern cities, and the double oppression imposed upon women and youth.

[. . .]

What was the response of Castoriadis's adversaries? The review did not publish their viewpoints—though these were amply expressed in the group's Bulletins Intérieurs—*for, to some degree, they were divergent and, above all, they constituted only a series of partial objections. Very schematically speaking, it can be said that Philippe Guillaume (not to the confused with the trivial [negationist] Pierre Guillaume), Véga, and Laborde reproached Castoriadis mainly for considering as resolved by capitalism itself, be it in a conflictual way, the question of laboring people's material situation and for underestimating the role wage demands can play in their willingness to struggle, be it only as a symbol of human dignity; and, more generally, for substituting, for society's division into classes, the hierarchical continuum characteristic of the bureaucracy and, therefore, for outlining a revolutionary perspective grounded no longer on the dynamic of class struggle but on the voluntarism of conscious individuals.*[14]

The already deep break with Marxism this text marks was going to be radicalized by Castoriadis on the philosophical level in a sizeable text published in the last five issues under the title "Marxism and Revolutionary Theory." Reprinted by Castoriadis in his work The Imaginary Institution of Society *(1975 [T/E: English translation 1987]), of which it constitutes the first part, this text is therefore available in full, and so it would not make much sense to offer here a few fragments of it.*

The excerpted articles that follow illustrate the new orientation the group intended to give to the critique of modern society by emphasizing the concrete content of hierarchical relations in work, everyday life, and the centers of radical struggle appearing in universities, particularly in the United States in the early 1960s.

Notes

1. T/E: This text was first circulated within the group in March 1963. Reprinted in *EMO2* and *EP3*. Translation by Maurice Brinton as *Redefining Revolution, Solidarity Pamphlet*, 44 (no date), 24, with a "Solidarity Introduction." The present version has been edited with a view toward standardizing terminology and providing a text more faithful to the original (Brinton's fine original translation was geared to Solidarity's working-class British audience). Footnotes added by the original translator have been eliminated. Translated in full in *PSW3*.

2. The ideas that follow have been developed in a number of texts published in *S. ou B.* See in particular the editorial, "Socialisme ou Barbarie" (no. 1) [T/E: partial translation of "Socialism or Barbarism" in the present *Anthology*]; "Les Rapports de production en Russie" (no. 2) [T/E: partial translation of "The Relations of Production in Russia" in the present *Anthology*]; "Sur le programme socialiste" (no. 10) [T/E: reprinted in *CS* and *EP2*]; "L'Expérience prolétarienne" (no.11) [T/E: partially translated as "Proletarian Experience" in the present *Anthology*]; "La Bureaucratie syndicale et les ouvriers" (no.13) [T/E: by Daniel Mothé]; "Sur le contenu du socialisme" (nos. 17, 22, and 23) [T/E: translated as "On the Content of Socialism I" in *PSW1* and as parts "II" and "III" in *PSW2*; "II" partially translated in *CR* and in the present *Anthology*]; "La Revolution en Pologne et en Hongrie" (no. 20) [T/E: Castoriadis is referring to a special section of this issue of *S. ou B.*, which included "Questions aux militants du P.C.F." (reprinted in *SB2*, *SB(n.é.)*, and *EP5* as "L'Insurrection hongroise: Questions

aux militants du P.C.F."); Claude Lefort, "L'Insurrection hongroise" (partially translated as "The Hungarian Insurrection" in the present *Anthology*); Philippe Guillaume, "Comment ils se sont battus"; Daniel Mothé, "Chez Renault on parle de la Hongrie"; and Pierre Chaulieu, "La Revolution prolétarienne contre la bureaucratie" (translated as "The Proletarian Revolution against the Bureaucracy" in *PSW2*)]; "L'Usine et la gestion ouvrière" (no. 22) [T/E: by Daniel Mothé; partially translated as "The Factory and Workers' Management" in the present *Anthology*]; "Prolétariat et organisation" (nos. 27 and 28) [T/E: first part translated in full in *PSW2* and partially for the present *Anthology*]; "Les Ouvriers et la culture" (no. 30) [T/E: by Daniel Mothé]; and "Le mouvement révolutionnaire sous le capitalisme moderne" (nos. 31, 32, 33) [T/E: translated as "Modern Capitalism and Revolution" in *PSW2*].

3. It is in a spirit of profound fidelity to this, the most important aspect of Marx's doctrine, that Lukács devoted the main part of *History and Class Consciousness* to an analysis of reification.

4. Several of the ideas summarized below have been developed or demonstrated in "Le mouvement révolutionnaire sous le capitalisme moderne" [T/E: see note 2 above].

5. *S. ou B.*, 1–8 [T/E: Romano's contribution to *The American Worker* partially reprinted in the present *Anthology*].

6. See "Sur le contenu du socialisme," no. 22, 56–58 [T/E: "On the Content of Socialism II," *PSW2*, 137–39], and "Le mouvement révolutionnaire sous le capitalisme moderne," no. 32, 94–99 [T/E: "Modern Capitalism and Revolution," *PSW2*, 267–71].

7. See "Sur le contenu du socialisme," no. 23, 84ff. [T/E: "On the Content of Socialism III," *PSW2*, 158ff.], and "Le mouvement révolutionnaire sous le capitalisme moderne," no. 32, 84ff. [T/E:"Modern Capitalism and Revolution," *PSW2*, 258ff.].

8. See Paul Romano and Ria Stone, "L'Ouvrier américain" (nos. 1–8) [T/E: see note 4 above]; Daniel Mothé, "L'Usine et la gestion ouvrière" (no. 22) [T/E: see note 1 above]; Roger Berthier, "Une expérience d'organisation ouvrière" (no. 20); and Pierre Chaulieu, "Sur le contenu du socialisme" (no. 23) [T/E: see note 2 above].

9. See "Le mouvement révolutionnaire sous le capitalisme moderne," no. 33, 77–78 [T/E: "Modern Capitalism and Revolution," *PSW2*, 299].

10. Developed in "Le mouvement révolutionnaire sous le capitalisme moderne," no. 33, 79–81 [T/E: "Modern Capitalism and Revolution," *PSW2*, 301–303].

11. "Les Ouvriers et la culture," no. 30, 37.

12. See "Prolétariat et organisation," no. 27, 72–74 [T/E: "The Role of the Proletariat in the Degeneration of Working-Class Organizations," a section of "Proletariat and Organization" in the present *Anthology*].

13. T/E: This fourth and final section, "Elements for a New Orientation," is an almost verbatim restatement of the eighth and final section of "Modern Capitalism and Revolution," titled "For a Modern Revolutionary Movement," with a few slight, but quite significant, alterations.

14. French Editors' Note; For more details, one can refer to chapter seven of Philippe Gottraux's work *"Socialisme ou Barbarie": Un engagement politique et intellectuel dans la France de l'après-guerre* (Lausanne: Éditions Payot Lausanne, 1997).

From Mr. First to Mr. Next

Daniel Mothé

"De Monsieur First à Monsieur Next.
Les Grands Chefs des relations sociales"
Socialisme ou Barbarie, 40 (June–August 1965): 1-20
Socialisme ou Barbarie—Anthologie, 297-308

Daniel Mothé's article, "From Mr. First to Mr. Next: The Big Chiefs of Industrial Relations," some excerpts of which we give below, analyzes in a satirical fictional mode the transformation in the style of "human relations" the management of a large industrial company endeavored during this period to introduce—without, of course, changing the profoundly inegalitarian and dictatorial nature of those relationships.

THE BIG CHIEFS OF INDUSTRIAL RELATIONS

Over the past two years, three people responsible for dealing with the shop delegates have come and gone in the overall management of the company.

These three characters, as we are going to see and contrary to what one might think, are quite different from one another both on the character level and on that of their respective principles—which does not fail to raise here a very important, if not fundamental, theoretical point. Indeed, in the space of these two years, no revolution has come to disturb the tranquillity of our factory and of our society. And yet, as we shall see, imperceptibly some changes in principle have insidiously been slipped in among the cogs of our relations with management. Given that the three people who have come and gone still represent—since there was no apparent revolution—the immutable and historical interests of the factory—that is to say, of the government, therefore of capitalist society[1]—it might be deduced that these interests have changed and that history has taken another course. Yet to claim that history is fanciful would risk shocking serious and dogmatic minds. That is why we shall only graze up against the problem while carefully avoiding taking sides. Also, it must be said that, against such a thesis, one observation exists that weighs fully on the other side of the scale. From our side, that of working-class representatives, nothing has changed, and we know full well that, history, however fanciful it might be, can do nothing without us. We have remained like granite, immutable in our habits, our language, and our already century-old clear-sightedness.

MR. FIRST

The first representative of management whom I encountered and who received us was a man around 35. His attire as well as approach called to mind balance and levelheadedness. He walked in even steps and dressed just as regularly—that is to say, impersonally. Not a button was left fancifully to chance: either they were all riveted tight in their buttonholes or all were left free. The man was impeccable, yet he was all the more so when he spoke, and since his role was to speak and not to walk about, it is especially with the former that we shall deal.

He spoke cautiously, but so cautiously that it was difficult for him to form sentences. And yet the French he employed was as rigorous and precise as a mathematician's. Metaphor, parable, even allusions were carefully banished as useless and dangerous artifices; the most harmless oratorical effects were absolutely nonexistent. This man must be praised on one account: he was no demagogue.

When, each month, as was customary, he stood at his lectern to answer questions from a learned assembly of more than 100 shop delegates, we knew that, for exactly three hours, he would not stray an inch from his calm levelheadedness. We knew that he would spend all that time constructing his sentences calmly but assuredly as if they were tiny cubes in a game of building blocks.

At each monthly session, there were around 45 questions, always similar, properly posed, and which Mr. First had had the leisure to study, since, in accordance with established protocol, a week-long waiting period was prescribed between the submission of the questions and answers thereto.

Obviously, three hours were quite inadequate to answer them, and this independent of the slowness of Mr. First's language, given the scope and importance of the questions themselves. At precisely 5 PM, Mr. First would rise anyway and the session would be over.

The slowness of the sentences of management's representative was in direct proportion to their conciseness.

Hardly had Mr. First finished constructing his last sentence, the one that was to be prominently displayed in the official report, when already in the hall several hands were raised to start the heckling and, especially, to manifest one's deep disagreement.

The dialogue often began as follows: "We, the workers, don't agree with you." Yet some other delegates, in order to liven up the dialogue, feigned astonishment at an answer known in advance since similar responses had been given for many years. There was thus always in the hall someone who began talking like this: "We, the workers, are very astonished to hear your answer."

Yet Mr. First glided above the astonishment or surprise. For him, such bits of dialogue could belong only to a bygone era or to an irrational system, for he had banished both from his language and from his concerns all surprise and manifested in his behavior no emotion of that sort. No misplaced raising of an eyebrow that might allow multiple interpretations, no shrugging of the shoulders or startled jump. First did not like to mime. He was there to respond, and respond he did.

So, once the wave of indignation, disagreement, and reproachful astonishment had passed, management's representative responded to the response's response. Of course, Mr. First was not going to go so far as to repeat verbatim what he had said previously; he had to innovate and give the appearance of something new in his language, and it is such creativity that became tiresome both for him and for us. Indeed, there are nothing but pitfalls and traps in the spontaneous creation of sentences and ideas. That is why Mr. First was so prudent. Jerky words, each moving aside the others with much difficulty but with precision and unassailable truth, responded to the responses.

The topic of the dialogue always rested on increasing wages. That was always the first question, but so were also practically all the other ones. People clung to this topic that was to be treated during the three hours of our discussion.

As one must have suspected, we in no way influenced Mr. First—who, moreover, was not paid for that—nor was Mr. First convincing, even when he provided us with figures, and God knows his language was never in short supply of those.

Things could have thus taken place in boredom and indifference, where each of the parties would have repeated themselves until the fateful hour amid the monotony of the usual etiquette. But the near-certain unfolding of this combat took a different course. A strange phenomenon occurred that must be described. Let us call it, to be clear, the phenomenon of passionate heat.

The fact that this man responded in a mathematical and ever so precise fashion that introduced no feeling or passion provoked an opposite effect in the hall. Mr. First's rationality seemed to be a sort of Machiavellian machination, a kind of hostility much subtler than language intentionally meant to hurt. I will go so far as to say that Mr. First appeared to us as a provocateur. So, faced with this wall of impersonal rationality, figures, and proofs, the hall began to react and heat up.

As it was practically impossible to attack the invulnerable words of Mr. First, each speaker tried scratching the smooth surface in order to discover all the stratagems hidden beneath. So, the more imperturbable Mr. First seemed, the more the audience attributed to him intentions he had not formulated. And many stated: "You seem to be saying, Sir, . . . " or "Hearing you, one would think that . . . " or "If one listened to you, one would have the impression that . . ."

It goes without saying that doubt enveloped the entire atmosphere and that soon suspicion would come to insinuate itself into every pore of the conversation, a bit like lice. The speakers turned themselves into detectives, discerning beneath each word the hidden intention or the snare. The dialogue unfolded on two quite different paths without ever meeting. There was, on the one hand, Mr. First, who clung to words like lifebuoys and tirelessly fit them together as in puzzles. Mr. First was ostensibly unaware of the ocean of intentions, so preoccupied was he with the mathematical assemblage of his sentences. On the other path, the speakers took into consideration only what did not appear and showed very little concern with the rhetorical edifices of their partner. They responded to the ideas and desires camouflaged behind Mr. First's constructions.

In acting thus, the speakers directly attacked Mr. First's logic and mechanics. He, on the other hand, in refusing to fight on another terrain, always responded imperturbably, without nuance, refusing to raise his voice a half tone even when it was drowned out by the noise of his adversaries' indignation.

Then, a rasher speaker, driven by demagogy, sounded off indignantly: "Mr. First, speak up, we don't hear you." The speaker doubtlessly hoped to start a quarrel over the power of First's voice, but nothing could upset the mechanics of his logic.

Mr. First responded that it was impossible for him to speak louder, without explaining the reasons for that and while carefully avoiding any raising of his voice when responding to the speaker.

Others expected that they would imprison him in his contradictions as one shuts up an insect in a box, and those speakers always began their talking with a promising preamble.

"Mr. First, what you say is in complete contradiction with what you stated during this or that session on some occasion or other."

Yet the oratorical effect often went no further, for Mr. First knew that his words had no flaws and he repeated verbatim what he had said at the session in question while stripping his words of their interpretation.

Here, I have no intention at all of judging the discussion itself, since, being a worker and shop delegate, I unconditionally line myself up behind the arguments of my fellow members. Yet I am trying to judge the climate which, itself, seems to be independent of the logic of the arguments and the rationality of the ideas. I am attempting to give to the reader an idea of this strange and passion-filled phenomenon that arose during those discussions; even though I obviously lay all the responsibility on Mr. First, it is difficult for me to give an explanation for that.

And yet, it was obvious that Mr. First's language was carefully targeted and rid of all clinkers that might hurt his adversary. Not an explosive or perverse word passed his lips. Not one insidious or hypocritically flattering phrase. Nothing. Nothing but a language as flat and arid as the desert, a language without oases, without harshness to cling to, to linger over, to pick up on, to nibble at some entertaining phrases or juicy jokes. No *faux pas*, either, that might give rise to a pun. No word one might take the wrong way so as to spin it into general laughter.

Mr. First offered nothing that would betray a hint of humanity, and quite often I thought that one could easily replace him with those wonderful electronic machines that, with the help of some punch cards, give you in clear and concise language an answer to any question.

The factory has already introduced somewhat similar machines for chewing gum. You just slip in a coin to be satisfied. I can easily imagine that such an invention could be called *the answer dispenser*, which would be placed in each shop. In this way, one would have contributed to the great enterprise of democratizing the factory, and the semiskilled worker, coming back from the toilets, would thus be able, at his leisure, to put in a token demanding a slowdown in his pace of work. He would receive, in exchange, the imperturbable and precise response of Mr. First. Yet under this hypothesis, it is likely that such machines would not withstand the collective fury. But Mr. First, he withstood it.

Sometimes, I had the impression that Mr. First was a large, well-trained dog that answered questions exactly like the ones that served in the experiments of the celebrated Dr. Pavlov. Now and then, one had the impression that some, competing audaciously, came closer and closer to the big dog, no longer in order to pose questions to him but in order to pull his tail. Forgive me for this image. But all this was still part of the Pavlovian experiment, and what some sought was no longer the answer but the bark.

Thus, I heard: "Mr. First, it seems that you are an engineer. Well, let me tell you that you are a funny one."

The *banderilla* was well placed, with an impeccable working-class Parisian accent, and a murmur passed through the hall as in an arena. We went silent, awaiting the riposte to the death blow. But nothing came and Mr. First, impervious to the bullfighting, simply remarked that this argument proved nothing and brought nothing positive and new into the dialogue.

Encouraged by the audacity of the *banderillero*, and not to be out-done, another guy shouted at Mr. First, reproaching him for a meeting he did not hold. The weary hall this time did not react, and the question perhaps did not even get a response.

We had, however, a distinguished *torero* in the hall, a talented tribune of the like one hardly ever finds these days. He rose from his chair, tackled Mr. First verbally, and a sort of joust began, it, too, promising. For a few minutes, questions and answers succeeded each other, and although our *torero* had the gift of posing embarrassing questions, Mr. First always responded to them so well that the duel always ended by wearying the speaker, who ended up sitting down, visibly sad. His talent was going to break like waves upon these imperturbable mechanics, his oratorical effects remaining unanswered, and, though they won the approval of the hall, the lack of echo removed a great deal of their flavor.

Every attempt to transform our meetings into Jacobin sessions ended in failure, for the enthusiasm was clearly on one side alone, and it was this feature that let loose such unbearable irritation on our part.

We knew all the answers, we knew everything that was going to be said, and especially we knew that no decision would be made in the course of the meeting, but we were expecting therein, certainly, a bit of illusion. And even this bit of simulated debate was taken away from us. Mr. First was stealing from us our *raison d'être*; he was pushing the affront to the point of not appearing to be an adversary but solely an impersonal mechanism. The discussion no longer could take on human dimensions; it remained below that level, and that wounded the participants to their very core. Yet all that happened as it did on account of what? On account of Mr. First. Everything was but a stratagem, a defiance of our function, a sort of humiliation.

Then, one day, Mr. First disappeared as he had come, swallowed up in the managerial apparatus and assigned to another post. He left us as impersonally as he had appeared to us. Perhaps he was worn out by our dialogues, as we really hoped so that we might still believe in the utility of language.

But if Mr. First was leaving for other reasons, then . . .

MR. S.

Mr. S., who replaced him, was a very different character. Highly pronounced were the lines on his face, which did not have the impersonal and chubby look of Mr. First's. Some longitudinal wrinkles made him resemble a hero in a Western, a bit like Gary Cooper, we thought. Yet it is not just the face that recalled this trait; his great stature and his determined approach gave him the appearance of a man of action.

[. . .]

Mr. S. knew of the divergencies and animosities that exist among the shop delegates themselves, and he did not miss a chance, when he so desired, to exploit that. When he wanted to bite, he knew that he could always use a few laughs that were there, available in the hall and ready to break out against one of us.

How much hate had been hatched in the minds of all my comrades who had thus gotten themselves immolated in public for nothing? How many cases of insomnia had Mr. S. perhaps induced among all those who were obliged to choke back their anger because they did not have with them the logic of the managers but simply the desire to transform their condition? And no weekly tract stigmatizing Mr. S. was going to change anything and bind one's wounds.

On his terrain, Mr. S. was unbeatable, but as he possessed the arrogance of all combative personalities, he sometimes dared to broach other problems and venture onto other terrains. He did all that in order to lead his enemy little by little into his fief and end up immolating him upon the great account book, always ready, wide open for the ultimate sacrifice.

What remained were but appearances of dialogue; reality was but a fierce combat behind this formal facade. Mr. S.'s smile was a sign neither of kindness nor of relaxation; it was the grin of cunning and victory, the neurotic smile that is a sign of the traditional maladies of our executives.

Appearances themselves crumbled, and only the name of the department can make one believe that we were dealing here with a body concerned with industrial relations.

Even though every sentimental criterion in this affair would be as superfluous as it was ridiculous and the laws of sportsmanship ordain that it is always the strongest that win, it goes without saying that here we are broaching a contradiction of sizeable importance.

Management had instituted an industrial-relations department in order to avoid clashes and thus serve as a shock absorber amid the irreducible antagonisms, and Mr. First, like Mr. S., had added just an additional note to this antagonism. One by his impersonality, the other by his fieriness, each had helped to bring some additional hostility to industrial relations.

Each time, a strange and unusual feature had inopportunely appeared within a rational universe: passion. Yes, passion, for it is always a matter of that. And yet, we had long ago triumphantly crossed the border from the Middle Ages, and here our industrial society is in the grip of such trivialities. Had we returned to the age of witches?

The utility of industrial relations, it turns out, was being challenged. Offices [*Les bureaux*] trembled on their foundations. The functionaries were anxious.

Basically, why humiliate quite decent people? Is it not enough to get them to produce? Humiliation has no commercial value; it is even costly.

Although this is the result only of some personal reflections, I can say that it is likely that some identical observations were made by our adversaries, and this is also what undoubtedly explains the reason why Mr. S. in turn disappeared through management's trap door.

Another man appeared, quite different from the two others. This was Mr. Last. Long live Mr. Last.

MR. LAST

Mr. Last was a man with a happy smile, irradiating affability as uranium does alpha particles, the skull so bare that his face, from chin to nape of neck, represents but a geometrical figure: the sphere, a symbol of harmony if ever there was one.

Mr. Last thus introduced himself to us, immodestly, with an easy-going baldness, revealing thereby the utter nakedness of his mind. It became obvious that Mr. Last could hide nothing from us, and, here too, he greatly contrasted with Mr. S., whose flowing locks presaged only warrior cunning and the mystery of a wily spirituality.

Mr. Last appeared before us plump, naked, and open like a book.

To begin the first session, Mr. Last spoke to us in an uncertain voice, his tone rather dull, and here again he contrasted so greatly with the metallic timbre of his predecessor. Mr. Last obviously possessed none of the qualities of a good orator, and that is why he spoke to us like a good *paterfamilias* rediscovering his children after a long absence.

He declared one thing that went unnoticed for an audience so weary of words and polite remarks. He told us that he would respond to all our questions, that he would endeavor to keep up a dialogue, and, though knowing in advance that it would be impossible for him to satisfy all our demands, he would try to get us to understand the reasons why.

This introduction left skeptical a hall of people whose objective was something other than understanding. Indeed, we had been elected to our posts in order to obtain benefits and not in order to grasp the hidden reasons that blocked our demands.

It was first of all his tone, devoid of rigor and floating like an indistinct thing, that reassured the hall. A few moments later, Mr. Last made a mistake about an important detail. Had he done so intentionally, in order to show that he belonged to humanity? Had he obeyed the irrefutable decisions of an electronic machine that forced him into conscious error? Had he followed the directives of operational calculus that strongly recommended him to do it? It is difficult to say. Yet Mr. Last, who listed our conquests—those of the workers—over the past few years, added to them some that were still far from achieved. Thus, when he spoke of retirement at 60, which we had victoriously snatched, the whole hall was moved to point out to him that he was mistaken, inasmuch as that figured not in the book of victories but in that of demands to which he had to respond.

This man, who wanted to make us more triumphant than we were, seemed strange to us.

Was Mr. Last then a poet? In jumping ahead and making a mistake, consciously or not, he contrasted with his predecessors by the liberty and, let us say, the fancifulness with which he responded to us.

He corrected himself, erased a phrase he had just stated, and thus the accumulation of his errors or gaffes had something kindly about it.

Oh, if Mr. First or Mr. S. had been mistaken, they would really have created a great stir in the hall. Each of the orators would, one after another, have clung to those errors in order to gnaw and chew at them for a good part of the meeting. Whereas Mr. Last, in being mistaken, gave proof to his interlocutors; he did not show himself to be the man of infallible knowledge but had the very humble look of someone making mistakes while chatting with us. Showing himself to be vulnerable already removed a great deal of the aggressiveness.

The phenomenon of heated passion about which I previously spoke did not manifest itself in the first sessions.

Of course, we laughed pretty hard when Mr. Last declared to us that we could already retire at 60, instead of 65, as is the reality. But our laugher was not malevolent; it forgave Mr. Last.

Suddenly, management's representative had switched places. He became our debtor. We were the ones who pardoned him for his ignorance. Relations had thus been somewhat overturned, and the climate clearly relaxed. We had before us a vulnerable and boyishly easy-going adversary; we were one step from thinking him a perfect idiot.

In pardoning him for being mistaken, we imperceptibly arrived at pardoning him for answering us "No," like his predecessors, since we knew that this was the only answer he would give us. Yet, deep down, we were reassured, thinking that perhaps he was mistaken in telling us "No."

It was, however, only when Mr. Last broached straight up the thorny, not to say taboo, questions that he had the greatest success.

In the hall, one of us spoke of that much-talked-about year 1936, as was commonly done in our circles. We evoked 1936 a bit like the English speak of Trafalgar or Waterloo; fortunately, they can vary things, as they have two victories to mention, whereas we have but a single one.

Mr. Last spoke of 1936 as he spoke of cars and the Auto Show—just as simply. That strange year was not banned from his calendar. He spoke of it even with a smile, as if it were an era as significant for him as for us. He also gave it the same interpretation, 1936 evoking for him, too, a workers' conquest. After such a declaration, there was a great silence in the hall, and friendly faces sought each other out. He, too, had confessed, like some guilty person who had just been made to tell his crimes. The triumphant smile of a victorious policeman passed over all the shop delegates' faces.

Just imagine! Management's representative stated that 1936 had existed. Many did not believe their ears.

As for Mr. Last, he looked like he found the thing so natural that he did not feel the need to emphasize what he declared and he did not exploit the thing with oratorical effects in order to obtain deserving cheers. Indeed, we had trouble explaining to ourselves his attitude. He could at least have prepared the audience by announcing that he was going to say something that was for him, personally, very painful to admit but that he was duty bound to state, for his conscience dictated that to him. He would thus have been able to create that sort of rapturous and attentive silence so marvelous for an orator. Yet he did not. Mr. Last was good-natured till the end, and a few among us were already asking ourselves whether he was a normal person.

However, it was still worse when Mr. Last, in an uncertain voice, himself asserted to us that we do indeed find ourselves in a capitalist system.

The hall became restless and we looked at one another. One of my comrades leaned toward me and, eyes bulging, repeated it to me, clearly thinking I had not understood.

"He said that we were under a capitalist regime; extraordinary."

Our arms fell to our sides. While murmurs were sweeping through the hall, Mr. Last, imperturbable and in no way troubled by his statements, continued to hold forth on the system in which one bought, sold, made profits, and competed—a system he described naturally with as little passion as he would have spoken of Niagara Falls.

I understood then that Mr. Last was a historical character. He was situated within the framework of a quite precise evolution in the relations between management and us. His place, his role was quite clear-cut, quite specific. He belonged among those personages who serve as the lubricant necessary to human relations and also to class relations.

Mr. Last was the oil.

But what was going to happen then? Was the flood of general animosity, the kind that is true as well as the kind that is feigned, going to crash against Mr. Last's good-naturedness?

Would the obscure sects, bloodthirsty and red, see themselves swept away by the oil? Would the rebellious no longer have their own language, would they see the whole of their originality stolen from them? Were those who had so much trouble explaining and reexplaining that we lived under a capitalist regime going to have this characteristic usurped by Mr. Last? And what about copyrights? You are stealing everything from us, even our '36, Mr. Last. What are we going to talk about now? You are but a thief.

But the obscure sects did not have the privilege of bathing in the warm, lubricated atmosphere of Mr. Last. They still moved within the world of brutal contacts.

So, will Mr. Last have to be denounced tomorrow before the world?

He's the one who is going to crush the age-old values of our traditional notions. He's the one who is going to deny the struggle and antagonism of our class enemies. We will then be submerged no longer by the violence of the armed riot police but by the oil that will engulf us.

If Mr. Last denies these values then, Comrades, what are we going to do and, especially, say? All will be oil, and we will chew our ideas and our words like chewing gum, slowly, and society will continue its imperturbable course without our aid.

And yet, beyond our contacts with Mr. Last, a more disturbing than painful question preoccupies us. It is that of the meaning of his personality.

When life is lived day to day without worrying what will become of things and your existence, these sorts of preoccupations do not affect you. But when you are a shop delegate, mandated by a trade-union organization and fed at the teats of some ideology floating about in society, what will become of our proletarian world raises a few concerns for you.

The question that was posed was therefore as follows: Who was Mr. Last? What did he represent? What was his function and, above all, his fate?

In industrial relations, as in business, a smile can never be interpreted as such. A word is never a word. Everything hides something, and it is this mystery that the most gifted—wily politicians—have as their mission to unveil.

Here, there were several interpretations.

For some, Mr. Last's smile did not exist. They paid no attention to all these contingent considerations that characterized Mr. Last.

[. . .]

For them, Mr. Last was part of an equation. His characterization was that of an *x* or a *y*. Specifically, Mr. Last was the officially recognized representative of capital. The smile, in this case, was no longer of any importance, and some, so imbued with this equation, had not noticed the change between Mr. First and Mr. Last.

[. . .]

There were also those who saw reality through attitudes, as one would see through a pane of glass. These were the sly translators. For them, Mr. Last's smile was but the translation of Machiavellianism. Nice words always amounted to ill intentions, and even Mr. Last's good-naturedness amounted to ill intentions. It signified only hidden hostility.

At bottom, these comrades' method of interpretation was simple: it sufficed to show that the hidden reality was exactly the opposite image of the one you saw. Yet this interpretation did not go so far as to systemize the thing, for when Mr. Last, with a huge smile, gave a negative answer to our demands, their exegesis did not translate the negative answer into an affirmation. Those comrades who interpreted things in this way gave to all Mr. Last's attitudes an orientation opposite to our hopes. This method was simple; it consisted in saying that everything Mr. Last said was good was bad and everything he said was bad was really bad.

There were also those who, thirsting for power, claimed that Mr. Last's good-naturedness served only to camouflage his fear. For them, this was the sign of his weakness in the face of our strength. That obviously did not explain why Mr. Last always said "No" to our demands instead of "Yes."

[. . .]

Between Mr. First and Mr. Last, there was, on the part of our management, a willingness to keep dialoguing and conversing with the shop delegates. That does not mean, of course, that the goal of such dialogue was to resolve the problems raised. No, in general, the questions that fed the dialogue are already resolved by other authorities or by other, less official paths. The goal is only to foster friendly relationships, a bit like when you try to connect with your neighbor by speaking to him each time you see him. It is obvious that, if you maintain these kinds of relations with him, the latter will have less desire to bang on the wall when you make too much noise.

It seems that the relations between management and us obey such imperatives. Management can talk, converse, but without us having the possibility of resolving anything at all. Dialogue takes on the same meaning as when you meet an acquaintance. You talk about rain and nice weather. This constitutes the richness of our civilization and our human relations, for, in most cases not having need of anyone to resolve our problems, we can all the better give free play to the refinement of human relations. Having nothing to say to each other, one can polish up and decorate the dialogue, which thus takes on the look of futile and desultory conversations having no effect whatsoever on either party's behavior or decisions.

Yet industrial societies have this in particular, that they strive hard by all means to recuperate [*récupérer*] what they have otherwise prodigiously wasted.

Industry recycles [*récupère*] old rags in order to put them back into circulation, along with used oil, bits of metal, and dirty water. It recycles, too, useless conversation in order to lubricate industrial relations. And here, we see the full importance and genius of Mr. Last, who is a past master in the art and manner of cooptation [*récupérer*]. But it would be inappropriate to reproach Mr. Last for that, since such recuperation was deep solace for us and the source of immense joy. May those who have never participated in such sessions imagine a situation in which each of the words that habitually fall into the oblivion of the day would be carefully gathered up, packaged, labeled and placed into the museum of countless reports that only the rats will have a right to destroy. Let them imagine for a single second all this wealth for posterity that the faculty of speech now offers us. A word flung out, a rejoinder, even an exclamation are thus taken into consideration, and it is to Mr. Last that we owe the boost in value of what each has thus abandoned. Mr. Last thus gives back to language the value it had perhaps known only in prehistory, when men used words only in order to communicate among themselves and when the notion of waste was still unknown.

Yet Mr. Last's power had its limits. He rehabilitated speech but nothing more. Mr. Last does not go beyond this task, and he always leaves a gaping hole between words and acts, between language and decision. He makes this notion of expression perceptible without going further. It is a bit as if Mr. Last were saying to his interlocutors:

Your words are words; I am taking them into consideration. Your language exists; I am its guarantor. It goes from you to me. What you say, I hear it; I understand it and I respond to it, but don't ask me for anything more. My function is that of understanding you and of answering you; that's all. It is not to transform your words into acts and give them material form. I am not an alchemist and I cannot transform words into anything other than words. What is abstract remains so, and I have no power to engage what you say into the factory's mechanism. Everything is to remain among us.

Thus will the interlocutors understand that the barrier of their impotence has moved back a few centimeters but that the barrier still exists between the apparatuses that decide and themselves.

So, the question becomes more burning. After Mr. Last, what will happen?

The shop delegates will still want to gnaw away at the wall separating them from the delights of decision-making. They will want to participate in this great joy, and Mr. Last will interest them no longer, for they will want to go beyond the stage of speech.

Notes

1. T/E: The vehicle maker Renault became government-owned after the end of World War II.

Hierarchy and Collective Management

S. Chatel

"Hiérarchie et gestion collective"
Socialisme ou Barbarie, 38 (October–December 1964): 38–43
Socialisme ou Barbarie—Anthologie, 309–18

S. Chatel's article, "Hierarchy and Collective Management," published in nos. 37 and 38, undertakes a critical analysis of a workplace setting little explored by the review till then: that of the offices charged with preparing and organizing actual production activity in a mechanical construction company. After having analyzed, both in their formal aspect and in their reality, the role of discipline, the hierarchization of skills, and labor organization, the fourth and last section broaches the question of the "Foundations for a Collective Management Perspective." It is this one that we reprint here.

[. . .]

FOUNDATIONS FOR A COLLECTIVE MANAGEMENT PERSPECTIVE

The business enterprise functions. It does what it sets out to do; it produces the objects it has decided to produce and the means necessary for transformations suffice for these transformations. One among those means, knowledge, is applied to define the object and prepare for production in such a way that a potential object and an executable manufacturing order result therefrom; the gap between forecast and fulfillment [*réalisation*] is significant, so control is possible. Via fear, ambition, or conformism, or through the effect of mere attachment to their labor, men are not content to suffer the law but become their own judges. A balance is thus attained between initiative and passivity, between responsibility and irresponsibility.

Logic of the System of Hierarchical Management
The business enterprise functions—and it functions with a given structure. It attains its objectives by defining and divvying up its functions in a precise way. It carves up all labor into phases, separates design [*conception*] from fulfillment, and carries on, within each phase, this same carving-up process, thus constituting some levels where decisions are made and others where men's sole function is to execute what has been decided for them and in their stead. And, just as it carves up labor into phases, it separates the content from the form, remits to certain levels the power to determine this form while depriving others of such power.

All that is divisible is divided, all that is separable is separated. Every phrase, as soon as it is recognized, becomes a moment apart, is solidified, is fixed in a definite site, acquires a structure and men, and calls for laws defining its relations with the other phases, from which it has been detached. Thus, design is separated from production; within production, manufacture of the means of production is separated from production proper, which in turn is divided according to specializations by product or by phase of elaboration. Thus, labor is divided and subdivided according to the mode and state of the product's transformation, and within each division other distinctions appear that ground, in turn, new divisions: the assemblage and arrangement of elements of labor, on the one hand, and, on the other, the execution properly speaking of the function's tasks; checking [*contrôle*] of labor and labor itself; checking of qualitative and quantitative aspects of labor, on the one hand, and that of the price and deadline objectives that, on the other hand, are attached thereto. Every intermediary product is recognized and defines a function, and, in order to elaborate this intermediate product, each function is in turn structured, divided into levels where fundamental decisions are made concerning the product and levels where the power to decide keeps eroding until one reaches the ultimate level, where it becomes nil.

The operation [*functionnement*] of the business enterprise assumes division: the divvying up of tasks in accordance with the functional carving up and divvying up of responsibilities—that is, of the power and duty to decide—according to hierarchical tiers. But its operation assumes, too, that these divisions are grounded in the whole. Production is a synthetic act; the intermediate products are abolished in the final product; efforts converge toward the same point.

The business enterprise is broken down into its component parts [*décompose*], but it is broken down only to be reconstituted [*recomposer*]. It carves up the productive act, but this is done so as to grasp it in its unity, in the mutual implication of its moments. It breaks down the final product into intermediate products, but each state of the project disappears in the following state, after having rendered it possible. Therefore, at every instant, there is in it something to ensure the coherency of the decisions made concerning the process and the product, and this coherency-function is precisely the function hierarchy accomplishes. It accomplishes this, first of all, because it is formed through a gathering of men who have the power and the duty to make fundamental decisions and who, consequently, can and have to ensure the coherency of those decisions. Yet the coherency of decisions is ensured as much through the hierarchy's structure as through its composition. Each level of the hierarchy is placed under the responsibility of a higher level that is responsible, by the very definition of its function, for the coherency of the decisions made at the lower level—so much so that, if the hierarchy of function B2 does not succeed in getting the C2 hierarchy to acknowledge that it has to modify its decisions in order to ensure their compatibility with the needs of B2, there is a level A1 not only that can settle the matter and establish in one way or another such coherency but that has to do so and is explicitly responsible for that.

Hierarchical structure signifies that all responsibility is under the control of a vaster responsibility. Decisions can be confronted with the general context; particular interests can be judged according to the general interest. Yet the hierarchy is not a man or an assembly of men: it is a tiering. Problems pass from one level to another, and it is through a dustcloud of carvings that they attain the point where unity appears and the decision is made. In the course of the ascent through the tiering of levels, the meaning of problems is modified beneath the effect, first, of conflicts proper to each level and next, from the mere fact that they are inserted into a framework of knowledge-forms and more general concerns. The meaning changes from one level to another without the basic data being falsified (falsification is to the operation of the business enterprise what crime is to normal social life): one and the same basic datum reported to frames of reference that are not shared receives different significations. For data to circulate, however, an explicit decision is required in this direction: even before the transformation of significations is effectuated, a selection is therefore made that chooses, once and for all, this while ignoring that. The effort to formulate problems therefore collides against the conflicts inherent in the hierarchy, against the displacement of signification, and also against the inevitable rigidity of a system designed to gather not all information (the sum of all possible pieces of information is nothing other than noise), but certain information alone, which is constructed on the basis of presuppositions about what was important to gather and what was to be disregarded. The same difficulties are to be found again at the level of the execution of decisions. The levels where execution occurs resist a modification of tasks, just as those who decide resist challenges to their decisions, unconsciously through the very inertia of the system of data gathering and consciously through explicit refusal; just as the summit ignores the letter, the base ignores the spirit, and since the summit possesses the future, the base entrenches itself in the past.

BREAKS IN THE SYSTEM'S LOGIC: COLLECTIVE ORGANS, AUTONOMOUS ORGANIZATIONS

Hierarchy makes possible the reconstitution of the unity on which labor and control of the business enterprise depend, but it turns this into an ongoing problem. And because there is this problem, because the hierarchical process does not absorb everything that happens in the business enterprise, other ways of doing appear that, whether official or not, whether established by an explicit decision of the hierarchy or not, nonetheless mark a break with the logic of division and hierarchization, and, though manifesting themselves within the system and even within the hierarchy, are no less alien to the meaning of this system.

Instead of fundamental decisions being the act of a definite level of the hierarchy, here and there they are reached haphazardly, according to the problems posed and the men involved, via collaboration between superior and subordinate: bits of information are shared, reasons explained, and the decision is the product of the group in its entirety, not of the sole chief of the group. The same collectivization appears, no longer vertically, within the function being carried out, but horizontally, at the level of the whole set of functions. Each function elaborates its product and furnishes it to the following function. But such elaboration occurs neither in solitude nor gratuitously; it is an elaboration for someone and, for that reason, it becomes at such and such a moment an elaboration with this someone. In order to ensure the coherency of their decisions and of their products, the functions unite, collectively examine the problems, and collectively work out [*élaborent*] solutions, traveling in a few instants through the long line of phases, anticipating the ultimate phase and discovering, from this point, what it is fitting to modify in this or that intermediate phase, obtaining, without any of the complex procedures that preside over normal operations, the intervention of such and such a function, such and such a skill, dominating therefore the division of labor instead of being dominated by it, and making it operate to their benefit instead of seeing themselves acted upon by it.

The elaboration of products is not totally and always absorbed by the procedure that best expresses the logic of hierarchical management: it is, on the contrary, necessary for it, at certain moments and when faced with certain problems, to take other paths. What is true for the content of labor is equally so for its form: the formal organization does not preside over all acts, nor does it settle all problems. People compensate for breakdowns (whether foreseen or not) in the organization or invent solutions they substitute for the official ones.

With the collectivization of decisions and autonomy in the organization, two notions appear that not only are new but, above all, deeply contradict the postulates on which the logic of hierarchical management is built: the notion of a constituted, deliberating, and acting collectivity, and that of a kind of labor that governs the diversity of its moments.

The collective organ that resolves its problems and organizes itself is profoundly different from the hierarchized one—for, in the former, the collectivity exists; it is not idea but reality; it is this organ at work, which poses questions, responds to them, decides, and executes, whereas in the latter the collectivity is necessarily a mere notion. Such and such a level of the hierarchy can very well, at this or that moment, affirm itself to be the "representative" of the collectivity; it can think the totality, make decisions that seem to it to be the best ones for the collectivity, but it remains the case that the collectivity itself is never present, that these decisions do not emanate from it, and that, *qua* constituted subject, it does not exist. As for collective organs, it is true that they do not allow the total collectivity of the establishment to constitute itself: it is a matter here only of small collectivities, about which one cannot even say that the members would be the representatives of larger collectivities. Yet, this being so, it remains the case that the constitution of collectivities of this type and the mode of operation that characterizes them mark a deep break from the principles on which the system of hierarchical management is grounded. Management by a hierarchy has no other ground, in modern society, than the fact that this type of management is the sole one that renders the execution and control of labor possible: it has a *raison d'être* only if it is constantly true that management by the collectivity is impossible—constantly true, therefore, that the elaboration and unification of decisions require hierarchization, and this not only on the scale of the collectivity in its entirety but also at the level of any sub-collectivity whatsoever. The existence of collective organs capable of self-determination outside all hierarchical structures is a contradiction to this condition.

The manifestations of autonomy have an analogous meaning. Management by a hierarchy has meaning only if each man is necessarily attached to a portion of labor and cannot at once execute his part and ensure the coherency of the whole. Now, each time a man exits from the narrow domain reserved for him, decides on the form and content of his labor himself, makes contacts himself, and himself gathers the information necessary for that, he restores to labor its unity, he proves that the organization of labor and the elaboration of coherent decisions does not necessarily go by way of the hierarchization of individuals, and proves, too, not only that the lower levels can achieve the unification presently conferred upon higher levels but that these lower levels feel the need for such a unification.

The very operation of the business enterprise prompts the appearance of organs and ways of doing things that mark a break with the official forms and that, by breaking the monolithism of the hierarchical system, allow new ideas and behaviors to appear.

EXPERIENCE OF THE COLLECTIVITY
AND OF LABOR AS VALUES

By participating in collective organs, in organs that really behave as such—that is, ones within which every man can express himself and express himself effectively, where the skills of each are utilized productively, where nothing else binds the participants but the constraints that flow from the finality of their tasks, where the rules of operation are elaborated by the collectivity itself, and where it is again the collectivity that exerts control over its own activities—by participating in such organs, men experience both the value and the power of operating collectively. *Value*, for, whereas elsewhere decisions are reached only at the cost of time and effort disproportionate to the result, they note here a way of doing things that is infinitely more rapid and economic and that, especially, culminates in results that break with the usual vague approximations and represent, on the contrary, a serious synthesis of needs concluded via an agreement made without reservations. Next, the *power* of this mode of operation, since it culminates in valid decisions and shows itself capable of utilizing the skills and profiting from the advantages of the division of labor and of specialization without, for all that, succumbing to them. Likewise, each time they take initiatives their job does not formally require or even rules out, men glimpse both that it is worthwhile to take such initiatives and that they can be taken. Labor then becomes for them something other than this necessarily limited activity, this participation in a whole they never perceive, this series of acts whose meaning they ultimately no longer even understand. They note, on the contrary, that, through their labor, they have access to the problems of the collectivity and they appreciate that, in participating in these problems, they develop themselves and grow, introduce responsibility and gravity into their lives, escape ridicule, and, in the same stroke, deliver themselves from the humiliation one feels in living a ridiculous life.

APPLICATION OF PSYCHOSOCIOLOGY AND CYBERNETICS, AND CRITIQUE OF HIERARCHICAL MANAGEMENT

In its daily operation, the business enterprise puts men in situations where they are obliged to decide collectively and to engage in self-determination, thus breaking with the official structures, escaping separation and irresponsibility, and having an experience of collective management and autonomy. With this experience an operating principle becomes apparent that is at odds with the inside-the-framework system and through whose very operation that principle becomes apparent. And now that this experience is there, settled in the business enterprise, repeating itself each day, it happens that men and ideas that, at first sight, seemed to have no relation either to the objective or to the notion of collective management draw close thereto, discover their truth in its light, and in return nurture it with what belongs to them.

Beyond those categories that concern the science and technology employed in the process of design and fulfillment, two categories of ideas circulate permanently within every business enterprise: those relating to the fate of man in work, to what he wants and to what is to be given him; and, on the other hand, those relating to management, to the objective, structures, and the methodology of such management. Now, those ideas, which are oriented toward men and the business enterprise such as it is today, cannot avoid encountering the phenomena of collectivization and autonomy and, if they are rigorously thought through, necessarily have to connect those phenomena to the official structure, show in what way they arise therefrom, and go beyond the limits of the system of hierarchical management by relativizing it and situating it within a vaster framework. Business psychosociology sees in the phenomena of collectivization and autonomy the manifestation of a fundamental need for communication and self-realization. Now, if that need is really fundamental, this means that a system that deprives men of the power to communicate among themselves and that assigns them to tasks through which they cannot realize themselves, because such tasks include neither unity nor responsibility—such a system mutilates men, denies them the satisfaction of their deepest needs, and ultimately oppresses them. Business psychosociology relativizes the structure with respect to needs and thus opens up a critique of the structure: for it, the business enterprise is not the reference to which every idea has to be related; it is not the definitive system of production but, instead, one system of production among others, whose characteristic is its denial of the satisfaction of men's fundamental needs. Business cybernetics culminates in an analogous relativization of the system of hierarchical management. Business management analysis (the kind of analysis a very large number of business enterprises presently do, often with a view toward automating the collection and elaboration, via computer, of the data necessary for management) brings out functions, input data, decisions, channels of transmission, and control feedback: it is carried out without once encountering the notions of hierarchy, power, command, or authority. Management analysis discovers that management is a matter of information, not of power; it discovers that it is the information grounding management that gives to decision its ordered character, not the hierarchical level at which the decision has been made. For such notions to become apparent, it is not necessary that they be explicitly formulated, since the product of the analysis speaks for itself. For, this product is nothing other than the completed analysis—that is, the breakdown of the management function into its constitutive moments, the enumeration of the bits of information from which it starts off, the characterization of the transformations to which this information is subjected by such analysis and the wording of the methodology employed, the listing of the products of these transformations, and their subsequent purposes. The mere act of performing such an analysis already culminates in a demystification of management and makes of it a moment of labor whose structure is analogous to the other ones—to design, preparation, and fulfillment—as well as analyzable and controllable like them.

The business enterprise cannot be thought either in terms of its interpersonal relations or in those of its overall management without, on the one hand, encountering the notions of human needs and information and without, on the other, conceiving the business enterprise as a particular system, one in which human needs and information receive a particular treatment. The business enterprise cannot be thought seriously—and the specificity of the modern business enterprise is that it seriously thinks through all that matters for it to think—without relativizing it, without discovering something more fundamental than it, that of which it is but one particular organization. The very movement of rigorous and informed thinking therefore creates, within the business enterprise, a category of individuals accustomed to thinking through the business enterprise's organization and its needs, people for whom hierarchical structure is not the horizon of all possible thinking but who have relativized this structure and have situated it and criticized it within the context either of a theory of needs or of some form of information theory.

True, these men live within the business enterprise, belong to its hierarchy, and are of a piece [*solidaires*] with it; they undergo pressures and develop conformist or ambitious attitudes that are those of hierarchy in general. For this reason, their thinking constantly swings between development and regression, between fidelity to its fundamental intuition and the betrayal thereof. The theory of needs falls back toward manipulative practices; since there can be no question of acting on how orders are communicated, and since the communication of the specifications necessary to the job and the return feedback of the results are narrowly determined by the task to be executed, the sort of communication one falls back on in order to satisfy the fundamental need for participation is the one that conveys only general information, opinions, and impressions about far-off objectives that, at this level, are of no effect and pose no danger; and since there can be no question of changing men's fate in work, one has to be content with conferring upon posts with no responsibility a false luster of responsibility, dressing up an unchanging reality with noble and beautiful words about whose content no one is under any illusions. And this is so to such an extent that, in the end, the theory of needs seems to ground, not the satisfaction of needs, but their exploitation, men receiving just enough dignity in labor and power to communicate that, having calmed their hunger, one might be able to deny them the fundamental dignity and communication of which they have need. Management theory undergoes an analogous distortion: its fundamental intuition resides in the reduction of management to a strictly defined phase of labor, in the notion that managing is nothing other than receiving, transforming, and emitting information, like any other form of industrial labor. Practice diverts theory from this intuition, for the kind of management of which it is matter in practice is that of hierarchy—that is, it involves a kind of structure that, though elucidation continues nonstop, ensures that obscurity, too, is ceaselessly coming back in where light had just dawned. The hierarchy has need of the notion of information, for without that notion the complexity of its managerial function escapes analysis. But to the extent that this notion requires a univocal definition of the terms and leads to a transparent system in which all activity is controllable, whatever the level at which it is exercised—to that extent the hierarchy, which maintains the obscurity and falls victim to it, has no need of it. The idea that managerial problems are definable, that one can speak of them, that one can say with precision what happens and what one wants—that idea is abandoned: management theory passes then from the notion of information to that of responsibility and no longer seeks to define the problem, or to work out a response, but only to find the responsible person, namely, the boss, that is to say that one flees the problem of management instead of broaching it as one had proposed.

Yet this deviation of theories from their initial meaning, it, too, is but momentary: the hierarchy can neither avoid thinking nor think things through thoroughly, and it can neither refuse to confront problems nor resolve them; it is condemned to a permanent reformism and, inasmuch as every brand of reformism is a mixture of lucidity and treachery, it is forever condemned to forget what it has just discovered, to use the truth in order to flee it, and to encounter always what it desires to avoid. For, not only does this hierarchy deal with a reality that does not allow itself to be ignored—with needs that are expressed, with a complexity that exists and that must be confronted—but again it is itself part of that reality: it is not just the category of people that manages and directs; each of its levels is subject to the management of the higher level; it is, as a whole, at once the subject of management and a part of the object of such management. The relations of executant to executive [*cadre*] are those of the executive to his own superior, and every executive is at the same time the executant of the higher level. The same dependency is to be found again here as well as there, and also the same reactions: frustration at the limitations to which each is subjected, discouragement at a structure that seems doomed to opacity, to endless flight from questions and responsibilities, and whose decisions, when they are finally made, look almost humiliating. And inside as well as outside the hierarchy, men experience the collectivization of decisions and autonomy—so much so that it is not only on the level of a critique of the system that the experience of hierarchy meets up with that of the executants. So, both because the facts are there and continue to be there and because the hierarchy appertains just as much to the category of the dominated as to that of the directors, this hierarchy constantly returns to—so as to leave it aside again—a way of thinking that interprets facts and expresses an experience of collective management in which it participates, a way of thinking that, for this reason, despite the treachery and distortions, ceaselessly continues to develop.

The permanency of this way of thinking is important for two reasons: because it attests to the existence, within the hierarchy, of a category of men that, all the while participating in hierarchical management, is nonetheless entirely available for an attempt at collective management; but also, in the second place, because management by the collectivity is meaningless if the ideas about which we have just spoken are not an integral part of the theory that grounds and inspires such management. To speak of collective management is meaningless if such management is not to be embodied in institutions, procedures, methods: the hierarchy can allow itself a certain degree of lack of organization, for the effect of its structure is to simplify a great number of problems, if only because it brings in the creativity of a limited number of men; collective management, because it is nothing other than decision by everyone, will be organized or will be nothing at all; it will be transparent to itself, will have its conditions, products, and phases defined or else it will be opaque, it will not dominate its own complexity, and, in that case, it will become again management by one category of people, and not by the whole collectivity. And, on the other hand, to speak of collective management without understanding that a modification in the management of activities has to be accompanied by a modification in the mode of execution of these activities is to imply that only the form of labor will change, but not its content. Now, such content, it, too, has to be modified if the problems that result from the present-day mode of carving up activities into independent functions and levels of skill are to be settled other than by creating categories of people that, by virtue of their skills, are capable of dominating the carving-up process, which is nothing other than the hierarchical solution.

* * *

The conditions for collective management exist. There is a frustration of needs—that is, there is suffering. There is an experience that establishes the might and the value of collective management and spreads that notion around. There are ideas that extend it and deepen it. And there are men who feel this frustration, who have this experience and think these ideas. Yet it is true that, among the category of people of which we have spoken here—that of employees and executives with some technical qualifications—an explicit demand for collective management does not manifest itself; no movement whose present existence we would be able to take note of seems to have to lead unambiguously to such a demand. Thought cannot lightly pass over this fact: Conditions cannot eternally pile up without proving in the same stroke that they are not the conditions for what one was awaiting; and, on the other hand, the absence of an explicit movement either toward collective management or toward a stage we could analyze as an intermediary step is particularly striking for us here, among this category of people, since this category seems to be the prefiguration of what the great majority of laboring people will be in a future, when tasks involving mere execution will give way, in number and in value, to tasks involving preparation, design, and management.

One cannot pass over the scandal represented by the absence of an explicit movement toward collective management, but neither can one ignore these conditions that are piling up, this experience, and these ideas. One cannot ignore the meaning that is apparent in all that: this clarification of the problem of management and direction, this demystification of a hitherto hidden activity, this pulverization, among the governed, of the function of governing. One cannot ignore the enormous quantity of men—members of the directorial category of people or executants and, in their majority, both at once—who know and confront each day the problem against which socialist revolutions have shattered: that of the direction of activities by men themselves. And neither can one ignore that, outside business enterprises, there exists a society that does not cease to make its problems explicit, not only those of its direction but all the others—those of education, of love, of aging, etc.—a society that questions itself about the meaning of work, of leisure, of life, doing so not in the secrecy of a few movements or through the works of a few writers, painters, or musicians, but overtly and in the face of everyone, and that, going beyond the mere problem of the direction of economic activities, raises the problem of the direction—that is to say, of the meaning and goal—of all activity and every relation.

The Free Speech Movement and Civil Rights

Jack Weinberg

"Le Mouvement pour la liberté d'expression
et les droits civiques aux États-Unis"
Socialisme ou Barbarie, 40 (June–August 1965): 72–75
Socialisme ou Barbarie—Anthologie, 319–23[1]

Contrary to the French Left and Far Left, which viewed American society overall as essentially reactionary, the group Socialisme ou Barbarie always took a passionate interest in this crucible for the modernity of social structures and social conflicts. The first issue included the first installment of The American Worker, *written by the metalworker Paul Romano; the fortieth and last issue of the review published an analysis of the Free Speech Movement and of the Berkeley student revolt in Autumn 1964. While in the United States workers' struggles had not ceased to occur during those nearly twenty decades of publication, the movements that shook university youth circles beginning in the early 1960s—and which continued to develop, as one knows, into the 1970s—appeared to the group to be particularly symptomatic of the new forms the crisis of capitalist societies was taking on as those societies entered into the so-called modern era.*

It will be noted that the text reprinted below was not signed by a member of the group but by an actual actor in the Free Speech Movement. This fact, which is not isolated (in the last issues of the review, the signatures of such outside collaborators as Edgar Morin, Georges Lapassade, and Marvin Garson appeared) testifies to the need, felt by the group after the 1963 split, to deepen the critique of contemporary society by diversifying the approaches thereto.

[French Translator's Note: The following article is an attempt to set the Free Speech Movement (FSM) back within its political and social context. The article's author is Jack Weinberg, a former teaching assistant in the mathematics department at the University of California who is presently the President of the local chapter of CORE (Congress of Racial Equality—one of the most radical organizations struggling against segregation) and a member of the FSM Steering Committee. It was his arrest that was at the origin of the incidents that arose at Berkeley in 1964; see *S. ou B.*, 39: 67–78.]

Those who view the FSM merely as an extension of the civil-rights movement, merely as a battle to enable student civil-rights groups to maintain the campus as a base for their operations, have a very incomplete understanding of the FSM, and probably an incomplete understanding of the student civil-rights movement. In this article we discuss the student civil-rights movement and its relation to the FSM, the FSM as an on-campus protest, and the implications of both the FSM and the student civil-rights movement for American society.

I. FSM AND THE CIVIL-RIGHTS MOVEMENT

Over the past few years, there has been a change, both quantitative and qualitative in Bay Area student political activity. Until 1963, only a relatively small number of students had been actively involved in the civil-rights movement. Furthermore, until that time, student political activity of all kinds was quite impotent in terms of any real effect it had on the general community. Organizations such as peace groups raised demands which were so momentous as to be totally unattainable. Civil-rights groups, on the other hand, often raised demands which were attainable but quite inconsequential; a job or a house for an individual Negro who had been discriminated against. In no way was student political activity a threat, or even a serious nuisance to large power interests. In early 1963, a new precedent in the Bay Area civil-rights movement was established, civil-rights organizations began demanding that large employers integrate their work forces on more than a mere token basis. Hundreds of jobs would be at stake in a single employment action. In the Fall of 1963, a second important precedent was established. Starting with the demonstrations at Mel's Drive-in, large numbers of students became involved in the civil-rights movement. And as they joined, the movement adopted more militant tactics. Thus with more significant issues at stake and with more powerful weapons available, the civil-rights movement became a threat, or at least a real nuisance to the power interests. Not only was the civil-rights movement, "a bunch of punk kids," forcing employers to change their policies, but it was also beginning to upset some rather delicate political balances.

Attempts were made by the civil authorities and the power interests to contain the movement: harassing trials, biased news reporting, job intimidation, etc. But the attempts were unsuccessful, the movement grew, became more sophisticated, and began exploring other fronts on which it could attack the power structure. Throughout the summer of 1964, Berkeley Campus CORE maintained a hectic level of continuous and effective activity. The Ad Hoc Committee to End Discrimination planned and began executing a project against the *Oakland Tribune*.[2] Since those who wished to contain the civil-rights movement found no effective vehicles in the community they began pressuring the university. Because a majority of participants were students, they maintained that the university was responsible. After initially resisting the pressure, the university finally succumbed and promulgated restrictive regulations with the intent of undercutting the base of student support for the civil-rights movement. The reactions to these regulations should have been predictable: immediate protest and a demand for their repeal. Since the civil-rights movement was responsible for the pressures applied to the university which led to the suppression of free speech and free political expression and their interests were the ones most seriously threatened, the civil-rights activists took the lead in protesting the suppression, and many concluded that the FSM is an extension of the civil-rights movement.

II. THE FSM AS CAMPUS PROTEST

But if we view the FSM simply as an extension of the civil-rights movement, we cannot explain the overwhelming support it has received from students who have been indifferent to the civil-rights movement and even from some who have been hostile to it. Civil-rights activists, those whose interests are really at stake, make up a very small part of the ardent FSM supporters. The vast majority of the FSM supporters have never before had any desire to sit at tables, to hand out leaflets, or to publicly advocate anything. The Free Speech Movement has become an outlet for the feelings of hostility and alienation which so many students have toward the university. Early in the movement, one graduate student who was working all night for the FSM said, "I really don't give a damn about free speech. I'm just tired of being sat upon. If we don't win anything else, at least they'll have to respect us after this." Clearly, his was an overstatement. Free speech has been the issue, and virtually all the FSM supporters identify with the FSM demands. The roots, however, go much deeper. The free-speech issue has been so readily accepted because it has become a vehicle enabling students to express their dissatisfaction with so much of university life, and with so many of the university's institutions.

The phenomenon we describe is not at all unprecedented, even though the FSM may be an extreme example. There have been wildcat strikes which in many ways are quite similar to the free-speech protest. The following pattern is typical: there is an industry in which the workers are discontented with their situation. The pay may or may not be low. There is hostility between the workers and the management, but it is hostility over a great number of practices and institutions, most of which are well established, and none of which have been adequate to launch a protest over the abstract issue. One of the greatest grievances is likely to be the attitude of the managers toward the workers. The union has proven itself incapable of dealing with the issue. Then one day a work practice is changed or a worker is penalized over a minor infraction. Fellow workers protest and are either ignored or reprimanded. A wildcat strike is called and the protest is on.

The same kind of forces which create a wildcat strike have created the FSM. Alienation and hostility exist but are neither focused at specific grievances nor well articulated. There is a general feeling that the situation is hopeless and probably inevitable. There is no obvious handle. No one knows where to begin organizing, what to attack first, how to attack. No one feels confident that an attack is justified, or even relevant. Suddenly there is an issue, everyone recognizes it; everyone grabs at it. A feeling of solidarity develops among the students, as among the workers.

The students at Cal have united. To discover the basic issues underlying their protest one must first listen to the speeches made by their leaders. Two of the most basic themes that began to emerge in the very first speeches of the protest and that have remained central throughout have been a condemnation of the university in its role as a knowledge factory and a demand that the voices of the students must be heard. These themes have been so well received because of the general feeling among the students that the university has made them anonymous; that they have very little control over their environment, over their future, that the university society is almost completely unresponsive to their individual needs. The students decry the lack of human contact, the lack of communication, the lack of dialogue that exists at the university. Many believe that much of their course work is irrelevant, that many of their most difficult assignments are merely tedious busy work with little or no educational value. All too often in his educational career, the student, in a pique of frustration, asks himself, "What's it all about?" In a flash of insight he sees the educational process as a gauntlet. Undergraduate education appears to be a rite of endurance, a series of trials, which if successfully completed allow one to enter graduate school; and upon those who succeed in completing the entire rite of passage is bestowed the ceremonious title, Ph.D. For those who cop out along the way, the further one gets the better the job one can obtain, with preference given according to the major one has selected. All too often, the educational process appears to be a weeding-out process, regulated by the laws of supply and demand. The better one plays the game, the more he is rewarded.

To be sure, there are some excellent courses at Cal; some departments are better than others. Although a general education is difficult if not impossible to obtain, in many fields the student is able to obtain an adequate though specialized preparation for an academic career. Furthermore, successful completion of a Cal education is quite a good indication that the student will be agile and adaptable enough to adjust to a position in industry and to acquire rapidly the skills and traits that industry will demand of him.

When viewed from the campus, the Free Speech Movement is a revolution, or at least an open revolt. The students' basic demand is a demand to be heard, to be considered, to be taken into account when decisions concerning their education and their life in the university community are being made. When one reviews the history of the Free Speech Movement one discovers that each new wave of student response to the movement followed directly on some action by the administration which neglected to take the students, as human beings into account, and which openly reflected an attitude that the student body was a thing to be dealt with, to be manipulated. Unfortunately, it seems that at those rare times when the students are not treated as things, they are treated as children.

III. THE IMPLICATIONS FOR AMERICAN SOCIETY

It is inadequate, as we have shown, to characterize the FSM as a purely on-campus phenomenon, as a protest stemming from a long overdue need for university reform, or as a response to a corrupt or insensitive administration. Invariably when students become politically and socially active, one can find that at the root, they are responding to their society's most basic problems.

Let us first consider why students have become so active in the northern civil-rights movement. The problem with which the civil-rights movement is trying to cope, the problem of the effect of our society on the Negro community, is exactly the problem of our entire society, magnified and distorted. Unemployment, underemployment, poor education, poor housing, intense social alienation: these and many more are the effects of our way of life on the Negro community, and these, to one degree or another, are the effects of our way of life on all of its members. When taking a moral stand, when doing what they can in the struggle for equality for all Americans, students invariably find that as they become more and more successful they come into conflict with almost all the established interest groups in the community. Students have turned to the civil-rights movement because they have found it to be a front on which they can attack basic social problems, a front on which they can have some real impact. In the final analysis the FSM must be viewed in this same light.

The University of California is a microcosm in which all of the problems of our society are reflected. Not only did the pressure to crack down on free speech at Cal come from the outside power structure, but most of the failings of the university are either on-campus manifestations of broader American social problems or are imposed upon the university by outside pressures. Departments at the university are appropriated funds roughly in proportion to the degree that the state's industry feels these departments are important. Research and study grants to both students and faculty are given on the same preferential basis. One of the greatest social ills of this nation is the absolute refusal by almost all of its members to examine seriously the presuppositions of the establishment. This illness becomes a crisis when the university, supposedly a center for analysis and criticism, refuses to examine these presuppositions. Throughout the society, the individual has lost more and more control over his environment. When he votes, he must choose between two candidates who agree on almost all basic questions. On his job, he has become more and more a cog in a machine, a part of a master plan in whose formulation he is not consulted, and over which he can exert no influence for change. He finds it increasingly more difficult to find meaning in his job or in his life. He grows more cynical. The bureaucratization of the campus is just a reflection of the bureaucratization of American life.

As the main energies of our society are channeled into an effort to win the cold war, as all of our institutions become adjuncts of the military-industrial complex, as the managers of industry and the possessors of corporate wealth gain a greater and greater stranglehold on the lives of all Americans, one cannot expect the university to stay pure.

In our society, students are neither children nor adults. Clearly, they are not merely children; but to be an adult in our society one must both be out of school and self-supporting (for some reason, living on a grant or fellowship is not considered self-supporting). As a result, students are more or less outside of society, and in increasing numbers they do not desire to become a part of the society. From their peripheral social position they are able to maintain human values, values they know will be distorted or destroyed when they enter the compromising, practical, "adult" world.

It is their marginal social status which has allowed students to become active in the civil-rights movement and which has allowed them to create the Free Speech Movement. The students, in their idealism, are confronted with a world which is a complete mess, a world which in their eyes preceding generations have botched up. They start as liberals, talking about society, criticizing it, going to lectures, donating money. But every year more and more students find they cannot stop there. They affirm themselves; they decide that even if they do not know how to save the world, even if they have no magic formula, they must let their voice be heard. They become activists, and a new generation, a generation of radicals, emerges.

Notes

1. T/E: According to the Free Speech Movement Archives http://www.fsm-a.org/stacks/weinberg.html, this article appeared in *Campus CORElator* in January 1965. *S. ou B.*'s French translation omits the opening line: "Over the past several months the relationship between the Berkeley Free Speech Movement and the civil-rights movement has become almost a cliche."
2. T/E: The French translator, displaying more political than geographical knowledge of this conservative Republican press outlet, identified the *Oakland Tribune* as a "racist newspaper of San Francisco [*sic*]."

APPENDIX I

TABLE OF CONTENTS OF *SOCIALISME OU BARBARIE*

"Table des matières de *Socialisme ou Barbarie*"
Socialisme ou Barbarie—Anthologie, 326–36[1]

Books:
Marc Foucault: *La Fortune américaine et son destin*, by Jean Piel
Letters

NO. 3 (JULY-AUGUST 1949)

Philippe Guillaume: War and Our Era
Pierre Chaulieu: The Temporary Consolidation of World Capitalism
Documents:
Paul Romano: The American Worker (Continued)
V. W.: Stakhanovism and Snitching in Czechoslovak Factories
The Life of Our Group
Notes:
The International Situation; Three Strikes; Strikes in French-Canadian
Asbestos Mines
Books:
Renée Sauguet: *La vie ouvrière sous le Second Empire*, by Georges Duveau

NO. 4 (OCTOBER-NOVEMBER 1949)

Peregrinus: The Kolkohz During the War
P. Chaulieu: The Exploitation of the Peasantry
under Bureaucratic Capitalism
Documents:
Paul Romano: The American Worker (Continued)
The Life of Our Group:
The Second Meeting of Readers of "Socialisme ou Barbarie";
Work Plan and Elaboration of the Program
Notes:
The International Situation; Overview of Events; The Repercussions
of the Russian Atomic Explosion; Devaluation and Vassalization;
Industrial Actions
C. Montal: Trotskyism in the Service of Titoism
Letters

NO. 5-6 (MARCH-APRIL 1950)

Pierre Chaulieu and Georges Dupont: The Yugoslavian Bureaucracy
Philippe Guillaume: War and Our Era (Continued)

Documents:
Paul Romano: The American Worker (End)
The Life of Our Group
Notes:
The International Situation; Industrial Actions;
Raymond Bourt: Renault Relaunches the Strike Movement;
Roger Bertin: The Strike at S.O.M.U.A.

NO. 7 (AUGUST-SEPTEMBER 1950)
Hugo Bell: Stalinism in East Germany
Philippe Guillaume: Mechanization and the Proletariat
Documents:
Ria Stone: The Reconstruction of Society
The Life of Our Group:
Political Declaration Drafted by the FFGC with a View to Unification
with the "Socialisme ou Barbarie" Group
Notes:
The International Situation: Korea, End of the Cold War; Henri Collet:
The Strike at Assurances Générales-Vie; Jean Léger: The Kalandra Trial

NO. 8 (JANUARY-FEBRUARY 1951)
Raymond Bourt: Voyage in Yugoslavia
Hugo Bell: Stalinism in East Germany (Continued)
Ria Stone: The Reconstruction of Society (End)
Notes:
The International Situation; J. Dupont: "Working-Class" Organizations
and the Korean War; P.C.: Nationalization and Productivity

NO. 9 (APRIL-MAY 1952)
War and the Revolutionary Perspective
A. Véga: The Class Struggle in Spain
The Life of Our Group
Claude Lefort: Pascal [Donald Simon]
Notes:
G. Pétro: The March 1951 Railway Strike; Pascal: An Adventurer in
the Bureaucratic World: *La vie et la mort en U.R.S.S.*, by El Campesino
[Valentín R. González's *Listen Comrades: Life and Death in the Soviet Union*]

NO. 10 (JULY-AUGUST 1952)

NO. 11 (NOVEMBER-DECEMBER 1952)

NO. 12 (AUGUST-SEPTEMBER 1953)

NO. 13 (JANUARY-MARCH 1954)

Documents:
G. Vivier: Life in the Factory
Discussions:
Henri Féraud: Trade-Union Unity
Notes:
Claude Montal: The New Russian Diplomacy; *Books:* F. Laborde: *Le mouvement ouvrier en Amérique* Latine, by V. Alba [Victor Alba's *Historia del movimiento obrero en América Latina*, later translated into English, in a revised version, as *Politics and the Labor Movement in Latin America*]; Meeting of Readers of *Socialisme ou Barbarie*; Letter from a Comrade The Workers' Press (Excerpts from *Correspondence* and *Tribune Ouvrière*)

NO. 18 (JANUARY-MARCH 1956)

Workers' Struggles in 1955:
J. Simon: The Summer Strikes
D. Mothé: Inaction at Renault
Georges Dupont: The Chausson Settlement
René Neuvil: A Strike in the Paris Suburbs
Wildcat Strikes in the American Automobile Industry
The English Dockers' Strikes
Pierre Chaulieu: Workers Confront the Bureaucracy
F. Laborde: The Situation in North Africa
Discussions:
Théo Maassen: Once Again on the Party Question
Notes:
Pierre Chaulieu: The French Elections; Claude Montal: Poujadism; René Neuvil: The International Situation; *Books:* Claude Montal: *Juin 36*, by Danos and Gibelin [Jacques Danos and Marcel Gibelin's book, later translated as *June '36: Class Struggle and the Popular Front in France*]; Meeting of Readers of *Socialisme ou Barbarie*; The Workers' Press: Excerpts from *Tribune Ouvrière*

NO. 19 (JULY-SEPTEMBER 1956)

Claude Lefort: Totalitarianism Without Stalin:
The USSR in a New Phase
Journal of a Worker: May 1956 at Renault
Pierre Chaulieu: Automation Strikes in England
Poznan

Question; Among the Postal Workers, A "Sector-Based" Strike; In Spain:
From Passive Resistance to Active Resistance; The Stockholm Revolt;
In Italy, the Revolutionary Workers' Left Gets Organized
by Y. Bourdet, S. Diesbach, G. Genette, Ph. Guillaume, F. Laborde, R. Maille

NO. 22 (JULY-SEPTEMBER 1957)

Pierre Chaulieu: On the Content of Socialism
D. Mothé: The Factory and Workers' Management
R. Maille: Khrushchev's New Reforms
D. Mothé: Agitation at Renault
The World in Question:
The French Situation; The Accounts of the "Loyal Manager"; The
April-May Strikes; The Counter-Revolution in Hungary; Six Months of
Kadarization; The Situation in Poland; The Awakening of Intellectuals
and Students in the USSR; Strikes in Great Britain
by R. Berthier, P. Chaulieu, F. Laborde, Cl. Lefort, M. Leroy, S. Tensor

NO. 23 (JANUARY-FEBRUARY 1958)

How to Struggle?
R. Berthier: July 1957 Bank Strike
D. Mothé: The Strikes at Renault
News from Strike Movements:
D. Mothé: How the Nantes and St. Nazaire Movement Was Killed Off
R. Berthier: A Strike in the Provinces
Ph. Guillaume: News Flash About the Postal Workers' Strike, or "Long
Live Lack of Organization"
Pierre Chaulieu: On the Content of Socialism
Claude Lefort: The Method of So-Called
"Progressive" Intellectuals: Samples
Ph. Guillaume: Facing the Artificial Russian Satellite
Documents:
Gabor Kocsis: On the Workers' Councils
"Trade Unions and Workers' Councils" (excerpt from *Nemzetör*)
The World in Question:
The Situation in Hungary; On *L'homme ne vit pas seulement du pain*, by
Dudintsev [Vladimir Dudintsev's *Not by Bread Alone*]; *L'Algérie en 1957*, by
Germaine Till[i]on; *La révolution qui vient*, by Yvan Craipeau; Expulsions
at the French National Primary-School Teachers' Union; Revolts; Mass
Man, or the ABCs of the Party "Militant"

by R. Berthier, M. Brune, P. Canjuers, A. Garros, M. Gautrat, C. Leroy

NO. 24 (MAY-JUNE 1958)

The French Proletariat and Algerian Nationalism
F. Laborde: Algerian Contradictions Exposed
P. Brune: The Class Struggle in Bureaucratic China
The World in Question:
The Role of Shop Stewards; Poland: Cold Kadarization; The Strikes
in Spain; Notes on England; The Lessons of Henri Lafièvre, Worker
Militant; *The New Wave*; René Neuvil: Working . . . Amid the
Chlorophyll; A Splendid Socialist Conscientiousness: Eugène Thomas,
Socialist Minister of the French Telephone and Telegraph Company;
Correction for the News Flash About the Lille Postal Workers' Strike; A
Left-Wing Meeting Devoted to Algeria; Reintegration of those Excluded
from the French National Primary-School Teachers' Union
Books:
La nouvelle classe dirigeante [*The New Class*], by Milovan Djilas;
Histoire du Premier Mai, by Maurice Dommanget
Films:
La Blonde Explosive [*Will Success Spoil Rock Hunter?*, by Frank Tashlin],
No Down Payment [by Martin Ritt]
Theater: Paolo Paoli, by Arthur Adamov
by Yvon Boudet, P. Canjuers, S. Chatel, Ph. Guillaume, M. Imbert, Cl.
Lefort, M. M., R. Maille, René Neuvil, S. Tensor
Letters

NO. 25 (JULY-AUGUST 1958)

The French Crisis and Gaullism:
S. Chatel and P. Canjuers: The Crisis of the Bourgeois Republic
F. Laborde: "Counter-Revolutionary" War,
Colonial Society, and de Gaulle
Cl. Lefort: The Power of de Gaulle
P. Chaulieu: Perspectives on the French Crisis
Testimonies:
D. Mothé: What We've Been Told; At the Mors Factory; Fifteen Days of
Agitation, Viewed by the Employees at a Large Company; A Primary-
School Teacher: Teachers and the Defense of the Republic; S. Chatel:
The Students of the Sorbonne and the Crisis; B.: Workers' Reactions
in Le Mans; The Big May 28 Demonstration (excerpted from *Tribune
Ouvrière*); A.G. and S. Tailor (workman): At the May 28 Demonstration

Documents:
Tracts published by *Pouvoir Ouvrier*; *Tribune Ouvrière*;
the *Revolutionary Action Committee*; the students of
Socialisme ou Barbarie; a group of employees

NO. 26 (NOVEMBER-DECEMBER 1958)
Assessment
G. Luk[á]cs: Critical Remarks on Rosa Luxemburg's Critique of the
Russian Revolution
The French Crisis:
P. Canjuers: Birth of the Fifth Republic
R. Maille: Objectives and Contradictions of the
French Communist Party
D. Mothé: At Renault, After the Referendum
S. Chatel: De Gaulle and Black Africa
André Garros: The "Union of the Socialist Left"
S. Tensor: The May, June, and July Strikes in England
Discussions:
Claude Lefort: Organization and Party
L. S.: Where is the Communist Opposition At?
The World in Question:
Interview with a Yugoslavian Worker; In England, the Shop Stewards
Make Life Difficult for the Trade-Union Bigwigs; Le Mans News Item;
Children's Remarks; A New Workers' Organization in England
Books:
Les idées politiques et sociales d'Auguste Blanqui, by Maurice Dommanget
by R. B., S. Chatel, Ph. Guillaume, C. P.

NO. 27 (APRIL-MAY 1959)
Rationalization on the Backs of the Workers
P. Canjuers: Sociology-Fiction for a Left-Fiction (Apropos
of Serge Mallet)
J. Delvaux: Social Classes and Mr. Touraine
Paul Cardan: Proletariat and Organization
S. Chatel: The Leopoldville Revolt
Documents:
Yvon Bourdet: The Strike at the Saint Frères Factory
The World in Question:
A New Khrushchev Report; The Strikes in Italy;

The Movement in the Borinage;
Excerpts from the Workers' Press
Letters

NO. 28 (JULY-AUGUST 1959)

Ph. Guillaume: With or Without de Gaulle
An Algerian Recounts His Life
Paul Cardan: Proletariat and Organization (Concluding Installment)
Documents:
Resignations from the UGS [Union of the Socialist Left]
Notes:
M. V.: Secularism in the Public Schools; How Mallet Judges Mothé
Books:
Pierre Brune: *La Classe ouvrière d'Allemagne Orientale*, by Benno Sarel
Excerpts from *Pouvoir Ouvrier*

NO. 29 (DECEMBER 1959-FEBRUARY 1960)

Jean-François Lyotard: The Social Content of the Algerian Struggle
An Algerian Recounts His Life (Concluding Installment)
P. Brune: China in the Time of Totalitarian Perfection
In Memory of Benjamin Péret:
Jean-Jacques Lebel: Moved, Address Unknown
Benjamin Péret: *Le Déshonneur des Poètes*
Documents:
Y. B.: Short-Time Working in the Textile Industry at Beauvais (Somme)
The World in Question:
The News; The English Elections; Khrushchev in the United States;
The Steel Strike; Poland: The Efficiency of Bureaucrats; China:
"Inexperienced Statisticians"; The Last Mendésist Congress; R. Maille:
Mendès-France and the New Reformism
Letters

NO. 30 (APRIL-MAY 1960)

D. Mothé: Workers and Culture
Jean-François Lyotard: The State and Politics in France, 1960
Sherwood Anderson: Lift Up Thine Eyes
Documents:
P. B.: The Kibbutzim in Israel
P. Journet: An Example of American-Style Industry: Péchiney

The World in Question:
The News (with Commentaries); S. Chatel: The African Masses and European Decolonization Plans; Interview with a Martiniquan; P. Canjuers: Apropos of *Come Back Africa*

NO. 31 (DECEMBER 1960–FEBRUARY 1961)
The Revolt of Colonized Peoples
S. Chatel: The Vacuum in the Congo
Jean-François Lyotard: Gaullism and Algeria
Ph. Guillaume: Ten Weeks in a Factory
Paul Cardan: Modern Capitalism and Revolution
Documents:
Kan-ichi Kuroda: Japan, June 1960; Unitá Proletaria: Italy, July 1960
Discussion:
The French Left Viewed by the Algerians
The World in Question:
Lay-Offs at Renault; After the American Elections; The Black Student "Sit-Downs" in the United States; *À bout de soufle* [*Breathless*], by Jean-Luc Godard
by S. Chatel, D. Mothé

NO. 32 (APRIL–JUNE 1961)
The Belgian Strikes:
Paul Cardan: The Signification of the Belgian Strikes
Testimonies and Reports on the Unfolding of the Strikes:
The Strike Viewed by Those on Strike; Martin Grainger: The Strike Viewed by an English Militant; The Strike Viewed by French Militants
D. Mothé: The Lessons of the Belgian Strikes
S. Chatel: The *Loi Unique* and "Structural Reforms"
Jean-François Lyotard: In Algeria, A New Wave
Ph. Guillaume: Ten Weeks in a Factory (End)
Paul Cardan: Modern Capitalism and Revolution (Continued)
Notes: News from England

NO. 33 (DECEMBER 1961–FEBRUARY 1962)
Jean Delvaux: Crisis of Gaullism and Crisis of the "Left"
Jean-François Lyotard: Algeria, Seven Years After
D. Mothé: The Young Generations of Workers
P. Canjuers: South-African Society

Paul Cardan: Modern Capitalism and Revolution (End)
The World in Question:
The News; The State of Civil Rights in the USA, 1961; International
Conference of Revolutionary Organizations

NO. 34 (MARCH–MAY 1963)

Jean-François Lyotard: Algeria Evacuated
Claude Martin: Student Youth
Student Testimonies:
Richard Dechamp: Student Life; Dionys Gautier: The Student Situation;
Alain Gérard and Marc Noiraud: Sexual Education in the USSR
The World in Question:
The News: The Simplification of Political Life in France; Fissures in the
Western Bloc; The Cuban Crisis; The Sino-Soviet Conflict; Acceleration
and Contradictions of the Thaw in the USSR; The Situation of
Underdeveloped Countries after the Liquidation of Colonialism
Films:
The Trial, by Orson Welles; *Le Petit Soldat* [*The Little Soldier*], by
Jean-Luc Godard; *Un Cœur Gros Comme Ça* [*The Winner*], by François
Reichenbach; *Ciel Pur* [*Clear Skies* (Soviet Film)]
Books:
La Raison d'État, by Pierre Vidal-Naquet
by P. Canjuers, S. Chatel, Jean Delvaux, Juliette Feuillet, J-F. Lyotard,
Claude Martin

NO. 35 (JANUARY–MARCH 1964)

Recommencing the Revolution
Paul Cardan: The Role of Bolshevik Ideology in the Birth of the
Bureaucracy (Introduction to *The Workers' Opposition*, by Alexandra
Kollontai)
Note on the Author of the Text
Alexandra Kollontai: *The Workers' Opposition*
Books:
Daniel Guérin: *Le Front Populaire*; Raymond Bourde: *L'extricable*;
Christiane Rochefort: *Les Stances à Sophie* [*Cats Don't Care for Money*];
Yvon Bourdet: *Communisme et marxisme*
by Serge Mareuil, Alain Gérard, Paul Cardan
Letter from Algeria

NO. 36 (APRIL-JUNE 1964)

Paul Cardan: Marxism and Revolutionary Theory

Serge Mareuil: Youth and Yé-yé Music

B. Sarel: Impressions of Brazil: The Tres Marias Peasant League

Marvin Garson: *Viva Stalino e Liberta*

Documents:

Alan Harrington: *Life in the Crystal Palace*

Discussions:

Serge Bricianer: Apropos of *The Workers' Opposition*

Chronicle of the Workers' Movement: The CGT Democratizes

Chronicle of the Student Movement: Toward a New "Decolonization"?

Books:

Herbert Marcuse, *Éros et civilisation* [*Eros and Civilization*]; The Marx Edition in the Pléiade Series; J.-B. Gerbe: *Christianisme et Révolution* by Hélène Girard, Yvon Bourdet, Maximilienne Jacques

Letters

NO. 37 (JULY-SEPTEMBER 1964)

S. Chatel: Hierarchy and Collective Management

Paul Cardan: Marxism and Revolutionary Theory (Continued)

Discussions:

Joseph Gabel: Mr. Garaudy, Kafka, and the Problem of Alienation (Apropos of the Essay: *D'un réalisme sans rivages*)

Chronicle of the Workers' Movement: The CGT Democratizes (Continued)

Chronicle of the Student Movement: The Toulouse UNEF (National Union of Students of France) Congress

The World in Question:

The News; The Doctor's Strike in Belgium; The Brazilian Coup d'État; The Sino-Soviet Controversy

Films:

Le journal d'une femme de chambre [*Diary of a Chambermaid*, by Luis Buñuel]; *Le silence* [*The Silence*, by Ingmar Bergman]

Books:

Les archives de Jules-Humbert Droz

by A. Garros, Paul Tikal, Benno Sarel, P. Canjuers, Louise Mai, Yvon Bourdet

NO. 38 (OCTOBER-DECEMBER 1964)

NO. 39 (MARCH-APRIL 1965)

NO. 40 (JUNE-AUGUST 1965)

Notes

1. For some very extensive columns or ones containing short notes, we give only the column heading. [T/E: Whenever the article's actual title differs from the one appearing in a table of contents, we have opted in this English translation for the former. A more in-depth version of the forty *S. ou B.* Tables of Contents is available in French at: http://agorainternational.org/toc.html and http://www.soubscan.org.]

APPENDIX II

LIST OF PSEUDONYMS

"Liste des pseudonymes"
Socialisme ou Barbarie—Anthologie, 337

BELL, Hugo: Benno **STERNBERG**

BRUNE, Pierre: Pierre **SOUYRI**

CARDAN, Paul: Cornelius **CASTORIADIS**

CHATEL, S.: Sébastien de **DIESBACH**

CHAULIEU, Pierre: Cornelius **CASTORIADIS**

LABORDE, François: Jean-François **LYOTARD**

MONTAL, Claude: Claude **LEFORT**

MOTHÉ, Daniel: Jacques **GAUTRAT**

VÉGA, Albert: Alberto **MASÓ**

APPENDIX III

AUTHORS' BIOGRAPHIES

"Biographies des auteurs"
Socialisme ou Barbarie—Anthologie, 337–41

HUGO BELL: BENNO STERNBERG

Born in 1915, Benno Sternberg, Romanian and Jewish, emigrated to France in 1936. He already was, before the War, Marxist and anti-Stalinist. He made contacts among marginal Far-Left groups and connected with the Trotskyists. During the Occupation, he lived clandestinely in France. He then traveled to Germany, as a militant and as a journalist in both West Germany and East Germany. Having experienced and studied Germany's transition under Soviet control, he analyzed the difficult struggles of former Communists who had survived Nazism and who experienced heavy oppression under the new regime run by Communist bureaucrats who had taken refuge in Moscow during the War. Upon his return to France, he joined Socialisme ou Barbarie in 1950 and published a series of articles on the Eastern-bloc bureaucracies. Some of these articles were to be reused in his book, *La classe ouvrière en Allemagne orientale* (Paris: Éditions Sociales, 1958), which was published under the pseudonym Benno Sarel.

Having become a sociologist, his areas of concern led him to study agrarian problems and potential ties between the peasantry in the Third World and a revolutionary movement. For several years and until his death in 1971, he carried out study missions for the French National Center for Scientific Research (CNRS) in Tunisia, Egypt, Brazil, and Iran.

PIERRE BRUNE: PIERRE SOUYRI

Pierre Souyri was born in Rodez, France in 1925. He joined the Resistance at a very young age as a member of the Francs-Tireurs et Partisans (FTP), participating in 1944 in the attack on and liberation of the Carmaux mines. He left the French Communist Party in 1944, spent some time among the Trotskyists of the Parti Communiste Internationaliste (PCI) and then in the Rassemblement démocratique révolutionnaire (RDR). He undertook his postgraduate work in Toulouse and became a professor of History, his first appointment being in Algeria, where he met Jean-François Lyotard. Returning to France, he joined Socialisme ou Barbarie in 1954 at the same time Lyotard did. His articles published in the review dealt with China. During the 1963 split, Souyri left S. ou B. and became a militant in Pouvoir Ouvrier, remaining there until 1967. He died in 1979. Several articles published in the monthly *Pouvoir Ouvrier* in 1965–1967 were reprinted in a mimeographed supplement to this newspaper under the title *Impérialisme et bureaucratie face aux révolutions dans le Tiers monde* (1968). He is also the author of *Le Marxisme après Marx* (Paris: Flammarion, 1970) and of *Révolution et contre-révolution en Chine*, written between 1958 and 1962 and published posthumously with a preface by Lyotard (Paris: Christian Bourgois, 1982).

PAUL CARDAN; PIERRE CHAULIEU: CORNELIUS CASTORIADIS

Cornelius Castoriadis was born in 1922 into a Greek family from Constantinople. His family settled in Athens a few months after his birth. As an adolescent, he participated in various clandestine activities during the Metaxas dictatorship, then under the German Occupation, first within the Greek Communist Party and then in the Trotskyist organization led by Spiros Stinas. He arrived in France in December 1945. In 1946, Castoriadis created with Claude Lefort the "Chaulieu-Montal Tendency" within the Parti Communiste Internationaliste (PCI). This tendency decided in July 1948 to break with the Trotskyist movement and to create the group and review *Socialisme ou Barbarie*. From 1949 until 1970, parallel to his political activities, he had a career as an economist at the Organization for Economic Cooperation and Development. He played a top role in the life of the group and in the development of its political orientation. Having become a naturalized French citizen in 1970, he was able, after the dissolution of the group, to publish under his own name most of his texts published in the review (eight volumes between 1973 and 1979, in the "Éditions 10/18" series [and widely translated in the three volumes of his *Political and Social Writings*]). A practicing psychoanalyst (from 1973 until his death in 1997), he was also a Director of Studies at the École des Hautes Études en Sciences Sociales (EHESS) from 1980 to 1995. In his classes, he developed the themes that had been presented in his main work, *The Imaginary Institution of Society* (1975 [English-language translation, 1987]). His ideas, centered around the notion of the *social imaginary*, were also expounded upon in the six volumes of his *Carrefours du labyrinthe* series [excerpts in English appearing in *Crossroads in the Labyrinth, Philosophy, Politics, Autonomy, World in Fragments*, and the *Castoriadis Reader*, as well as in online translations available at: http://www.notbored.org/cornelius-castoriadis.html] and in various posthumous works [see: http://agorainternational.org/englishworksb.html and: http://www.notbored.org/cornelius-castoriadis.html]. Although he devoted most of his time after the end of the group to his philosophical work, he never stopped taking an interest in political and social problems and defending what he called *the project of autonomy*, as can be seen in the posthumous volume *A Society Adrift* http://www.notbored.org/ASA.pdf, among others.

S. CHATEL: SÉBASTIEN DE DIESBACH

Sébastien de Diesbach was born in 1934 in Paris. He discovered Socialisme ou Barbarie through a talk organized by the group after the crushing of the 1956 Hungarian Revolution. He was, along with Daniel Blanchard ("Canjuers"), one of the representatives of the younger generation of militants who entered the group in the late 1950s; he was to remain there until 1963. In addition to his contributions to the review, he actively participated in the preparation and dissemination of the monthly *Pouvoir Ouvrier*. After studying philosophy at the Sorbonne, he worked in industry in the fields of labor organization and training. He later ran a consulting business.

F. LABORDE: JEAN-FRANÇOIS LYOTARD

Jean-François Lyotard was born in 1924. Obtaining his teaching certificate in Philosophy in 1950, he first taught in Oran, where he made friends with Pierre Souyri, read Marx, and became highly critical of the Soviet totalitarian regime. He was appointed in 1952 to teach at the Prytanée National Militaire (military prep school) in La Flèche. In 1954, Lyotard became, along with a group of students, a member of Socialisme ou Barbarie at the same time Souyri joined the group; having had, along with his friend, direct experience of colonialism, Lyotard was an active militant against the Algerian War. His articles in the review, often signed Laborde, developed a critical analysis of the Front de Libération Nationale's struggle as well as of the FLN's bureaucratic attitudes. Appointed to the Sorbonne in 1959, his courses were a great success, and several of his students during that period joined the group. His articles in the review followed developments in the Algerian war of independence in detail and, irrespective of his principled support of the Algerians, allowed a glimpse of trends that were sure to come to the fore as soon as the country became independent in 1962. These positions can be found in his book *La guerre des Algériens* (Paris: Galilée, 1989 [English-language translations in his *Political Writings*, 1993]).

After the 1963 split in the group, Lyotard was a militant in Pouvoir Ouvrier until 1966.

Teaching at the University of Nanterre and then at the University of Vincennes after 1968, he devoted most of his time, until his death in 1998, to his philosophical work: *Discours, Figure* (1971 [English-language translation 2011]), *Économie libidinale* (1974 [English-language translation 1993]), *La condition postmoderne* (1979 [English-language translation 1984]), and *Le Différend* (1983 [English-language translation 1988]), which established him as a theorist of the "postmodern" current of thought and brought him a certain amount of notoriety in intellectual circles, particularly American ones.

CLAUDE MONTAL: CLAUDE LEFORT

Claude Lefort was born in Paris in 1924. As early as 1946, he contributed, along with Castoriadis, to the creation, within the French Trotskyist party, of the "Chaulieu-Montal Tendency," which was to lead to the birth of Socialisme ou Barbarie. Most of his texts published in *S. ou B.* were reprinted, along with other, more recent ones, in *Éléments d'une critique de la bureaucratie* (1971) and *L'invention démocratique* (1981). A student and friend of the philosopher Maurice Merleau-Ponty (1908–1961), some of whose unpublished work he edited and commented on, Lefort collaborated in the latter's review, *Les Temps Modernes*, from 1945 until 1954. He left that review after a violent polemic with Jean-Paul Sartre over the question of Stalinism and the politics of the French Communist Party. He also participated in the reviews *Textures* (1972–1975), *Libre* (1975–1979), and *Passé-Présent* (1982–1985). Obtaining a teaching certificate in Philosophy (1949), he taught Sociology in various university establishments, in particular in Caen (he took part in the May '68 movement in that city), before becoming a Director of Studies at the École des Hautes Études en Sciences Sociales (EHESS) from 1976 to 1990. He developed an interest in the political philosophy of the Renaissance, and especially in Machiavelli, to whom he devoted a major work: *Le travail de l'œuvre* (1972 [*Machiavelli in the Making*, 2012]). After his departure from S. ou B. at the time of the split that led to the founding of Informations et liaisons ouvrières (ILO)—which later became Informations et correspondances ouvrières (ICO)—and then his break from that group, he continued to work on the relation between totalitarianism and modern democracy. In addition to the works mentioned above, he has published: *Un homme en trop: Réflexions sur "l'Archipel du Goulag"* (1976), *Essais sur le politique: XIXe-XXe siècles* (1986), *Écrire à l'épreuve du politique* (1992 [*Writing: The Political Test*, 2000]), and *La complication: Retour sur le communisme* (1999 [*Complications: Communism and the Dilemmas of Democracy*, 2007]). [T/E: Collections of his writings have appeared in English as *The Political Forms of Modern Society: Bureaucracy, Democracy, Totalitarianism* (1986) and *Democracy and Political Theory* (1988). He died in 2010.]

DANIEL MOTHÉ: JACQUES GAUTRAT

Jacques Gautrat was born in 1924 in the suburbs of Bordeaux. He left school at the age of 15 to learn and practice the trade of upholsterer. While earning his living under the Occupation, he was clandestinely active, in Mazamet, among the Trotskyists of the Revolutionären Kommunisten Deutschlands (RKD). He next became a miner in Albi. Then, in 1945, he was a dockworker in Marseille, became a Bordigist, and collaborated with the organ of that group, *L'Internationaliste*.

Gautrat moved to Paris and was hired, in 1950, at the Renault factory in Boulogne-Billancourt. There he became a milling-machine operator/ toolmaker and remained there as a wage earner until 1972. He joined S. ou B. in early 1952. Starting in 1954, he ran, along with Gaspard (Raymond Hirzel), a factory-floor newspaper, *Tribune ouvrière*. His analyses, first published in *S. ou B.*, were reused and developed in two books: *Journal d'un ouvrier* (Paris: Minuit, 1959) and *Militant chez Renault* (Paris: Le Seuil, 1965). He decided in 1963 to become a union activist within the Confédération Française Démocratique du Travail (CFDT).

An accident prevented him in 1971 from returning to his position at Renault. He then completed his third book, *Les O.S.* (Paris: Le Cerf, 1972), and received a diploma from the École Pratique des Hautes Études, his thesis becoming a book: *Le métier de militant* (Paris: Le Seuil, 1973). He then carried out research on labor conditions for the French National Center for Scientific Research (CNRS), first as a part-time lecturer and then, starting in 1979, as a tenured researcher in Sociology. He partic- ipated in the creation of the Center for Research and Information on Democracy and Self-Management (CRIDA) and continues to collaborate with the reviews *Esprit, Autogestion*, and *La Revue du MAUSS*.

PAUL ROMANO

We know practically nothing of the American worker "Paul Romano" be- sides what he himself tells us in his long text, *The American Worker*, which was published as a booklet in 1947 by what was then called the "Johnson- Forest Tendency" and which was translated for the first six issues of the review *Socialisme ou Barbarie*. This "young worker in [his] late twenties" was working at the time in a small production unit at General Motors on the East Coast of the United States, after having had work experience in several other major factories.

The "Johnson-Forest Tendency," to which he belonged, was close to Socialisme ou Barbarie starting in the late Forties. Greatly affected by the importance of wildcat strikes during World War II and by the wave of strikes that occurred in the immediate postwar period, this tendency made the autonomous activity of workers the central axiom guiding its efforts.

The "Tendency," which issued from Trotskyism as did S. ou B., functioned as a tendency within various parties before becoming an autonomous group. The three main leaders and theorists of the group—C.L.R. James (Johnson), Raya Dunayevskaya (Forest), and Grace Lee (Ria Stone [later Grace Lee Boggs], author of the second, more theoretical part of the booklet, whose text was published in translation in the seventh and eighth issues of the review)—were later to separate from one another in 1955 in order to found two groups, Correspondence and News and Letters (the latter still in existence). [T/E: "Paul Romano" was in fact the pseudonym for Phil Singer; it was "only Martin Glaberman's 1972 preface to the pamphlet which finally reveals that Phil Singer worked at General Motors factory in New Jersey" (see: http://www.viewpointmag.com/2013/09/27/workers-inquiry-a-genealogy/#fn25-2809).]

A. VÉGA: ALBERTO MASÓ

Alberto Masó was born in 1918 in Barcelona. At age 16, he took part, along with the action groups of a small Catalan Marxist party, the Bloque Obrero y Campesino (BOC), in the urban battles conducted in support of the general strike in Asturias. With the BOC, he participated in the formation of the Workers' Party of Marxist Unification (POUM), within which he opposed the influence of the Trotskyists. In July 1936, he took part, in Barcelona, in the workers' counterattack against the pro-Franco uprising, then in all the combats of the POUM column and, later on, those of the 29th Division. He was wounded on three occasions and his armed engagement continued until the last days of the Spanish Republic. His political commitments were established at the same time that his political education occurred. In October 1936, he was witness to the first arrivals of Soviet armaments as well as to the beginning of the infiltration of the Republic by the Communists; he also witnessed the GPU's early efforts to liquidate independent revolutionary forces. In May 1937, he was on the barricades erected in Barcelona against the Stalinists' efforts. Upon the Republic's defeat, he reached France and was interned in the camp at Argelès. After his escape, he went underground in occupied France. At the end of the War, he drew close to the Fraction Française de la Gauche Communiste Internationale (FFGCI), a group drawing its inspiration from Amadeo Bordiga, the founder of the Italian Communist Party. Rejecting, after a few years, the FFGCI's backward-looking rigidity, Masó brought along with himself a small group of militants who joined Socialisme ou Barbarie (1950). In the controversy over the organization question, he defended the line closest to the Leninist standpoint. Masó gradually became the main leader involved in the group's monthly supplement *Pouvoir Ouvrier*, which in 1958 began to be distributed inside companies, and then, starting in 1963, in the P.O. group that issued from the S. ou B. split. In 1977, some young Spanish militants approached him in the hopes of reviving POUM. He left Paris and resumed militant activity in Spain for two years; he put an end to that activity when the young people from the new POUM refused to condemn the terrorism of Euskadi Ta Askatasuna (ETA) in the Basque Country. He returned to Paris, where he died in 2001.

APPENDIX IV

ABBREVIATIONS OF CASTORIADIS VOLUMES[1]

ENGLISH

CR *The Castoriadis Reader.* Ed. David Ames Curtis. Malden, MA and Oxford, England: Basil Blackwell, 1997.

IIS *The Imaginary Institution of Society.* Trans. Kathleen Blamey. Cambridge, MA: MIT Press and Cambridge, England: Polity Press, 1987.

PSW1 *Political and Social Writings.* 1: 1946–1955. *From the Critique of Bureaucracy to the Positive Content of Socialism.* Trans. and ed. David Ames Curtis. Minneapolis: University of Minnesota Press, 1988.

PSW2 *Political and Social Writings.* 2: 1955–1960. *From the Workers' Struggle Against Bureaucracy to Revolution in the Age of Modern Capitalism.* Trans. and ed. David Ames Curtis. Minneapolis: University of Minnesota Press, 1988.

PSW3 *Political and Social Writings.* 3: 1961–1979. *Recommencing the Revolution: From Socialism to the Autonomous Society.* Trans. and ed. David Ames Curtis. Minneapolis: University of Minnesota Press, 1993.

FRENCH

CMR1   *Capitalisme moderne et révolution. 1: L'impérialisme et la guerre.* Paris: Union Générale d'Éditions, 1979.

CMR2   *Capitalisme moderne et révolution. 2: Le mouvement révolutionnaire sous le capitalisme moderne.* Paris: Union Générale d'Éditions, 1979.

CS   *Le Contenu du socialisme.* Paris: Union Générale d'Éditions, 1979.

EMO1   *L'Expérience du mouvement ouvrier. 1: Comment lutter.* Paris: Union Générale d'Éditions, 1974.

EMO2   *L'Expérience du mouvement ouvrier. 2: Prolétariat et organisation.* Paris: Union Générale d'Éditions, 1974.

EP1   *Écrits politiques 1945-1997. 1: La Question du mouvement ouvrier.* Tome 1. Paris: Éditions du Sandre, 2012.

EP2   *Écrits politiques 1945-1997. 2: La Question du mouvement ouvrier.* Tome 2. Paris: Éditions du Sandre, 2012.

EP3   *Écrits politiques 1945-1997. 3: Quelle démocratie?* Tome 1. Ed. Enrique Escobar, Myrto Gondicas et Pascal Vernay. Paris: Éditions du Sandre, 2013.

EP4   *Écrits politiques 1945-1997. 4: Quelle démocratie?* Tome 2. Ed. Enrique Escobar, Myrto Gondicas et Pascal Vernay. Paris: Éditions du Sandre, 2013.

EP5   *Écrits politiques 1945-1997. 5: La Société bureaucratique.* Ed. Enrique Escobar, Myrto Gondicas et Pascal Vernay. Paris: Éditions du Sandre, 2015.

SB1   *La Société bureaucratique. 1: Les rapports de production en Russie.* Paris: Union Générale d'Éditions, 1973.

SB2   *La Société bureaucratique. 2: La révolution contre la bureaucratie.* Paris: Union Générale d'Éditions, 1973.

SB(n.é.) *La Société bureaucratique* (nouvelle édition). Paris: Christian Bourgois Éditeur, 1990.

SF *La Société française*. Paris: Union Générale d'Éditions, 1979.

Notes

1. T/E: This list of abbreviations of Castoriadis volumes is provided to simplify the *Anthology*'s apparatus. Only Castoriadis volumes in French and English that are referenced in the publication notes or endnotes or that otherwise contain *S. ou B.* texts by Castoriadis appear here. For a complete twenty-language bibliography of writings by and about Castoriadis, including other Castoriadis volumes published in French and English, see: http://www.agorainternational.org.